LIFE PICTURES

FROM

THE BIBLE,

OR

ILLUSTRATIONS OF SCRIPTURE CHARACTER.

BY

LE ROY J. HALSEY, D. D.

AUTHOR OF THE LITERARY ATTRACTIONS OF THE BIBLE, &C.

PHILADELPHIA:

PRESBYTERIAN BOARD OF PUBLICATION,

No. 821 Chestnut Street.

WILLIAM W. HARDING, STEREOTYPER.

PREFACE.

THE object of this volume is to commend the book of God to the favourable attention of all those, both parents and teachers, who are charged with the education of youth, and especially to the attention of the young themselves, as a book of permanent historic and biographic interest; and as such, furnishing the richest store-house of example, and the surest guide in the formation of character. It cannot be, that a book which deals so much in illustrations of life and character, as the Bible, should be devoid of interest to the young, or fail to furnish them with important aid in the development of their own characters, and the regulation of their own lives.

But to do this, these characters must be known, studied, and appreciated. It is manifest, that they are not known, studied, or appreciated, as they ought to be, even by our best educated youth. A large portion of the historical and biographical Scriptures is, in fact, seldom read, and of course little known.

And yet God certainly had a purpose in making history and biography the broad basis of all Scripture. Is it not manifest, that, by putting so large a portion of his word into this narrative form, he thereby sought to attract and interest the youthful mind? If so, it is well to profit by the indication. It is wise to follow, in our own instructions, the divine pattern thus set us. Religion never speaks more gracefully, than when she speaks by example. It is chiefly through the living voice of example, that she speaks to the young in all the Scriptures. To inculcate Bible truths, through Bible characters, whether from the pulpit, the press, or the teacher's chair, is to adopt the Bible's own method of instruction. And, certainly, it is one which experience proves to be the most effective, as it is the most pleasing.

Believing that there is an attractive power, as well as rich stores of instruction, in all the sacred biographies, even when presented singly, the writer of these pages has thought that he could not do a better service for the young Bible reader, and indeed for parents, teachers, and all others, who have at heart the education of our youth, than by classifying, arranging in groups, and so presenting at one view, as large a number of these Scripture portraits, as could thus be brought together without making too cumbrous a volume. By selecting, and grouping together such prominent characters as would be most likely to interest the young, and by clothing them somewhat in our modern style of thought and phraseology, he has hoped that the narrative portions of the Bible might be presented, if not in a new, at any rate, in an attractive and useful light. But while freely comparing ancient with modern characters, and often discussing the former in the most familiar current language of our times—deeming that the only way to make antiquity fully intelligible to the young is to modernize it—the writer has studiously avoided everything, that might offend the taste of the scholar on the one hand, or the piety of the devout Christian on the other.

He has not sought to make these ancient characters attractive at the expense of the truth. He has not aimed to embellish them by any attempt of pen-painting. With this divine method ever before him—a method which leaves the deeds of the life to tell the story of the character—he has not sought to eulogize, but simply to set forth, Scripture characters, as they are in the book itself; giving them only that development which their recorded deeds would justify, or that prominence which their virtues demand. Not one jot or tittle of Scriptural truth has been anywhere knowingly sacrificed for the sake of making any scene the more impressive, or any character the more attractive; but the single aim from first to last has been, to let the Bible speak, and utter its voice of wisdom, through its own real personages. Of course only a part of this great cloud of witnesses could here be brought into view; but that part has been selected, which seemed to speak with a voice of spiritual interest to the young. The writer can only hope, that those who may recognize the voice of truth in these pages, may wish to hear that voice again, and be induced to follow it to those living oracles where God himself speaks. It may be proper to say, that in addition to the aid derived from books, the author has been indebted, for many valuable thoughts and suggestions, to his brethren of the ministry, whose oral and sometimes unwritten discourses he has been permitted to hear during the last fifteen or twenty years. If, in these pages, any of them should find their own ideas reproduced without the credit which is due, it is only because he was unwilling, by special references, to make them responsible for what they had not themselves published, and what he has reproduced here only from memory.

CONTENTS.

CHAPTER I.

GENERAL INFLUENCE OF THE BIBLE ON HUMAN CHARACTER.

CHAPTER II.

PORTRAITURE OF CHILDHOOD IN THE BIBLE.

CHAPTER III.

THE HEROIC CHARACTERS OF THE BIBLE.

CHAPTER IV.

KINGS AND STATESMEN OF THE BIBLE.

CHAPTER V.

THE PROPHETS AND APOSTLES OF THE BIBLE.

CHAPTER VI.

INCIDENTAL CHARACTERS, OR THE LESSER LIGHTS OF BIBLE BIOGRAPHY.

LIFE PICTURES FROM THE BIBLE.

CHAPTER I.

GENERAL INFLUENCE OF THE BIBLE ON HUMAN CHARACTER.

I. STATEMENT OF THE SUBJECT.

AT whatever point we open the Sacred Scriptures, we are at once struck with a spirit, tone, and character, in all their utterances, separating them entirely from all other writings. Almost all persons, even the most superficial, can tell when they hear a quotation from Scripture, by its very sound. It comes with a tone of authority, a simplicity of style, a plainness of speech, an earnestness, sanctity, and reverence for God, which may indeed be imitated, but, otherwise, can never be mistaken for anything else in the world. This total isolation of the Bible, and unlikeness to all other books, while it arises from its very nature as a revelation from God, and is doubtless salutary in its general effect upon our minds, may also have the effect of driving some from its sacred pages altogether, under the impression, that its truths are too mysterious, and its characters too awful and unapproachable, for the apprehension or imitation of ordinary minds. But this would be a great mistake;

and a great abuse of what God intended for our good. For nothing can be plainer, than that the Bible is intentionally adapted to all classes of men; and though it stands alone in the grandeur of its truths, and the holiness of its characters, yet all are invited to approach it with the most perfect freedom and familiarity. The air we breathe, the crystal fountains where we drink, the genial sunlight in which we live, can be understood, in all their deep mysteries, only by the philosopher; but God made them just as much for the child and the humble artisan as for the philosopher. The policy which would withhold the word of God from the people, on the plea, that it is too mysterious or holy for common minds, is just as insane, as that which would restrain them from undue familiarity with the air, the water, and the sunlight, which God has as certainly made for all, as he has made them at all.

Owing partly to a vague dread of its mysteriousness, and partly to the antique dress in which its characters are clothed, the Bible is to many a sealed book; and yet it is the great book of living character to which all are invited to come, that they may learn the most important lessons of life. It is our purpose in the following chapters of this work, to group together and portray, in language adapted to our current style of thought, some of the most prominent characters that adorn the annals of Scripture history and biography. But it seems to us an appropriate introduction to such an undertaking, to devote its opening chapter, to a brief, but comprehensive survey of the general influence which the Bible itself, in all its characters and all its revelations, has, from the beginning, wielded over the character of the world. It seems to us that we shall be all the better prepared to appreciate and admire its wonderfully diversified characters, and to derive from them the great practical lessons which God intended, when we see how much this book has had to do already in the formation of all rightly formed human character, and what stores of yet unexhausted power, for all time to come, God has treasured up in its sacred pages. The subject is a wide and difficult one: difficult however only from its fulness. The Bible has had so much to do in raising the character of men and nations up to its present standard, that it is not easy, in our limited compass, to say all that should be said on so great a theme. We hope to give, at least, a distinct outline of its influence, and, at the same time, unfold the reasons of that influence in the present chapter.

II. INDESTRUCTIBLE CHARACTER OF THE BIBLE.

"The grass withereth, the flower fadeth: but the word of our God shall stand for ever." Thus spake the inspired prophet, Isaiah, when foretelling the advent and glory of Immanuel, seven hundred years before his manifestation to Israel. This claim of perpetual duration for the word of God, in contrast with the fleeting nature of man and all earthly things, holds good, not only for each particular declaration which the Lord then made by the mouth of his prophet, but also for the whole inspired canon which we call the Bible. Of each word in particular, and of all together, it may be affirmed, that its truth shall stand for ever. Heaven and earth may pass away, but not one jot or tittle shall pass from the law or word of God, till all be fulfilled. And even then, its fulfilled and finished truth shall still stand for the instruction and admiration of all the good. "For ever, O Lord, thy word is settled in heaven."

Now, in a world of endless change and shadows, such as ours, this enduring character of the word of God is no mean vindication of its truth. Ultimately it will amount to a demonstration complete. For nothing but truth can finally withstand the tooth of time. Error may flourish for a season and win a partial triumph, but truth is bound to come out victorious at the last, as surely as God is on the throne. Of ancient errors that survive, the number is already few; and it is becoming constantly less with the progress of ages. If time be a sure and searching test of truth, how much more eternity! But here is a book which challenges beforehand the test of all time and of all eternity—a book, whose principles, it is predicted, shall withstand decay's effacing fingers to the end of time, and then pass unscathed through the fires of the last judgment into the clear light of an eternal day. This is its claim from the beginning—that it shall stand for ever: and we, in admitting its validity, have all the advantage of knowing that it has stood already, in one form or other, upwards of thirty centuries.

We must all confess that this is just as it ought to be, in case the Bible be from God. Once admit its Divine origin, and it is easy to believe that it will abide for ever. Such a cause must produce just such an effect. On the other hand, arguing back, from effect to cause, if we see in the Bible this enduring and indestructible character—if we see it standing fast through all the ages, while all other things perish and pass away as the withering grass and the fading flower—then are we constrained to say, this is God's finger, this is God's truth: here is a wisdom and a power far above the reach of man. And all that the argument needs to make it complete is just a few more centuries, to sweep away every vestige of the world's idolatries, and leave this book standing alone in its glory. This phenomenon of durability in the midst of decay, the word of God has been presenting to the world ever since Moses closed the first five books of it. And it is one which is becoming more and more remarkable the longer the world stands. Nothing would, at first sight, appear more ephemeral than such a book—written in different ages, in different nations, in diverse tongues—some of it in Hebrew and some in Greek, some in Jerusalem and some in Babylon, some in the desert and some amid the islands of the sea, some in a Grecian workshop and some in a Roman prison. And yet see how it has outlived, not merely the perishable parchments and tables of stone on which it was written, but the very nations and races whose destiny it records, and whose memory it alone has kept from utter oblivion.

In a world where all things fade as the flower, and perish as the grass, this book remains from age to age the same, as indestructible as if endued with the power of an endless life. All the material monuments that ancient Israel erected to commemorate the mighty deeds of Jehovah have been swept away. The stones of memorial at Gilgal, the stony tables that received the law from God's own finger, the ark of the testimony that so long enshrined it, the glorious tabernacle and temple that enshrined the ark—all these have been utterly obliterated, whilst the word of the Lord still abides, fresh and vigorous as at the beginning. And how often have its enemies leagued together with kings and rulers of the earth for its destruction! How often has the bare reading of it been punished with confiscation and death! Since the day in which the wicked King Jehoiakim burnt the roll of the book which the Lord had delivered by the mouth of Jeremiah, in how many lands has the whole Bible been committed to the flames, in the hope of obliterating it for ever! But it has only been to give it a deeper hold upon the heart of man, and a wider diffusion through the world. The burnt Bible has sprung to life again, like the fabled Phœnix from its ashes. The burnt Bible has been like the ashes of Wickliffe, when his enemies thought to drown his memory, by drowning the poor relics of his mortal part.

> "The Avon to the Severn runs,
> The Severn to the sea,
> And Wickliffe's dust shall spread abroad,
> Wide as the waters be."

III. ITS GENERAL INFLUENCE ON MAN.

But the main point, to which we would here direct attention, is not the mere fact, however remarkable, that this book abides with men, but the far higher and more remarkable fact of its permanent and abiding influence over them. It lives in the lives of men. It has interpenetrated all the affairs of civilized nations. It has given a new life to the world. There is a silent, yet all-pervading and irresistible power, which has gone out from it over the earth, that may be best likened to the influence of the sun in the heavens. There is no influence more distinctly marked, none more easily traced along the track of past ages, than that which the Bible has exerted. It is an effect everywhere answerable to its producing cause; an effect obvious, salutary, and great, just in proportion as the Bible has been known and circulated freely amongst men. Where the word of God has been unbound, there light, liberty, and virtue have always abounded. Where it has been fettered or excluded, there light, liberty, and virtue have languished and died; and their opposites flourished. The lines that divide the moral darkness from the light, the night from the day, may be traced all around the globe by the progress of the Bible.

The only lines of this sort that can be found on the globe, are such as the Bible has drawn. And perhaps there is at this day no single demonstration of the truth of the Bible, more tangible and more satisfactory than just this potent influence for good which it has everywhere been shedding over the world, like the genial rays of the sun, or like the emanations of divine power, that went out from Immanuel's person.

As the old Greek mythology, though dead as a religion, still lives and breathes in the literature of all civilized nations—all that was true and beautiful in it still surviving; as the Aristotelian philosophy, though long since exploded as a system, has yet left its impress on the thinking mind of the world—but growing less and less every day because of the little truth it ever had; as each great name amongst the sons of genius—Homer or Plato, Bacon or Shakspeare—may be traced through all the generations succeeding them, by their influence on literature,—even so may the book of God be traced in all that influence which it has exerted over the character and institutions of man. It has left a track of light and beauty, even in the darkest periods of human history, which for breadth of outline and profound occult glory may be compared to the Milky Way across the heavens. As of all books known to man, it has, at least in portions of it, existed the longest, and been diffused the widest, it would be strange if its influence had not been deep and enduring. It would seem impossible for any one at all acquainted with the general history of civilized nations, and accustomed to trace effects to their causes, not to see that the word of God has been the great light of the world. If there is any such thing as the philosophy of history, this we take to be at once the widest and the grandest fact in the philosophy of modern history; namely, the influence of the Bible upon the character of man. In that fact lies the main spring of our modern civilization. In that fact lies the secret of all our pre-eminence over the ancient civilization. Any attempt to thread the labyrinth of history, to solve its problems, to explain its progress, and show its issue without the Bible, would be as insane as to study astronomy, ignoring the existence of the sun. A Cosmos without the Bible is not the real Cosmos, that God has made for man.

And yet, in this restless, rushing age, when the human mind is on the lookout for new truths, and has been trained by an exact, experimenting science, to contemplate chiefly proximate and secondary causes, there is no little danger of losing sight of the more remote and grander truth, that the book of God has created this new state of things, that it has been, and is now, the mighty moving power of all our high modern civilization. "The entrance of thy words," says the Psalmist, "giveth light; it giveth understanding unto the simple." What is true of its effect on the individual, has been true of all society. This is the true light, shining in darkness, that lighteth every man who cometh into the world. "The grass withereth, the flower fadeth, but the word of the Lord endureth for ever."

IV. SPECIAL LINES OF INFLUENCE.

But to take a nearer view; let us here briefly indicate some of those special lines or channels of influence, by which the Bible has made its plastic power felt in all the institutions, characters, and fortunes of civilized men. There are many such lines, each beautiful and glorious, radiating from this holy book: and it is by the combination of all together, that it has wielded its whole power over the world.

There is first its influence upon man as a religious being, and upon all his religious interests; his opinions, belief, character, hopes, fears, conduct, and destiny as an immortal being, a citizen of two worlds, a possessor of two natures, and a candidate for eternity. This is the highest and most important of all its influences, just as man's spiritual nature is the controlling element of his being, and governs all other interests. On this exhaustless theme volumes are yet to be written, as volumes have been in all past ages.

There is, in the next place, its influence upon all the great interests of morality and virtue; upon man as a moral and social being, a citizen of this world, in all his human duties, and in all his relations to his fellow-man, private and public, domestic and national. And it would be easy to show from all the past, that simply as a system of ethics, or code of moral duty, founded on Divine sanctions, and adapted to every condition of human life, the Bible has exerted an influence in ameliorating the character of man, deeper and more lasting than that of any other book.

There is again its influence upon civil government and legislation; upon the political rights and interests of man; upon the formation and development of all national institutions, the progress of religious liberty, the defence and promulgation of all true constitutional freedom and equality amongst men. In the great battle which freedom has had to wage against leagued oppression and tyranny, in every age and every land, the Bible has ever wielded an arm of power. And no man is competent to tell the story of civil and religious liberty on earth, who is unacquainted with the history of the Bible.

Then again, distinct from these, we have its influence as a great elevating and refining power, upon all the useful and fine

arts; upon man in all his industrial relations and pursuits, as God's chief worker and master builder in the world; upon trade and commerce, agriculture and manufacture, the wealth of nations, the spread of families, and the support of human life; upon all the arts of peace and even the dread necessities of war. "Put up thy sword, for they that take the sword shall perish by the sword." In an age when the thirst for military glory ruled the world, our Saviour indicated that the true policy of the world was peace. In the arts of peace lies the secret of wealth and glory both for the nation and the individual. And for eighteen centuries, under the growing influence of the gospel, the world has been coming more and more to a clear understanding of this profound maxim—Peace on earth, good will amongst men. If the great social problems of capital and labour, master and servant, the rich and the poor, which have so long perplexed the minds of political economists, and so often disturbed the peace of society, are ever to find a satisfactory solution, it must be, as it ever has been so far, under the guiding influence of this book.

And still further, we have its influence upon all the great educational interests of man; upon the whole circle of human science and literature; upon the rudimental instruction of the young, the popular diffusion of useful knowledge, the spread of a spirit of philosophical inquiry, and the general advancement of learning in the world. It is not to be denied, nor concealed, that ever since the Bible became a power in the earth, it has been marching at the head of all these things, the champion of all high culture, the pioneer of all popular education, the friend of universal knowledge. As such it has led the advanced column of the world's civilization in every land. And as such, it has now gained such headway, and risen to such power, that we behold it sending forth, over the whole world of letters, a divine and quickening energy that shall ere long awake all its slumbering powers, heal all its imperfections, consecrate its genius, and baptize its whole science and literature in the name of Jesus.

Let us look at this last point a little more fully. Each of the great nations of Christendom has its own classical or polite literature, consisting chiefly of works of taste and imagination, but covering the whole range of history, biography, eloquence, criticism, poetry, romance, and fiction. A portion of this literature is indigenous, and peculiar to each nation; and a portion of it, being borrowed, is common to others, it may be to all. But whether indigenous or borrowed, peculiar or common, this literature, all together, constitutes the sum total of the literature of the civilized world as distinguished from the uncivilized. And this, along with another vast department which we call science, may be said to embrace its whole learning, except so far as it is contained in a third great department which we call religion or theology. But regarded simply as so much writing, existing in books, all science and all theology may be comprehended under the general term, literature, taking the word in the broad sense of letters, or written composition. Now, in the rise and progress of the literature, or learning, of each of the nations composing the present Christian world, especially of the great Protestant nations, and still more those of the Anglo-Saxon race, speaking our own tongue, there has been a constant growth and development from their earliest beginnings to the present time. And the point here under consideration, is, that the Sacred Scriptures have exerted a plastic, creative power through all this growth and development, deeper and more enduring than other writings whatever, those of Homer not excepted.

Upon the whole body of this literature, the Greek and Roman classics have, indeed, exerted a mighty and undying influence. And a man would be insane to deny it. But we think it would be easy to show that the influence of the Bible has been far greater. The very fact that our literature is Christian and not heathen, shows it. Its very letter and spirit have both been baptized in the name of the Lord. Directly or indirectly, the Bible has fashioned and controlled all the great leading minds, that have in turn controlled and fashioned the world of letters. The poets, orators, sages, heroes, historians, statesmen, artists, jurists, divines, who have written, or sung, or acted, the living history of the last fifteen centuries, and especially of the last three, have all, or nearly all, drunk inspiration from its sacred pages. To this mount of vision they have been perpetually coming for new supplies of grace and glory. They have been great, and they have done great things for God and their fellow-men, just in proportion as they have ascended to these glorious heights of Zion. On these sublime summits they have lighted the torch of genius with more than Promethean fires; they have drunk at gushing crystal fountains sweeter than any Pierian springs.

V. THE CHIEF ELEMENTS OF ITS INFLUENCE.

Having now pointed out the principal lines of influence, or channels, through which the book of God has been steadily shaping the character and fortunes of mankind, we come to consider next the great elements, or sources of power, that have given it such supremacy. These are to be learned only from the book itself. And here it is obvious, that our subject opens into a wide field—wide as the whole contents of the inspired volume. In such a field we must here select only the most prominent points. And in doing this, we must remark at the outset, that we shall select only those elements, which are to be regarded as means or instruments, in the hand of God, by which he has made his word to man so effective for good. The great source of power and influence in the Bible is God himself—God, by his providence, ever protecting and opening the way for his word, and God, in the person of his Spirit, ever accompanying that word, and opening the heart of man to receive it. There is no intrinsic power in the Bible itself, standing alone and bereft of Divine influence, to do all the great things which it has done, and shall yet do, in the world. Its efficiency is all of God. But as God works by means, and has everywhere wrought mightily through his written word, we accordingly open the book to see what are the great elements of its power, as God's instrument—as the sword of God's Spirit, as the text-book of God's teaching, as the medium of God's influence over the world.

VI. ITS SUBLIME DOCTRINAL SYSTEM.

The first thing that strikes us here, as an element of its power over the human mind, and consequently over human character, is its sublime doctrinal system. When we consider the vast variety of the contents of this book—written by so many different authors, running through so many long centuries, embracing so many diversities of style and method, from the grave historical narrative to a song of praise for the choirs of the temple; it is remarkable with what facility and beauty all its facts and principles range themselves into one grand system of doctrine, having the compactness and harmony of the most exact science of positive truth. Now a man may not study the Bible long enough to see this, and consequently may live and die knowing nothing about it. But such minds as Newton's and Bacon's have been filled with mingled emotions of wonder and adoration, as they have contemplated it. This system runs through the whole Bible. It is addressed to the human understanding, as containing all the truth essential to salvation, and as something to be believed on God's testimony. When fully and cordially embraced, it is the power of God and the wisdom of God unto salvation. It is that which is so often, in the Scriptures, denominated the truth—the truth as it is in Jesus. "Sanctify them through thy truth; thy word is truth." "To this end was I born, and for this cause came I into the world, that I might bear witness unto the truth; every one that is of the truth, heareth my voice."

It would be impossible, in our present limits, to give any thing like an adequate outline of all the great truths that make up the doctrinal system of the Bible. Every careful reader will find them everywhere reiterated and illustrated in a thousand different forms; shining most brightly of course when viewed all together in the aggregate; but yet shining brightly, each one by itself, like the broken particles of a true diamond, or the scattered fragments of a true mirror, each of which will reflect the same image as the whole. But it is easy to give a brief, yet comprehensive, summary of these great doctrines, as they now constitute the common faith of the church, and the accepted belief of our whole Christian literature. There are certain great facts and doctrines, which may be regarded as constituting the very nucleus of the Bible system, the life and essence of its whole scheme of salvation; and which belong to it as they belong to no other book, ancient or modern. For they belong to it by a right which stands good against all the world—the right of prior discovery. They are revelations from God alone. They were not struck out by Grecian or Roman, Egyptian or Chaldean sages. They are doctrines which the world did not possess before the Bible came; could never have discovered without its aid; and can now nevermore let die.

In this sublime system, we have first the great and unfathomable doctrine of the existence, character, and perfections of God—of God as a Spirit, infinite, eternal, and unchangeable in his being, power, wisdom, justice, goodness, holiness, and truth—one God in three persons, "over all blessed for ever." We have the doctrine of Divine providence—God's universal and eternal government, general and special, moral and physical, over all worlds and creatures, the greatest and the most minute. We have the doctrine of the supreme divinity, mediation, incarnation, humiliation, death, resurrection, exaltation, and intercession of Jesus Christ—God manifest in the flesh—God a Saviour, delivered for our offences, and raised again for our justification; and along with this, the doctrine of immaculate perfection as exemplified in his life and character. We have the doctrine of the personality, office, agency, and work of the Holy Spirit of God—the author of all special divine influence in the hearts of men, enlightening their minds to understand the truth, inclining them to turn from sin unto God, enabling them to repent and believe the gospel, and thus regenerating and sanctifying the soul. We have the doctrine of the apostasy, depravity, ruin, and death of our race through sin, and of the redemption, recovery, restoration, and eternal salvation of a large part of it through the intervention and atoning sacrifice of the Son of God, and the quickening, saving influences of the Spirit of God. We have the doctrine of the forgiveness of sins through the blood of Christ—of peace, pardon, reconciliation, and justification before God, for every soul that cometh to God in the exercise of a true repentance for sin, and a true faith in our Lord Jesus Christ. We have the doctrine of the church or kingdom of God, militant on earth, triumphant in heaven, consisting of all those who in every age and land are called to be saints of God, or who believe and obey the gospel. And, in addition to these, we have, summarily, the doctrine of the second coming of Christ, the conversion of the whole world, the resurrection of the dead, the judgment of the last day, the endless punishment of the wicked, and the life everlasting in heaven for all the righteous. Such are the main features of a system which might be amplified into the whole body of our theology; and is, in fact, spread through all the Scriptures—a system whose grand final cause is God's glory, whose immediate end is man's salvation, and whose great central truth is Jesus Christ crucified, the power of God, and the wisdom of God unto salvation.

Now the crowning glory of the Bible is that it is a system of truth unto salvation. It contains just so much knowledge from God, and so much knowledge of God and man, as is needful to save us. This is its greatest attraction to sinful, dying man. This gives it its deepest hold upon the human heart. It alone unlocks the mysteries of our existence, solves the great problems of life and death, and answers the most earnest longings of the soul, by opening the way to life and immortality beyond the grave. Without this knowledge we should be in hopeless ignorance of God, of ourselves, and of the future.

It is not surprising, then, that a volume which brings us such knowledge and such glad tidings from God, should speak in a voice of authority and power to the world—speak as never man spake. It has, indeed, many and various other attractions, calculated to win our hearts. It is a broad land of indescribable beauty, of inexhaustible wealth. It is full of learning, eloquence, poetry, philosophy, and history, surpassing all the dreams of fiction and romance. And it is well for us at times to consider these—"to walk about Zion, to mark her bulwarks, to consider her palaces, to tell the towers thereof." For these may lead us on to that spiritual glory which shines within. These should be as morning stars that usher in the day. These are but the decorations on the outer wall, which God has flung out to catch the view of the uninitiated, and to allure them upward and onward, until they get such glimpses of glory from the inner sanctuary, that they shall be "filled with reverence and awe, and drawn in humble adoration to its very shrine." But all these outer attractions are as nothing compared with the one grand and all-pervading idea, that the Bible is a book of revealed truth—"the truth as it is in Jesus"—the truth by which God proposes to save our souls from everlasting death. This is the one supreme, precious, and infinitely glorious attraction, before which all others fade away, like morning stars before the opening day. We shall not cease to appreciate these lesser attractions. They have their importance, else they had not been in God's book. They all have their place, just as the stars of the firmament have. But they are not the sun. For all man's bodily wants on earth, one sun is worth a thousand stars. And for all the wants of the soul, one Divine Saviour is worth all the other characters, merely human, in the Bible. Thus it is, by the sublime doctrine of God our Saviour, and the whole system of truth circling around it, that the gospel has won the heart of man, and wielded its mightiest influence over the world.

The Scriptures tell us, that we are to be saved through sanctification of the Spirit and belief of the truth. And it is easy to see how such a system of truth, as the Bible reveals, when fully and cordially believed, must control the whole life and character of the believer. "Be it unto thee according to thy faith," said the Master; and this has ever been the measure of the Bible's influence over the heart of man. It is a grand system—incomparably the grandest every way, that was ever propounded to the human mind—and it cannot be believed and accepted as such, without producing the greatest results. These results, too, are always in exact proportion to the strength of our faith, and the amount of the truth believed. By this we do not mean, that there is any power in the truth itself, aside from the Spirit of God, to sanctify and save. The effective power of the battle lies not in the sword of the victor, but in the right arm of him who wields it; or rather in the indomitable will that moves both arm and sword. All the swords in the world could never win a battle—would be but so much inert and harmless steel—without an active agent to wield them. And so this truth of God in the Bible, though formed of purest metal, and attempered to the keenness of a Damascus blade, and throwing back the very sunlight of heaven from its polished surface, is but a sword in the hand of the Divine Spirit, deriving all its power from him who wields it. Still, as we can see how the sword of battle is adapted to its purpose, so it is easy to see how this system of Divine truth is fitted for its great work—piercing to the inmost recesses of the heart, and mighty through God to the pulling down of the strongholds of sin and Satan. Because it is in this system, and here alone, that we find motives adequate to restrain men from sin, and constrain them to holiness of life; here alone, that we find any possible remedy for the ruins of sin and death, or satisfactory knowledge of a better world beyond the grave; here alone, that we find the full proof of those great facts and doctrines, which make the gospel remedy for sin efficacious on the one hand, and its motives to holiness powerful on the other.

VII. ITS PURE PRECEPTIVE SYSTEM.

This brings to our view another great source of influence in the Bible. It is that incomparable preceptive system, which we find interwoven throughout, with its sublime doctrines, and in fact founded upon them. There are, indeed two grand systems, running side by side, through all the Scriptures, the counterparts and supplements of each other: namely, the doctrinal system, and the ethical or preceptive system, and both are essential to the full development of the power of the Bible, in moulding the character of man. The one is a system of truth, addressed to the human understanding, to be believed on God's testimony. The other is a code of duty, enforced by God's authority, and addressed to conscience, or the moral sense. The great demand of the one is faith, or trust in God. The great demand of the other is practice, or obedience to God. And the connection of the two is so intimate, being akin to the connection between our intellectual and moral nature, that there can be no true faith without practice, and no right practice without faith. Works without faith are just as dead as faith is without works. So that the true gospel of God, under every dispensation in the Old Testament and the New alike, has consisted of doctrines and precepts, belief and duty, faith to accredit all that God has said, and obedience to do all that God has commanded.

It is interesting to notice how these systems of doctrine and duty everywhere interpenetrate and support each other, "with line upon line, and precept upon precept, here a little, and there a little." There is no doctrine which does not call for some corresponding duty; and there is no precept or command which is not founded on some great doctrine. Moreover, we find these closely interwoven systems everywhere revealed and illustrated after the same peculiar method. It is the method, not of abstract scientific formulas, but of concrete cases and examples.

God seems to have sown the whole field of revelation broadcast, precisely as he has sown the truths of science in the great field of nature. Wherever we enter the field of nature, we behold, at first sight, a wild aspect of irregularity and diversity, which seems to preclude the possibility of any science or system there. And it is not until we have carefully studied the field, that we see all its elements of apparent disorder shaping themselves into the most beautiful scientific systems—truth after truth taking its rightful position, and science after science unfolding itself to view. And just so, wherever we open the Bible, we find a vast array of facts, doctrines, precepts, promises, threatenings, examples good and bad—not arranged in so many separate scientific drills, like the straight rows of a garden or orchard, but growing all together without any apparent method, like a field that had been sown broadcast with every kind of grain, or the wild forest of nature which God's own hand has planted. To the eye of science, we know, there is as profound an order in the scattered field and in the wild forest of nature, as there is in the well-arranged garden and orchard. Precisely so is it in the Bible; and it is the province of him, who would rightly interpret, and teach it to others, to find all the order, beauty, and system of a divine science everywhere revealed in this broadcast field of Scripture truth.

Now this is just as applicable to the precepts of the Bible, as to its doctrines; for they are both taught after the same method. As we have just contemplated the power of the book in the light of its sublime doctrinal system, so also may we now regard it in this other light—as containing a pure and exalted ethical or preceptive system—the law of the Lord—the only true and infallible code of moral duty for man.

The sacred writers themselves often refer, in glowing terms, to this great characteristic of the Bible as a book of holy and salutary precepts. Says the Psalmist, "I esteem all thy precepts concerning all things to be right. I have longed after thy precepts. Through thy precepts I get understanding; therefore I hate every false way. Oh! how I love thy law; it is my meditation all the day." Says Paul, "The law is holy, and the commandment holy, and just, and good." Says John, "His commandments are not grievous." Says Solomon, " My son, forget not my law; but let thine heart keep my commandments. Bind them about thy neck; write them upon the table of thine heart. For they shall be an ornament of grace unto thy head; and chains about thy neck. So shalt thou find favour and good understanding in the sight of God and man." And to the whole preceptive code of the Bible may be applied that beautiful description which David gives of a part of it in the nineteenth Psalm—" The law of the Lord is perfect, converting the soul; the testimony of the Lord is sure, making wise the simple. The statutes of the Lord are right, rejoicing the heart; the commandment of the Lord is pure, enlightening the eyes. The fear of the Lord is clean, enduring for ever; the judgments of the Lord are true, and righteous altogether. More to be desired are they than gold; yea, than much fine gold; sweeter also than honey and the honey-comb. Moreover by them is thy servant warned, and in keeping of them there is great reward."

As already indicated, the precepts of the Bible, like its doctrines, are spread over its whole surface, taught in every variety of form, and illustrated in the character and actions of men. Still we have many brief, but comprehensive, statements of them; and, sometimes, as is the case also with the doctrines, we find summaries of all the precepts, which seem to condense into a few profound and pregnant words, man's whole duty. Thus we have the ten commands of the moral law, promulgated and written on tables of stone at mount Sinai, which may be regarded as the nucleus of all the precepts of the Old Testament. Thus we have our Saviour's sermon on the mount, which we may regard as the foundation of the whole preceptive system revealed in the New Testament. And not to mention many other shorter expositions of duty, such as those two great commands of love to God, and love to our neighbour, on which all the law and the prophets hang, or our Saviour's golden rule—"Whatsoever ye would that men should do to you, do ye even so to them"—we have a beautiful compend of the ethical system of the gospel in the following passage from Paul, "Whatsoever things are true, whatsoever things are honest, whatsoever things are just, whatsoever things are pure, whatsoever things are lovely, whatsoever things are of good report; if there be any virtue, and if there be any praise, think on these things."

But whether we consider the moral or the positive precepts of the Bible—whether we regard them as briefly comprehended in the decalogue, or in the sermon on the mount, or in the golden rule, or in the apostle's summary just quoted, one thing is manifest, that for purity, spirituality, and power, there never has been any code of ethics, or system of morality, known amongst men, comparable to that which the Bible reveals. Regarded simply as a book of morals, intended to form the character, and direct the conduct of man in all his duties and relations, the Bible has taken a deep and abiding hold upon the heart of the world. And to no other book is the world under such obligations for all the virtue that is in it.

The reason of this superior influence is found, first, in the exceeding clearness and certainty of its teachings. On the whole subject of duty, not less than of doctrine, it speaks as never man spake; because it speaks with the voice of a teacher come from God. It knows what is in man; and it knows what is in God. It gives no surmises, no conjectures, no mere guesses at the truth. Its words are yea and amen—verily, verily, I say unto you—we speak that we do know, and testify what we have seen. It speaks in all the consciousness of superior wisdom and of infallible certainty. And hence it draws with absolute precision a line which the greatest and best men of ancient times, unaided by its light, could never draw clearly—the line between good and evil, virtue and vice, holiness and sin. So that the least in the kingdom of God here has a knowledge of duty which Socrates, Plato, and Aristotle might have coveted. There is, perhaps, nothing in the Bible so plain as the path of duty. The way-faring man, though a fool, need not mistake it. It is fenced along on both sides all the way to heaven by landmarks both negative and positive—directions both of injunction and of prohibition—precepts commanding all that is right, and forbidding all that is wrong.

Another reason of this superiority is found in the extent and spirituality of its requirements. As a rule of life, the Bible addresses itself directly to the conscience. "Thy commandment," says the Psalmist, "is exceeding broad." It is described as quick and powerful, sharper than any two-edged sword, a discerner of the thoughts and intents of the heart. It not only reveals God to man, but man to himself, as no other book was ever able to do. Speaking directly to the conscience, it seeks to control the outward actions of men, by controlling their inward thoughts and feelings. Its high aim is to bring every thought into subjection to the law of Christ. All human laws, from their imperfection, must stop with the overt actions of men. And all merely human systems of morality fail, because there is a large and important class of our duties, especially towards God, on which unassisted reason can shed no light, and lay down no rule. It is at this point that the word of God comes to our relief with its brightest light. Where all other teachers fail us—where reason falters and philosophy is silent as the grave—the Bible presents itself as a safe and infallible guide. Its requirements cover the whole ground of human duty in all our complex relations to God and our fellow men, time and eternity. And such is the compass and spirituality of its requirements, that they have power to control our whole spirit, and soul, and body.

And a still further reason of this superior influence of the moral code of the Bible is found in the Divine authority with which it is enforced. No other system, known amongst men, was ever enforced by such sanctions, or could appeal to such motives, legal or moral. The whole truth of the doctrinal system of the Bible is, as it were, but one vast storehouse of motives to enforce its precepts. Every doctrine is an argument pleading in God's great name for the fulfilment of duty. All that is august and awful in these revealed truths of God stands as an incentive to man, ever urging him to do all that God has commanded. And we cannot conceive of anything in the way of motives or sanctions, enforcing obedience, more perfect and powerful than those sublime and awful sanctions, legal and moral, by which the whole preceptive system of the Bible is supported. This point has been forcibly presented by Dr. Thornwell, in one of his admirable discourses on truth. "Whatever certifies the rule, or illustrates the misery of disobedience, assaults temptation in its strong hold, and strips transgression of its favourite plea. The certainty of the law is put beyond question in the Scriptures, because it rests upon the immediate authority of God. It is not a deduction of reason to be questioned, but a Divine command to be obeyed. The power of the sanctions is found in the unlimited control which He who promulgates the law possesses of the invisible world. The legal motives of the Scriptures are projected on a scale of inconceivable grandeur. The Bible deals with the vast, the awful, the boundless. If it addresses our hopes and proposes the prospect of future happiness, it is an exceeding, an eternal weight of glory it dispenses. Does it remind us of a judgment to come? God is the judge, earth and hell the subjects, angels spectators, and the complexion of eternity the doom. Does it address our fears? It reminds us of a worm that never dies—a fire that is never quenched—the blackness of darkness forever. It is a grand system; it springs from the bosom of an infinite God, and opens a field of infinite interests. Eternity in the emphasis it gives to its promises, the terror it imparts to its curse. Conscience under the tuition of nature, may dread the future; it is the prerogative of revelation alone to lay it bare. Conscience may tremble, but revelation alone can show how justly its fears have been excited. Hence the Bible is without a rival when it speaks in the language of command. It wields the thunder of infinite power, as well as utters the voice of infinite righteousness."

We regard the ethical system of the Bible alone, as furnishing a complete demonstration of its Divine origin. All experience proves that its tendency everywhere has been to make men better—restraining them from vice, constraining them to virtue. We feel, as by an intuition, that what is so good must be true—cannot be false. But if true, in this case, then Divine, because what is thus vindicated as true claims to be Divine; and, in admitting its truth, we admit its Divinity. God's truth ought to be good—ought to promote man's highest happiness. The moral code of the Bible does it—and that in exact proportion to the extent in which it is embraced. There is not one thing required in it, which would not promote our present and eternal good; and there is not one sin prohibited which would not ruin us, if indulged. All its injunctions and all its prohibitions are alike salutary. Its unvarying language to every being on earth, created in God's image, and capable of understanding right and wrong, is, "Do thyself no harm; seek that which is good: and let thy soul delight itself in fatness." To the individual and the family, to the little child and the man, to the community, to the nation, and to the whole world of mankind, it says—Embrace me, obey me, follow me, I will do thee good, I will lead thee to peace, plenty, and happiness here, to glory, honour, and immortality hereafter.

From the day in which Moses said to Israel, "See, I have set before thee life and good, in that I command thee to love the Lord thy God, to walk in his ways, and keep his commandments," down to the present hour, the word of God has vindicated itself as a good and wholesome rule of life to all who have endeavoured to live according to its precepts. It has verified all its promises. It has led men to usefulness and honour here, and given them peace in death and the hope of a blessed immortality beyond the grave. If there is any one great lesson of human experience, settled beyond the shadow of a doubt, demonstrated by the history of Israel, and every other nation that has possessed the Bible, illustrated in the happy lot of every good man, and the sad and bitter end of every bad one—it is that life and blessedness have been found in obedience to God's commands, wretchedness and ruin in the road of transgression. "Wisdom's ways are pleasantness, and all her paths are peace." And there are no others that are so. All others go astray. All others end in death. It is the Bible that asks and answers the greatest problem in morals —"Wherewithal shall a young man cleanse his way? By taking heed thereto according to thy word."

The history of the world, ever since the Bible has been in it, demonstrates this preceptive system, in all its requirements, to be a reasonable service—a thing to do us good, to make us happy, to keep us from manifold and infinite evils. It is profitable for all things, having the promise of the life that now is, as well as of that which is to come. The world cannot dispense with the morality of the Bible, any more than with its salvation. There never was a time, even under the most rigorous exactions of the ceremonial law, when the service of God was not immeasurably better than any thing else in the world, at the time, claiming to be a moral and religious system. Under every dispensation of the church ancient and modern, but especially under the gospel of the New Testament, the people of God have been able to compare both the doctrinal and the ethical systems of the Bible, with the moral codes of heathenism, and the schemes of sceptical philosophy, and to say, with overwhelming triumph, as did the great lawgiver of Israel—"Their rock is not as our rock, even our enemies themselves being judges."

VIII. THE BIBLE A FOUNTAIN OF SENTIMENT AND SYMPATHY.

There is another source of influence in the Bible, not often mentioned as such, and perhaps somewhat difficult to distinguish from those already referred to, which, nevertheless, seems to us one of exceeding importance. It is the power which it has to affect our whole emotional and sympathetic nature. It is the influence, which it exerts, as a book of sentiment and feeling, over the whole current of human thought, feeling, and character. Now, whilst it is mainly by the doctrines it reveals and the precepts it enjoins, though not exclusively so, that the Bible has power to affect the human heart, still this does not hinder our regarding it as a deep fountain of sentiment and feeling. If there were nothing in it but doctrines and precepts, even these alone might make it a book of sentiment: that is, of thought imbued with feeling and passion. But these are not all; these are everywhere intermingled with other elements. There is character in the Bible; character in all its moods; character human, angelic, and divine. There is nothing more obvious than its graphic delineation of character.

There is consequently feeling, sympathy, passion there, in all its varying hues, in all its intensest forms. And these things, incorporated throughout with its doctrinal and preceptive systems, make the Bible a deep and inexhaustible fountain of the finest sentiment.

Our meaning here may be readily illustrated by the difference between a church creed and a book of devotion. We have all the doctrines of the Bible summarily comprised in a Confession of Faith or an orthodox Catechism. But this is not a book of sentiment. On the other hand, we may have all these doctrines incorporated into a hymn book, or complete system of psalmody. And in this latter case, we may have all the doctrines which we had in the former; but they are doctrines fraught with feeling, and so forming a book of devotion and sentiment. Now, such is the Bible throughout, but especially so in some parts of it—a book of doctrines truly, but doctrines not in the dry form of a Catechism, but clad with feeling, and breathing out the living soul of sentiment.

As such, it could not fail to exert a deep and controlling influence over the sentiments of mankind; to give colouring to the whole current of human thought, and tone to human character; and, consequently, to that which is the sure exponent of all these, the world's literature. As a book of sentiment and feeling, the Bible has had this advantage, over all other books of sentiment; that being Divine, it has been the truest to nature, and therefore the most influential; and being Divine, its sentiments have been clothed with an authority which nothing else can claim. Hence we are prepared for that which modern history proves to be a fact: namely, that the literature of every nation which has received the Bible, is found imbued with its sentiments, just in proportion as the Bible has been studied.

If we look at society, as it now exists, in this, or any other Christian land, we shall find a vast body of our fellow-men, and among them often the most gifted and intelligent, who make no profession of religion, belong to no branch of the visible church, and cannot be said, either to have embraced the doctrines of the Bible, or to have obeyed its precepts. But has the Bible no influence over them? It has a most potent influence—an influence just as real and obvious, though not as full and saving, as that which it exerts over those within the pale of the church. They feel that influence every day and hour, in every opinion and sentiment they have ever adopted. That influence has been at work from their earliest childhood. To them the Bible has been, and is, the great fountain of sentiment and sympathy, out of which have been flowing all the deepest currents of their intellectual and moral character. They appreciate and admire the Bible as a book of sentiment and feeling, even while denying its doctrines, or refusing to obey its precepts. They might not be able to state a doctrine of the book correctly, but they have read with delight its graphic descriptions of nature, its glowing delineations of character, its passages of moral sublimity and beauty, its scenes of thrilling power and pathos: in a word, all those things that distinguish it as a book of genial sentiments and sympathies; and they have, either consciously or unconsciously, adopted them as their own. Upon this whole class of minds, the world over, the Bible has thus exerted an influence of sentiment, wholly distinct from that direct moral and religious influence which it has exerted over those who have truly believed and obeyed it. And so it has fashioned and controlled the thoughts and feelings, and to some extent the character, of that large class of men, who live without the pale of the visible church.

And this will serve to illustrate the manner in which the Bible has influenced the whole current of our literature. For our literature, in all departments, is to a very great extent the product of just this class of minds. A large proportion of our ablest writers, such, for example, as Shakspeare and Walter Scott, have been of this class; men who were certainly Christian in sentiment, as proved by all their writings, but not Christian in the full sense of living up to the doctrinal and preceptive systems of the gospel. And hence we find that a vast body of our literature which cannot be claimed as orthodox or evangelical, may be most justly regarded as Christian, because thoroughly imbued with Christian sentiment. In this way it is evident that the Bible has been a great well-spring of influence, whose salutary streams have been diffused through the whole literature, and public mind of Christendom. We find these sentiments of the Bible scattered, like its doctrines and precepts, through all parts of it; but especially in its sublime, impassioned poetry, its lofty eloquence, its thrilling narratives, its masterly delineations of character, its beautiful parables, its preceptive proverbs, its affectionate epistles, and above all, in its touching story of the cross. But the books of Job, the Psalms, and Proverbs may be taken as an example of its sentiment.

It has not only given us new conceptions of truth and duty; but it has filled the world with new sentiments and sympathies, the counterpart and reflection of these grand revelations. Its doctrines have been more than the dry abstractions of philosophy; they have been clothed with living power; its duties have all been illustrated in the living actions of men. As a vital quickening spirit, or as a sacred purifying fire, it has diffused itself into the very heart of the world; and it has created or developed there a whole class of exalted, heroic, and ennobling virtues, which found but little place, if any, in the old Greek and Roman literature, and have not existed at all in modern heathenism. It has been a little leaven at the first; but it has wrought mightily, until it has now well-nigh leavened the whole lump.

Do you ask, what are those sentiments that have thus sprung from the Bible? Of course, all of them cannot be pointed out here. But they are such as the following, which may be sufficient to illustrate our meaning: the love of God to our race, and all those sentiments which are suggested by the paternal character of God; the love of man to his fellow-man, and all its kindred ideas of fraternity, equality, and universal philanthropy; the sentiments of personal humility, condescension to the poor, liberality, beneficence, charity, mercy, religious toleration, and forgiveness of injuries; the feeling of responsibility to God, of respect for the aged, of reverence for law, gallantry to the weak, care of the sick, tenderness towards children, sympathy with the suffering, and companionship with woman; the sense of honour, of independence, patriotism, public spirit, moral courage, and self-denial even unto death for the good of man and the glory of God; the love of truth, the love of justice, the love of liberty, fortitude in affliction, temperance, patience, regard for human life, the sacredness of home, and the inviolate obligation of the marriage covenant. These, together with all the deep sympathies that gather around the story of the cross, may serve to illustrate what we mean, when we speak of the Bible as a fountain of sentiment and feeling. For all these lofty sentiments and godlike virtues, though now forming part and parcel of all modern literature worthy of the name, came from the Bible. They were either first created and vindicated by it; or else, when known before, they have been here taught on a scale of grandeur, and enforced with a clearness and authority, utterly unknown before.

In nothing has the triumph of the Bible been more brilliant and complete, than in the extent to which it has impregnated the common thought of the civilized world with all these heaven-born sentiments and sympathies. By these, all our greatest authors, in poetry, philosophy, criticism, history, biography, romance, as well as in morals and religion, stand elevated and distinguished above everything that classical antiquity, at its best estate, ever attained. This remark holds good, not only of those great lights of the inner temple, such as Milton, Cowper and Young, Johnson, Addison and Coleridge, whose genius was confessedly kindled at the divine altars, and who loved to sit in adoring homage at the feet of Jesus; but also of those of the outer court, who, like Shakspeare, Pope, and Scott, have seemed to stand at a greater distance from the shrine of God, but still near enough to catch the spirit of its worshippers; and even of those, few in number, who, like Byron, have striven to get as far off as possible, and to speak as little as they could in the language of Zion. All of these classes, though in very different degrees, have constantly reproduced the sentiments of the Bible in their writings, and thus illustrated its influence upon the human mind. So strong has been its hold upon the current literature of the world, that it has been impossible for any great writer, whose genius has been at all in sympathy with nature, truth, and beauty, wholly to emancipate himself from its powerful attractions, however sceptical his creed, and however strenuous his efforts. Consciously or unconsciously, all have bowed, in admiring homage, before the superior lustre of its sentiments and the majesty of its virtues. Some, like Hume and Gibbon, have reproduced its peculiar beauties while attempting to vilify or refute its claims; and some, like Rousseau, have gone so far as to confess it.

Take some illustrations of this reproduction of the Bible's sentiment. Pope is one of the most sceptical and unevangelical of all the great English poets. And yet we can hardly read a page of his more serious poems without finding sentiments which were evidently borrowed from the Bible; some of them so striking that he seems merely to have paraphrased the words of Scripture so as to suit his measure. For instance, take these two lines from his "Universal Hymn"—a hymn latitudinarian enough in its creed, to commend the worship of "Jehovah, Jove, or Lord," as alike good, and therefore the more strangely contrasting with some of its Christian sentiments

> "The mercy I to others show,
> That mercy show to me."

That certainly is a noble sentiment, and most assuredly not borrowed from the religion of Jove. Whence did it come? You perceive it is but a new translation of a single petition in the Lord's prayer: "Forgive us our trespasses, as we forgive those who trespass against us," modified by the words of the apostle James, "He shall have judgment without mercy, that hath showed no mercy."

Take another illustration from Shakspeare—one of those innumerable passages in which he adopts the very sentiment of the Scriptures without making the slightest allusion to them, or perhaps even thinking about them. It is in the Merchant of Venice, where Portia utters these wholesome words for Shylock's benefit:—

> "The quality of mercy is not strained;
> It droppeth as the gentle rain from heaven
> Upon the place beneath: it is twice bless'd;
> It blesseth him that gives, and him that takes:
> 'Tis mightiest in the mightiest; it becomes
> The throned monarch better than his crown;
> His sceptre shows the force of temporal power,
> The attribute to awe and majesty,
> Wherein doth sit the dread and fear of kings;
> But mercy is above this sceptered sway,
> It is enthroned in the hearts of kings,
> It is an attribute to God himself;
> And earthly power doth then show likest God's
> When mercy seasons justice. Therefore, Jew,
> Though justice be thy plea, consider this—
> That in the course of justice, none of us
> Shall see salvation; we do pray for mercy;
> And that same prayer doth teach us all to render
> The deeds of mercy."

What is this but the reiteration of our Saviour's memorable words, "It is more blessed to give than to receive." "Blessed are the merciful, for they shall obtain mercy." "Freely ye have received, freely give;" and of the oft-repeated proverbs—"The liberal soul shall be made fat; and he that watereth shall be watered also himself." "There is that scattereth, and yet increaseth; and there is that withholdeth more than is meet, but it tendeth to poverty." "The merciful man doeth good to his own soul!"

No one would suspect Byron of writing under the inspiration of the Bible. And yet how true to all its descriptions of the frailty of life, the vanity of the world, the depravity and ruin of our nature, are the following stanzas from Childe Harold, which he evidently wrote without once thinking from what quarter he was borrowing the sentiment:—

"Alas! our young affections run to waste,
Or water but the desert; whence arise
But weeds of dark luxuriance, tares of haste,
Rank at the core, though tempting to the eyes,
Flowers whose wild odors breathe but agonies,
And trees whose gums are poison: such the plants
Which spring beneath her steps as passion flies
O'er the world's wilderness, and vainly pants
For some celestial fruit forbidden to our wants.

We wither from our youth, we gasp away—
Sick—sick: unfound the boon—unslaked the thirst,
Though to the last, in verge of our decay,
Some phantom lures, such as we sought at first—
But all too late, so are we doubly curst.
Love, fame, ambition, avarice—tis the same,
Each idle—and all ill—and none the worst—
For all are meteors with a different name,
And death the sable smoke where vanishes the flame.

Our life is a false nature—'tis not in
The harmony of things, this hard decree,
This uneradicable taint of sin,
This boundless upas, this all blasting tree,
Whose root is earth, whose leaves and branches be
The skies which rain their plagues on men like dew—
Disease, death, bondage—all the woes we see—
And worse, the woes we see not—which throb through
The immedicable soul, with heart-aches ever new."

Alas! that understanding our malady so well he should not have better known its only cure! In what glowing numbers then might he have sung, with Cowper, Montgomery, and

Kirke White, of that balm in Gilead, and of that great Physician, provided of God, for the taking away of this "uneradicable taint of sin," and the healing of all the heart-aches of this "immedicable soul."

IX. ITS FUND OF HISTORICAL AND BIOGRAPHICAL FACT.

We come now to another, and in our present survey, the last great source of influence in the Bible. It is its vast fund of fact—biographical and historical fact. It has wielded the sceptre of authority over all other books, because it has come with the power of superior information, touching the origin of man, and the history of the world. It tells us what we greatly desired to know, and what can be learned from no other quarter. Across the wide waste of otherwise forgotten centuries, it comes to us with the burden of a great history, with every voucher of truth, which Divine inspiration can impart. It is a history, the earliest, the widest, the most curious, the most important, that ever engaged the attention of men. It is a history without which all the early annals of our race would be lost in fable, and history itself remain a strange and inexplicable riddle. It is the history of the ever-widening stream of human existence from its origin, through forty centuries of its progress, down to that great point, the cross of Christ, which alone could give it power to expound the past, interpret the present, and become the prophet of the future. It is accordingly the only history which makes any history intelligible. Was ever such a record, such a treasure, embosomed in any other book?

History has been appropriately called philosophy teaching by example; nor does philosophy ever speak more impressively than when she speaks to the living through the venerated voices of the dead. This maxim which holds good of history in general, is most signally true of that long line of history, which has been recorded for us by the pen of inspiration. There is scarcely any characteristic of the book of God more striking than this, of its being a history—a history of the world's creation, of man's existence in it, of God's providential dealings with man, of the kingdom of Christ on earth, and of the grand scheme of redemption from its opening to its close. It was certainly not without some high purpose that the truth of God necessary to salvation should be made known in this historical and biographical form, its revelations filling a period of forty centuries, its stupendous doctrines gradually unfolded in the events of Providence, its sublime precepts and sentiments all enforced and exemplified in the living actions of men. It is preëminently a book of facts—such facts, both in multitude and grandeur, as the historic muse of Greece never collected. Its doctrines are facts, or deduced from facts; its precepts are built on facts; its sentiments are all illustrated by facts.

There is something grand and imposing in this historical character of the Bible; that it should be a revelation from God, and yet should take the form of a human history. Think of any other book as undertaking to reveal the character of God and the plan of salvation, through the facts of history and the lives of men! Think of any other historian as telling the tale of forty centuries before reaching the grand climax which first led him to take his pen in hand, and, through all those ages, deliberately weaving a web of human story, which should be but as the prologue of a drama, to introduce its chief character. But you cannot think of any other; for since Herodotus began to write, there never was another that did it or even attempted it. Suppose we had no Bible, and no revelation from God whatever; and that God should begin from this time forward to reveal himself to mankind; and should do it through the medium of a carefully recorded history of Great Britain or the United States. Would not such a thing be marvellous in our eyes? But this is just the texture of our Bible. Its long, broad warp is history—first, the history of the whole world—then, of one great race and nation—then, of one Divine man, who concentrated in himself all the glory of that race—and then, a prophecy supplementing the history to the end of time; while the thickly woven woof of this long story, from first to last, is biography or the lives of the saints of God.

It is in keeping with the biographical character of the book throughout, that of the first good man that died on earth, righteous Abel, we should have this declaration—"He being dead, yet speaketh." God ordained that he should be a teacher to all the generations of men. And this was the method of his instruction. He was to speak, as so many others did afterwards, by having his name, and holy life, and martyr's death, inscribed upon the oracles of God. And this earliest example of God's method of teaching man, by his fellow-man, is but an illustration of the influence, which has gone out over all the earth, from the Scriptures, as a book of history and biography.

But there is scarcely any thing in the Bible, with which an unbelieving criticism has found more fault, and against which it has been readier to level the shafts of its ridicule, than these recorded lives of the servants of God. Scepticism considers them very imperfect characters at best, and very bad models for us. Scepticism, however, forgets the main point of their introduction to the sacred pages; forgets that the book, which records these imperfect lives, teaches throughout and by these very examples, that all men are, by nature, ruined sinners; that there is no such thing as human perfection, or salvation by morality and deeds of law; that no man can be justified before God, by what he has done, or for what he is in himself; and that every one who is saved at all, must be saved through the atoning blood of Jesus Christ. These lives of the holy men of old, from Noah to David, and from David to Paul, are just histories of great sinners redeemed from all their sins by a great Saviour. As such they are in perfect harmony with all the other teachings of the Bible. They are what they were intended to be, eminent illustrations of man's apostasy and God's grace; and all the more so, because they are, sometimes, what infidelity would call hard cases. A hard case is the very case in point, when the point is to show the sovereign power and grace of God; just as a dangerous disease is the best case to test the virtue of the medicine. Such a sinner as Manasseh, or David, or Paul, when saved, only proves the more signally, that where sin abounded, grace did much more abound. Let scepticism remember that they are not held up to be admired as models of angelic virtue. There is no such model in the Bible, save one, the man Christ Jesus. But the grand design of all these historical and biographical sketches, which constitute so large a portion of the Scriptures, is to reveal the way of life by the gospel, and to display, for our learning and encouragement, the glorious grace of God in the salvation of sinners.

And who can say, that any other method could have been devised, so effective and impressive, so adapted to different capacities, so easy for the learner, and so enduring in its influence over him, as this method of teaching by living examples, infinitely diversified through a period of four thousand years?

As it is, the Bible is a vast picture gallery, where every face may find its likeness, and every character its counterpart. It is a rich store-house of instruction to which every reader may come perpetually, to draw lessons of wisdom for all the duties and trials of life. It is an inexhaustible fund of fact and illustration, from which the pulpit of Christendom may continue, till the end of time, to derive its most powerful arguments and appeals. Thus we find the Old Testament histories and biographies, with all their teeming wealth of incident and character, constantly referred to in the New, to illustrate the saving faith of the gospel. "These all died in the faith, not having received the promises, but having seen them afar off, and were persuaded of them, and embraced them, and confessed that they were strangers and pilgrims on the earth." These are the ensamples set for our learning. These constitute a part of that great cloud of witnesses, whom the apostle conceives as looking down from the skies to cheer us on our race for glory. These, though dead, yet speak to us through all the Scriptures; and when we hear them, it is but to hear God's own animating voice;

Up from the dust, thou child of sin and sorrow,
  Ten thousand voices bid thee weep no more;
Though dark the night, 'twill bring a bright to-morrow—
  The day of peace and joy for evermore.

It is obvious at a glance, that as a book of history and biography, the Bible holds the very first rank among books. It has so interwoven its biographical characters into its historic narrative, everywhere enlivening the general with the detailed description, as to give the whole, the sustained interest of a great drama. It has thus imparted the vivacity of living characters to its history; and the dignity of history to all its minutest biography. In this respect it is a model for the world. It has not only taught men how to live, but how to write. We know not where Macaulay got the idea of his charming method; but we have been reminded of the Bible history, as we have seen his life-like biographical sketches, and his dramatic shifting of the scene constantly coming in to relieve the long line of his narrative. The chief characteristics of the Bible biography are simplicity of style, brevity, impartiality, truthfulness, and the absence of eulogy. The faults of men are as faithfully stated as their virtues. Character is drawn to the life, not by words of description, but by its living actions. Men are praised only as their deeds of virtue praise them. There is every variety of character given, from the immaculate purity of the Son of God, to the deformity of the prince of darkness; from the fidelity of the loved disciple, to the treachery of a Judas; and it is drawn with every varying degree of fulness, from a whole book on the life of Jesus, to the passing touches of a single verse. There is certainly nothing in the whole range of literature, more wonderful, and more worthy of imitation, than this life-like, biographic history of the Bible.

X. THE BIBLE COMPARED WITH WORKS OF GENIUS.

Having now pointed out the four great collateral sources of power, by which the book of God diffuses its influence over the world in its doctrines, its precepts, its sentiments, and its facts; or those things which characterize it successively as a theology, a morality, a religion, and a history, and make it altogether the most remarkable thing in the world—it remains for us, in conclusion, to set before the reader, as distinctly and yet briefly as we can, our own impressions, as to the extent and value of this influence. And this we shall be best able to do by an illustration. Though the Bible is so unlike other books that it is difficult to compare them, yet other books may be taken as the best measure of its excellence. We can judge of its merits most easily, when we bring it, side by side, with the great works of human genius. And for this purpose, we shall take the works of Shakspeare as our standard. Of ancient authors, Homer would be the best illustration. But we regard Shakspeare as a greater genius than Homer; all things considered, the very greatest that has appeared in any age. And as our object is to measure the Bible by the greatest uninspired genius, we accordingly select the works of the bard of Avon.

Now it would seem, at first sight, a little incongruous to put the two in comparison, owing to their many points of total dissimilarity. But on examination there will be found, between the Scriptures as a whole, and Shakspeare's writings as a whole, many points of striking resemblance, and such too as exactly suit our present purpose of illustration.

In the first place, let us get a distinct idea of what constitutes the real greatness of the bard of Avon. We open his writings, and find them, like our Scriptures, to be a large collection of comparatively short and separate pieces, each as completely finished in itself, as if it had no connection with the others; but all written by one man, whereas the Scriptures were written by many. We find all these pieces, making up the book, written in what is confessedly the most ephemeral and perishable form of literature, that is, in the form of dramas or plays for the stage. Consider for a moment the nature of such compositions. The poet writes for a particular occasion,

5

to please some particular audience, in some special locality. For, as his plays are to be acted, and he has to live by his genius, he must make them popular, so as to draw the multitude, even the illiterate multitude, at the given place and time. But if they must be thus local and popular, how shall they be immortal? How shall the bard, writing under these conditions of disadvantage, please the populace, satisfy the local critics of the time, and yet write for all men and all times? What suits one place and one audience may not suit others. What suits one generation may not suit all. What suits one race and nation may not suit the world. Can the bard then make these ephemeral productions universal and enduring? That he has done it is enough to vindicate the greatness of Shakspeare. These apparently ephemeral productions, composed for the entertainment of a London audience two hundred and fifty years ago, overstepping all the boundaries of time and place, have spread with an ever-widening popularity, from generation to generation, from race to race, from language to language, until they have filled the whole civilized world with the most profound and undying admiration. So that men of all classes and conditions, the learned and the rude, nations of different tongues and different eras, the grave and the gay, have all agreed in extolling the genius of Shakspeare.

Nor is this all. When we examine these marvellous dramas —so perishable in their form, and yet so universal and undying in their influence over the world—we find them entitled to this high distinction. We find in them an originality, versatility, and combination of great talents, for which it would be hard to find an equal in any other writings. That is to say, we find many different kinds of endowment of the very highest order, meeting, and all coming to perfection in Shakspeare; any one of which alone would make him a full match for any other man, who has ever written in each special department. And this is enough to prove the transcendent greatness of his genius. For example, take him simply as a dramatist; and, for power of invention, originality, insight into human nature, and skill in the delineation of passion, he is fully equal, if not superior, to any other writer. Take him simply as a poet; and you will find passages of sublimity, beauty, and pathos, with a range of imagination, fully up to any thing to be found in Homer, Virgil, Milton, Burns, or any poet that ever wrote. Take him as a wit, a humourist, or a satirist; and he is a full match for any other wit, humourist, or satirist in any language, ancient or modern. Take him as a moralist; and you will find a fidelity to nature and common sense, a range of observation and experience, and profound insight into human character, not surpassed by men who have spent their lives on the study of morals. Take him on the deepest philosophy of man—the nature and working of the human mind—and you will find him equal to all the books and all the schools, ancient and modern. You will find a profound and far-reaching knowledge of man, in all his powers, relations, and destinies, which has suggested to some of the German critics, the idea that he was a philosopher in disguise, who, in advance of his age, was seeking to teach the world lessons of wisdom and virtue through the only channel which it could then appreciate—the stage-play. But be this as it may; our main point cannot be denied—that if you single out from the whole range of literature, those passages which you consider the highest efforts of unassisted genius, in all the diversified fields of sublimity, beauty, pathos, eloquence, fancy, invention, wit, humour, satire, description, dialogue, romance, fiction, wisdom, or philosophy, you may find a match for every one of them, somewhere in Shakspeare. That is to say, Shakspeare, in several important departments of literature, has achieved the very highest perfection of his art, and is, in all of them, fully equal, if not superior, to all other writers, who even singly have been most distinguished in those departments.

Now these two considerations alone—that he has taken the most ephemeral form of literature, and breathed into it that which is universal and immortal, and that, in this form, he has reached an excellence in several distinct kinds of writing, beyond which no human genius was ever able to go—justify us in taking his works as the highest standard of what man can do. And this is the standard by which we would measure the Bible. Let us now see how it applies.

When we open the Scriptures, we find them, as just stated, to be a collection of separate pieces, all complete in themselves, and for the most part written at different times and places. Some of these pieces are grave historical treatises or prophecies, large enough to bear the name of books; but the most of them were written for some definite local purpose, and are, in fact, as short and apparently as ephemeral, as any of the pieces of Shakspeare; being either brief prophecies for the times, or songs of praise written for the choirs of the temple, or current letters addressed to churches or to individuals. But, if these pieces that make up the Bible, be not all quite so ephemeral in form as his, yet, humanly speaking, they were far more unlikely ever to become universal and immortal as a whole, from the important fact that they were nearly all written by different authors, through a period of fifteen centuries; whereas his were all the productions of one mind. If the more ephemeral form of stage-plays makes the wonder, that they should live and become immortal, the greater in his case, this great diversity of authorship, in the case of the Bible, along with the perishable form of much of its contents, would vastly augment the wonder, that a book, thus composed by piecemeal, should ever live and become immortal. And if a single human genius in the greatness of its triumph, could take these local and temporary dramas, and so endow them with immortality, that all the world should admire them, what genius shall take some sixty different pieces, written by some forty different hands, and not only make them a unit, but breathe into its whole composition a universal and immortal life?

But this is just the life which the Bible is living in the world. These, once local, apparently ephemeral, and still greatly dissimilar productions, like those of the great dramatist, have transcended all the boundaries of time and place, race and language, climate and country, sea and continent; and to say the least, have become as completely universal and immortal, as any thing on earth. For theirs is a triumph and dominion, not like his, of two hundred and fifty years, but of eighteen centuries. If great success triumphing over great difficulties be the measure and the proof of great ability, as it undoubtedly is in the bard of Avon, what must be our estimate of the greatness of the Bible, triumphing over still greater difficulties, and achieving a much greater success? Judged simply as a human production, is it not manifest, that the rule which requires us to rank Shakspeare, as we think justly, above all other works of genius, will require us to place the Bible even above Shakspeare?

But this is not all. Our judgment rests not solely on the principle, that what has been received as great, always, everywhere, and by all men, must be great. We are permitted to examine and judge for ourselves. And so, when we look fully into these apparently ephemeral tracts that make up our Scriptures, what do we see? We find just that sort of wonder, which was so remarkable in Shakspeare, only on a still grander scale. We behold a combination of excellences, of rare and extraordinary powers of different kinds, and in many different departments of writing, such as never did meet before, to the same extent, and we venture to say, never will meet again, in any other book. In poetry, eloquence, history, and biography; in sublimity, beauty, pathos, and imagination; in concentration of thought, in grandeur of imagery, in the portraiture of character, in the delineation of passion, in descriptions of nature, in power of reasoning, in the inculcations of truth, and the illustrations of the principles of virtue, not to speak of its high revelations of religion, we find passages in the Bible, which are fully equal, and often superior, to any thing of the kind to be found in the whole compass of literature. We have not space here to prove this by examples. We have had occasion to illustrate it at length, in another work—"The Literary Attractions of the Bible;" and all thorough students of the Bible will bear us out in the statement. These books of Scripture, not claiming to be works of genius at all, nor intended by their respective authors to be contributions to literature, but all written for the one specific purpose of revealing the religion of God to man, have nevertheless given us, examples and models of excellence in almost every department of literature, beyond which no human genius, in any age or nation, has been able to go. As we can find a match for almost all other writers in Shakspeare, so we can find a match for them and Shakspeare himself in the Bible.

But perhaps you are ready to think in all this, that we are

exaggerating the superiority of the Bible. No doubt, some will think, we have also exaggerated the superiority of Shakspeare. But his admirers, especially those who have studied him the longest and deepest, will not think so. They know from profound acquaintance how much there is in him. And thus only, from long and deep study, can any man know how much is in the Bible. We have no fear, that any thorough student, in either case, will dissent from the view we have taken. The superficial may in both cases, but it is for want of a full acquaintance with the subject. For not every man knows the Bible, who thinks he knows it. The greatest truths in nature always lie the deepest; and the whole history of science, both before and after Newton's day, shows how long some of them have had to lie there unknown for want of an interpreter who could read them. So there are many things of truth, of beauty, and of grandeur, that lie in the Bible; just as there are in Shakspeare; and it requires some study, as well as taste, to appreciate and bring them out. We do not mean, by all this, that you shall find a grand Epic, like Paradise Lost, all written out, in the Bible; but, that there are passages in the Bible, of power and beauty, fully equal to any thing in Paradise Lost; and so of other works of genius with which it may be compared.

These, then, are the two grounds on which we vindicate the superiority of the Bible, even as a human book alone, compared with the greatest works of genius: namely, that, under the most unfavourable conditions it has become universal and immortal; and that, in all those fields of thought, which human genius has called its own, and illustrated by its greatest achievements, the Bible contains models of sublimity and beauty, fully equal, if not superior, to any of them.

And now, what is the bearing of all this superior excellence upon the truth and divinity of the Scriptures? Let us see. In the case of Shakspeare, the facts of which we have been speaking demonstrate, beyond the shadow of a doubt, that he was endowed with the very highest inspirations of human genius. In the case of the Bible, the analogous facts must be held to prove, with equal certainty, that its writers were also endowed, either with the highest inspirations of genius, or else, with something higher still. Any thing else would be wholly inadmissible, as not accounting for the wonderful character of the sacred writings, even as human compositions. And we do not see, how any man, who denies the Divine inspiration of the Bible, and rejects every thing higher than the inspiration of genius, can escape from the conclusion, that the sacred writers were all endowed with the highest gifts of genius; any more than he could resist that conclusion respecting Shakspeare, Homer, or Milton. Now, if these facts respecting the Bible were the only ones to be taken into account, we should rest in this first part of the conclusion: to wit, that the Bible is the product of the highest human genius. And the argument in favour of that conclusion, as we have seen, would be even stronger for the Bible, than for Shakspeare.

But these are not all the facts, nor even the most important. We find another class of facts, rising entirely above the province of human genius. And it is on the basis of these other facts, that we have the great argument for the Divine origin and inspiration of the Scriptures. Here it is that we find the witness of a power and inspiration with which mere human genius was never endowed. And here the analogy between Shakspeare and the Bible ends. We find in these same Scriptures what is not to be found in his or any other work of genius, a system of revelations direct from God, supported by a vast array of mighty miracles, making known to us an august system of doctrines and duties—in a word, a new religion, which was intended to supplant, and has, in fact, supplanted and abolished all other religions in the world wherever it has gone. This makes an immeasurable difference between the Bible and all other books; so that, if the first class of facts, namely, those which belong to the Bible in common with such works as Shakspeare's, shut us up to the conclusion that the Bible could not be the product of anything less than the greatest human genius; this other, far higher, class of facts, will also shut us up, with equal certainty, to the other conclusion, that it must be the product of something more; and, if more, then Divine. For it is not more certain that none but a great genius could write what Shakspeare wrote, than it is certain that neither Shakspeare nor any other man could have written, except by inspiration of God, what we find in the Bible, on all those high and awful themes. To appreciate the force of this remark, you have only to imagine that, in addition to what you now have in Shakspeare, you should find there such miracles, such doctrines, such precepts, such revelations from God, and such institutions as you have in the Bible; and, in addition to all these, should see the whole civilized race of man, as a matter of unquestioned historical fact, tracing its whole system of religion and morality to his writings as the origin, and starting point. For it is not a particle more incredible that you should find all these things in a mere human writer such as Shakspeare, and find all these grand world-wide effects, flowing from him as the source, than it would be to find them all in the Bible as we do, and trace them all to the Bible, as the world does, and yet regard the Bible as a mere human book. If you feel, in your very soul, that such a thing would be impossible in Shakspeare's case; that is, just the impossibility which lies in the way of the Bible's being anything else than a Divine Book.

XI. CONCLUDING REMARKS.

In view of considerations such as these, how insane is the folly that would withhold the Bible from the daily reading of the people, and how atrocious the wickedness that would banish it from the schools of education! It is the hapless fate of our modern infidelity to extol a book which it will not admit to be true, and yet cannot prove to be false. It is the still sadder inconsistency of the Papal church, and her more damning guilt, to hate the very book which she knows to be from God, and to the extent of her power, to extinguish its light among men. No error is so fatal as that which rejects and despises the only possible method of having its mistakes corrected. There is hope of a man so long as he will read what God has written, even though he read it in a doubting, cavilling spirit. But what possible chance is there for truth or salvation, when, so far from searching the Scriptures, men pronounce it a mortal sin even to hear what God has said? In this war against the Bible the Papal church is infinitely worse than infidel. Not merely does it reject the light, and the truth, and the bread of life which God in his bounty has provided for the world; but it seeks, by all the terrors of priestly power to prevent the world from ever knowing what God has revealed in his word. Is it a crime to put out a man's eyes, or to withhold the light of truth from a single human mind? Here is a power which is chargeable with the unnatural and unparalleled crime of standing between God and the souls of men, and which, if its success were only equal to its intention, would entail upon the world a reign of spiritual darkness as deep, as wide, and as perpetual, as that natural night which would follow the extinction of the sun, or the putting out of every human eye. Infidelity is a great error, and a great wrong. But it has never, even in the days of its pride and power, devised a more gigantic wickedness than this.

Infidelity reads but to doubt the more. And yet it is often constrained, in defiance of its doubts, to admire and confess the preëminent wisdom and beauty of the sacred pages. One of the most remarkable things in the history of this sceptical philosophy is its frequent and often high-wrought eulogium of the Bible. Does it seek, by fine-spun compliment to Christ and the Gospel, to make amends for the injury it has done through the advocacy of unbelief? Very likely, a sort of poetic justice has prompted those unasked tributes of commendation, which it has been the fashion, at least since the times of Rousseau, to offer to the Bible on the part of those who dispute its claims. Most assuredly there is no such book in the world, infidels themselves being judges. Testimony coming from such quarters is, of course, not to be undervalued or refused; but the mode of treatment in giving it, is very much like that of Joab when he slew Abner, or of Judas when he said, "Hail, Master, and kissed him."

One of the most recent tributes of this kind we have met with, and perhaps as strong and decided as anything since the famous confession of Rousseau, is the following from Mr. Francis Newman, as cited by Henry Rogers in the Eclipse of Faith. The devoutest believer in the world could scarcely say more of the book of God than this champion of modern unbelief. "There is no book in all the world," says he, "which

I love and esteem so much as the New Testament with the devotional parts of the Old. There is none which I know so intimately, the very *words* of which dwell close to me *in my most sacred thoughts*, none for which I so thank God; none on which *my soul and heart have been to so great an extent moulded.* In my *early boyhood*, it was my private delight and daily companion; and to it I owe the best part of whatever wisdom there is in my manhood." After praise like this, it seems to us that infidelity might afford to adjourn the question of a Divine origin, and even on the ground of common philanthropy, aid the Bible society in printing and circulating so blessed a book!

But it is not alone from the circles of unbelief that we hear high and just encomium on the Bible. The noblest genius of the age in which we live bows in graceful and willing homage before its claims. Take one example out of many as an evidence of the truth, and a fitting close of these remarks—it is the tribute of our distinguished American orator and statesman, who is doing so much to embalm his own honoured name with the memory of Washington. "Apart from its direct claims upon our reverence as the depository of a Divine Revelation," says Mr. Everett, "we cannot but respect the Bible as the great fountain of our civilization. Strike from the political, moral, and intellectual condition of modern society, all that has flowed directly or indirectly from this source, and you would reduce European and American Christendom to the state of the barbarous and semi-civilized countries, whose character has been formed, or powerfully influenced by the Koran, or other religious codes of the East. The highest historical probability can be adduced in support of the proposition that, if it were possible to annihilate the Bible, and with it all its influence, we should destroy with it the whole spiritual system of the modern world—all our great moral ideas—refinement of manners—constitutional government—equitable administration of law, and security of property—our schools, hospitals, and benevolent associations—the press—the fine arts—the equality of sexes, and the blessings of the fire-side—in a word, all that distinguishes Europe and America from Turkey and Hindostan."

CHAPTER II.

PORTRAITURE OF CHILDHOOD IN THE BIBLE.

I. HOW THE BIBLE ADDRESSES CHILDREN.

In the very spirit of the book, whose excellences we have been seeking to describe, and which seems to delight in nothing more than a tender care for the young, let us begin our survey of Bible characters, by looking at the lives of its little children. It has much to tell us, everywhere, of childhood and youth. It would not have been true to the living world, as we find it, if it had left them out. And any illustration of its biographical characters, would be incomplete, without, at least, a passing glance at its numerous groups of children. Their constant presence amid all the scenes of Scripture history, gives the same delightful air of life and variety to the sacred pages, which may be found in the real world around us, wherever home is made happy, and the hearth-stone joyous, by the companionship of sons and daughters. This world would be a sad one, indeed, much sadder than it is, were it not for the ringing glee of childhood, heard at morning, noon, and nightfall, through all its hills and valleys, alike in its mansions of wealth, and its humble dwellings of the poor. Other things being equal, we regard those families, the world over, as the happiest, which are the largest—most blest with the presence of children, like olive plants round about their table. We have no sympathy, and we are very sure the Bible has none, with that wretched misanthropy which grudges childhood an existence in the world, and hails exemption from its care and trouble as a great blessing. There is not one line in the Bible, which represents the presence of children as a burden and hardship. On the contrary, the Psalmist expresses the view of all the sacred writers in those gladsome and beautiful words: "Lo, children are a heritage of the Lord; and the fruit of the womb is his reward. As arrows are in the hand of a mighty man; so are children of the youth. Happy is the man that hath his quiver full of them."

We are in perfect harmony, then, with the whole spirit of the Bible, in assigning its children a prominent place in our present undertaking. But there are certain general characteristics of the Bible method of dealing with childhood which it may be well to notice, here, in the foreground. Before we attempt to set forth those individual characters, or those groups of children, that figure in the sacred pages, let us point out some things in the manner of address, by which the Bible speaks to children more effectively than any other book, even when it does not speak of them. For it would be a great mistake to suppose, that only those parts of the Bible which are about children, are addressed to them.

Now, without any disparagement to the merits of such books for childhood as, "Æsop's Fables," or the "Arabian Nights," or "Robinson Crusoe," we may justly claim, that the Bible, when rightly used, is the most interesting book to children in the world. And its great attractiveness arises from these two causes: first, from the kindly manner in which it speaks to children; and secondly, from the frequency and fulness, with which it speaks of them. It speaks to them and of them, as no other book has ever done, except those which have spoken in its name. It presents to our view various groups of children, experiencing all the diversified and often opposite fortunes, which are to be found on the great stage of life. It portrays minutely and graphically many living characters among them, passing through all the degrees of good and evil, joy and suffering, that can mark the career of childhood in the world. And all this is attractive to the youthful mind. But besides this, it has everywhere adopted a style of address, well calculated to win the heart, excite the curiosity, please the fancy, and instruct the understanding of the young. And in this way it has, in all ages, gained an influence over them, which no one can deny or disregard. We all know, as a matter of history, that it has gained and retained its mastery over the adult mind of the world, in great part, by means of that early, all-controlling influence, which it has wielded over the young mind of each successive generation. What is there in the Bible to give it this influence? We have endeavoured, in the foregoing chapter, to show what there is, as it regards man in general. But in what lies the secret of its power and the charm of its fascination over the tender mind of childhood?

II. FIRST CHARACTERISTIC.

We may mention, first, that wonderful simplicity of language, and naturalness of imagery, by which it oftentimes brings down its loftiest themes to the comprehension of a child. There is a plainness of speech about the Bible, which reveals itself even unto babes. To the child, it often "speaks as a child, thinks as a child;" and that without any approach to puerility. And sometimes what is hidden from the wise and prudent, is here made radiant with heaven's own light to the opening eyes of childhood. As the winds of heaven play gently around the tender grass of the field, as the sunbeams bend themselves down to kiss the lowliest lily of the valley, so does the word of God stoop, in condescending kindness, to the capacity of the infant of days. It has words of profoundest learning for the great and the wise; and yet, like the eastern sages at Immanuel's birth, it brings its richest treasures of truth—its gifts: gold, frankincense, and myrrh, and lays them down at the feet of humble, docile infancy.

You are well aware, that books for children, as a general rule, have to be constructed on a different plan from those intended for adult minds. What suits the young, does not often suit the aged. The same book of science, or literature, or religion, will not interest the minds of the young and the old, the educated and the uneducated, alike. But there is something in the very language of the Bible, as well as in its subject-matter, which seems to adapt it, at once, to all periods of life, all stages of scholarship, all degrees of mental capacity. The same story, or character, will rivet the attention of learned men and of little children, and be read with equal and undying interest, by every class and condition in life. All its high and holy themes, even its most mysterious and sublime revelations of the Divine character, while furnishing food for the life-long contemplations of philosophy, have yet enough on the surface, that is plain and patent to instruct both the little child and the unlettered man.

Beautifully has it been remarked, that "there are in the Bible shallows where a lamb may wade, and deep waters where an elephant might swim." But the wonderful thing is, that the elephant and the lamb may both feel at home in the same waters; may drink together at the same great fountain, just as though its life-giving virtues had been made for each alone. The text which interested Sir Isaac Newton at sixty, will interest a child at six years old. Can this be said of any other book in the world? Now, it is this wonderful characteristic of simple, unadorned grandeur, running through all the Scriptures, clothing the greatest thoughts in the plainest words and symbols; it is this, that enables them to speak in an attractive voice to the children of every land and every age. In the language of Dr. Brown: "They are transparently clear, and they are unfathomably deep. There is much important truth on the surface: there is more, much more beneath it. Much meaning meets the ear; but more meets the mind. The words express much—they suggest more. They are replete with emphasis, and rich in reference." Hence, a man may read the Bible all his life, and still find something new in the old familiar words, whose import he thought he had exhausted when a child. The words expand in meaning, as the mind expands in capacity.

III. SECOND CHARACTERISTIC.

Again, the Bible is full of interest to children, because it addresses them in the great name of God; and, at the same time, speaks with an endless variety, both of style and of subject. From beginning to end, God Almighty is present in all the sayings and doings of the Bible. He is its grand theme, its Alpha and Omega. It tells us of a thousand other things, but they are all connected with God. It is the fashion of many book-makers in our day, especially the fictionists, who are reaping an ephemeral popularity, at the cost of anything like enduring fame, to leave God out of view as much as possible. Verily they have their reward—much laudation and much money now! But coming generations will not hear of them. The most popular novelist of the day, a hundred years hence, will be read by no one except the antiquarian; and by him only, to see how much could be made of nothing. It is in the power of human genius, even when perverted, to achieve wonders, but it will hardly be able to withhold from oblivion, a literature which has no better basis than fiction, and no better religion than atheism. How different is it with the Bible—built on the enduring basis of truth, and reared to the glory of God! Beginning and ending with God, it lays hold of the youthful mind by a grasp, corresponding somewhat to its great theme. For there is nothing which the ingenuous mind of a child is more delighted to hear about, than God.

But while God himself is the main subject of the Bible, there is an endless variety in the detail; precisely as there is in all the manifestations of God in the book of nature. A devout mind can feel the presence and behold the glory of God in every field of nature, and every event of life; but so variously displayed as never to weary the attention. And so is it in the Bible. The scene is constantly changing; the style is constantly changing; the subjects are changed; the speakers themselves change. It is not Homer all the time, nor Milton all the time; nor even Moses and Paul all the time; but some forty different historians, bards, and sages, in alternation and succession. The diversity is as great as the history of forty centuries, embracing the fortunes of individuals and of nations, can make it. The book borrows variety and wonder from all the greatest transactions and interests of three worlds, heaven, earth, and hell. It is a grand drama of real life and character, where the highest representatives of these worlds, human, angelic, and divine, are seen and heard, speaking and acting in their own appropriate spheres.

This point has been strikingly presented by Professor Gaussen. "The Bible instructs all conditions; it brings on the stage the humble and the great; it reveals to them equally the love of God, and exposes in them the same miseries. It addresses children; and they are often children, who there show us the way to heaven, and the greatness of the Lord. It addresses herdsmen; and they are often herdsmen, who there speak, and reveal to us the character of God. It speaks to kings and to scribes; and they are often kings and scribes, who there teach us the miseries of man, humility, confession, and prayer. Domestic scenes, avowals of the conscience, secret effusions of prayer, travels, proverbs, revelations of the depths of the heart, the holy career of a child of God, weakness unveiled, falls, revivings, intimate experiences, parables, familiar letters, theological treatises, sacred commentaries on some ancient Scripture, national chronicles, military pageants, political censures, descriptions of God, portraits of angels, celestial visions, practical counsels, rules of life, solutions of cases of conscience, judgments of the Lord, sacred songs, predictions of the future, accounts of the days which preceded our creation, sublime odes, inimitable poetry. All this is found in turn; and all this is there exposed to our view, in a variety full of charm, and in a whole, whose majesty is captivating like that of a temple." How could such a book fail to fascinate the young?

IV. THIRD CHARACTERISTIC.

A third striking characteristic of its method with children is found in its incomparable short stories, its multiplied and beautiful parables and allegories. Its symbols, figures, and similitudes are drawn from the most familiar objects in nature. And in this way, the whole outer world around us becomes a teacher, conveying, through the language of Scripture, its lessons of truth and wisdom. In its unique and inimitable parables and allegories, the Bible possesses all the charms of fiction, without losing the higher charms of truth.

We all know how strong and abiding is the impression, which the language of fable and allegory makes upon the young mind. Of all the books which have come down to us from the ancient classical world, what one, think you, is most attractive to the young? No doubt, every school-boy would answer at once, "Æsop's Fables." And of all the books that have ever been written in the English tongue, what one, do you suppose, has been read by the greatest number of persons, and been most pleasing to children and youth? It would be difficult to tell. But of religious books next after the Bible, we suppose, the "Pilgrim's Progress" has been the most popular. But what is the Pilgrim's Progress, and what the secret of its popularity? It is a dream, an allegory, a prolonged parable, founded from first to last upon the Scriptures, and deriving therefrom all its materials, its peculiar conceptions, and its wonderful interest. But for the Bible, Bunyan's genius never would have been awakened, for the production of that immortal work. Now, the reason why the Pilgrim's Progress has such power over the minds of the young, is because it has virtually reproduced the Bible. It has spoken to them on Scriptural subjects of the deepest interest, in the very style and manner and spirit of the Scriptures. But for the parables and allegories, the dreams and visions of holy writ, the world would never have heard either of John Bunyan, or his Christian Pilgrim.

Nothing in human literature can exceed the force and beauty of our Saviour's parables in the New Testament. In these, as in all his discourses, "he spake as never man spake." This speaking in parables seemed to be one of the peculiar and wonderful characteristics of his preaching. There are about thirty of these parables recorded at length by the Evangelists, besides those familiar comparisons and analogies, which he was in the habit of employing on all occasions. Similar to these parables of Christ, we find in the Old Testament, Isaiah's parable of the "Vineyard," Ezekiel's allegory of the "Valley of dry bones," Nathan's parable of the "Ewe Lamb," and Jotham's sarcastic "Fable of the Trees," in the book of Judges, which last may be regarded as the earliest example of a regular parable in the Scriptures.

From this first fable of Jotham down through all the allegories of the prophets, and the impersonations of the poets, even to the thirty recorded parables of Jesus, in what a multitude of diversified forms and shapes, colors and disguises, has Divine Truth presented herself to the human mind in the Scriptures! Why has she done it? Why has she thus spoken in parable and symbol? Why has she thus borrowed drapery from every object in nature? We answer, in order that she might be the more attractive and the more intelligible to all the generations that should follow. For after all, figurative language is the language of nature, and the easiest to be understood. As the prominent objects of nature—the sea, the sky, the rain, the sunshine, rocks and hills, rivers, trees, and mountains, are the same the world over, and through all ages; so the language of simile and comparison, where it is drawn from the actual living world, as it always is in the Bible, is not only the most striking language, but also the most easily understood. Who could ever doubt, in any age or nation, what the Bible means when it calls God a rock, or a shield, or a sun; or Jesus the good Shepherd? Hence the book of God, written for all the world to the end of time, has dealt little in the language of abstractions, and much in figures and symbols drawn from living nature. And thus it—

> "Finds tongues in trees, books in the running brooks,
> Sermons in stones, and good in everything."

This thought has been brought out with great vivacity by Gilfillan, speaking of the case of Jotham. "Whence this strange evasiveness of truth?" says he: and most beautifully does he give the answer: "It is partly because Truth, like all her true friends, loves to unbend and disport herself at times; because Truth herself is but a child, and has not yet put away childish things; because Truth is a beauty, and loves, as the beautiful do, to look at, and show herself in a multitude of mirrors; because Truth is a lover of nature, and of all lovely things; because Truth, who can only stammer in the language of abstractions, can speak in the language of forms; because Truth is a fugitive and in danger, and must hide in many a bosky bourne, and many a shady arbour; because Truth, in her turn, is dangerous, and must not show herself entire, else the first look were the last; and because Truth would beckon us on, by her very bashfulness, to follow after her to her own land, where she may still continue to hide in heaven, as she has hid in earth—but amid forests, and behind shades of scenery so colossal, that it hath not entered into the heart of man to conceive thereof."

V. FOURTH CHARACTERISTIC.

Another great source of attraction, in the Bible, to the youthful mind, is the multitude of its mighty miracles. It is a book of wonders, a record of stupendous works, all ascribed to the mighty hand of God. It does what no other book can do—it tells when, and how, and by whom, the worlds were made. This element of the wonderful occupies an important place in books written for the young. It is the charm of Sheherazade's "Thousand and One Nights," of "Robinson Crusoe," and of many popular romances. But the Bible possesses this element in a higher degree than any other book, because its wonders are all wrought by the finger of God, and narrated as the veritable facts of history. In all other books of stupendous wonders, the wonderful is mingled with the false. And whenever a suspicion of their fictitious character creeps into the mind of the young reader, the charm is broken. Not so is it with the Bible. It carries an air of perfect truth and sincerity through all its narrations; and what is of the utmost importance, it carries a complete voucher and explanation of all its wonders, in the fact, that it recognizes Jehovah's hand in all of them.

You perceive that there is an infinite difference between a book of signs and wonders, all the creations of imagination, and a book full of mighty miracles, all ascribed to God. This book, which has "God for its author, truth for its basis, and salvation for its end," is so written, as never to raise a suspicion of its veracity in the heart of a child. We do not believe, that any child was ever made a sceptic by reading the Bible. When children become sceptics, it is not from reading about its wonderful miracles, but from associating with older sceptics. The doubts of childhood, where any doubts exist, are, for the most part, prompted by unbelieving parents and teachers.

Now the Scriptures, from Genesis to Revelation, are full of these mighty works of God which we call miracles—that is, things which are above all human power. For the proper idea of a miracle is not that of a violation, or even suspension of the laws of nature, as it has sometimes been called, but of something superhuman—something done, which man could not do. The original word for miracles in the Greek Testament means powers—Divine powers. The Roman Catholic church translated it by a word in the Vulgate, meaning *prodigies*, and thus have confounded all true ideas of a miracle with the silly and lying wonders of pretended miracles in modern times. The creation of the world out of nothing, was no suspension or violation of any law of nature known to us; and yet it was a true miracle. And so the true idea of all the miracles of the Scriptures, as remarked by Archbishop Whately, is just that of superhuman power, as implied in the words of Nicodemus to Christ: "No man can do these miracles, that thou doest, except God be with him;" and also in his own words, "Miracles which none other man did."

The Bible, being a history of creation, providence, and redemption, is, in its very nature, a history of God's greatest works and greatest manifestations to man. Is it surprising that such a history should contain many and great miracles? Indeed we do not see how it could have been otherwise. In such a history and in such works of creation, providence, and redemption, we should expect to find mighty miracles, at every step, asserting the presence of Jehovah. And so it is. The Bible is full of them. We find them in every part of it, from its opening to its closing chapter. Our Saviour's whole public ministry was a succession of stupendous miracles. Of these thirty-three are distinctly, and many of them minutely recorded in the four Gospels. Many, also, wrought by his apostles, are recorded at length, or briefly referred to, in the book of Acts. The recorded miracles of Moses have been computed at seventy-six. All the signal, circumstantial miracles, recorded in the Old Testament, have been set down at one hundred and fifty. But it is evident that these specific cases, numerous as they are, must be taken only as the prominent specimens of an order of events and transactions, which distinguished the whole period of the Bible history.

If then, as all know, the young love to read of wars, battles, and heroic achievements; if they are attracted by the myths, fables, and incredible prodigies of Grecian mythology; if they are charmed with the daring deeds of adventure that marked the chivalry of the middle ages; if they are held spell-bound by all the strange things that crowd upon each other in the Arabian Nights; if they are pleased with the stories of modern fiction just in proportion to their stock of marvellous deeds; why should they not have their curiosity, and love of the wonderful, as well as their love of the truth, excited and gratified by the Bible? Such, in fact, is, and ever has been the case. And to appreciate the full force of these things in the Bible, you have only to imagine what would be the sensation created in the world of young readers, if a new book should be published to-morrow in every land, making known for the first time, and on undoubted evidence, a class of facts, just equivalent to the following—the creation of the world, the universal deluge, the dispersion at Babel, the destruction of Sodom and Gomorrah, the judgments in Egypt, the passage of the Red Sea, the giving of the law, the manna of the wilderness, the crossing of the Jordan, the fall of Jericho, the stopping of the sun, the chariot and horsemen of Elijah, the raising of the dead by Elisha, the overthrow of Sennacherib's army, the feast of Belshazzar, the dreams of Nebuchadnezzar, the preservation of Jonah in the fish, Samuel's return after death, the fiery furnace at Babylon, Daniel's night in the lions' den, the casting out of devils, the appearance of angels, voices from heaven, walking on the sea, opening the eyes of the blind, the resurrection of Lazarus, the crucifixion, rising, and ascension of Jesus, the wonders of the day of Pentecost, Peter's deliverance, Ananias' and Sapphira's death, the earthquake at Philippi, the doom of Herod, the conversion of Paul, together with all the mysterious seals, vials, trumpets, and thunders of the Apocalypse. These are, indeed, all amazing things; but what child ever thought it incredible, that God Almighty should perform them? And what child ever heard of them with indifference, when properly presented?

VI. FIFTH CHARACTERISTIC.

In addition to all these attractive modes, through which the Bible addresses the young, we must mention yet another characteristic, which is well adapted to win the heart of childhood. It is the manifest interest which the book everywhere seems to take in the welfare of little children. No one can read it, without seeing with feeling that God cares for children. Indeed, sympathy with childhood, as before stated, is one of its prominent and distinctive sentiments. If God cares for the sparrow in its fall, if he clothes the lilies of the field, if he feeds the young ravens when they cry, how much more must he love little children! The world may overlook and leave them, as being too small for its philosophy, but Jesus tells us, that in heaven, their angels do always behold the face of his Father. "Whosoever shall offend one of these little ones that believe in me, it were good for him that a mill-stone were hanged about his neck, and he cast into the depths of the sea." Did any other teacher of the ancient world ever utter a sentiment of such yearning sympathy for children? In all the extant learning of the Grecian and Roman classics, can any single book be found, breathing love like that, towards helpless, suffering infancy? No; the Bible stands alone among ancient books, in this tender regard for children. And if the literature of the modern world has learned to unbend itself, and stoop to converse with childhood, it is because the Bible has first taught the lesson. Nearly all the juvenile literature in the world may trace its origin to the Bible. It does not neglect or pass them over, in dignified silence and reserve; it condescends, with matchless grace, and with infinite kindness, to their low estate. It includes them in all its promises, in all its covenants, in all its blessings. Its most affectionate counsels, its most beautiful promises, its most encouraging instructions, its sweetest invitations, are addressed to children. It opens for them the richest provisions of the gospel of Jesus; it assigns them to the tender maternal care of the church on earth; it throws around their pathway, the special guardianship of angels; and it, at last, peoples heaven, with numbers without number of their happy spirits. The God of the Bible endears himself, most of all, to our hearts, by being the very God and Father and Saviour of little children.

He speaks to them on this wise: "I love them that love me, and they that seek me early shall find me." In the Old Testament, David expresses the feelings of every pious parent under that dispensation, and the feelings of God himself, when he says: "Come ye children, hearken unto me; I will teach you the fear of the Lord." Moses, indeed, had long before declared the tender care of Jehovah, for the instruction and welfare of children, when he laid down the following law, to be a perpetual ordinance for all the families of Israel: "These words which I command thee this day, shall be in thine heart, and thou shalt teach them diligently unto thy children, and shalt talk of them, when thou sittest in thine house, and when thou walkest by the way, when thou liest down, and when thou risest up." The Old Testament writers often speak, with manifest delight, of the ample provisions, which God had everywhere made, for the instruction and salvation of their children. Thus speaks the Psalmist Asaph: "For he established a testimony in Jacob, and appointed a law in Israel, which he commanded our fathers, that they should make them known to their children: that the generation to come might know them, even the children which should be born: who should arise and declare them to their children."

When we turn to the New Testament, we hear the same voice of tender, parental love for the little ones, breathing itself out, in all the commands, all the promises, and all the institutions of Jesus. How could it be otherwise, when the God who speaks, was once incarnate in the form of childhood; when the great founder and lawgiver of the gospel, condescending to the very lowest degree of our helpless humanity, had been once wrapped in swaddling bands and laid in a manger? We hear him speaking on this wise: "Suffer the little children to come unto me, and forbid them not, for of such is the kingdom of heaven. Have ye never read: Out of the mouths of babes and sucklings thou hast perfected praise? I thank thee, O Father, Lord of heaven and earth, because thou hast hid these things from the wise and prudent, and hast revealed them unto babes." And we hear that beloved disciple, who caught so much of his Master's spirit, and who records the injunction, "Feed my lambs," saying: "I rejoiced greatly when I found of thy children walking in truth. I have no greater joy than to hear that my children walk in truth."

Thousands upon thousands of children, in every age and every land, have felt the attractive power of this gentle, loving spirit of the Bible. From lisping infancy to blooming youth, and on to ripening manhood, they have read the Bible with the feeling that it was their friend—that its God was their Father, its Saviour their brother, and its heaven their home. Thousands of them, with no other friend to help, and no other teacher to guide, have been so taught and blest of God in the simple reading of it, that they have there found the pearl of great price; have chosen the good part like Mary, have been made wise unto salvation like Timothy, and have worked the works of God like Jesus himself at the age of twelve. And perhaps there are no triumphs of divine grace on earth, more remarkable and more precious in the sight of heaven, than those which it has won over the heart of childhood through the reading of the Scriptures. How many little ones, not only in life and health, but in their dying moments, have breathed forth a loving, child-like faith, in response to all the Divine love of the Bible!

"I know I'm weak amd sinful,
But Jesus can forgive,

For many little children
  Have gone to heaven to live.

Dear Saviour, when I languish
  And lay me down to die,
Oh, send a shining angel
  To bear me to the sky."

Yes, it is this great feature of salvation from sin and death—salvation and eternal life in heaven through the mediation of the Son of God, for all that believe in him—it is this more than anything else that gives the Bible its strong hold upon the heart of childhood. It is the powerful attraction of the cross that children feel, when they read the Bible. It is the influence of a Divine and dying Saviour that wins their gentle, loving hearts. "And I," said our Saviour, "if I be lifted up, will draw all men unto myself." But he draws them for the most part in early childhood. The infant dead are all saved. But most of those who live, and are saved, are doubtless saved by being converted in childhood and early youth. Even the aged sinner, if ever converted at all, must be brought back to the simple, loving, and confiding faith of childhood. "Except ye be converted and become as this little child, ye shall in nowise enter into the kingdom of heaven." It is a great truth, it is a precious truth, that the great salvation of God, as wrought out by the death of Jesus, applied to the heart by the Holy Ghost, and revealed through all the book of God, is a salvation provided for children, offered to children, and levelled down to the capacity and belief of children even in their tenderest years. Upon children it makes its earliest, deepest, most lasting impression; and from the ranks of children it wins its most illustrious trophies.

VII. THE CHILDREN OF THE BIBLE.

But it is often through the life and character of its own children, that the book of God thus speaks to the children of all generations. And of these living examples we are now to speak. If our attention has been arrested by the incomparable method of Scripture in winning its way to the youthful heart, we shall find still more to admire, in the fulness, with which it has set before us, illustrations of childhood, in all the different stages of its career, from opening infancy to ripening manhood. Leaving all its adult characters, for the present, in the background, let us fix our view upon its long line of little ones, as they march in rapid procession, across the sacred pages; sometimes in large groups, sometimes in little families, and sometimes one by one, either preparing for the great duties that awaited them on earth, or sinking into an early grave, to join the larger and happier company in heaven. We cannot, of course, in the brief limits of a single chapter, present all the examples of childhood to be found in the Bible; it will be sufficient to bring together into one view, all, or nearly all, the prominent examples. And, for the sake of some definite order, let us take those first who appear in groups; next, such as are found in striking contrast in the same family; and, last of all, the most remarkable individuals.

We turn our attention first to that infant train (we cannot tell how many) who perished, at different times, under the cruel edicts of kings—Pharaoh king of Egypt, and Herod of Judea. Although separated by the long interval of fifteen centuries, these two martyred bands may well be associated together in any portraiture of the children of the Bible. They are not usually classed with the noble army of martyrs. But they were, in fact, the victims of a bloody persecution of the people of God; one company being destroyed by a tyrant who sought thus to exterminate the church, and the other by one who sought the life of Him who was the King and Head of the church. And being thus slain for the sake of Jesus, they well deserve to hold a place in that uncounted throng of martyrs, or witnesses for the truth, who have fallen by the hand of the persecutor, from righteous Abel, even down to those dear little ones of our missionaries who so recently fell in India, under the rage of the bloody Sepoys. If there are crowns of glory in heaven for the martyred dead, it should stir our hearts to think, how large a share of that glory will crown the infant dead. Childhood will not be without its honours there; for it has never been without its service here, to the cause of God.

This destruction of their children, on the banks of the Nile, and through all the coasts of Bethlehem, was indeed a bitter cup to the weeping mothers who had to drink it, but it was in each case a memorable and instructive lesson to the church of God; for in each, it was an illustration of that overruling Providence, which has ever made, as it did then, "the blood of the martyrs the seed of the church." The first was but the means of raising up Moses to be the great leader, lawgiver, and benefactor of Israel; and out of the second, unharmed by all the machinations of Herod, came forth the Son of God, with infinite blessings for the whole world. The wrath of man was made to praise him, and the remainder of wrath he did restrain. And so the unoffending victims of these two royal murders, though so widely sundered on earth, have their memorial in the book of God; and they will stand associated together for ever in the bond of a common innocence and common destiny—

brothers in their early death on earth, and in their glorious crown of martyrdom above.

"Every son that is born ye shall cast into the river, and every daughter ye shall save alive." This was the infamous decree with which Pharaoh charged his own people with the work of infanticide. He had failed in his first plan, which was to make the Hebrew midwives kill all the male children; because these women feared God more than the king of Egypt. And this well illustrates the sacred regard for human life, which has ever characterized the people of God, even before the giving of the Mosaic law. What the God-fearing Hebrew women shrank from, as an atrocious murder, the Egyptians were ready to do. We know not what numbers of lovely babes, torn from their heart-broken mothers, by this cruel decree, found a watery grave in the Nile, or were devoured by its crocodiles. We only know with what difficulty Moses was preserved for three months by parental care, and then, as the last resort, committed for safety, in his frail ark of rushes, to that very river which had swallowed up so many others. The Bible, with its usual brevity, has just stated the command of the king, and then mentioned a single example, leaving the imagination to fill up all the sad scene of woe. The sacred writer could well appreciate the peril, having himself so narrowly escaped it.

Nor can we tell the number that perished in the parallel massacre at Bethlehem, from which our Saviour was delivered by the protecting hand of God. Dr. Kitto remarks, that "the Greek church canonized them as fourteen thousand innocents; and another notion, founded on a misconception of Rev. xiv. 4, swelled the number to one hundred and forty-four thousand." He considers even the smallest of these numbers utterly absurd, as Bethlehem was merely a village, in which the number of infants under two years old must have been very small; and he thinks it would be extravagant to suppose that more than twenty-five children perished on this occasion. But when we remember that this ferocious order of Herod was executed not only in the village of Bethlehem, but in "all the coasts thereof;" and when we remember further, that Bethlehem, at that time, was crowded by many strangers, some of whom may have been detained like the parents of Jesus; and still further that his order would be unavailing unless executed on all the young children in that region; it seems to us much nearer the truth to suppose, that at least a hundred, perhaps several hundred infants were slaughtered by the bloody tyrant. The well known character of Herod, who seemed to revel in the shedding of blood, and the words of the sacred writer, certainly agree best with our supposition. For we are told, that "he was exceeding wroth, and sent forth and slew all the children that were in Bethlehem, and in all the coasts thereof, from two years old and under, according to the time which he had diligently inquired of the wise men. Then was fulfilled, that which was spoken by Jeremy the prophet; saying, In Ramah was there a voice heard, lamentation and mourning, Rachel weeping for her children, and would not be comforted, because they were not."

Alas! how often has that wailing cry been heard on earth, since the banks of the Nile, and the rocks of Ramah echoed back its full chorus of woe! In how many lands besides Egypt and Judea, has the prophecy been fulfilled! How many sorrowing mothers, from Rachel's day to ours, have returned from the desolate grave to their desolate, vacant homes, to pine in anguish over the loss of their little ones! How many happy family-circles of earth, even when there was no persecuting Pharaoh, or cruel Herod to disturb them, have yet been broken up by the great enemy, and called to part with these jewels of the heart! Who hath not lost a child? and who is safe from losing?

> "There is no flock, however watched and tended,
> But one dead lamb is there:
> There is no fireside, howsoe'er defended,
> But has one vacant chair."

VIII. THE WICKED CHILDREN OF BETHEL.

From this company of the "early lost and early saved," we turn now to look upon another group of the children of the Bible, of a character wholly different. They form one of the darkest pictures of youthful depravity, to be found in the Bible. They appear before us, not as helpless infants, murdered in the days of their innocence, but as children of sufficient age to know good from evil. 'Tis a rude band of mockers, profanely reviling a prophet of the Lord, that we are now to look upon.

Your thoughts will at once recur to the wicked children of Bethel, who are mentioned in the second chapter of the second book of Kings, as coming out to mock Elisha the prophet, and as meeting with a sudden and awful destruction from the Lord. In order to understand the full import of this terrible visitation on a class of offenders so young, it is necessary to notice carefully the circumstances attending it.

Elijah, as the crowning wonder of his eventful and remarkable life, had just been taken up to heaven in a chariot of fire, in the full light of day, and in full view of Elisha and fifty of the sons of the prophets—a number of witnesses sufficient to establish any fact beyond question. Elisha, having received the falling mantle of his great master, and being now his acknowledged successor in the prophetic office, first performs two signal miracles—the dividing of the Jordan, and the healing of the waters at Jericho; thus giving the highest possible proof of a Divine commission from that God with whose honour Elijah had been so long charged before the face of all Israel. This done, he passes on, in prosecution of his ministry, to the capital of Israel; and it is important to bear in mind the high and sacred character which he now bears as the commissioned, and divinely accredited prophet of Israel.

On this journey he must needs pass through Bethel; a town which, from being one of those ancient and revered places where the patriarchs had so often worshipped the true God, had now degenerated into the vilest seat of idolatry in all the land; being the very spot where Jeroboam had set up one of his golden calves. And no doubt the idolatrous inhabitants of the place, having heard the recent story of Elijah's ascension (during the three days' search for him), and knowing that his successor was to pass that way, conspired together and instigated their children to inflict upon him the public and disgraceful insult which followed. All the circumstances of the case, as well as the words of insult, show clearly that it was a deep laid and premeditated plot on the part of the Baal-worshipping Bethelites, to pour contempt upon the person and office of the newly installed prophet of Jehovah. For we are not to forget the overwhelming defeat and destruction of the false prophets of Baal by the hands of Elijah some years before this at Mount Carmel. How fine an opportunity then would this be to the Bethelites, using their children as their tools, to visit upon Elisha, that old grudge which they had never been able to settle with his great master!

The record is in these words: "And as he was going up by the way (probably intending to pass the place without stopping), there came forth little children out of the city and mocked him, and said unto him, Go up, thou bald-head; go up, thou bald-head! (that is, in bitter, unbelieving derision and irony, Ascend to heaven, thou impostor, as Elijah did). And he turned back, and looked on them, and cursed them in the name of the Lord. And there came forth two she-bears out of the wood, and tare forty and two children of them."

This was an awful doom for children. But it was an awful provocation; especially so, as there were others more guilty behind the scene, who were using these children as their tools. Many have found it difficult to reconcile a judgment so dreadful with the humanity of the prophet and the goodness of God. But you must observe two things in this account. The first is that the prophet did not inflict the punishment; he did not call for the bears, nor any other messengers of death; and it is clear that he could have no natural power over them. All that he did was to "turn, look upon them, and pronounce a curse in the name of the Lord;" and you must remember, that one great department of duty in this ancient prophetic office, was to declare these Divine judgments, burdens, or curses, not only upon sin in general, but upon particular sinners, both individual and national. With that Elisha's agency ended in this matter. The other thing to be noticed is, that what followed this curse, took place, to all human appearance, not as a special and miraculous interposition, but in the ordinary course of Divine Providence. These were probably not the first, nor the last children, that have been destroyed by raging bears, robbed of their whelps. And how is it any more difficult to reconcile, with the Divine goodness, this destruction which can be traced to a particular sin, than it is to reconcile all those other destructions, constantly occurring, which can be traced to no such cause, but must be set down to the account of sin in general?

We get the idea very clearly, from the narrative, that this speedy and terrible execution of judgment was from the Lord; and that it was visited upon these young offenders because of their blasphemy and shameful insult to a holy prophet of the Lord. But it is no more difficult to vindicate than any other case of the punishment of sin in childhood. Thousands of cases have occurred, and do still occur, in the ordinary course of Providence, all teaching the same great lessons which this case taught: namely, that we belong to a sinful race, and inherit a depraved nature; that folly is bound up in the heart of a child at a very tender age; and that it is an evil and bitter thing, even for a child, to sin against God.

Some learned commentators, to escape the apparent difficulty of the passage, tell us, that the word rendered, "children," in our version, ought to be translated, "young men." This meaning, indeed, it will very well bear, being so translated in other parts of the Bible. But it seems to us utterly improbable, under all the circumstances of the case, that forty-two grown young men could have been torn in pieces by two she-bears. This would be to take the case out of ordinary providences, and put it into the class of miracles, merely to get over an appearance of harshness and severity. We prefer to take our version as it stands. Our own opinion is, that these irreverent and profane mockers were neither young men on the one hand, nor very young children on the other; but, half-grown boys, past the age of thirteen, at which the Jews fixed the period of moral responsibility. And though they had been taught by their idolatrous parents to utter this blasphemy, and to insult the God of Israel in the person of his prophet, still they were of sufficient age to know and love the wrong they did.

As such, this case contains an awful warning both to parents and children. These wicked children of Bethel, in their boisterous derision of sacred things, may be taken as the early types and representatives of a very large class of youth, who have never lacked a succession to the present hour. We have seen boys of this very class, enacting on a smaller scale, the same sad scene of youthful depravity, and gradually ripening into the same hardened characters, which these young Bethelites exhibited. Childhood is, indeed, a lovely thing, when it grows up in the fear of the Lord. Its fresh, young breath of love is sweet and grateful as the morning fragrance of spring flowers. An ingenuous and manly boyhood, that fears God and honours man, that shrinks from all that is mean and low, and reverences all that is sacred and noble, is an exhibition of character, which finds nothing on earth to eclipse it, except the highest beauty of woman's virtue. But when, alas! blooming boyhood puts on the hardened vices of mature age, learns to laugh the hollow laugh of the sceptic at sacred things, and to vent its young breath in oaths, and blasphemies, and ribald jests, there is not to be found on earth, a spectacle more shocking and mournful. For there is not this side of the judgment-seat, any indication more sure of a ripening doom, and an already ruined character. As profanity is, of all sins, that which is committed with the least provocation or excuse, so it is, of all, the surest index of a wicked heart. Ordinary sinners, it is said, must be caught with a baited hook—riches, pleasures, honours;—but the profane swearer swallows the naked hook.

This scene at Bethel reads us another solemn warning. The parents did not escape punishment. They suffered in the loss of their children. And this often occurs. If children are often doomed in the course of nature and Divine Providence to suffer for the sins of their parents, it perhaps as often occurs, that wicked parents live long enough to be punished in their children. Here is a tender mother, who, instead of restraining the naturally selfish and violent passion of her darling boy, only takes all occasions to inflame them; teaching him not to forgive but to resent injuries; teaching him to look out for insults, and to fight when they are offered. And what is the result? The tender boy of the nursery becomes a pugilist at school, and ere long a duelist; and in some fatal hour, for some fancied insult, kills his former friend and inherits a murderer's remorse for life; or else becomes himself the victim, dies as the fool dieth before his time, and leaves that mother, whose declining years he should have lived to honour, to drag out a miserable existence, with the bitter thought that her own folly did it all. If the iniquities of the parent are often visited upon the children, they are very apt to come back again, for payment where they first issued.

And so the swift and unexpected judgment, which overtook these young blasphemers at Bethel, was no doubt intended to bear a public aspect towards all the Bethelites, and towards all that idolatrous generation. The seed of transgression which they had been so long and so sedulously sowing, had not only budded, but bloomed and ripened for destruction; when young children must be put forward to scoff at age, to deride virtue, to desecrate the most holy things, and blaspheme the God of

Elijah. We mistake altogether the spirit and import of this transaction, if we look upon it as a private affair. It was not a matter of mere personal feeling with the prophet; but a great public demonstration, made and executed "in the name of the Lord," for the good of Israel, and of all generations to come. Was it not time to strike a blow at Bethel that would be felt? Was it not time to rebuke such heaven-daring impiety? Was it not time for the God of the prophets to vindicate the sacredness of the prophetic office, ere these young mockers should grow emboldened by impunity, and learn to imbrue their hands in a prophet's blood? If such things were done in the green tree, what would be done in the dry? If as boys they could mock with impunity, what might they not do as men? And who can say to what extent they would have gone with Elisha, had not their bitter sport been thus cut short in sudden judgment? We cannot read the sad story of persecution, written as it is in the blood of the prophets, from righteous Abel down to Zacharias, and from Zacharias to Stephen, without feeling that the world needed to be taught the great lesson, that irreverence for age, derision of sacred things, and mockery of God's servants, are sins against God himself which cannot always go unpunished.

When God has said, "Touch not mine anointed and do my prophets no harm;" "The hoary head is a crown of glory, if it be found in the ways of righteousness;" and when the Saviour has told us, that every idle word shall be accounted for at his judgment-seat, we need not wonder at the quick and terrible retributions, which, in an age when God was giving lessons for the benefit of all generations, sometimes fell upon the ungodly sons of ungodly families, who dared to vilify a character so sacred, and an office so Divine as Elisha's. Who can say how much the world has profited by these awful warnings? And though such immediate judgments from heaven are no longer visited upon transgression, and perhaps for this very reason, that we have enough of them already in the book of God to teach the lesson, still it would be well if a certain class of half-grown boys in our times, who desecrate the Sabbath, profane the name of God, and ape the vices of men, in mocking at sin and trifling with sacred things, would consider well whether their own eternal doom be not distinctly shadowed forth in the fate of these wicked sons of Bethel.

IX. THE GOOD CHILDREN OF JERUSALEM.

From this dark picture of youthful depravity, the darkest perhaps in the Old Testament, we turn with relief to its opposite in the New; we listen to the joyful songs of a group of young worshippers, praising God, and shouting welcome to a far greater prophet than Elisha. These are the good children of Jerusalem, mentioned in the gospel history, who on the day of our Saviour's public and triumphal entry into the holy city, a little before his last suffering, received him into the temple, with the loudest, sweetest acclamations of joy and praise their young lips could raise, crying, "Hosanna to the Son of David."

It was a glad day in Jerusalem. The whole city was astir to see this great prophet of Galilee, whose fame had so long preceded him, and whose mighty power had been so fully confirmed, in the estimation of the multitude, by the recent resurrection of Lazarus. Such a prophet had not been heard of in Israel since the days of Malachi; nor indeed for centuries before. It is not strange that the thronged city should be moved at his coming; and that every street and highway should pour forth its multitude, all eager to meet and to greet him, as he rode slowly onward, over the Mount of Olives. His disciples and followers were elated with joy. The whole multitude of them began to rejoice and praise God, saying, "Hosanna in the highest; Blessed is he that cometh in the name of the Lord." Thousands thought, that this would be the day of Israel's glory; that as the true and long promised Messiah of the prophets, he was now about to establish his royal power in Jerusalem, and set up the long fallen throne of his father David.

It was fit, that childhood—eager, loving, admiring childhood—should be there to see this wonderful prophet, to behold his glory, and to lay down its own joyful offerings at his feet. Such a scene of rejoicing would have been incomplete without th glad voice of childhood. Nor was it wanting. And we have reason to believe, that in all the multitude of friends and followers, who thus heralded his approach, there was no voice so sweet and grateful to the sorrowing heart of Jesus, as this spontaneous outburst of the children—"Hosanna to the Son of David."

The rulers at Jerusalem, chief priests, scribes, and Pharisees, were sorely offended with this youthful burst of enthusiasm in favour of Jesus. Unable to control it themselves, they came to him with words of complaint and expostulation. "Hearest thou what these say?" Jesus, however, so far from yielding to their complaint, accepts and commends the children's hosannas, justifying all their childlike devotion and enthusiasm by a quotation from Scripture; "Yea, have ye never read, Out of the mouths of babes and sucklings thou hast perfected praise?"

Beautiful and timely was this pure offering of the little ones to Jesus. It was probably their first and last opportunity, thus publicly to honour that great and good prophet of Galilee, of whom no doubt they had heard many wonderful things. It had been predicted by the old prophets, that the great Messiah should come in this very way—combining the extremes of grandeur and humility in his coming—though a King and the Son of God, yet meek and lowly, "sitting upon a colt, the foal of an ass." And it seemed in striking accordance with his character that he should be thus welcomed by the children of the Holy City, to that temple which was but the earthly symbol of his glory. Whilst their blind and hardened rulers were engaged in plotting his destruction, and whilst the populace in the streets were rending the air with shouts of applause in expectation of a temporal throne, these children in the temple poured forth their sincere and affectionate homage to him, in songs of admiration and joy. It was a tribute worthy of the great teacher, the healer of diseases, the restorer of the dead, the friend of the poor, the comforter of the widow and the fatherless. The incident was trivial in itself, but taken in its connections, it seems to tell us, that whilst devils and wicked men were leagued to oppose the Son of God, the generous, loving heart of childhood, like that of woman, was everywhere, and to the last, beating in holy sympathy with his Divine character and his heavenly mission. It is a pleasing thought, that childhood, loved and honoured as it had ever been by Jesus, should be permitted, as a sort of prophetic type of what it should thenceforth do to the end of time, to come forward and bear this sweet incense of praise, in return for all that he was doing and suffering for its eternal salvation.

What a contrast between this heart-felt outburst of love from the children of the temple, and that ruffian-like profanity, which we have just been contemplating in the young scoffers at Bethel! And what an illustration does this contrast give us, both of the great evil and the great good which children may do in the world, merely by their words! Who will say, with such cases as these before him, that God does not hold children accountable for their conduct, and for the words they utter? The words are but the index of the heart; and the heart is the fountain of the character. "By thy words thou shalt be justified, and by thy words thou shalt be condemned." What did the children of Bethel, and of Jerusalem do? They only spake certain words—one to the prophet of the Lord, the other to the Lord himself. But how different the spirit of these words—how different their import—how different the character they displayed—and how different their end! For their sweet words of praise, one of these youthful bands was approved and blest of Jesus; for their taunting words of derision and blasphemy, the other was accursed of God and devoured by wild beasts. As depravity never appears more shocking than when it speaks from the lips of the young; so on the other hand piety never appears so lovely as when its young voice is lifted to the Lord amid the hosannas of his temple.

"Grace is a plant, where'er it grows,
Of pure and heavenly root,
But fairest in the youngest shows,
And bears the sweetest fruit."

There are many other groups of children, mentioned in the Scriptures, of which we might speak in this connection; but we shall refer to but one more at present. In some respects it is the most interesting company of children to be found in the Bible. It is the little band who were brought to Jesus, we cannot tell where, but, no doubt, by their believing mothers, that he might lay his hands on them and bless them. They are called young children, and evidently belonged to that tender age which we call infancy. We associate them also, with that little child, whom Jesus, on another occasion, took up in his arms, and then set down in the midst of his ambitious disciples, when he rebuked their strife, with the emphatic declaration—"Except ye be converted and become as this little child, ye shall in no wise enter into the kingdom of God."

When the little ones, of whom we are now speaking, were brought to Jesus, his disciples rebuked those who brought them, and tried to prevent their coming. We know not what was the ground of this opposition. It may be they thought their exalted Master had more important business to attend to, than the reception of babes. Men, whose thoughts ran on the great things of an earthly kingdom, would be apt to think so. Be the cause what it may, Jesus was much displeased, and rebuked the rebukers with the memorable words, "Suffer the little children to come unto me, and forbid them not, for of such is the kingdom of heaven." And we are told, he took them up in his arms, put his hands upon them and blessed them.

Happy babes! happy mothers! thrice happy partakers of such Divine compassions and condescension! There are no words in the book of God, none in human literature, none ever spoken by mortal tongues, that have healed more bereaved and breaking hearts than these. No single sentence, we suppose, ever spoken by man, or to man, hath breathed a sweeter consolation into the ear of parental sorrow, or shot a brighter ray of hope across this dark world of death. There is no act or incident in all the life of Jesus, not even his weeping at the grave of Lazarus, which more effectually wins our hearts than these words of tender sympathy and love for little children. No pen or pencil can picture, no imagination conceive, no history in the world furnish, an act of condescension more attractive, a scene of tenderness more pathetic, and a proof of sympathy more perfect, on the part of God, than this. It has been the admiration of ages. It has won the homage of the world. It is the good Shepherd folding the lambs upon his bosom. It is the angel of mercy unfolding the gates of glory to our babes. It is Divinity incarnate in parental love. It has been the standing theme of poetry, and painting, and sculpture, and of every eloquent tongue. It has elicited the highest endeavours of genius and art in every age, and wrung reluctant praise from the very lips of infidelity and scepticism.

The names of these little ones have been lost in oblivion, but their introduction to Jesus will be held in grateful remembrance, to the end of time, by every bereaved parental heart, as the occasion which reveals the Son of God in his loveliest, gentlest, most endearing character; for it reveals him in the personal exercise of that watchful, ministering care of the young, which he was so explicit to enjoin upon his disciples, when he said, "Feed my lambs."

"See Israel's gentle Shepherd stands
With all engaging charms,
Hark, how he calls the tender lambs,
And folds them in his arms.

"Permit them to approach, he cries,
Nor scorn their humble name,
For 'twas to bless such souls as these
The Lord of angels came."

X. GOOD AND BAD CHILDREN IN THE SAME FAMILY.

One of the most striking points in the portraiture of childhood in the Bible, is the frequency with which we find good and bad children in the same family. Some of the most remarkable contrasts of character, portrayed in the Bible, are exhibited in children of the same household, born of the same parents, and to all appearance, educated under the same influances. It is true that, in such cases, for the most part, very little is said of the period of early childhood. Such examples are presented to us, chiefly, at the age of adolescence, or in their years of opening manhood; and we are left to infer what their early childhood had been, by knowing some of their first actions as young men, or half-grown boys. As we generally know the man by the boy; so it is a safe rule to learn what the boy has been, by the man we see. And on this principle, it is not difficult to determine the character of the childhood of Cain and Abel, in the family of Adam; of Ishmael and Isaac, in the family of Abraham; of Esau and Jacob, in the family of Isaac; of Joseph and his brethren, in the family of Jacob; and of Solomon and his brothers, in the family of David; and many others.

It is a significant fact, that the first example of this contrast of character, should be found in the first two children born into the world. It seemed to be a sort of foreshadowing of the future—the early beginning of that broad line of distinction, and that close conflict, between the evil and the good, which may be traced through all the families of the earth. The Bible does not describe for us the childhood of Cain and Abel. We are left to infer what they must have been as boys, by that awful act which made one a murderer and the other a martyr. No doubt this radical difference in their moral character had manifested itself in their earliest years. Character, in the young and the old alike, is formed as the mountain is climbed, not at a bound, but step by step. Character is the result, not of some sudden impulse, or some single act, but of sentiments long cherished and habits long indulged. If, when occasion offers, it manifests itself in some resplendent deed of virtue, or some atrocious wickedness that makes our very ears tingle, this is only because of that preceding work of preparation in the heart and habits of life, which had been going on, it may be privately, through many years. If Cain hated his brother, and sought his injury, however secretly, he was, in heart, a murderer, long before he had stained his hands with his young blood. And so the brethren of Joseph, long meditating his destruction, and at last actually intending to kill him, were murderers in the sight of God, although no blood was shed. "Whosoever hateth his brother is a murderer." The great lesson which this first example of childhood in the world teaches, is a lesson of warning to all the young. It is to resist temptation early. It is to oppose the very beginnings of evil passion. For it is manifest that these extremes of human character—the one a saint of God, and the other a child of the devil—could not have met thus in young men of the same family and with equal privileges, had it not been that they began, even in their earliest years, the one to yield to the good, the other to yield to the bad.

In Isaac and Ishmael we have another example of the same

contrast of character, though not to the same extent. Their history, though briefly told, is interesting as affording an early illustration of the truth, that the boy is but the type of the man. The lines of destiny which finally bore them so far asunder, and separated their posterity still farther, began to diverge in their early childhood. They were sons of the same great father Abraham, the friend of God; but of different mothers—the one born of a bond-woman, the other the favoured son of Sarah. And they seem to have been as unlike and antagonistic to each other in the dispositions of their youth, as they afterwards became in the pursuits and habits of their riper years.

The character of Ishmael, as a child, is portrayed by the sacred writer, in a single expression, revealing in him the same proud and overbearing spirit which had often shown itself in his Egyptian mother. "He mocked his brother." This occurred at the feast given by Abraham to celebrate the day of Isaac's weaning. It was probably his birthday also; and as Ishmael was fourteen years old when Isaac was born, he could not have been less than sixteen at the time he thus mocked his little brother. As it was evidently done in a spirit of arrogance and rivalry, it may be taken as the keynote of his character. The boy of sixteen, or it may be eighteen, was but acting out that fierce, selfish, ungovernable temper, which had once driven his haughty mother into the desert, and was finally to drive him, "a wild man, his hand against every man, and every man's hand against him." Infancy is always an object of attraction and fond endearment to a well disposed heart, whether among the old or the young, and it augured badly for the character of Ishmael, whether prompted on this occasion by his own heart, or his mother, that he should have indulged in mockings, when there should have been nothing but kindness and caresses. His conduct was probably but the result of his mother's instructions. But this did not make it either virtuous or lovely. And mothers would do well to remember that selfishness and cruelty in their children are still wrong and hateful things, although their own gentle voices may have early instilled the poison.

On the contrary, the character of Isaac's boyhood is beautifully revealed to us; and that also at a single stroke. He was, when he reached the same age, the very opposite of Ishmael. His whole character as a child shines out in a single, but important transaction, which must have taken place when he was on the very verge of manhood; at any rate, as old as Ishmael was when he himself was an infant. But at whatever age it occurred, whether in his later boyhood, or his opening manhood, it is an event that throws a strong and beautiful light back over his whole pathway from earliest childhood. By a single action, we are made to feel that we understand fully, what Isaac was, and what he had been all his life. His whole preceding history is clearly mirrored in this one great occasion. We refer to his proposed immolation on Mount Moriah. His ready acquiescence in the will of his father, his uncomplaining submission to the appointment of God, and the heroic spirit of self-denial which made him willing to be offered up as a burnt sacrifice on the altar, when he certainly had the power to resist and escape—all this goes to show, even more impressively than any mere words of eulogy, what virtues had from the beginning adorned the character of Isaac. He had learned obedience as a son, though he was the honoured subject of prophecy and heir of all the promised blessings of the covenant. All the great essential virtues of obedience, patience, fortitude, courage, self-denial, and faith in God, shone forth resplendently in this one act of cheerful submission to his father. Like gold from the furnace so he came forth from the fiery ordeal—a noble illustration in the son, of that same faith which distinguished the father of the faithful. And thus he was a fitting and beautiful type of Him, who was called to endure a far greater trial—the holy Lamb of God—who on that very mountain in after ages, was offered up as a sacrifice for the sins of the world. The whole story of Isaac is full of wonder and full of instruction, and should be carefully studied by the young. We need not recount it here, as no words of ours could add to the touching pathos with which it is told in the Bible. We only refer to it now, to show the striking contrast of moral character exhibited in these two sons of Abraham; in one the rebellious, intractable spirit which found its only congenial home in the wilderness; in the other, the docile, loving, yet heroic heart, which shrank not from the sacrifice of life itself.

And this will serve to illustrate a point in character which is sometimes forgotten. It is, that gentle, loving spirits are often the bravest. The meek, mild man will often endure trials, and face dangers, at which the proud and noisy would be utterly appalled. What character in all the Old Testament appears more humble and unassuming than Isaac? And yet who ever passed through a greater trial of faith and fortitude? In nothing more than in character does the proverb hold true, that "still water runs deep, and the bird that flutters least is longest on the wing."

We might go on to notice a similar contrast of character between Esau and Jacob in the family of Isaac, and also in many other families. It would be tedious however, to delineate all the examples. It is enough for our present purpose to have referred to these cases, as illustrations of the whole; and to leave the topic to the reader's own study, with two practical lessons which may be deduced from all such examples in the Bible.

The first is for parents. It is, that nearly all these wide contrasts of character, in children of the same household, while they have their deep root in the two great principles of nature and grace, which began to be developed immediately after the fall, and have never ceased to work, may nevertheless be also traced to some defect in family discipline, to some error or violation of God's law in parents themselves. It is worthy of notice that most of the evils in the patriarchal families flowed from polygamy. The multiplied domestic troubles that marred the tranquillity of home, and embittered the old age of Jacob, of David, of Solomon, and even of Abraham, may be traced to their violation of the great primeval law of marriage, which from the first allowed only one wife. For the hardness of their hearts and the darkness of the times, God permitted polygamy to exist even in these good men. But still the evil tree was always sure, even in good men, to bear its bitter fruits, apples of Sodom and grapes of Gomorrah. One reason of its permission, doubtless, was to teach the world by example, a lesson which should never be forgotten. For you will observe, that these domestic troubles increased just in proportion to the multiplication of their wives. So that Solomon, who tried polygamy on the largest scale the world has ever seen, left but one poor, half-imbecile son, whose first act on coming to the throne, was to play the tyrant in so absurd a way as to rend asunder for ever the tribes of Israel.

Even in those families where the great law of marriage was strictly observed, as for instance in those of Adam and Isaac, the widely different moral characters of their children were probably connected with some want of concert and co-operation on the part of the parents. It is a significant fact, that even the exemplary Isaac and Rebekah, who never departed from the original ordinance of marriage, had yet each a favourite son, and perhaps a different theory of domestic discipline.

The other lesson is for the young. After all, these wide contrasts of character cannot exist in children of the same household, without the agency of the children themselves. With them must rest the final decision, to them is left a free choice, in all cases, between the evil and the good. No parents, however good and faithful, can choose the good for them, if they deliberately choose the bad. Thousands of examples, in every age, show that children, even of the best parents, may resist and defeat, by their own wilful opposition, all that can be done by mortal man to save them; and thus press their way down to perdition from the very gates of the sanctuary, and over all the covenants of God. The same great alternative of life or death, which the dying king David set before his son Solomon, is set before every other child: "Know thou the God of thy father, and serve him with a perfect heart and a willing mind; if thou seek him, he will be found of thee, but if thou forsake him, he will cast thee off for ever." And this is the great problem of life, for the most part decided in childhood—to choose the good part like Abel, Isaac, Jacob, Timothy, Mary; or to despise the heavenly birthright like Cain, Esau, Absalom, and a thousand other sons of pious parents.

XI. CHILDHOOD OF JOSEPH AND MOSES.

Joseph and Moses, as men, will come before us in other connections. We have now to speak only of their childhood and youth! They stand out in bold relief on the sacred pages, even from infancy to old age. And no enumeration of the remarkable children of the Bible would be complete without some allusion to them.

The lovely, helpless infancy of the one, and the ingenuous, unsuspecting boyhood of the other, as narrated in the Bible, are perfect pictures in themselves. We see the weeping babe, and the tender boy; we follow them through all their exposure to death, and their preservation in the midst of death; and, at each step, we behold the hand of God, keeping them as the very apple of his eye. What scene in fiction, what drama of real life, can be more touchingly beautiful, than the brief record of the unsheltered infancy of Moses! There lies the great lawgiver of Israel; we see the goodly child, in his secret hiding place at home, narrowly watched and tended, for three long months, by all the fond anxieties of parental love. There, at last, in his frail ark of bulrushes, when the precious charge can be no longer kept, we see him reluctantly, yet prayerfully, launched, by a mother's own hands, upon the turbid waters of the Nile. There, adown the current, through the flags of the river's brim, the precious little treasure, all unconscious of that mother's last kiss and falling tears, is floating slowly away, whilst a sorrowing but yet hopeful sister is watching in the background to see the end. There again on the bank, in the uncovered ark, we behold the lovely little stranger, lying beneath the pitying eye of the king's daughter, and by its tears appealing unconsciously to all the womanly instincts of her nature. And there, at length, in the wonderful providence of God, we see the fortunate child, an adopted son of the princess, remanded back to the fostering care of his own mother, who, but for her faith in God, had given him up for lost.

Surely there is nothing in the early fortunes of Cyrus the Great, as related by Xenophon in the Cyropœdia, and nothing in the famous story of Romulus and Remus, nursed by the wolf, half so striking and beautiful as this. At the distance of three thousand years, the infancy of Moses is a subject of unabated interest to the poet and painter, the musician and the preacher. "And behold the babe wept; and she had compassion on him." Though a king's daughter, she was a true woman. What a theme for description—the weeping babe, the pitying woman! What a text for woman's mission! what a proof of her power! what an appeal for childhood! what an argument for the training and salvation of the young!

Here was a child to be educated for the great purposes of God; to be educated in such a way that he shall be prepared ere long to accomplish a greater work than had ever been done on earth before. And behold the method of it. Behold the agency of woman in it. All other agents are sunk out of view, and three women appear on the scene, to bring about the peculiar, yet important instruction of that child—one a king's daughter, one a sister, and one its own mother. And had either been absent from the scene, or failed to act well her part, Moses had never been learned in all the wisdom of the Egyptians, nor prepared to act well his part in the grand drama of Israel's deliverance. But woman was there with all her watchful care to bear a part in this important work. The noble hearted Egyptian princess was there clothed with authority to save from death, and moved with compassion at the sight of the weeping, homeless babe. The ready-witted and courageous sister was there, just at the auspicious juncture, to take advantage of these good impressions of the princess, and to speak a word in season for her little brother—"Shall I go, and call to thee a nurse of the Hebrew women, that she may nurse the child for thee?" And the Hebrew mother herself was there, near enough to come at a moment's warning, and to hear, as she came, and with a joy, no doubt, that thrilled her inmost soul, the command—"Take this child away, and nurse it for me, and I will give thee thy wages."

The whole incident occupies but little space in the sacred narrative; took indeed but a few moments of time when it occurred. But how important were its issues to Moses, to the world, and to the church of God! Yet a mother, a sister, and king's daughter, were the instruments of Providence, in all that was done. "And the child grew, and she brought him unto Pharaoh's daughter, and he became her son." This child, who became, all things considered, the greatest man that lived in the first four thousand years of the world's history, and did the greatest work that was done in all that time, owed his whole education, under God, to these three women. He was taken by Divine Providence and sent to school in his little ark of bulrushes. He was sent to a king's court in order that he might obtain all that knowledge of Egyptian wisdom, which otherwise he could not gain, but which was yet so essential to him. And yet his Hebrew mother was sent with him, to see that, even in an idolatrous court, he shall be faithfully instructed in the knowledge of the God of Abraham. And thus the important point was secured, that Moses should be trained in all the learning, both of the Egyptians and Hebrews; should have all the advantages of the secular and classical learning of the one, and the sacred, revealed wisdom of the other.

"Take this child and nurse it for me, and I will give thee thy wages." How impressively do these words set forth the duty, the work, the responsibility, the reward, and the high calling of the educator! No duty can be more urgent, no task more delightful, no calling more honourable, no wages more certain, than that of the educator. Was there a human being in all the land of Egypt, more honourably or usefully employed than this Hebrew mother, during all the years she was nursing and training this child for the king's daughter? But the educator, however humble, who is true to his high calling, is doing his work not merely for earthly wages, nor solely at the bidding of a king's daughter; but for God, for the church, for an immortal crown. This charge is to us, no longer the mere voice of Pharaoh's daughter, but one of the most solemn and sacred calls of Divine Providence. God is saying, the Church is saying, the State is saying, the Sabbath-school is saying to us all, wherever children can be found—"Take this child and train it for me, and I will give thee thy wages." Did the mother of Moses receive her wages? Not more certainly, than every faithful mother, every Sabbath-school teacher, every true hearted educator, shall receive a sure and just recompense for all the labour and care bestowed on the young.

While on this subject of education, we may remark that there are three distinct parties, each equally interested in it. These are the Parent, the Church, and the State. There are three Divine institutions in the world: first the family, the foundation of all, then the church, and then the state. Every man is, or ought to be, a member of each of these. Now there can be no question, that the education of the child is a matter which belongs primarily to the parent. It is at once his right and his duty to educate his child. The great responsibility is upon him, and no other agency can divest him of it. But then the parent is at the same time a citizen and a member of the church; and may also act through both these Divine ordinations in the work of education. He may employ their aid. He may call upon them to help him. And they are both bound to help him, for this is a great work; and the parent, single-handed, is often too weak for it. And still further, there are always children who are orphaned; and it is the duty both of the church and the state, to act the part of a parent to them. Hence, the necessity of education by the state, and at the same time by the church, both to help the parent in his weakness, and to help the child, when there are no parents. And though originally education is the appropriate and incumbent work of the parent, as ordained of God; still it is easy to demonstrate the necessity of state schools, and of church schools, just so long as there are any children in a community who have no parents, or any parents, who from poverty, ignorance, or any other cause, are incompetent to educate their own children. In the existing state of things, we hold the true doctrine to be, that all three should be educators, the parent, the church, and the state, each in its proper sphere. As to what part of the work of education, the church and the state as such shall perform, that is for the parent as such to determine. But all experience proves that it is best here to make a separation—giving to the state that part of education which is secular, and to the church that which is religious, but to both always that which is moral and Christian on the broad basis of the Bible.

But not to pursue this suggestive theme, let us return to Joseph. Of his infancy we know nothing, save the bare mention of his birth. But who is not familiar with the record of his childhood and youth? What child has not read in Genesis, the long, and yet for him too short, story of Joseph? What child has not heard the story, even before he could read it? And what good child ever heard it, without wishing to hear it again? The favourite son of his father's old age; the gentle, unsuspecting boy; the brother hated without cause; the artless dreamer telling his dreams; then buried in the deep pit, sold as a slave, carried to a far country, and given up for dead by his poor, heart-broken father. What young heart has not mourned with Jacob, and suffered with Joseph through all these sad changes?

How does the youthful imagination picture him in all his peculiar trials—now arrayed in his coat of many colours; now alone in the fields with his father; now recounting his singular dreams to his brethren; now on his solitary journey to Dothan, and thence to Shechem; and at last, seized, stripped, hungry, haggard, and it may be, wounded, by being forced into the pit; and to crown all, carried away into captivity and exile! Whose heart has not burned with indignation against the false and cruel brothers, when the venerable and desolate patriarch, deceived by the blood-stained coat of his darling, refused to be comforted, saying, "Joseph is without doubt, rent in pieces. I will go down into the grave unto my son mourning?"

And after the long lapse of years, when that boy had grown to be a man in Egypt, who has not rejoiced with the desolate old man, in his distant, dreary home, when the strange tidings reached him, that the lost was found, and the dead was alive again? Who has not rejoiced that God is on the throne, and works all things well, when reading that passage of surpassing pathos, in which the heart of the patriarch alternately faints and revives at the tidings; until at last, gathering strength enough for utterance, he pours forth the ruling desire of his soul in the hope of seeing that long lost son again? Leaving out of view all the honours, and all the great things that had been told him of his son's exaltation, and true to the deepest instincts of human nature, it is enough for him that he still lives. He utters all his aged heart in one great hope—in one simple and touching expression: "It is enough; Joseph my son is yet alive; I will go and see him before I die."

No master of human passion, no moral or dramatic bard, ever gave a truer touch of genuine human feeling than this. The thoughts of the patriarch centered not on the governorship of Egypt, nor its riches, nor its honours, nor all the wonders of the story; but solely on the image of his long lost son.

It was enough for him, an ample compensation for all his past woes, that Joseph was yet alive, and he should see his face once more. Old as he was, he was not too old to encounter any dangers of the way, to meet that son again. "I will go and see him before I die."

XII. LITTLE SAMUEL AND THE SONS OF ELI.

But of all the children of the Old Testament, little Samuel is probably the one that makes the deepest impression on the heart of a child. There is a peculiar interest in his history, even as there was a peculiar beauty in his childlike piety, and early consecration to the Lord. Next to our Saviour in the New Testament, he is, perhaps, the very best type of what piety in childhood ought to be, which the Bible gives. He seems to have been sanctified from the womb, to have grown up in the nurture of the Lord, without ever going astray. He seems, like Timothy, to have known the Scriptures; like Mary, to have chosen the good part; and, like Jesus, to have been about his heavenly Father's business from his earliest years. His opening character appears all the brighter too, from the fact of its shining out from the dark back-ground of depravity in the sons of Eli.

We need not recite here the story of his birth, his early ministrations at the Lord's tabernacle, and his remarkable revelations from the Lord by night, up to the time, when it is said, "All Israel, from Dan to Beersheba, knew that Samuel was established to be a prophet of the Lord." With all this every young reader of the Bible must be presumed to be as fully acquainted as with the story of Moses or of Joseph. But we may remark, as a thing worthy to be remembered, that Samuel has the high distinction of being the first child mentioned in Scripture, who received direct revelations from the Lord, and was endowed with the prophetic spirit, even while a child.

He was pre-eminently the child of prayer—of earnest, importunate prayer and holy vows preceding his birth. He came into the world in answer to the prayers of his godly mother. And he was brought by her, at a very tender age, probably when only seven years old, it may be only three, and given to the Lord as a perpetual loan, to be trained up by Eli, in the service of the Lord's house. We know not how old he was when the Lord called to him by name, and at night, in the tabernacle. The probability is that he was about twelve, as stated by Josephus. The writer of the first book of Samuel tells us, that he "ministered before the Lord, being a child, girded with a linen ephod." It is repeatedly stated, that he "grew on, and was in favour both with God and man." His humble and devoted mother, herself one of the most lovely female characters in the Bible, made him an annual visit in Shiloh, bringing such presents as were prompted by maternal love and the fear of God.

What an admirable model for children is the artless, devout Samuel! And what a noble model for mothers is the faithful Hannah! In prayer and faith, she devoted her son, her first born, and, at the time her only son, to the service of the Lord for life. She gave her all—the very jewel of her heart to the Lord. And how amply was she repaid! Not merely did she live to have other sons and daughters, but she had the unspeakable pleasure of seeing this very child of her tearful vows rise to the highest post of usefulness and honour in all the land of Israel. What a blessing would it be to the church of God, if each Christian mother, in the spirit of Hannah, would dedicate one son to the service of the Lord in the work of the gospel ministry! Her prayer for this child may have been regarded as a small affair among the great events of the times. But who now can calculate the amount of holy influences which, for three thousand years, have been flowing upon the world from that one agonizing prayer of the humble woman? Who can tell how much the humblest mother in our Zion might bless her own household and bless the world, by giving a single son to God for the ministry of reconciliation? When the whole world shall have been evangelized, and all the martyrs of truth, and faithful heralds of the cross, of every age and every land, shall stand before God to give up their account and receive their immortal crowns, who can say, whose crown of glory shall be the brightest—that of the labourers themselves who went forth in the gaze of the world to toil for Christ, or that of the humble, faithful mothers, who toiled at home, with ceaseless prayer and watchfulness, to train such labourers for the service of the church?

The noble son of Hannah, growing in favour with God and man, stands forth in strong contrast with the degenerate sons of the high priest, Hophni and Phinehas, whose awful doom was revealed to him from the Lord. The whole story of these depraved and wicked young men, is one of the most tragical in the Bible. They rushed madly upon their fate. Their sins were open beforehand, going before unto judgment. Though exalted to heaven in point of privilege, they yet practised iniquity till it was found to be hateful; and the judgments of God could slumber no longer. The virtues and the advancing years of Eli should have restrained them; the solemn warning by Samuel should have checked them. Their unbridled licentiousness, and early ignominious doom, tell a fearful tale to the ungodly sons of pious parents, and a no less fearful one to the parents themselves, who, like Eli, with excessive leniency and false indulgence, only admonish softly, when they should govern with the rod of authority. It would be easy to trace the steps of their ruin. Parental neglect and their own wilful self-indulgence did it all. First we see two ungoverned and spoiled children; next two rash and self-willed noisy boys; and then two profane and hot-headed young men; and, last of all, the infliction of the Divine threatening—"If his children forsake my law, and walk not in my judgments; if they break my statutes and keep not my commandments; then will I visit their transgression with the rod, and their iniquity with stripes." The visitation, in this case, though speedy and terrible, was but a type of what it has been in many others, and, sooner or later, will be in all.

We need not stop to recount the sad story of the battle in which these young men fell, and paid the penalty of their crimes. We need not tell how all the words of the Lord by Samuel, were fulfilled to the very letter. They lived just long enough to bring death upon their aged father, ruin upon all his house, defeat and disaster upon their country, and uneffaceable infamy upon themselves. They left the world with no legacy for their orphaned posterity, but the sad heritage of an ominous name: "Ichabod," the glory is departed.

But the manner in which the tidings are revealed to Eli, is worthy of our special notice. It is one of the most remarkable specimens of tragic, descriptive power in the Bible. It is plain prose, as simple and brief as words can be made. But it has been admired by eminent classical scholars, as surpassing in natural, unstudied grandeur, anything to be found in the range of dramatic and epic literature. The passage is in these words:

"And there ran a man of Benjamin out of the army, and came to Shiloh the same day, with his clothes rent, and with earth upon his head. And when he came, lo, Eli sat upon a seat by the way side, watching; for his heart trembled for the ark of God. And when the man came into the city and told it, all the city cried out. And when Eli heard the noise of the crying, he said, What meaneth the noise of this tumult? And the man came in hastily, and told Eli. Now Eli was ninety and eight years old; and his eyes were dim that he could not see. And the man said unto Eli, I am he that came out of the army, and I fled to-day out of the army. And he said, What is there done, my son? And the messenger answered and said, Israel is fled before the Philistines, and there hath been also a great slaughter among the people, and thy two sons also, Hophni and Phinehas, are dead, and the ark of God is taken. And it came to pass, when he made mention of the ark of God, that he fell from off the seat backward by the side of the gate; and his neck brake, and he died; for he was an old man and heavy. And he had judged Israel forty years." Then follows that last affecting scene, where the young wife and mother gives name to her new-born babe and dies—repeating to the last, "The glory is departed from Israel, for the ark of God is taken."

XIII. THE DYING INFANT.

The next example which we select for a few remarks, is the child of David and Bathsheba. It is the fullest narrative of a dying infant in the Bible. The tender bud was smitten, and withered away ere it bloomed. The little light was extinguished, just as it began to shed its cheering beams over an earthly household. But small as it was, it was an event sufficient to send desolation and penitential grief into the most exalted family circle of the land.

The child was sick, and the stern warrior king, whose heart had never yielded in the hour of battle, fasted and wept, and lay all night upon the bare earth, beseeching God to spare it. But when, at the end of seven days, it died, he went into the house of the Lord and worshipped. He comforted his bleeding heart with those precious words of faith and hope, which have since cheered so many others in affliction. "Now that he is dead, wherefore should I fast? Can I bring him back again? I shall go to him, but he shall not return to me."

This little one, though born in sin, was taken home to God. The early lost was the early saved. Washed in a Saviour's blood, and clothed in a Saviour's righteousness, it was soon introduced into that heavenly kingdom of which he so often spake as the loved abode of little children. It had not sinned after the similitude of Adam's transgression. So that, where sin abounded, grace did much more abound. It had committed no actual sin; and yet it was wholly born in sin. Its death was a judgment and punishment from God. It was smitten of God and died on account of the sins of its parents. It was done publicly before the sun, that all Israel might know that the thing which David had done, had displeased the Lord. The king was humbled and chastened and made a holier man by the stroke. The child was taken from the evil to come. Thus the death and salvation of this child early illustrated the true Scriptural ground on which the church of God has placed both the death and salvation of all who die in infancy. The whole doctrine of the Bible on the subject of the infant dead, is briefly comprehended in this: They died because Adam sinned; they live again because Jesus died.

Nothing more impressively proclaims the fallen condition of our race, and the sad inroads of sin, than an infant's grave. Without the Bible, no mystery would be greater than the suffering and death of infancy. Nature has nothing to account for such a disaster. It is in the very face of all that is natural. Why should the pure and fresh young rosebud be blasted in its very opening? Why should the kindly cultured and beautiful flower wither even as it blooms? Why should a light just kindled go out so soon; a life just begun so suddenly cease? We might expect the sere leaf of autumn to fall, the aged oak of the forest to decay, the hoary head of the patriarch to be bowed down. But why should the most loved and cherished plant in all the garden die? Why must this most precious jewel of my heart—this beautiful boy—and this angel of my household—the loved and loving daughter—be snatched away?

> "'Twas bright, 'twas heavenly, but 'tis past!
>
> Oh! ever thus from childhood's hour,
> I've seen my fondest hopes decay;
> I never loved a tree or flower,
> But 'twas the first to fade away.
> I never nursed a dear gazelle,
> To glad me with its soft black eye,
> But when it came to know me well,
> And love me, it was sure to die!"

Surely death never appears so unnatural, and but for the Bible so mysterious, as when the blooming infant dies. And yet it is estimated that about half our race die in infancy. Ah! what a destroyer is death! What desolations hath he wrought in the earth! What a harvest of tears and of broken hearts has he been reaping! How many hills and valleys has he planted thick with little graves! The whole earth has been but a Bochim—a valley of tears for the infant dead. Tears have never flowed oftener and more freely than when they have fallen around the infant's suffering bed and new made grave.

> "Leaves have their time to fall,
> And flowers to wither at the north wind's breath,
> And stars to set; but all,
> Thou hast all seasons for thine own, O death!"

But blessed be the name of the Lord, there is consolation in the Bible, and relief in heaven, for all these tears. There may be joy in the desolate dwelling even now; for there is hope in this early doom of childhood, the same that sustained the penitent David. "He may not return to me; but I shall go to him." The most precious belief of the church of God is the salvation of the infant dead. Perhaps the greatest of all the triumphs of the cross of Christ will be found at last to be this, that it has saved half our race in a body, by calling them away from the world in infancy. Perhaps the greatest joy that is now felt in heaven, in view of all things done on earth, is caused by this one event which creates the deepest, widest wave of sorrow here, the infant's death. For if there is joy in the presence of the angels of God over one sinner that repenteth, can we doubt that there is joy there, at the happy release of each little sufferer, as they pass death's iron gates, one by one, into the heavens, to be for ever blest on the bosom of their God? "Precious in the sight of the Lord is the death of his saints." How beautiful and glorious must be the infant dead!

"Oh, when a mother meets on high,
The babe she lost in infancy,
Hath she not then, for pains and fears,
The day of woe, the watchful night,
For all her sorrows. all her tears,
An overpayment of delight?"

With the word of God in our hands, and the hope of heaven in our hearts, there is no death on earth so blessed, so consolatory, so hopeful as the death of a little child. An infinite gain to the child, it often becomes an instrument of the greatest spiritual blessings to the parent. Many a mother will praise God for ever, that the death of her darling babe was made the means of her greater sanctification; or it may be, of her conversion to God. When the good Shepherd would draw his wandering sheep away from danger, and gather them safely into his fold, he has no more effective mode, than to take the little lambs up in his arms. Then the sheep will follow him. So he wins our worthless hearts. He takes our lambs away. He allures to brighter worlds, by removing our brightest objects of affection here. Where our treasure is, there will our hearts be also. He cuts the ties which bind us down, that our affections may be free to aspire upward to things above. How near the gate of heaven seems, when we know that our children have just passed through it! And how precious the Saviour seems, when we feel that our lambs are in his bosom! The ties which bound our hearts to earth, will thenceforth bind them to heaven. Who would not follow the good Shepherd to that house of many mansions, where he has been gathering these children of our love? Where is the Christian parent, who has the precious memory, and the unspeakable honour, of a child ascended to God, who has not thereby been made to drink in more of the beauty and power of the gospel? And when the image of that sainted one has been obliterated here, by lapse of time, from all other hearts, how will it still linger, like the fragrance of crushed flowers, around his own! And though long years may pass, and distance intervene, he will still love to breathe forth the tenderest sympathies of the soul in memory of the infant's dying couch, and lowly tomb.

I saw him oft at play,
  As no more I see him now,
With the roses on his cheek,
  And the lily on his brow;
His lisping notes so sweet
  And his laugh so full of joy,
As the sparkle of his eye
  Told the merry hearted boy.

I stood beside the bed,
Where the little sufferer lay,
Long struggling with disease
Till he breathed his life away.
No rose was on his cheek then,
Nor sparkle in his eye;
Oh, how it crushed my heart
For the darling one to die!

In a robe of snowy white,
We adorned him for the tomb,
And laid upon his breast,
A sweet rosebud half in bloom;
A smile of beauty lingered
Upon a face so fair,
It seemed as if an angel
Were softly slumbering there.

We laid him down to rest,
In the consecrated ground,
Where little ones before him,
Were sleeping all around;
Amid the summer flowers,
Beneath the bending skies,
We left him in his beauty,
Till God shall bid him rise.

I saw him once again,
In the visions of the night,
He seemed a little cherub
In his robe of snowy white;
A harp was in his hand,
And a garland on his brow,
For evermore an angel,
Oh, such I see him now!

XIV. TWO CHILDREN RESTORED TO LIFE.

The next two children that claim our attention in this survey, are those who were raised from the dead, and given back to their mothers, by the two great prophets of Israel, Elijah and Elisha. Each of them was an only son. We know neither their names nor their ages. But they were evidently children, somewhat advanced beyond the tender years of infancy. The one was the son of a very poor woman, a widow of Sarepta, with whom Elijah lived for a season during the great famine in Israel. The other was the child of affluence, being the son of a "great woman of Shunem," who had shown distinguished kindness to Elisha. It is a somewhat singular fact that God should have given to children this distinction of being the first of Adam's race, that were ever raised from the dead. Indeed, these two little boys are not only the first examples, but, with one exception, the only examples to be found in the Old Testament, of persons who were restored to life, after being dead So far as we know from the Bible, they were the earliest resurrections in the history of the world.

It was an amazing triumph of faith on the part of these prophets of God, thus to raise the dead. It must have been peculiarly so with Elijah, who was, probably, the first man in the history of the world, that ever made such an attempt, or, perhaps, even entertained the thought that God would restore the dead to life again at the request of mortal man. And what an illustration too, of the power of prayer, the fervent, importunate, effectual prayer of a righteous man! For you will observe that, in both instances, these children were restored to life in answer to earnest, wrestling prayer. "Elias," says the apostle James, "was a man subject to like passions as we are, and he prayed earnestly that it might not rain, and it rained not on the earth by the space of three years and six months. And he prayed again, and the heaven gave rain, and the earth brought forth her fruit." He who could thus, by his prayers, prevail with God to give or withhold the rains of heaven, was in like manner able to raise the dead by prayer.

The Scripture account of both these cases is so touching and beautiful, that varying our method a little, we propose to give you all we have to say further about them, in the very words of the Bible. They stand recorded, one in the seventeenth chapter of the first book of Kings, and the other in the fourth chapter of the second book. It was while Elijah was in concealment from the wicked king, Ahab, living with the poor widow, and her little son, on the unwasting barrel of meal, and the unfailing cruse of oil, that the event took place.

"And it came to pass, after these things, that the son of the woman, the mistress of the house, fell sick; and his sickness was so sore that there was no breath left in him. And she said unto Elijah, What have I to do with thee, O thou man of God? Art thou come unto me to call my sin to remembrance, and to slay my son? And he said unto her, Give me thy son. And he took him out of her bosom, and carried him up into a loft, where he abode, and laid him upon his bed. And he cried unto the Lord, and said, * * * O Lord, my God, I pray thee, let this child's soul come into him again. And the Lord heard the voice of Elijah, and the soul of the child came into him again, and he revived. And Elijah took the child, and brought him down out of the chamber into the house, and delivered him unto his mother; and Elijah said, See, thy son liveth."

She was the first mother, doubtless, that had ever known the joy of receiving a child back from the dead. And now let us turn to the somewhat fuller account of the second, the wealthy Shunamite:

"And it fell on a day when the child was grown, that he went out to his father, to the reapers. And he said unto his father, My head, my head! And he said to a lad, Carry him to his mother. And when he had taken him, and brought him to his mother, he sat on her knees till noon, and then died. And she went in, and laid him on the bed of the man of God, and shut the door upon him and went out. And she called unto her husband and said, Send me, I pray thee, one of the young men, and one of the she asses, that I may run to the man of God, and come again. And he said, Wherefore wilt thou go to him to-day? it is neither new moon nor Sabbath. And she said, It shall be well. Then she saddled an ass, and said to her servant, Drive and go forward; slack not thy driving for me, except I bid thee. So she went and came unto the man of God to Mount Carmel. And it came to pass, when the man of God saw her afar off, that he said to Gehazi, his servant, Behold, yonder is that Shunamite; run now, I pray thee, to meet her, and say unto her, Is it well with thee? Is it well with thy husband? Is it well with the child? And she answered, It is well. And when she came to the man of God, to the hill, she caught him by the feet; but Gehazi came near to thrust her away. And the man of God said, Let her alone; for her soul is vexed within her; and the Lord hath hid it from me, and hath not told me. Then she said, Did I desire a son of my lord? Did I not say, Do not deceive me? Then he said to Gehazi, Gird up thy loins, and take my staff in thine hand, and go thy way; if thou meet any man, salute him not; and if any salute thee, answer him not; and lay my staff upon the face of the child. And the mother of the child said, As the Lord liveth, and as thy soul liveth, I will not leave thee. And he arose and followed her. And Gehazi passed on before them, and laid the staff upon the face of the child; but there was neither voice nor hearing. Wherefore he went again to meet him, and told him, saying, The child is not awaked. And when Elisha was come into the house, behold the child was dead, and laid upon his bed. He went in, therefore, and shut the door upon them twain, and prayed unto the Lord. And he went up and lay upon the child, and put his mouth upon his mouth, and his eyes upon his eyes, and his hands upon his hands, and he stretched himself upon the child, and the child waxed warm. Then he returned and walked in the house, to and fro; and went up and stretched himself upon him; and the child sneezed seven times, and the child opened his eyes. So he called Gehazi, and said, Call this Shunamite. So he called her. And when she was come in unto him, he said, Take up thy son. Then she went in, and fell at his feet, and bowed herself to the ground, and took up her son, and went out."

Who of the millions upon millions that have lost children in infancy, would not have freely given all earthly treasures for the blessedness of that mother as she bore away her living son? When we have watched through the long, silent nights at the couch of the loved one; when we have done all that human skill can do, all that parental love can prompt to give relief, and all in vain; when we have gone to our closet to mingle our tears with our prayers in wrestling supplication to God for its life; when we have caught the last look, and heard the last accent of the dear little dying sufferer, never more to be effaced from our thoughts; and when, at last, he is gone—the light of our eyes, the brightest jewel of our hearts, gone—so still, so calm, so pale, so cold, so dead to us and all the world; oh! who but a parent can ever know the desolation, the hopelessness, the crushing tenderness of such an hour? Alas! the poor, stricken parent strives in vain to fathom it. There is a tide of feeling overwhelming his soul, too deep and strong for all the dikes of reason. No words, no thought, no human conception can measure the griefs of such an hour. It seems almost impossible to realize that it can be so—that our loved one, so bright and beautiful, so pure and joyous, so long and tenderly cherished, is, indeed, dead—dead and gone from the sight of our eyes, and the embrace of our hearts.

"And thou art dead, sweet child!
Ah yes! we ne'er shall see thee smile again!
We ne'er shall hear thy voice, which was to us
A music and a charm, until we meet
Away beyond life's stormy ocean's shore,
Where thy pure spirit on immortal wings
Hath flown!
But oh! I scarce can think that thou
Art gone from earth for ever; yet, oh! yet
They tell me thou art dead."

Well do we recall, as though it were yesterday, (for the scene is painted on the heart's retina to last for ever,) one touching example of such sorrow. It may no doubt stand as the type of thousands. It was a child of prayer and promise. It was a child marked out from all the others of the family by many things of peculiar and touching interest. Like little Samuel of old, whose name he bore, he had been dedicated to God, from his birth, to be a minister, if such might be the will of heaven. But he was a tender plant; frail in body as a flower transplanted into ungenial soil, yet, sprightly in mind and strong in spirit, in proportion to this outward frailty. An eminent servant of God who baptized him, inscribed his name in a beautiful little Bible, a token of his love, accompanied by the fervent prayer, that he might live to preach the gospel from that very book. And as the little one grew to intelligence, that baptismal Bible became the object of his fondest affections, which he often asked to see and handle before he could read. Twice was he stricken down by painful and dangerous illness, and twice did the Lord restore him in answer to wrestling prayer. His peculiar and manifold infirmities, and the lamb-like patience with which he bore them, had made him doubly dear to every heart of the household; so that he had become the pet, both of affection and of anxiety, to all the family. As he entered his seventh year, he seemed to have safely passed all the clustering dangers that had hitherto lurked along his little pathway of life—and parental hope grew bright, that now with a stronger step, answering to the inner progress of his mind, he would make his way up to man's estate. But how soon and suddenly was the promise blighted! God's ways are not our ways; nor his thoughts our thoughts. A third time was he stricken with disease. After a struggle of twelve days, which seemed to concentrate the sufferings of years, he breathed his little life away—and left a loving household in sadness and desolation—a sadness and desolation unrelieved except by the assurance that little Samuel was now in the bosom of the good Shepherd. In such an hour, it is faith's province to look up, and, though it be with tearful eye and bleeding heart, to say, It is well—He shall not return to me, but I shall go to him.

Dear child of my heart's love, how precious to me,
The thought that in heaven thy spirit is free,
Thy head is now pillowed beneath the cold sod,
But thou art at home on the bosom of God.

For six fleeting summers, sweet seraph, thy love
Illumined my life as a beam from above,
While thy budding beauty did win on each heart,
And year after year new graces impart.

With heaven I pleaded to spare thee áwhile,
And cheer my sad heart with thy sweet sunny smile,
To greet me at morning and bid me good night,
And gladden the hours with thy childish delight.

But alas for my hopes! the bright vision is gone;
The good Shepherd marked the dear lamb for his own,
He needed an angel to join the blest band,
And called him away to that bright, happy land.

The casket is broken and moulders in dust,
The jewel alone hath escaped from its rust,
But jewel and casket are precious to God,
And beauty immortal shall wake from thy sod.

XV. OTHER EXAMPLES FROM THE OLD TESTAMENT.

It is interesting to notice, as showing the diversified conditions in life, of the children of the Old Testament, that three of them, at least, were exalted to the throne of David, while as yet children of tender years. These were Manasseh at twelve, Josiah at eight, and Joash at seven. Nothing at first view seems more unnatural and absurd, than the crowning of little children, as rulers over a great nation. The New Testament tells us that "the heir, as long as he is a child, differeth nothing from a servant, though he be lord of all; but is under tutors and governors until the time appointed of the father"

So it ought to be with all young kings. But under the Jewish monarchy, many of their sovereigns fell by the hand of violence, before they had lived out half their days: and hence their successors were sometimes raised to the throne at an early age, some at sixteen, some at eighteen, and others still younger.

The history of little Joash, as related in the eleventh chapter of the second book of Kings, is full of romantic interest. He was hid for six years in the house of the Lord, by the wife of Jehoiada the high priest, when every other descendant of David had been put to death by the bloody queen Athaliah. He was then suddenly brought out in his seventh year, anointed and crowned king of Judah in the presence of an armed soldiery, and an enthusiastic multitude, who clapped their hands and cried, "God save the king," or, "Let the king live." Possibly the very tender years of their little sovereign, along with the fact that he was the last link in David's line, which till now they had looked upon as lost, suggested to the people, these ardent desires for his welfare. Certainly, no child ever stood more in need of the saving grace and help of God than this infant monarch. But he had a wise friend and counsellor in his faithful priest Jehoiada; and he made a good king as long as his old protector lived.

It is not, however, our purpose to trace his history; nor that of the idolatrous, blood-thirsty, and at last penitent Manasseh; nor indeed the far more inviting history of the pious and noble Josiah. The introduction of Josiah's history in the twenty-second chapter of the second book of Kings, is instructive as referring to his mother. It is in these words—"Josiah was eight years old, when he began to reign, and he reigned thirty and one years in Jerusalem And his mother's name was Jedidah, the daughter of Adaiah of Boscath. And he did that which was right in the sight of the Lord, and walked in all the way of David his father, and turned not aside to the right hand or the left." If we might infer anything from a name, we might infer from Jedidah's name, *the beloved one,* that she was a good and lovely woman. But we have more here than a name, though nothing is said about her directly. The fact, however, that she is mentioned at all, in this connection, as if to give us some clue to the lovely character and noble reign of so young a sovereign, and the fact that Josiah's father Amon and his grandfather Manasseh had been two of the worst of all the Jewish kings, seem to make it very safe to conclude that Jedidah was a faithful woman, and had done her whole duty in the training of such a son. As a general rule, great and good men, the world over, have faithful and noble mothers; and it would be very difficult to acconnt for such a character as Josiah under the circumstances, if Jedidah had not been, as her name imports, the "beloved one," honoured of God and man.

We barely direct the attention of our young readers to these three royal children, raised so prematurely to all the responsibilities and dangers of a throne. And while it may be a pleasing thought for childhood that there never was a better king on David's throne than young Josiah; it is also a sad fact that there scarcely ever was a worse one than young Manasseh. The history of these three young princes shows very clearly that it is not good for children to be exalted to power Even the good Josiah with all his piety and wisdom, and after all his great services in reforming his country, betrayed an inconsiderate rashness and folly in waging the war which cut him off so early in the fatal battle of Megiddo. This an older and more experienced sovereign would have avoided. His valuable life paid the penalty of his youthful self-confidence. So also, the penitential old age of Manasseh was but a poor compensation to his country for all the innocent blood he had shed in his childhood and youth. And even the good and wise reign of young Joash was sadly over-balanced by the cruel crimes which disgraced his old age. Evidently it is the wise ordination of divine Providence, that children should be kept, as the Scripture says, "under tutors and governors," and not placed upon the throne of responsibility and power.

Another interesting case for childhood is that of the young and good Abijah, son of king Jeroboam. He died early because the Lord loved him, and would thus remove him from the corrupting influence of his father's bad example. The Lord loves them that love him, and those that seek him early shall find him. It is sometimes remarked, that children of extraordinary piety are apt to die early. And why should they not, if the Lord loves them, and has already prepared them by his grace for heaven? This case of Abijah teaches us very clearly, that the Lord may remove a child from this wicked world, just because he loves it too well to leave it here to be ruined by contact with unhallowed influences. As Abijah was thus taken from the idolatrous court of Jeroboam, so, no doubt, many a child now sickens and dies, because a gracious, loving God is determined to save it from the ruinous influence of ungodly parents. How often do such parents prevent their children, as they grow up, from becoming pious! And how little do they consider, that they are thus, as it were, compelling God to remove their children to heaven; and thus save their souls from the ruin that would await them if permitted to grow up here under parental influence! And is it not a mercy to the child when the Lord cuts short that process by taking it away in infancy? Is it not better to die and enter heaven early, than linger here under such influences, to forget God and at last perish?

In the present instance, Abijah is sick and ready to die. It is a tragic and affecting story, as narrated in the fourteenth chapter of the first book of Kings. Jeroboam has done many wicked things against the God of Israel, but he knows that He alone reigns, and has the power over life and death. In his deep distress, conscious of his many crimes, and anxious for the life of his son and heir, he sends the mother of the child to Shiloh, loaded with presents, but in disguise, lest she should be known there as the wife of Jeroboam. There is an old prophet of Jehovah, Ahijah by name, still living there—the same who many years before had predicted his exaltation to the throne, and who will now be able to divine the result of this sickness, and tell what will become of the child. The mother, as directed, makes the sad and weary journey, in all probability alone; reaches the sacred city; and at last, no doubt with a trembling heart, stands at the threshold of the house of the man of God. Ahijah recognizes her as soon as the sound of her feet is heard at the door; for though dim with age and unable to see, he has already been informed of the Lord, that it is the wife of the rebel monarch who is now come to inquire of him. He has nothing but heavy tidings for her. He has no greetings to utter, but the bitter wages of long continued transgression. She hears first the dreadful doom of all the race of Jeroboam, his kingdom rent away, his seed utterly destroyed, "for the Lord hath spoken it;" and then the fate of her child in these words: "Arise thou therefore, get thee to thine own house; and when thy feet enter the city, the child shall die. And all Israel shall mourn for him, and bury him;

for he only of Jeroboam shall come to the grave, because in him there is found some good thing toward the Lord God of Israel in the house of Jeroboam."

And so was it fulfilled to the letter. All Jeroboam's posterity, sooner or later, were cut off by a violent and ignominious death, except this little one, who was but taken from the evil to come. His sorrowing mother returned, more sad and dreary than she went, and reached her home only in time to see it breathe its last. As she crossed the threshold of her door, its little spirit, released from toil and pain, was wafted away to the mansions of the blest.

> "Though no pious parents' care
> Young Abijah e'er had known,
> God had heard his early prayer,
> And had marked him for his own.
> Happy child, by God approved,
> Early taken to his rest,
> From the abodes of sin removed
> To the mansions of the blest!"

Another beautiful story for children is that of the little captive maid in Syria. It comes as an episode in the drama of Jewish history, along with the remarkable cure of Naaman the Syrian captain, who was cured of his leprosy through her humble instrumentality. The whole account is given in a single chapter—the fifth of the second book of Kings. The whole story is interesting and instructive; but the most touching incident in it, is that which recounts the part enacted by this little maid of Israel. She had been taken by the Syrian bands, and carried away into exile from her native land, and had become a servant in the household of this valiant soldier of the Syrian army.

Hard, indeed, seemed to be the lot which tore this little girl away so early from all the endearments of home, and doomed her to servitude not only in a land of strangers, but idolaters. But like Joseph in Egypt, she was made, in the providence of God, the honoured instrument of bringing great blessings upon her master's house; for while in her native land she had heard of Elisha, the wonder-working prophet of God; and no doubt she now, like Joseph, remembered and served the God of her parents in this land of idolatry. The brief narrative simply mentions the kind and seasonable part which she acted in leading Naaman to visit Elisha; and then drops her entirely out of view. We should like to know more of her. We can hardly think she lost her reward for so great a service to her master. For aught we know, the generous and thankful captain on his return, may have raised her to honour and affluence in Syria, or in after years, restored her to her parents and her native land. Be this as it may, though nameless, she has her record in the word of God. Her memorial is in three verses: "The Syrians had gone out by companies, and had brought away captive out of the land of Israel a little maid; and she waited on Naaman's wife. And she said to her mistress, Would God, my lord were with the prophet that is in Samaria; for he would recover him of his leprosy. And one went in and told his lord, saying, Thus and thus said the maid that is of the land of Israel."

But we need not recount the story. You know what great results flowed from this little word so fitly spoken—how he went to Elisha, bathed seven times in the waters of Jordan, was cleansed of his leprosy, and returned to his home rejoicing. We cannot, however, dismiss this striking Old Testament narrative, without noticing how beautifully it illustrates the whole way of salvation through Christ, as it is revealed in the Gospel. By nature we are all together, whether old or young, like Naaman, afflicted with a dreadful malady. It is the fatal leprosy of sin. And like him, we must be cured, or perish. But there is no help for us except in Israel. As there was then, so there is now a great prophet, and but one who can cure us of this malady. It is Jesus Christ. As Naaman went to Elisha and believed his word, and followed his directions, and was healed; so we must come to the great Prophet of God, Jesus Christ, believe in him, and obey his word, if we would be saved. If we stay away, we perish. If we refuse to believe and obey, we perish. "None but Jesus can do helpless sinners good." There are a thousand things to hinder our coming, or make us unwilling to believe and follow his directions. We may feel, as Naaman did at first, that God ought to do some great miracle for us; that the thing which he requires us to do is too simple. We may say as he did, "Are not Abana and Pharpar, rivers of Damascus, better than all the waters of Israel? may I not wash in them, and be healed?" Still we must do the thing—we must believe God's word—we must come to Jesus Christ, or perish. We must come just as we are, and come now.

"Just as I am! without one plea,
Save that thy blood was shed for me,
And that thou bid'st me come to thee,
O Lamb of God, I come.

"Just as I am, and waiting not
To rid my soul of one dark blot,
To thee, whose blood can cleanse each spot,
O Lamb of God, I come."

XVI. CHILDREN OF THE NEW TESTAMENT.

We must reserve a little room to notice the prominent examples of childhood in the New Testament. And yet we have not said all we wished to say about the children of the Old. There are many other interesting cases. We might speak of Daniel and his three companions, the God-fearing children of the captivity. Although it is chiefly in their character, as heroic young men, that they act a prominent part in Bible history, still it must not be forgotten that the lustre of their virtues shone forth with remarkable power in their very childhood. They never could have braved the lions' den and the fiery furnace, as young men, had they not been trained to the fear of God and the self-denying discharge of duty, from their earliest years.

But for want of space, we must pass them by, and all other children of the Old Testament, in order to mention a few prominent examples in the New; and so complete our sketch. And perhaps the first name here, occurring to every youthful mind, will be that of John, the son of Zacharias and Elizabeth, who became the forerunner of our Saviour. Like Isaac, he was an only son, and the son of his parent's old age. Like Isaac, he was also the child of prophecy and Divine promise. We need not now relate the many extraordinary circumstances attending his birth and early infancy, as recorded in the first chapter of the gospel by Luke. The angel, who announced his birth, predicted, that he should be great in the sight of the Lord; should drink neither wine nor strong drink, and should be filled with the Holy Ghost, even from his mother's womb. And so it is stated by the Evangelist, that all who heard of the wonderful things attending his birth, "laid them up in their hearts, saying, What manner of child shall this be? And the hand of the Lord was with him. And the child grew, and waxed strong in spirit, and was in the deserts, till the day of his showing unto Israel."

Another child brought to our view in the New Testament, though but little is said of his childhood, is Timothy, to whom the Apostle Paul writes two of his epistles. All that we know of him would lead us to suppose that he was a good child, and that he possessed a lovely character from his early years. The great Apostle, when his own mortal race was almost finished, looked upon the still youthful Timothy with peculiar joy, not only because he was his own son in the gospel, but because he had been his most faithful and trusty companion in labour and tribulation. He never speaks of Timothy but with affection and delight. In one place he makes the following honourable allusion to his early studies and attainments: "From a child thou hast known the Holy Scriptures, which are able to make thee wise unto salvation, through faith which is in Christ Jesus."

What a tribute was that to young Timothy! How much of early piety, how much of patient study, how much of manly character even in childhood does that single sentence reveal to us! "From a child thou hast known the Holy Scriptures." He had known them, moreover, not with a bare theoretical knowledge, but with an experimental saving acquaintance; for the Apostle, in another place, speaks of the "unfeigned faith," which, from the first, had dwelt in Timothy, and also in his mother Eunice, and his grandmother Lois, before him. This indicates to us the secret of Timothy's early knowledge of the Scriptures, his noble character, and his career of usefulness His faithful mother and grandmother were at the bottom of it.

Eunice and Lois had been his teachers, and had done their duty in sowing the seeds of Divine truth in the heart of the child. What an encouragement is this to parents! And what an illustration of the truth of God's words: "Train up a child in the way he should go; and when he is old, he will not depart from it!"

Blessed promise! blessed precept! the one as binding, and the other as unfailing, now, as in the days of Eunice and Lois. Aye, train up the little ones in the nurture and admonition of the Lord; make them wise in the Holy Scriptures. For there is no work in this world which fathers and mothers are bound to do, more important, more hopeful, or more certain of a blessed recompense. They may not all become, like Timothy, wise and pious from their early childhood. They may not all, like Mary, choose the good part and sit at Jesus' feet in their youthful prime. On the contrary, they may long neglect the one thing needful. They may wander far away from the fold, in many a forbidden path of sin and folly. They may almost cause the fond parental heart to break in despair, ere they return. But still the promise shall not fail. The seed long buried, and to all appearance dead, shall take root, and spring to life again. The prodigal shall return from his wanderings; for a covenant keeping God shall bring him back.

Be not discouraged, then, faithful, Christian parent. Eunice and Lois may be dead; and yet the children shall be saved. They may seem impervious to all good impressions at first. Though children of much prayer, and many kindly counsels, they may, for a season, disappoint the fondest hopes, and when ripening age comes on, may seem to have lost every early religious impression. But all is not lost that appears to be lost. There are some things which a child rightly trained can never forget The sanctuary where he was first taught to worship the God who made him; the household altar where, evening and morning, he was wont to hear a father's earnest prayers, and a mother's gentle counsels; the spot, the day, the hour, in which, for the last time, he received the parting benediction, or the dying charge of that father and mother—these are things that shall cleave to him as long as life or memory remains. He may go to the ends of the earth; he may travel every bright pathway of joy, or thread every dark labyrinth of danger and death, the foot of man hath ever trod; he may sail the trackless seas like John Newton, or be cast upon some lone and desolate isle like Alexander Selkirk; he may pitch his last tent, like Henry Martyn, upon the scorching sands of some Persian desert, or be left to perish alone, amid Alpine glaciers, like the poor drummer boy of the French army; like Richardson and Lander, his mortal career may be cut short in the wilds of Central Africa, far beyond the abodes of civilized men; or he may die encased in polar ice and be shrouded in darkness, like the heroic Franklin; he may be called to lay down his life at the bidding of some bloody tyrant, like Freeman and his martyred brethren at Cawnpore, or to fall like Hammond, Havelock, and Hedley Vicars on the ensanguined fields of war, where the soldier rushes to glory or the grave—but still, go where he may, and die as he may, these loved scenes of his childhood and his home will cling to him even in death. Faithful memory will bring to him then, if never before, that last yearning look, that solemn benediction, and that distant home and hearth-stone, where the voice of morning and evening devotion first greeted his ear, and the warm gushings of a mother's love bathed his infant cheek. And even then and there too, while the life blood is ebbing low, he may be able, through Divine grace, like the dying thief upon the cross, to cast all his sins on Jesus, and die in peace. Or if, like some of those just mentioned, he had long before learned to cast his sins on Jesus, death itself will then be welcome, as but the gate to glory.

Among the children of the New Testament, we must not omit to notice the extraordinary case of one who died and lived again. It is, indeed, one of the only three persons who are mentioned, as having been raised from the dead by our Saviour. This was the child of Jairus, a ruler of the synagogue, and, as we are told, his only daughter. Her name is not given; but she is described to us in the narrative very distinctly, by a few expressive terms. She is called damsel, maiden, little daughter, and one twelve years old. Her father left her at home, sick, and at the point of death. Coming to Jesus, he fell at his feet, and besought him to go and heal her. Jesus at once started with him, but was detained by the crowd that thronged his way, and by a poor woman who had come to be healed. Whilst they tarried, the child died, and Jairus was met by a messenger from home, saying—Thy daughter is dead; trouble not the Master. But Jesus encouraged his sinking faith, and hastened on to the house of death. There he found all weeping, and wailing, and lamenting her. At his bare suggestion that something might yet be done for her, we are told, they all laughed him to scorn, knowing that she was dead. Jesus was there, however, by the father's request; and he always acted, on such occasions, as one clothed with authority. He accordingly put them all out of the room where the little girl was lying, except the father, and mother, and his three disciples, Peter, James, and John. He then took her by the hand, and called, saying, "Talitha cumi, Maiden arise," and her spirit came again, and she arose straightway and walked.

In what other book could we have found such an event recorded, (in case there had been such to record,) in terms so brief and unpretending? It must have been a thrilling scene. How short the recital! How simple the word of command! How immediate its execution! How sublime the power that could thus awake the dead! How composed the demeanour of him who wielded it! What must have been the joy of the parents of the child! With what lofty hopes of coming grandeur must the disciples have been filled! With what mingled wonder and delight, the little maid herself! But of all this not one word is said. All this is left to the imagination. All this the genius of the greatest masters of the fine arts may fill up. But what skill, either of the chisel or the pencil, what descriptive powers either of prose or poetry, can ever adequately portray these wonderful Scripture scenes? The genius of our American poetry, like that of other lands, has sometimes essayed to translate them into its own measured lines of beauty; and never perhaps more successfully than in the present instance, by Willis.

"The Saviour raised
Her hand from off her bosom, and spread out
The snowy fingers in his palm, and said,
Maiden! arise!—and suddenly a flush
Shot o'er her forehead, and along her lips
And through her cheek the rallied colour ran,
And the still outline of her graceful form
Stirred in the linen vesture, and she clasped
The Saviour's hand, and fixing her dark eyes
Full on his beaming countenance—arose."

XVII. THE CHILDHOOD OF JESUS.

But it is time to conclude this survey of the children of the Bible. And how can we do so more appropriately than with a brief reference to the childhood of our blessed Saviour! He was indeed the great antitype of all other children. He was like Isaac, in being the child of promise—the very seed in whom all the families of the earth should be blessed. He was like Joseph in being betrayed and sold by his brethren. He was like Moses in being providentially saved from the decree of a cruel despot. He was like Samuel in his early knowledge of Divine things and his early consecration to his Father's work. He was like Josiah and Joash in coming of David's royal line. And yet he was in many important points unlike every other child of Adam's race.

He was the child to whom every other child, from the first-born of Eve, had in a manner pointed. He was the long promised child, to whom the daughters of Abraham through all generations had been looking forward with eager desire, that they might enjoy the distinction of being its highly favoured mother. He was the child of whom all the ancient prophets had spoken—the child born of a virgin—given of God—the Wonderful—the Counsellor—the Mighty God—upon whose shoulders the government of earth and heaven should rest. The highest honour that was ever conferred, or can be conferred on childhood, is surely this—that the Son of God was once a child; that he passed through all the stages, endured all the hardships, felt all the weaknesses, tasted all the joys and sorrows of a child. Among the many wonders of the incarnation is this fact of the infancy of Jesus.

Had we been told beforehand, that the Son of God was

coming into the world to assume a human form, how little should we have calculated on his taking the form of an infant! Instead of his condescending to be born, like other children, we should have expected him to avoid all the ills and infirmities of helpless infancy, and to appear at once from heaven, as a full grown and perfect man, or like Adam fresh from the creative hand of God. Or if told, that he must be born of a woman, in order to fulfil his great redeeming work, we should have at least expected to find him in some splendid mansion of the great. We should have looked for a palace as his birth-place, a queen his mother, the nobles of the earth his attendants, with crowns and sceptres as the playthings of his youthful years.

But how different from all this, the story of Bethlehem! How amazing the contrast between this and the story of the inn, the manger, the flight to Egypt, the carpenter's shop at Nazareth! And is it not best that it should be as it is? As it is, the poorest man on earth, the humblest woman, the most helpless child, may look upon the Son of God as a brother. For there is no stage of life which Jesus has not passed: no depth of poverty, no vale of humiliation, no condition of helplessness to which he has not gone down. He trod them all. He proved them all. And he is therefore able to feel towards us all, the tenderness of a brother's heart.

And yet, amid all these outward circumstances of humiliation in the childhood of Jesus, there was a strange mingling of other elements of surpassing glory. There was an unearthly grandeur attendant upon his very infancy. There was a more than regal dignity belonging to him from his mother's womb. There was a sense in which no man could call him son, and no angel regard him as inferior, even when he lay a babe in Bethlehem. When the heir to an earthly throne is about to be ushered into the world, nobles and ministers of state are summoned to attend, while a whole nation waits in eager anticipation for the earliest tidings of the event. A hundred cannon announced to France the joyful news, when the king of Rome was born and Napoleon had an heir. But when Jesus, the Son of God, was born, there was nothing unusual done on earth; no outward demonstrations proclaimed it: no high officers of state came to welcome it; no princes and nobles attested it to a rejoicing people. Nevertheless, though earth was silent, heaven was joyful. There were signs and wonders and glad voices in the firmament. The angels of God sung his natal hymn in the skies. Bethlehem's shepherds came in from their night watchings to behold the wonder; and wise men, from a far country, poured their offerings at the feet of Him, who, though his bed was a manger, was yet entitled to a throne—the King of kings and Lord of all. When did ever the extremes of weakness and grandeur meet so wondrously as in the babe of Bethlehem?

> "Cold on his cradle the dew drops are shining,
> Low lies his head with the beasts of the stall;
> Angels adore him in slumber reclining,
> Maker, and Monarch, and Saviour of all."

We need not recount the incidents of his infancy. They are familiar even to the youngest readers. For what Christian mother has not recited them, and sung of them, to her little ones long before they could read? It is enough to say, that Jesus was a perfect child, just as he was a perfect man. No sinful thought or desire ever found a home in his young heart. No sinful word ever escaped his tender lips. No sinful deed ever defiled his pure hands. No neglect of duty to God or man, could ever be laid to his charge. As a child, not less than as a man, he magnified the law and made it honourable. All other children of the Bible, however amiable and lovely, in many instances, were yet sinful, either by nature or practice. Jesus alone, of all born of woman, came into the world absolutely holy—free from all taint of original sin when he was born, and free from all actual transgression while he lived. "He did no sin, neither was guile found in his mouth."

In him, therefore, the children of the world have a perfect model of all virtue—of obedience, gentleness, truth, prudence, courage, industry, benevolence, patience, piety, wisdom, zeal,—all that childhood, without sin, would be capable of being, doing, and attaining in our world. And think what our world would have been, or would now be, if all the children, ever born into it, had been just like Jesus Christ! What a beautiful illustration of his perfect character—his sublime obedience both to God and man—is that which is recorded of him at the age of twelve, when he said, "Wist ye not that I must be about my Father's business?" and yet, though having such work to do, went back as a dutiful, loving child, to his humble home at Nazareth!

Such was the childhood of Jesus. And how cheering to our hearts is the thought of it! We love to think of the relation in which the Son of God has stood, and will for ever stand to children. It throws the warm glow of love over the whole history of redemption. The Son of God a child! It seems to be the very crowning proof of the infinite and everlasting compassions of God towards our fallen nature. There is no fact in all the story of Immanuel, that should more encourage our approach to God as a loving Father, than that his own well-beloved Son was once a child, even as we have been. And answering to this cheering fact, is the great and precious doctrine that he was, and is for evermore, the children's Friend and the children's Saviour. By his death he has secured the eternal salvation of all that die in infancy. How different would be our feelings, if, when we looked into the Bible, we found no provision in the covenants of God, no love in the Saviour's heart, and no promise of a dwelling place in heaven for the little children!

But in Christ Jesus the dark enigma of the infant's death is for ever solved; for death is but the gate of glory. In him an infant's grave is a blessed earthly destiny, because there the earliest lost is the soonest saved. In the light that shines forth from his cross, the dying infant is seen to be associated with all that is sacred in the love of Jesus, all that is blessed in the life of heaven, all that is beautiful and glorious in the companionship of God, of angels, and of just men made perfect. If our hearts burn with grateful, adoring love to him, because of his sympathy for the poor, his condescending kindness to men of low degree, his tender regard for suffering woman, how much more should he win our hearts by his yearning affection for little children, and his amazing grace in becoming himself a child! That he should bear all the griefs and carry all the natural infirmities of childhood; that he should take up the little children in his arms and bless them; that he should rejoice in spirit when he thought of them as the favoured subjects of his grace; that he should shed his blood as an atonement for their sins, and thereby open the gates of Paradise to countless millions who had never heard his name till they heard it in heaven in the new song of redemption—these are things that should bind our hearts in sweet and willing bonds of love to the person of Immanuel. And these are things that should make every child love to read the Bible.

"I think when I read that sweet story of old,
When Jesus was here among men,
How he called little children like lambs to his fold,
I should like to have been with them then.

I wish that his hands had been placed on my head,
That his arms had been thrown around me,
That I might have seen his kind look when he said,
Let little children come unto me.

Yet still to his footstool in prayer I may go,
And ask for a share in his love;
And if I thus earnestly seek him below,
I shall see him and hear him above."

CHAPTER III.

THE HEROIC CHARACTERS OF THE BIBLE.

I. THE HEROIC IN HUMAN AFFAIRS.

THERE is scarcely any class of characters who stand out in bolder relief along the line of Bible history than its military and moral heroes. And there is perhaps scarcely any channel through which the Bible history has exerted a more marked influence over the lives of men, than through the mighty deeds of these mighty men of old. No one who has read the Bible or any other history of the world attentively, can fail to see, that the heroic has been one of the most potent elements of good or evil in the affairs of men. No one who has read the Bible, and at the same time studied the promptings of his own heart, can fail to feel, that a profound admiration for heroic characters is one of the most deeply seated, as it is one of the most common sentiments of human nature. It is amongst the earliest inspirations of our childhood. We all pay the instinctive homage of our applause, and our very love to the man who proves himself a real hero. We may hate his crimes and pity his errors, but his true courage we cannot forbear to honour and admire. In the world's estimation, a brave heart has often availed to hide a multitude of sins. It may be questioned whether any other trait of character will go so far to cover the imperfections of its possessor as real heroism. The widest and the highest term for virtue among the old Romans originally denoted simply strength and courage. And we have a striking illustration, in Napoleon Bonaparte, of the extent to which a heroic character of the highest order has been able to throw a mantle of glory over deeds of selfishness and ambition, which otherwise would have been regarded as infamous. But so it is, and always has been. Right or wrong, the world canonizes the heroic character. Whether it be displayed upon the battle field of the soldier, or in the cabinet of the statesman; whether on great public occasions when empires are lost and won, or in those sufferings for conscience' sake, which the martyrs of truth and liberty endure; sooner or later the world is sure to honour the memory of the man who dares to do, or die—who nails his colours to the mast, either to stand by them till he conquer, or to perish with them.

It is the heroic, not less than the philanthropic element, which the world so much admires in the character of John Howard and men of that class. Could you divest their philanthropic labours of all personal danger, and exhibit this benevolence on a field where there is no risk to run, and no sacrifice to make—in a word, where no moral heroism was called for—you would take away one of its greatest charms. The same is true in the case of Luther and Knox and all great reformers. It is the daring, self-sacrificing spirit of the hero, as much as the burning zeal of the missionary, that wins our homage in the career of such men as David Brainerd and Henry Martyn, Duff and Livingstone. And so also it was the bold adventure, not less than the brilliant success of the achievement, that crowned the name of Columbus with imperishable glory. The same was true of Washington. It was not alone his love of country and of liberty that has rendered his name as immortal as liberty itself; but an unfaltering heroism that could look suffering and death in the face, and maintain itself alike in success or disaster, victory or defeat. Of this heroic spirit, and of the world-wide admiration which it inspires, we have had a recent striking exemplification in the search for Sir John Franklin. Who has not read the story of that last forlorn hope of humanity under Dr. Kane? With what a thrill of interest did the whole civilized world look on, and watch the result of those heroic endeavours to ascertain the fate of the lost? And when, after two winters of stern encounter with the terrors of the Polar regions, the brave young commander with his little band of heroes emerged again to the view of the world, who would not have accorded them a prouder triumph than any Roman conqueror ever won from his grateful country?

Real heroism is not necessarily restricted to great men and to great public occasions. The earth has many other theatres for its display, besides the red fields of war, the perilous paths of adventure and the rough routine of political life. There is a sublime sense in which life is all a conflict, and every man who has a heart for it may be a hero in the strife. The world is one wide battle-field, and every day brings its trials, its conflicts, its victories or defeats. There is no condition in life so lowly or obscure as to call for no brave and generous action. But still, it is always the great man, endowed with more than ordinary courage and genius, who stands up boldly and perils all for the public good, that reaps the largest harvest of the world's applause. Be it his labour, his eloquence, his suffering, or his sword, which he consecrates to the welfare of his fellow men; be it that he lives long like Lafayette to enjoy his triumphs, or returns from his toil only to die like Kane amid the hosannas of his country, or falls in the deadly breach like Leonidas or De Kalb, still he wins for himself the freely accorded title of hero—a veritable noble of the earth and rightful king of men. And this heroism honoured by all, has an especial charm for the young. To ardent, enthusiastic youth, there is no attribute of human greatness, which makes a more powerful appeal.

Accordingly, in holding up to the young the chief attractions of the Bible, as a book of taste and genius, of history and biography, we should leave out of view one broad field of instruction, and lose one important argument, if we failed to portray its heroic characters—its mighty men of valour, and its still mightier champions of truth and righteousness. The Bible would not have corresponded to the great world we live in, nor indeed to the little world within ourselves, had it ignored the existence of such a thing as heroism. On the contrary we shall find, that it has furnished some of the finest specimens of the heroic character to be found in history, has developed all the elements of that character on its grandest scale, and at the same time pointed out the method by which that character may turn all its mighty energies from purposes of destruction, and employ them for the glory of God and the good of man.

II. HEROIC CHARACTER OF THE BIBLE HISTORY.

It cannot have escaped the notice, even of a superficial reader, that a very large portion of the Old Testament history, like almost all ancient history, is a record of wars and bloody battles. Several of the larger books are made up of narratives of revolutions, conquests, and fierce collisions, not only of the tribes of Israel, one with another, but with all the surrounding nations. Indeed, the first book of their national history, that of Joshua, which recounts their settlement and conquests in the promised land, is but a succession of battles and victories, fought and won in the name of the Lord. It would be difficult to find in all history a more martial and heroic people than ancient Israel, at several stages of their national career. They had to fight their way to the land of Canaan, to fight their way inch by inch into possession of it, and through long centuries to maintain that possession by the sword, till the long military reigns of Saul and David at last gave them peace by the utter annihilation of all their old enemies. And then, after the peaceful reign of Solomon, which formed the culminating point of the national career, and divided it into two great periods, we find another succession of wars and battles, onward almost to the coming of Christ. The whole ascending history of the nation was warlike and heroic, from the departure out of Egypt to the death of David; and the whole descending history from the reign of Rehoboam to the Babylonish exile, was very much of the same character; save only that, in the latter period, the two kingdoms were as often found in arms against each other, as against their common foes. And so this whole history, running through eight or ten centuries, and embracing so large a portion of the Old Testament Scriptures, is a history of heroes.

The pages of Homer are not more crowded with daring deeds and garments rolled in blood, and all the dread scenery of war, than are some of these inspired annals of the Jewish history. Much of it was both written and enacted in what may be called the heroic ages of the world—the age of Hercules, Achilles, Agamemnon, Ajax—the age of the mythological heroes and demigods of Greece—the age both of the fabulous and the real giants of the earth—the age when men living under the open sky, breathing the fresh air, and blest with athletic bodies and long life, loved to exercise their souls by looking danger in the face till danger died. It could not be, that a book recounting so large a portion of the actual history of the ancient world as the Bible does, and dealing so largely in the facts of real life during the progress of these heroic ages, should have been lacking, or even sparing in its record of military glory, and its illustration of the most heroic character.

Let no one suppose, however, that it is a mere catalogue of savage war-chiefs and blood-stained conquerors, which the Scriptures of the Old Testament call us to contemplate. They were mighty men of valour; but they were something more. Along with their heroism, they possessed the true religion, and often the inspiration of the Almighty. And when they drew the sword, it was mainly for the defence and vindication of these that they fought. They stood upon a vantage ground, fought for a prize, and aspired after a glory, which the heroes of Greece and Rome knew not of. There were, indeed, some of this character—mere soldiers of the battle-field who fought for the love of fighting—heroes fashioned after the Grecian and Roman style, whose inspiring genius was military glory—men like Joab and Abner, who knew no law but their swords, no right but might, and no God but ambition, and who, had opportunity been given on a wider field, might have become the rivals of Alexander and Hannibal, Cæsar and Napoleon.

But the heroes of the Bible history are for the most part of a different order. In them the soldier of valour is also the soldier of the cross; the hero of the battle-field is crowned with the higher glory of the hero of faith. Alongside with these mere soldiers of the camp, such as Joab and Abner, the Bible has given us models of a much higher order, in its great moral heroes. In truth, it often portrays the two characters —the military and the moral hero, as exemplified in the same man; and then it is the highest style of heroism. Of this we have striking examples in Joshua, in Gideon, in David, and even in Moses and Abraham. For it is certain that Abraham had once to gird on the stern armour of battle for the rescue of Lot; and there can be no doubt, that Moses, "mighty in words and deeds," had done the same in Egypt, long before he was called to lead the armies of Israel to the promised land. These heroes of the old covenant had to fight the battles of the Lord in a double sense. They had to wield both a spiritual and a material sword. And the great principle by which they waxed valiant and conquered with both was faith in God. An apostle of the New Testament has given us the clue to their heroic character in the eleventh chapter of the Epistle to the Hebrews, where he closes a sketch of their mighty deeds, with these remarkable words—"Through faith they subdued kingdoms, wrought righteousness, obtained promises, stopped the mouths of lions, quenched the violence of fire, escaped the edge of the sword, out of weakness were made strong, waxed valiant in fight, turned to flight the armies of the aliens."

Even in the Old Testament, where the warlike element predominates, there are abundant examples of the sublimest moral heroism, planting itself on unshaken faith in God, holding fast its integrity against a world in opposition, and though standing alone, yet doing battle to the last against all the powers of sin and darkness. Such were Enoch and Noah, Abraham and Joseph, Moses and Samuel, Elijah, Daniel, Jeremiah, and all the prophets of God. But it is chiefly in the peaceful pages of the New Testament where no sound of war or smell of battle ever comes, that we behold this character in its noblest manifestations. Here in the great mission of its apostles and martyrs, we are permitted to look upon a type of character, which is as justly entitled to the term heroic, as any thing in human history, and which, both for its intrinsic grandeur, and its blessed influence upon the world, outshines all mere military glory, as the rising sun does the morning star.

And hence there can never be any danger of imbibing too much of a military spirit from the Bible. Because we have on every page the check and the antidote; especially on every page of the New Testament. We may safely invite the young to the study of these old military chieftains of the Bible, even when most gorgeously arrayed in all the outward "pomp and circumstance of war." Along with all these the Bible reveals a better way, a higher glory, a nobler character, in its moral heroes. The best cure for the love of military glory, is the "expulsive power of a new affection"—even admiration for that higher style of glory which shines forth from the arduous, but ascending and triumphant pathway of the moral hero. So that if there were any tendency to catch too much of the martial spirit, from the war-clad heroes of the Old Testament, it would be at once corrected by the mild majestic characters of the New; just as our first acquaintance with that violated law which speaks out its thunders to the guilty is soon conjoined with an insight into that gospel, which, in "strains as sweet as angels use," whispers peace to the believing penitent.

III. WHY THE BIBLE HISTORY IS SO HEROIC.

It has, no doubt, often occurred to the thoughtful to ask, why the book of God, whose grand mission is peace on earth, good will to men, should deal so much in the heroic and the warlike? Some, perhaps, may be ready to imagine that these old chronicles of Jewish wars and battles were once instructive, but have now lost all practical significance to us, and may be treated just as any other ancient and uninspired record. We are far from being of this opinion. As satisfactory reasons may be assigned why the word of God should take the form of a human history, so there are reasons why, being intended for all ages and all races to the end of time, it should take this particular form of a heroic history, and set before us, not only its suffering martyrs of peace, but its warlike champions of right and justice. We believe that the world has needed the one class of heroes about as much as the other; and that it has as much to learn from the one as the other. There have been many epochs in modern history—such as our own Revolutionary struggle for independence, such as the Scottish struggles for civil and religious liberty, and such as the civil wars in England—when these old Scriptures were as applicable and inspiring to Christian heroes as they ever were to the Jews themselves. We cannot tell when such times may return.

War is, indeed, a dreadful evil, even when a nation is driven to it in self defence. It is a thing to be prevented, if possible, by all fair and honourable means. But war is not the greatest calamity that can befall a people. Awful as it is, it must sometimes be resorted to for the cure or prevention of still greater evils. Whilst injustice and oppression reign, there must be war. Whilst there are tyrants and barbarians on earth, bent only on destruction, and ready to trample in the dust the dearest rights and liberties of mankind, there will be, and there ought to be, war—at least defensive war. It is one of the highest duties which a free and civilized nation owes to God and man, to protect itself against such enemies. We have no sympathy with the monstrous, unnatural dogma of non-resistance to tyranny, and vice, and crime. God has none, and does not require his rational creatures to have any. We find nothing in the Bible, not even the loving spirit of that gospel which preaches forgiveness of injuries, seeks to save the lost, and teaches that all men are brothers, that requires, or even permits a Christian nation to quietly fold its arms, and be trampled down by the iron heel of despotism, or the Goths and Vandals of barbarism. Christianity proclaims peace on earth and good will to men; but it, at the same time, proclaims truth, and right, and justice; and it is by the establishment of the latter, that the former is to be, at last, fulfilled and realized. The teaching of the New Testament does no more require that civilized and Christian man should give up the world to the unconditional rule of the wicked, than that he should surrender it to the wild beasts of the forest. No! the doctrine of the whole Bible, from first to last, ever true to the highest instincts of nature and common sense, is, that those enemies of God and man, who can neither be disarmed by love, nor won by truth, nor controlled by justice, shall be resisted, if need be, by the strong arm of power. The true Scriptural sentiment on this subject is well expressed in the stirring lines of Cowper, the most evangelical of all the great English poets:

"Let laurels drenched in pure Parnassian dews
Reward his memory, dear to every muse,
Who with a courage of unshaken root,
In honour's field advancing his firm foot,
Plants it upon the line that justice draws,
And will prevail or perish in her cause
'Tis to the virtues of such men man owes
His portion in the good that Heaven bestows;
And when recording history displays
Feats of renown, though wrought in ancient days,
Tells of a few stout hearts that fought and died,
Where duty placed them, at their country's side,—
The man that is not moved with what he reads,
That takes not fire at their heroic deeds,
Unworthy of the blessings of the brave,
Is base in kind, and born to be a slave."

So long then as the world remains what it is, and a necessity for defensive war remains, so long will a martial and heroic spirit be found needful for every free and civilized people who have anything to lose from the aggressions of tyrants and barbarians. And so the word of God, being a heritage intended for all free and civilized people to the end of time, among all its other great lessons and great characters, has given us some of the sublimest illustrations of courage and heroism. The spirit of the Bible is peace—its tendency is to make the men of all nations brothers, and if it were fully received into every human heart, the nations would beat their swords into ploughshares and their spears into pruning hooks, and never fight again. But if men must fight, then the Bible has heroes, who have fought to some purpose, who knew when and how to gird themselves for the battle; and who, though dead, can yet teach their fellow men, on what principles, and for what ends, and in whose name to wage war. For this is the grand distinction of the Bible heroes, that they never drew the sword except in Jehovah's name, that they recognized his hand alike in victory and defeat, and that both in girding on their armour and in putting it off, they were impelled by a high sense of duty to God and their country. And there can be no question, for the history of all modern warfare proves the point, that here, as in all other things, the influence of the Bible has been most salutary, not only as restraining men from fighting, but as making them fight when they must, on higher and better principles. The best soldier in the world, and the bravest, is the Christian soldier. The heroic characters of Cromwell's day, were moulded by a deep and familiar study of the Bible. And we have seen in our day, how it can take those who would otherwise have been soldiers only of ambition or vengeance, and transform them into humane, conscientious, and yet invincible heroes, like Havelock, Hammond, and Hedley Vicars.

But there is perhaps a deeper reason for this warlike character of the Bible history. These old wars and battles of the chosen people were but the prelude of another and greater warfare—the outward types and symbols of that great conflict of ages, begun in the garden of Eden, and to be ended only with the end of time, between God and all the powers of light on the one side, and Satan with all his powers of darkness on the other. In the kingdom of God, and all through the word of God, the material and the temporal are always the signs and figures of the spiritual and eternal. As ancient Israel was set forth to be a type of the church militant through all ages, so those incessant conflicts with the enemies of the Lord which had so often to be decided by the sword, only prefigured that great spiritual battle which the true gospel must fight in every nation and in every age, against all the devices of the Devil, and all the oppositions of wicked men, and all the deceits and iniquities of the human heart. And so Joshua and Gideon and David, and all these heroes of the old covenant, who led the hosts of Israel to battle, became but the forerunners and ensamples of that innumerable army of Christian heroes—soldiers of the cross of Jesus Christ, who with weapons not carnal but spiritual—the sword of the Spirit, the shield of faith, the breastplate of righteousness, and the helmet of salvation, have come up to the help of the Lord against the mighty. For though the weapons are changed, the mode of warfare changed, and the arena of conflict changed, the battle is still the same, the parties at issue are the same, the heroic character demanded for the fight the same, the grand interests at stake the same. The contest, bequeathed to us by all the centuries that are gone, only deepens and widens with the lapse of time. It is for the possession of the world. It is for the dominion and glory of Jesus Christ. It is for the pulling down of the strongholds of sin and Satan. It is the fight of faith. It is the holy war of God against the man of sin, against the prince of the power of the air, against all the works of darkness. And these old Scriptures with their din of battle and their shouts of victory, with their Red Sea triumphs and their lion-hearted heroes—one chasing a thousand and two putting ten thousand to flight of the enemies of Israel—are written for our learning, to inspire us with fresh courage, zeal for truth, confidence of success, and faith in God, as we gird on the whole armour of the gospel.

Thus we find the New Testament writers constantly referring to these warlike characters of the Old, as types of the saints of God and illustrious examples of a true and saving faith in Christ. In fact we find this whole imagery of the church as a militant host, of the Christian as a soldier encompassed with enemies, and of the Christian life as an incessant warfare against sin and Satan, everywhere reproduced in the pages of the New Testament—thus forming the exact counterpart in spiritual things, to that heroic character in temporal things, which was displayed on so many battle-fields of the Old. Thus has God taught us how to fight the great battle of life—how to contend earnestly for the faith once delivered to the saints—how to gain the great victory that overcomes the world—how to conquer all his and our enemies, until Satan shall be put under our feet, and death, the last enemy, shall be destroyed. It is to be done on a thousand fields. It is to be done against foes within and foes without. It is to be done with the whole armour of the gospel. It is to be done in the strength of Jehovah. It is to be done under the lead of the great Captain of our salvation. He is a conqueror, and all his followers must conquer with him. He shall go forth conquering and to conquer, until all the kingdoms of this world shall be given to him for his inheritance, and the uttermost parts of the earth for his possession. With the sword of his Spirit, with the truth of his word, with the influence of his love, with the offers of his grace, and with the rod of his omnipotent power, he shall fight, and all his people with him; until every heathen altar shall be pulled down, and every human heart be brought into captivity, till every knee shall bow and every tongue confess, that he is Lord to the glory of God the Father. The battles of the Lord could not have been fought and won in ancient times without heroes—faith's heroes. Nor can they now. We should have heard of no Red Sea triumphs, no Miriam's songs, no sun standing still upon Gibeon and moon over the valley of Ajalon, no proud Goliath falling by the sling and the stone of David, without a heroic courage and trust in God. And we shall have nothing now corresponding to them in the spiritual field without the same high qualities—no conquests over sin at home, and no aggressions upon the dark domains of the enemy abroad. Courage and a self-renouncing trust in God, are essential elements of the soldier of the cross in every dispensation. The heroic character is as needful to the church now, as it was in the days of David.

But this is not all. Not only is the whole Bible history so constituted as to develope a heroic Christian character in our warfare against sin, and our efforts to evangelize a world lying in wickedness; but we may perhaps go still further and say that God has constituted human nature as it is, with a view to this same great end. He who saw the end from the beginning—saw what a world we must live in, what enemies we must encounter, through what conflicts we must pass to reach the crown of life, seems to have endowed us with capacities and energies, fitted for this great work and battle of life. These great and warlike energies, so deeply planted, so early developed, and so universal in man—this admiration of the heroic, love of military glory, and capacity to wage war—have all been sadly abused and perverted by the apostasy of our race—directed in wrong channels and to wrong ends, even to the destruction of our race and the dishonour of God. These energies however are the most mighty for good, when they run in proper channels, and to proper objects. The gospel of the Son of God, in such a world as this, needs them all, and does in fact make them bend in contribution to its grand designs. It seeks to employ them all in that great battle which it is waging against the enemies of God and man. It calls Paul off from his persecutions and his mad war against the church of God; but it does not seek to eradicate his zeal, his energy, his courage, his heroic spirit; because it has other battles for him to fight, and it would employ his great powers to build up that which he once destroyed. These very capacities for destruction, which made his name a terror to the church of God, will be all the more needful and the more useful to him, when, sanctified by grace and directed by the Spirit of God, they are turned in holy and mighty conflict against the strongholds of sin and Satan. The gospel had a field, and ample work for all the heroic and warlike energies of Paul. He had been fighting against the church with carnal weapons—henceforth he was to fight for it with spiritual weapons.

And so could this gospel now lay its arresting hand upon the veteran heroes of a hundred battle-fields, and enlist them for life, as soldiers of the cross, in that greater battle of truth and holiness against the darkness of this world, which Immanuel is carrying on, it would not destroy but only turn to good account, all the high qualities of the hero, as that for which they were originally intended. It would take the iron men of the old armies of Cromwell and Gustavus Adolphus, and show them a higher and nobler field on which to fight. It would take the war-worn Havelock, or the young Hammond and Hedley Vicars, and make them, as in fact they were, true heroes of the cross. But it would take them from the blood-stained fields of war, where they sacrificed their lives for their country, and give them a bloodless field, on which to employ all their powers, as ministers and missionaries of the cross. As Christian heroes, they did good, as it was; but what might not such heroes do, in such a field as that which engaged the great Apostle of the Gentiles? And what might not such heroes as Kane and Franklin do, if willing to devote their talents, treasure, courage, health, and life itself to carry the gospel to a ruined world, as they were to explore the Polar seas?

Yes, God has made man capable of great things, by endowing him with courage, energy, perseverance, heroism, and public spirit. And the Gospel calls for all these attributes on a scale of grandeur, such as nothing else beneath the sun can equal. And, though all men are not called, like Paul, to these great deeds, yet all are called, who have the Bible in their hands, to possess and cherish this self-sacrificing and heroic spirit. We must bear the cross if we would wear the crown; we must fight, if we would win eternal life. There is no discharge in this warfare, except with death. The kingdom of heaven suffereth violence, and the violent take it by force. Like the Captain of our salvation who was made perfect through suffering, we must all endure this fight of afflictions, this struggle with sin, this battle with the adversary of our souls. For thus alone can we be made entire in virtue, and become fitted for the rest and glory of heaven.

IV. NO HERO WORSHIP IN THE BIBLE.

A distinguished writer of our times Mr. Carlyle, has a book on "Heroes and Hero-worship," in which with no small approach to an idolatrous exaltation of great men, he traces the hero of modern history, through all his changing aspects of divinity, prophet, priest, poet, reformer, man of letters, king, and conqueror. Understanding by the term hero, the greatest, ablest man of his age, Carlyle singles out the following as the most notable types of heroism that have appeared in modern history—namely, Odin and Mahomet, Dante and Shakspeare, Luther and Knox, Johnson, Rousseau, and Burns, Cromwell and Napoleon, each reaching the highest distinction in his peculiar way, and all being but so many separate impersonations of the one great heroic element of our nature.

Now it is important to observe that, whilst there are heroes in the Bible, there is no such thing as hero-worship in all its pages. When this book gives us examples of human greatness, it gives us also an infallible standard by which to measure those examples. The Bible is the only book in the world containing an original religious system, which teaches us how to admire and honour great men without idolatry—without exalting the creature above the Creator. Hero-worship has been one of the most debasing forms of idolatry, and it has existed in every nation on earth, whose moral sentiments have not been moulded by the Bible. The old Greeks and Romans not only honoured their heroes, but deified and worshipped them, mostly after death, but sometimes even before. Among the Roman emperors from Julius Cæsar to Constantine, some sixty persons received the honours of deification, either dead or living. What would they not have done, if their national annals had given them characters, wielding the mighty, miraculous powers of Moses and Joshua?

But it is a remarkable fact that, although the Hebrews gloried in a history abounding in the most miraculous and heroic materials, and, although they often fell into idolatry of the grossest kinds, yet they were never guilty of hero-worship. No Jew, living or dead, ever received Divine honours from his countrymen. And when the degenerate Herod was, on one occasion, willing to receive them from the Gentiles, he was immediately smitten by an angel and devoured of worms. The race of Abraham never has, even to this day, given to man or woman any title or decree of canonization and apotheosis. And when we find but one exception to this remarkable fact, in the whole history of the race of Abraham: that is, when we see Jesus Christ, alone of his race, both claiming and receiving those Divine honours, which no mortal Jew had ever dreamed of arrogating, how can we fail to feel that Jesus was more than a Jew—was, indeed, no less than God?

It was fit, and it seemed to be so ordered in the wisdom of Providence, that the only nation of antiquity which had never polluted itself by any species of man-worship, should be the one in which the only Divine man should appear, and lay the foundations of that throne before which all on earth and all in heaven should bow.

It is because the Bible reveals the infinite excellence of God, and consequently the infinite difference between God and man, that it cuts up the roots of all hero-worship. What is man whose habitation is in the dust—what are princes whose breath is in their nostrils, that they should be worshipped? The Bible allows us to admire and honour great men, but it is an effectual antidote to every form of man-worship. It allows no idolatry of the living or the dead—no worshipping of man, of woman, or of angel. Would it not be strange then, if it tolerated that stupendous system of deception by which Papal Rome has substituted the worship of a virgin-mother for the worship of God? But there is no such toleration in all the book. Its whole spirit is as much opposed to woman-worship as to man-worship—as abhorrent to the Mariolatry of modern Rome, as to the idolatry of ancient Rome. That ancient cry at Ephesus—"Great is Diana of the Ephesians," did not more certainly convict its authors of idolatry, than the universal worship of Mary brands the Church of Rome as an idolator in the sight of God. For if Mary be not a Divine being, it is as unlawful to worship her, as it is to worship Diana, or any other fabulous or real woman.

Whilst, therefore, we repudiate and condemn everything like hero-worship in man or woman, let us turn for a brief survey of those types and specimens of real greatness which figure on the pages of sacred story—sometimes illuminating the darkness of the past with the red glare of war, and sometimes casting forward a stream of purer light, in the superior glory of the moral hero.

V. THE HEROIC CHARACTER OF ABRAHAM.

At the head of the list stands Abraham, the father of the faithful and the friend of God. Perhaps, you may be ready to meet us with an objection at the start, and to ask, with what propriety he can be ranked as a hero, who, on more than one occasion, was guilty of manifest duplicity, not to say pusillanimity, in trying to save his life, by a denial of his devoted and beautiful wife Sarah? We answer, that this conduct of Abraham did not spring from any want of courage. The bravest of men may be cautious and prudent when they think their lives in danger. And although the measure of safety which the patriarch adopted on these occasions was an unwise and impolitic one, as the result proved; and although it involved a breach of strict veracity which must now be admitted to be wrong, still it is plain, that it did not arise from cowardice or pusillanimity. It is clear, that in Abraham's judgment there was no issue at stake, as to Sarah's preservation. In the precaution to which he resorted, he never once thought of losing his wife, much less of endangering her life or person. Had he done that—had he deliberately risked her life or character to save his own, we would not call him a hero. No man is entitled to be called a hero, who would not be willing, in case of necessity, to lay down his life in defence of his wife, his child, his country, or his religion. But mark the condition: it must be a clear case of necessity—one in which a direct issue is made, and must be met. Where a man's own life or that of another must be sacrificed, or where there is an unavoidable issue between truth and falsehood, in a case where the vital interests of truth and virtue are at stake, and where the world has a right to the testimony, a man ought to die, and a real hero will die, before he will tell a lie. The man who creates a crisis when there is none, who on the plea of courage risks his life when there is no call for it, instead of proving himself a hero, only proves himself a fool. A brave man will wait till necessity is laid upon him by the demands of truth and duty. For this is the precise condition of case, which, in every age, has called forth the heroic spirit of the Christian martyr, who might easily have saved his life by a falsehood, but chose rather to tell the truth and die.

But there was no such issue as this in Abraham's case. His expedient of keeping back a part of the truth, touching his relation to Sarah, must indeed be condemned as a breach of veracity, because it was intended to deceive and did deceive; but it is in no way inconsistent with his magnanimity and courage as it regards Sarah. His subsequent heroic conduct wipes away from his brow every charge of cowardice or selfishness. Who can doubt, that the man, who was ready to sacrifice his beloved son at the bidding of Jehovah, or to rescue his brother Lot at the risk of his own life, would have been willing to lay down his life also for Sarah, had he deemed such a sacrifice needed? But this is the key for the solution of the whole matter. She was in no danger. And when the means, which had been adopted to secure himself, proved to be but a snare, and, contrary to all expectation, not only did him no good, but endangered her, then that was done which would have been much the best policy from the first—the whole truth was told. The incident beautifully illustrates the great truth, that honesty is always the best policy, even for the brave.

There are three passages of heroic interest in the life of Abraham: two of a moral, and the other of a military character. His first act of heroism was his voluntary expatriation from his native land at the command of Jehovah, to wander as an exile in distant, unknown countries, seeking "a city that hath foundations whose builder and maker is God." This was heroic in a double sense—in that sublime, unfearing faith which could so implicitly trust in God as to give up all at his bidding, and in that uncomplaining endurance of all the toils, trials, dangers, privations incident to such a migratory life. We are told, in the epistle to the Hebrews, that "he went out, not knowing whither he went." But he had even then a faith which enabled him to surrender all that was seen, and to rely upon the Divine promise for all those great future blessings, temporal and spiritual, which were both unseen. Thus he exemplified the great fundamental principle of the gospel, which is to walk by faith and not by sight. He believed God—believed what God said, and it was counted unto him for righteousness. By faith he was justified; and thus living so long before Christ, he rejoiced to see the day of Christ, and became the father and the type of all them that believe.

The second great act of moral heroism in the life of Abraham, was his unquestioning surrender and almost immolation of Isaac, the child of his old age and his love, the son and heir of all the promises. This was the trial of his faith and the great test of his obedience—immeasurably more difficult than that which was propounded to Adam in Eden, and under which he fell. The sacred writers celebrate this as one of the most triumphant and sublime of all faith's victories. But it was as triumphant and sublime as a work of obedience, as an act of faith. If ever there was among men, an exercise of faith and obedience, which was entitled to the term heroic, it was this virtual immolation of Isaac. If it had occurred in classic Greece, it would have been heralded to the world as an example of virtue worthy of the gods, and old heathen poets would have exhausted all their best powers of description and pathos upon the scene; even as has been done in the celebrated case of Agamemnon sacrificing his daughter Iphigenia. But we cannot see why it should be less sublime and heroic, standing on the sacred pages, than if it had stood on those of Homer. None but a strong arm, a brave heart, and a soul whose strength was in God, could ever have come off conqueror from such a trial. If we consider well the circumstances—what strength of purpose it required, what nerve of the physical and moral man to execute such a purpose, what absolute mastery of the mind over all the strongest instincts of nature—we must regard Abraham, in this one act, even if there were no others, as having fairly won, not only the title of Father of the Faithful, but the right to be called the first great heroic character in human history. There were doubtless heroes before him, but no previous record tells of any such deed as this. Even the far-famed case of Agamemnon was enacted (if indeed it ever occurred) and certainly reduced to writing many centuries later.

Nothing can exceed the simplicity and natural pathos with which this story is told in the Bible. It occupies only nineteen verses in the twenty-second chapter of Genesis. But each verse opens to us a graphic and impressive scene. First we have the brief introduction—God did tempt, that is, try, Abraham—the word of the Lord came to him and he answers, Here am I—ready to hear, ready to do. Then we hear the command—Take thy son—thine only son, thy loved son Isaac, and go into the land of Moriah, and offer him there for a burnt offering upon one of the mountains that I will show thee. A long journey is to be made, the loved child carried away, and there offered in sacrifice. Next we have the prompt morning preparation—He arose early in the morning, saddled his ass, took two servants, his young men, clave the wood, ready for burning, and started to the appointed place. Then follows the long journey of the four travellers—On the third day, Abraham lifted up his eyes and saw the place afar off. It was a mountain summit, probably one of those long afterwards occupied by the Holy City. Then we have the precautionary separation of the party—And Abraham said to his young men, Abide ye here with the ass, and I and the lad will go yonder and worship, and come again to you.

Then we have the impressive scene of the father and son, ascending the mount together for the execution. The venerable patriarch, now probably some hundred and twenty years old, lays the wood of the burnt offering upon the unconscious victim, the son of his love, bearing the fire and the knife in his own hands, and the two go on together, for a while at least in silence; because there were thoughts evidently too deep for utterance in the patriarch's heart. Then we have the brief dialogue, Isaac breaking the silence with words, whose full im port could be revealed only by the inquiring look and earnest tone, with which he uttered them—"My father! And he said, Here am I, my son. And he said, Behold the fire and the wood; but where is the lamb for the burnt offering? And Abraham said, My son, God will provide himself a lamb for a burnt offering." So they went both of them together; and came to the place which God had told him of. Then follow in quick succession the altar, the preparation, and the solemn crisis of execution—He built an altar there—laid the wood in order upon the altar—bound Isaac his son—laid him on the altar upon the wood. And Abraham stretched forth his hand and took the knife to slay his son. A moment more, and that precious blood would have crimsoned the ground which in process of time was to be wet with the blood of a still dearer Son and costlier Lamb—the Son and Lamb of God. But at this awful crisis the patriarch's arm was stayed, his work arrested, and deliverance granted to the child—" And the angel of the Lord called to him out of heaven, and said Abraham! Abraham! and he said, Here am I. And he said, Lay not thine hand upon the lad, neither do thou anything unto him; for now I know that thou fearest God, seeing thou hast not withheld thy son, thine only son, from me."

Then we have the substituted victim; for this transaction had a meaning and a bearing on the great atonement of Christ; the sacrifice was typical and could not be set aside. The child of the patriarch is delivered from death, but delivered only by the shedding of blood—the blood of the vicarious victim which the Lord himself had provided in the mount. "And Abraham lifted up his eyes and looked, and behold behind him a ram caught in a thicket by his horns; and Abraham took the ram, and offered him up for a burnt offering in the stead of his son. And he called the name of that place Jehovah-jireh, as it is said to this day—"In the mount of the Lord it shall be seen." We are told by our Saviour that Abraham rejoiced to see his day. This was doubtless the time, and this the place of that glad vision. Well might he rejoice in the deliverance of his child from death; and well might he rejoice, with a double joy, in that great doctrine of grace and salvation, then made plain to him—the substitution, the vicarious offering, the shed blood of the great victim of the cross on whom all our iniquities were laid.

Then again we have the blessing and the renewal of all the promises of the covenant—"And the Angel of the Lord called unto Abraham, out of heaven, the second time, and said, By myself have I sworn, saith the Lord, because thou hast done this thing, and hast not withheld thy son, thine only son, that in blessing I will bless thee, and in multiplying I will multiply thy seed as the stars of heaven, and as the sand which is upon the sea-shore; and thy seed shall possess the gate of his enemies. And in thy seed shall all the nations of the earth be blessed; because thou hast obeyed my voice." This was now the fifth time in the life of Abraham, when the Lord appearing and speaking from heaven had solemnly assured him of the great blessings of the covenant. The first and second occasions were when he was called to leave his native land, and when he had separated from Lot, in the land of Canaan, at both of which the blessings were guarantied to him on the Divine promise or word of God. The third was on the announcement that he should have a son, when in addition to the simple promise, God covenanted these blessings to him in sacrifice, confirmed by the miraculous sign of the smoking furnace and the burning lamp. The fourth was when he was ninety-nine years old, at the announcement of Isaac's birth, the seal was given to all these promises in the covenant of circumcision. And last of all is this memorable day of Isaac's deliverance on the mount, when the promises and covenant are all confirmed by the solemn oath of Jehovah. Thus was the one great covenant with Abraham developed and confirmed through a series of years; not, as some strangely imagine, by different covenants, but by one grand covenant, the foundation of the visible church, gradually unfolded, enlarged, and perfect—from the promise to the oath of God—from the plains of Chaldea to the mount of vision—from the faint hope of an earthly heir, to the full manifestation in sacrifice of Him, the Son and Heir of all, in whom all the families of the earth were to be blessed. Thus we see the significance of this great transaction on Moriah. And now the scene closes with the joyful re-union and return of all the parties. "So Abraham returned unto his young men, and they rose up and went together to Beersheba."

But it is not our purpose to dwell on these two acts of heroic faith. There is a third occasion in the life of Abraham in which he appears in the double character of military and moral hero. As this is a combination not always to be found in warlike characters, it may be instructive to notice its existence in this man of peace. For the first and only time in his life, we find him leaving his flocks and herds, buckling on the helmet and the sword, and showing that he had a heart, as courageous before the face of man, as it was humble in the sight of God. He, who had been too cautious of his life in Egypt, when there was little or no danger, now had an opportunity of looking danger in the face, such as might have appalled even the bravest of those critics who sneer at the timidity of Abraham. The occasion that called forth this new and noble display of the patriarch's character, was the war of the nine kings, who, at last, joined battle in the vale of Siddim.

It has been remarked that this was the first war of which we have any authentic record in history. Doubtless there had been wars, and battles, and "mighty ones," like Nimrod, long before. But upon the dark and distant background of this first recorded war of human history, which was a war of ambition and conquest, it is pleasing to behold the character of Abraham shining out in all the lustre of true moral greatness—shining indeed as a "light in a dark place." It is instructive to find, in this first war of the Bible, an example of moral blended with military glory, which is as perfect a model of what a conqueror ought to be, and as clear an index of what constitutes lawful war, as the world has ever seen. The fourteenth chapter of Genesis, with its long hard names, you have read perhaps a hundred times, and wondered why it should be there. But viewed in its true light you perceive it is one of the most instructive chapters of human history. It is put there to teach the world when war may be lawfully waged. It is put there to tell us, even so early, what is the end of pride, and ambition, and the lust of conquest. It contains the first great lesson, as to what constitutes a true military and moral hero.

The four confederate northern kings had come down like a whirlwind, and swept everything before them in the fruitful vale of Sodom. They had vanquished the five opposing kings in a pitched battle. They had taken Lot and his family captive, and carried off the spoils of war. And they were already far away on their return to Damascus, before any tidings of the disaster reached the quiet tent of Abraham in Hebron. Not a moment was to be lost. No cost or danger was to be counted. The liberty, it might be the life, of his kindred was at stake. Unused as he was to war, he musters a little band of three hundred and eighteen men, servants of his household, and pursues the victors, all flushed and elated with their recent successes. Overtaking them after a forced march of several days, and dividing his little band for a night attack, he falls upon their encampment at different points, routs their whole army, pursues the flying foe almost to Damascus, and having retaken the spoil, and rescued his kinsman from the grasp of the oppressor, returns in triumph.

Thus impelled by a generous, exalted sense of duty, he performed a deed of valor and personal prowess, which is fully entitled to the term heroic, which would not have been unworthy of the military fame of Joab or David, and which, had it occurred in the time and country of Homer, would have been celebrated in immortal verse, and ranked with the deeds of Hector and Achilles. As it is, the pen of inspiration has left its record in the following brief and modest words:

"When Abraham heard that his brother was taken captive, he armed his trained servants, born in his house, three hundred and eighteen, and pursued them unto Dan. And he divided himself against them, he and his servants by night, and smote them, and pursued them unto Hobah which is on the left hand of Damascus. And he brought back all the goods, and also brought again his brother Lot, and his goods, and the women also, and the people."

Never was a military expedition prompted by better principles, or executed with more signal success. And then to crown the whole, when met and congratulated by Melchisedeck, priest of the Most High God, and when urged to receive a recompense for what he had done, he freely offered tithes of all to Jehovah for his victory, but refused to touch anything in the semblance of pay for himself. When did king or conqueror more gracefully wear the honours of war? With a generous magnanimity, not surpassed by Epaminondas, Cincinnatus, or Washington, he refused to receive of the spoil "from a thread to a shoe-latchet," that no one might say, "I have made Abraham rich." He had been great in peace; he was now great in war; and, in this last act, the great warrior stands forth invested with the crowning glory of true moral heroism. In the generous motives which prompted his expedition, in the bravery which achieved it, and in the magnanimity of self-sacrifice, with which it closed, Abraham deserves our admiration as a model man and a hero.

All these military operations were, doubtless, on a small and insignificant scale, as compared with the exploits of modern generals, and the dread machinery of modern wars. The field was contracted; the forces were small; the campaign was brief. But that makes no difference. Be the scale ever so small or ever so large, the principles and characters may be the same. He who is a hero in the least, would be a hero in the greatest. The Bible is a miniature of the world—an epitome, in advance, of all its history. As such it contains the types of all its grand events and all its great characters. And so, those principles which made Abraham a warrior and conqueror at Dan, and far more than a warrior at Salem, and Mamre, and Moriah, would have enabled him, on a larger theatre and a grander scale, to do anything that mortal man ever did. The hero of Dan might have been a Wellington at Waterloo, or a Washington at Yorktown.

It was no selfish and ambitious love of military glory, but a sense of justice and of duty, that impelled Abraham to buckle on the armour of war. This distinction is radical, and it has existed in all ages of the world. We have had a remarkable illustration of it in the present century. The two greatest military leaders that have figured in the wars of the nineteenth century, are confessedly Napoleon and Wellington: one the hero of glory, the other the hero of duty. The lives of Plutarch's heroes and statesmen do not furnish any more wonderful parallel and contrast than that which is presented in the career of these two great champions of Waterloo. Each of them born in the same year 1769—each born on an island of the sea, which was a mere dependency of the great nation whose fate he was to hold on the point of his sword—each trained to arms from his very boyhood, and rising to distinction in the foreign service of his country—each on distant theatres of Europe passing through a succession of hard-fought battles, which seemed but a preparation for some grand and final issue—their destinies at last met on the field of Waterloo, and trembled for a moment in the scales of war, and then separated for ever. For the first and the last time, the orbits in which their mortal life revolved crossed each other. But how strange the spectacle after death! How strange that the year 1852, as it closed, should leave the nations of Europe, still ringing with those very names, which, in 1815, had sent forth from Waterloo, a thrill of joy or a wail of woe, through all their borders! How wonderful that the name and empire which Wellington seemed to have crushed for ever at Waterloo, should appear again above the ground in the person of Louis Napoleon, at the very moment when the sun of Wellington was going down! How mysterious that, whilst the country of the one was preparing a gorgeous funeral pageant over all that was mortal of her greatest general, the country of the other was startled by the sudden apparition of all that remained of her grand emperor—the prestige of his great name, the shade of his departed glory, the "stat nominis umbra" of Bonaparte? Where is the prophet that had foretold this?

It has been said, though we cannot vouch for the accuracy of the statement, that Napoleon never wrote a despatch in all his campaigns in which he did not use the term "glory," and that Wellington never wrote one without using the word "duty." Be this as it may, it is manifest, that the two words strikingly illustrate the two characters, and reveal to us a distinction which lies at the foundation of the widely different destinies of the two great antagonistic heroes. The love of glory made the Corsican boy a hero; but it landed him, at last, an exile from his ruined country, on the bleak rocks of St. Helena. The sense of duty made the Irish boy a hero; but it saved England from foreign invasion, made Arthur Wellesley the "Iron Duke" of Britain, and kept the dictator of France from consolidating a universal empire over Europe.

Now it is easy to see, even if history did not tell us, which of the two rival heroes had his character mostly modelled after the pattern of the Bible. It cannot be said that either was much imbued with the true spirit of the Bible hero. But Wellington was as much nearer to that standard than Napoleon, as the heroic Scotch Marshal Macdonald was nearer than all the other marshals of France. And it is easy, also, to see, whatever may be the appearance of success at first, that, if you will give the two a fair conflict and an open field, the hero of duty will be, in the long run, more than a match for the hero of glory. Waterloo is not the only field where this superiority has been attested. Every battle field of Washington is a trophy of its truth. If Washington had fought for glory, no glory would he have reaped. He drew the sword from a sense of duty, as a true Bible hero, and glory was the result. But Abraham's victory was the earliest trophy of this great principle.

If we have dwelt long upon the character of Abraham, it has been because of its great excellence, and of the great lessons of life which it inculcates. The contracting party to that great covenant with God by which the visible church was first organized, and the progenitor of that remarkable race and nation of whom the Messiah came, was well worthy of such distinction. Bnt with all his pre-eminent virtues, and his exalted station, he was not infallible. And this may suggest to us two important reflections:

The first is the folly of confiding in any thing human. The Bible does not allow us to trust in man—though that man should be a hero, a prince in Israel, and the very friend of God. If ever the descendants of any man had cause to glory in the flesh, to boast of high nobility, and claim to be the favourites of heaven, they were the children of Abraham. We know in fact that many did thus glory, in being the seed of Abraham. But how signally was this folly rebuked by the great Teacher? "Think not to say within yourselves, We have Abraham to our Father. For verily I say unto you, that God is able of these stones to raise up children unto Abraham." And how is it rebuked when we look at the record of his life! Even he who was in special covenant with God, who talked face to face with the angels of God, who had so many tokens of Jehovah's constant presence and blessing, and was so valiant in battle, could more than once prevaricate, and resort to unworthy expedients for protection. With such an example of fallibility and imperfection before us in the life of this great man, what are we to think of that Romanism which boasts of an infallible church, and claims perfection for the erring, sinning, and deluded mortals, who sit, not in the seat of Abraham or Moses, but of Peter at Rome?

The second is the impossibility of salvation, except through a Divine Saviour. If salvation could have been by man at all —by any mere man that has ever lived from Adam to the present hour, we should say, it would have been by Abraham, the friend of God, the father of the faithful, the contractor of the covenant. So great was Abraham, and so intimate his relations to God, that in the current language of the Jews, Abraham's bosom became the very symbol of heaven. But although the Jews of our Saviour's times had come to regard themselves as being in a state of grace and salvation, the special favourites of heaven, because they were Abraham's seed; yet how is that folly everywhere rebuked in the New Testament, by our Lord, by John the Baptist, by Paul and all the apostles: "Ye are of your father the devil," said our Saviour to those very Jews who boasted of their salvation through their great father Abraham. And what are we to think of those in our day, who still talk of salvation by man—no longer the man Abraham, but the mere man Jesus Christ? How much better is that Socinianism which sees nothing but a man in Jesus Christ, worships him as such, and boasts of his salvation, than that Judaism which trusted in Abraham, and was denounced by Paul and Christ himself as an utter perversion of the grace of God! If Jesus were merely human, salvation would be as impossible by him as by Abraham. And the very fact that he is a Saviour at all —that he has power to save, and that salvation is ascribed to him in the Scriptures, as it never was to Abraham or any other man, is the one all-sufficient and overwhelming proof that he is Divine. As a mere man he never could have answered the question of the Jews—"Art thou greater than our father Abraham?" It was only in virtue of his being God as well as man that he could say, "Before Abraham was, I am." And it is only in virtue of his being God as well as man that he can do for a world of sinners, what Abraham, with the whole world to help him, could never do for a single soul—give salvation. The man, who under the plea of logical reasoning can believe that Jesus Christ is a mere man, and yet a Saviour of the soul to all that shall be saved, has either no conception of what salvation means, or no conception of what logical reason demands. God out of Christ is a consuming fire, and Christ without God is no Saviour. In either case salvation is impossible. God in Christ and Christ in God is the only Saviour given under heaven whereby we can be saved. This is the central sun of the whole Gospel—the supreme Divinity in the humanity of Jesus Christ. And the soul, that, through pride of reason, and boasting philosophy, and a self-complacent sense of its own righteousness, denies and rejects this most essential and glorious truth of all the Scriptures, can have no more hope of salvation, than those apostate angels for whom no Saviour ever died.

Till God in mortal flesh arrayed
  My soul with love and wonder sees,
No works achieved, nor ransom paid,
  Can give the guilty conscience ease.

Immanuel! a glorious name!
  The only hope for dying men!
A Saviour God the heavens proclaim,
  Let all on earth respond Amen.

On this great mystery of love
  Where God and man so strangely blend,
My soul, let all thy passions rove,
  And all thy hopes of heaven depend.

VI. THE HEROIC CHARACTER OF MOSES.

The next great character after Abraham, which we select as an illustration of all the high attributes of the true hero, is that of Israel's lawgiver and leader, Moses. Josephus tells us, that as the adopted son of the king's daughter, and heir presumptive to the throne, he had been promoted to a high rank in the armies of Egypt, and had already in early life distinguished himself as a soldier by his brilliant victories. It may be that Stephen the martyr, in his speech before the council, as given in the seventh chapter of the Acts, refers to this Jewish tradition, when he tells us, that "Moses was learned in all the wisdom of the Egyptians, and was mighty in words and in deeds." For he evidently refers to the earlier stages of Moses's life, prior to his flight from Egypt. So that these "mighty deeds," were things that he had done long before his miracles in Egypt, the wonders at the Red Sea, and the great transactions at Mount Sinai, and through the march to Canaan. If he had been thus trained to war, and had proved himself a hero on many a hard fought battle-field, he was only the better prepared by this, for that great commission of Jehovah, greater and more difficult than any uninspired warrior ever received, to be the head and leader of a whole nation in an armed march of forty years, alternately through desert wastes and hostile bands, from Egypt to the promised land. If it required military skill and courage of the highest order in Xenophon to lead back ten thousand veteran soldiers from Babylonia to Greece;

if it required a skill and courage that even the great Napoleon was not quite equal to, to lead back the most formidable army that ever marched, from the central wilds of Russia to the confines of civilized Europe, we cannot think that either genius or courage, the highest the world ever saw, would be at all out of place, even along with the miracles of God, in such a generalship as this of Moses.

But it is not of the warlike character of Moses that we wish to speak. It is of his moral heroism—his self-sacrificing spirit, and discharge of duty, in the face of every danger that could appal a human heart. The very responsibility that was laid on Moses, and whose accumulating weight he bore for forty years, almost without a murmuring thought, is enough to indicate the greatness of his heroism. Such a responsibility would have crushed any ordinary man. None but a brave heart—and that heart fast anchored on God—could have borne it for a single day.

Now there are several memorable occasions brought to view in his history, when this heroic character shone forth with extraordinary lustre. One was that referred to by Stephen, when, forty years old, he undertook, single handed and uncommissioned, to avenge his suffering countrymen and deliver them from the Egyptians, but was repelled by his brethren, saying, "Who made thee a ruler and a judge over us?" Another was that celebrated by Paul, as the turning-point in his destiny, and the crowning evidence of his faith: "By faith, Moses, when he was come to years, refused to be called the son of Pharaoh's daughter, choosing rather to suffer affliction with the people of God than to enjoy the pleasures of sin for a season; esteeming the reproach of Christ greater riches than the treasures in Egypt; for he had respect unto the recompense of reward. By faith he forsook Egypt, not fearing the wrath of the king; for he endured as seeing him who is invisible." Another was, when, forty years later, he came back to that same haughty court, with the high behests of Jehovah, and attended only by his brother Aaron, stood from day to day before the monarch, fearless, alike, of all the wisdom and power of Egypt, and urged their claims, until amid signs, and wonders, and terrific judgments, every jot and tittle was conceded, and Pharaoh was compelled to let Israel go. And still another was at Mount Sinai, when thunderings and lightnings, and the sound of the trumpet, and the mountain smoking, caused all the people to shrink back in terror, whilst Moses alone drew near to the thick darkness where God was.

But the occasion which displayed his heroic character on the grandest scale, was the passage of Israel through the Red Sea. In vain we search the annals of the human race for any other occasion parallel to this—a whole nation delivered from their foes by a march through the depths of the sea, and those foes buried beneath its waters. We may safely challenge the literature of the world to produce anything which, even on the score of sublimity and moral grandeur, can be compared with this. And think of the man who led the host, and executed the purpose of Jehovah in all that scene! True, he was but an instrument in the hand of God, and acted only as he was commanded. Still he was a mere man. And the command he obeyed had never had a precedent. A nation of millions, led by him to that awful crisis—standing in consternation on the narrow sea shore, with an avenging army just behind and no chance for flight on either side, upbraiding him with their destruction, and crying to heaven for help! Such was the scene. "Why criest thou unto me? Speak to the children of Israel that they go forward." If ever there was a command which it required heroic faith to execute, it was that. But it was done. Moses stretched out his hand over the sea. It was cleft asunder. Israel passed dry shod. Safely on the other shore, he again stretched forth his hand and the waters closed in upon their pursuers. Then sang the daughters of Israel that most ancient of all heroic songs, which we have in the fifteenth chapter of Exodus.

VII. JOSHUA AS A SOLDIER.

The next prominent example which we select from the military and moral heroes of the Bible, is Joshua the son of Nun, successor of Moses, and captain-general of the armies of Israel. We purposely pass over other illustrious examples of moral heroism, such as Joseph: partly because these may come before us in other connections, and partly because it is impossible to embrace all the illustrations of any one character in a single chapter. We select Joshua as one of the finest exhibitions of a "servant of the Lord," when he appears in the character of a soldier.

His occupation was war; his mission was conquest; but, unlike all others, he was a conqueror by express Divine command; his chief distinction was, that he always conquered in the name of the Lord, so that all his victories of the sword were, at the same time, victories of faith. We behold in him a great military leader, who, for the larger period of his life, stood at the head of an army of six hundred thousand fighting men, and who had the good fortune of never losing a battle when leading any portion of that army in person. For you must bear in mind that Joshua's military career had commenced long before the death of Moses and the passage of the Jordan. Those thirty-one battles which he fought in Canaan, and those thirty-one kings and cities which he overthrew, as recounted in the book that bears his name, were the battles and the trophies of his advanced years. They were not his only, or even his greatest victories. It is very evident that he was the military leader, as we would say, the commander-in-chief in all those great battles and campaigns against the Amalekites, the Amorites, the Midianites, and the Moabites, through which the children of Israel had to fight their way to the promised land, and which long afterwards were celebrated in the patriotic psalms of David. Moses does not appear, from the Scriptures, to have been a soldier. The Jewish traditions, as reported by Josephus, represent him as distinguished at an early age, for his military achievements in Egypt; but he never appears in Scripture history as acting the part of a soldier. He is always presented as the prophet, judge, law-giver, mediator, deliverer, and civil governor of Israel; whilst Joshua, before, as well as after, the death of Moses, seems to have been in command of the army, and to have done the fighting. The probability is, that when the Israelites marched out of Egypt, through the Red Sea, Joshua, who was called "Moses' minister," and who was then about forty-five years of age, from his superior courage and military genius, already held this high command as chief of the six hundred thousand. For if you will look into the seventeenth chapter of Exodus, when the Amalekites attacked Israel at Rephidim, in the first year of their march from Egypt, you will find Moses saying to Joshua, "Choose out men, and go fight against Amalek." Accordingly, on the next day, whilst Moses stood on a neighbouring hill-top, with outstretched rod and uplifted hands, supported by Aaron and Hur till the going down of the sun, Joshua and his chosen warriors discomfited Amalek and all his hosts with the edge of the sword.

The great work to which Joshua was appointed in the conquest of Canaan, required a man of invincible courage, and of ripened experience, not less than it did an implicit heroic faith in God. And we see how admirably qualified for such a work he must have been, by reason of his forty years' march and discipline in the wilderness. And this leads us to remark that it is always the order of Divine providence, when it has an extraordinary work to be performed, not only to prepare an extraordinary man for the occasion, but to prepare the man himself for his work in an extraordinary way. So was it with Joshua in the conquest of Canaan. That war of aggression and of extermination against the idolatrous inhabitants of Canaan, who were themselves invaders and usurpers, and whose cup of iniquity was now full, is not to be judged of by the rules of ordinary warfare, nor to be pleaded as a precedent for any ordinary war.

Joshua was commissioned to wage it in the name of Jehovah, on much the same principles, with which some centuries before, in that very vicinity, Jehovah himself had waged war, in a rain of fire and brimstone on the doomed cities of the plain. He who can understand the equity of the one, may, if he will, understand the equity of the other. He who can comprehend the equity of that flood which once drowned the world, or of that judgment-day which will one day burn it up, need have no difficulty in reconciling either with the justice of a sin-hating God. Joshua was empowered, as a special executioner of the wrath of heaven, to punish the Canaanites, "to the intent that all the earth might know and fear the mighty hand of the Lord"—a lesson indeed which the idolatrous nations of that day needed much to learn, and one which there seemed to be no other mode of teaching them. No ordinary man would have been equal to such a war, especially when he had to take the place of Moses. But all the solemn charges which he received from the lips of Moses, and afterwards from the Lord himself, were so many agencies preparing him for his mission. Those charges generally ran in these words—"Be thou strong and very courageous; be not afraid nor dismayed, for the Lord thy God will be with thee." His whole preparatory training and career of forty years in the wilderness, eminently tended to develope a character of the highest heroism.

One of the most remarkable illustrations of faith to be found in the Bible, and of a meeting of divine and human agency in the same act, is that which occurred in the first military operation of Joshua after crossing the Jordan—the overthrow of Jericho. "By faith," says the apostle, "the walls of Jericho fell down;" that is, faith in the power of God, on the part of Joshua and his army—a faith which trusted in God so implicitly, that it diligently used all the appointed means, even when those means appeared wholly inadequate to the occasion. To use means at the bidding of Jehovah, which have no earthly power to produce a desired result, and yet expect that result, is one of the highest manifestations of true faith. It was this sort of faith, which, small as a grain of mustard seed, saved Naaman the Syrian. And it was this faith that caused the walls of Jericho to fall.

It may be doubted whether there would have been faith enough in Israel to march their whole army around the city thirteen times, if they had not so recently witnessed the mighty power of God in their passage through the Jordan dry-shod. As it was, they seem to have followed Joshua's orders without a murmur or misgiving. Seven days in succession did the vast host encircle the beleaguered city in solemn silence and awe, save only as that silence was broken by repeated blasts of the trumpets, and the ceaseless heavy tread of such a multitude. Seven times on the seventh day, did they perform the same strange and faith-trying circuit. And then the long looked-for crisis comes. The last circumference is completed; and for a moment all Israel stands in awe and expectation, awaiting the command of Joshua, and the intervention of God. The signal is given; the blast of the trumpets is heard long and loud from the spot where the ark of the Lord stood still; the whole army raise the shout to heaven as the voice of one man; the walls of the city are levelled to the dust; and the men of Israel rush in, sword in hand, and find an easy victory over its dismayed and doomed inhabitants.

It would be hard to conceive of any combination of circumstances more awfully sublime than these. The slow and measured march around the city so often repeated—the dread and ominous silence of the procession—the critical moment of suspense at the close of the last circuit—the simultaneous shout of such a multitude, lifted up like the voice of many waters—the instantaneous falling of the walls—the impetuous onset of the whole army:—all are fitted to inspire the mind with emotions of wonder or of terror. The shout of an army in the onset of battle, under any circumstances, must be a sublime and terrific thing. We talk of the sublimity of concerts and oratorios and orations. But probably there is no occasion on earth, when the mighty music of the human voice produces so great an effect, either to inspire courage, or to strike terror to the heart, as in the shout of battle. This was pre-eminently the case in ancient times, when there was no noise, or smoke of fire-arms; when hostile armies grappled face to face in personal conflict; when all their passions were inflamed by close contact with the foe; and when they rushed together from two neighbouring hills, with the watchwords of glory, or patriotism, or vengeance on every tongue. And this accounts for the great destruction of human life which attended the ancient battles. For instance, in one of the wars between Judah and Israel, mentioned in the second book of Chronicles, where the king Abijah at the head of 400,000 chosen warriors attacked an army of 800,000 under Jeroboam, and joined battle with a shout in the name of the Lord, we are informed that 500,000 of the latter were left dead on the field. Modern warfare recounts no such wholesale slaughter as this, even in the maddest campaigns of Napoleon. There can be no doubt that the introduction of fire-arms, by which men fight at a greater distance from each other, has done as much to mitigate the horrors of war, as the humane conventional principles themselves on which it is now conducted. If civilized men had to grapple in mortal combat as they once did, no doubt they would still fight as barbarians. But this is one of the cases in which scientific discovery has been the helper of humanity, and the handmaid of religion.

But to return from this digression to Joshua; the most wonderful of all his battles—the most wonderful truly that history records—was the battle of Gibeon, in which he destroyed the allied armies of five Canaanitish kings, when it is written that the "Lord cast down great hailstones from heaven, which destroyed more than fell by the sword." Excuse us, if we do not stop to explain these wonderful things. You can explain them as well as any one, if you will refer them to the place they belong to—the miraculous power and justice of God. The only explanation we could give, would be by citing analogous cases. He who sent down these destructive hail stones, once sent hailstones upon Egypt, and fire and brimstone upon Sodom.

It was at the battle of Gibeon, that Joshua paused in the midst of the combat, and seeing the sun about to go down and leave his victory incomplete, first addressed a prayer to Jehovah, and then, in the presence of all Israel, uttered the memorable command—" Sun, stand thou still upon Gibeon, and thou, moon, in the valley of Ajalon!" And the sun stood still in the midst of heaven; and the moon stayed until the people had avenged themselves upon their enemies. " And there was no day like that, before it or after it, that the Lord hearkened unto the voice of man; for the Lord fought for Israel."

You have doubtless read the short and thrilling speeches of many a great military commander on the field of action, which have sometimes turned the tide of battle and sealed the fate of empires. But it must be admitted in this case of Joshua, that the Bible has given us the climax of military speeches and orders of battle. We may safely defy all history to bring its parallel. Never before or since, did the lips of mortal man offer such a prayer, and utter such a command so awfully sublime, so fearfully effective. And what an illustration of the power of a heroic faith and confidence in God! Conceive, if you can, what attainments in faith and holiness a mortal man like ourselves must make, before he could utter that prayer and issue that command—" Sun, stand thou still upon Gibeon; and thou, moon, over the valley of Ajalon." That Joshua should have prayed such a prayer and uttered such a command, seems to us almost as wonderful as that the Lord should have wrought such a miracle. No doubt it was intended to teach the great lessons, long afterwards taught in the New Testament, that nothing is impossible with God—that "all things are possible to him that believeth."

But here we must leave this great military character, who, to the glory of a soldier always invincible in battle, added the higher moral glory of a servant of the Lord who never swerved from the line of duty. His moral heroism is evinced in the fact, that he and Caleb alone, of all that generation which came out of Egypt, were found faithful and worthy to enter the promised land. His whole life was a beautiful commentary on those memorable words of decision and energy, which he uttered in his last charge to Israel—"Choose ye this day whom ye will serve; but as for me and my house, we will serve the Lord." We cannot better close our sketch of him, than by quoting the following just and striking remarks of Dr. Kitto: "The character of Joshua is not only one of the finest in Scripture history, but one of the most remarkable that the world ever saw. There is scarcely any other great conqueror, and certainly no Asiatic conqueror, like him—without personal ambition, without any desire of aggrandizement. His whole heart was in the highest degree patriotic, under a system which required patriotism to take the form of religious obedience. In the distant view, the personal and even public character of the man is overshadowed by the very greatness of the events and circumstances in which he is placed. The events are greater than the man, and engage the attention more; and hence individually he appears with less eclat, and attracts less attention than an inferior man among events of less importance. This, when rightly viewed, is not a dishonour to him, but a glory; for it shows how accurately he measured, and how truly he understood, his right position. A lesser man in all the attributes of true greatness would have been seen and heard more; but it is the magnanimous character of real greatness, to shroud the power it exercises."

Many object to the character of Joshua, on account of the bloody conquests which marked his career. But when was war ever any thing but bloody and terrible! Look at the great and fearful conflict which, with letters of blood, has marked these years in the middle of the nineteenth century. What a sad drama of woe, what a tragedy of horrors was that of the Crimea! A spectacle to angels and to men! a stage on which have been turned the eyes of the civilized world, where the great Powers of Europe marshalled their armies, and with all the modern arts of destruction, struggled for the mastery! Alas! how different this exhibition, from that which only a few years ago, these very nations made at London in the peaceful arts of industry! The world needed another argument against war; and we had it in the Crimea.

VIII. GIDEON AND THE WARRIOR-JUDGES.

Leaving Joshua, we come now to speak of the heroes of the book of Judges—a class of men who have so little in common with those of other ages and nations, that it is almost impossible for us to understand or appreciate their character. The book closes with a remarkable declaration, which seems to be intended as a sort of clue to the very curious history, and an apology for the somewhat doubtful and eccentric characters, which it contains: "In those days there was no king in Israel; every man did that which was right in his own eyes."

The period of some three or four centuries, which is embraced in this book, and which extends from the death of Joshua to that of Samson, was a period of great and terrible wars in Israel, carried on from time to time, not like those of Joshua, against the aboriginal inhabitants, but against the surrounding nations far and near, that successively invaded and oppressed the land. It gave rise, accordingly, to an order of men, called Judges, whose chief distinction was that of warrior; who, for the most part, endowed with extraordinary strength and courage, were directly raised up, and called, and inspired of God to become the deliverers of their down-trodden country, and who, in virtue of such services, exercised as long as they lived the highest civil and judicial authority known to the theocracy of Israel.

From the Epistle to the Hebrews we learn, what otherwise we should not have known, that many of these war-clad champions of their country were at the same time "faith's worthies;" that they wrought their daring deeds of personal prowess, not solely by the help of a material sword, but with that sword of the Spirit which nothing ever wields but a devoted and heroic faith in God. Such were Gideon and Barak, Jephthah and Samson. With the high endorsement which the New Testament has given to their character, we must hold their names in honourable regard as valiant champions of faith. But, at the same time, it must be borne in mind, that in no characters of the Bible, do we find such a mingling of good and evil, of lights and shadows, of physical strength and courage with intellectual and moral weakness, as in these strange heroes of the book of Judges. Their lives often illustrate how much ignorance, and folly, and even criminality, may co-exist in a character which is mainly in the right, and in the end, faithful to the cause of Jehovah; and they call to mind the declaration of that same apostle who ranks them on the list of faith's victors—"The times of this ignorance God winked at." From Othniel the nephew of Caleb who heads the list, down to Samson who (if we leave out the peaceful characters, Eli and Samuel) closes it, these valiant war chiefs of Israel stand before us in all the stern mysterious grandeur and sometimes doubtful reputation of a knight of the Middle Ages. As we gaze upon them, we at once think of a mail-clad, helmeted crusader, like Richard the Lion-hearted, whose soul was symbolized in his sword, and whose sword was the infallible interpreter, as well as defender, of his faith. We have read of the famous Peter Francisco, a man of gigantic strength, who fought as a soldier in our Revolution, and who, at the battle of Guildford Court-house, is reported to have cut down eleven men with his single brawny arm and terrible broad-sword. But where would he have stood before such men as Shamgar, and Samson, and other heroes of the book of Judges?

But all were not of this character. Of the fifteen personages, who bore the title and filled the office of "Judge in Israel," some possessed the very highest characteristics both of the military and the moral hero. Of this description was Gideon, whom we select as the representative of his order, and who, with one exception, was by far the greatest genius, the truest hero, and the most faultless character of them all. There is one exception; and that one is a woman—a mother in Israel—the patriotic, the inspired, the heroic Deborah, who judged Israel, sustained the sinking cause of her country against the most powerful foe that it had yet encountered, and triumphantly avenged its wrongs, when there was not a man, from Dan to Beersheba, who, without her presence, dared to strike a blow. We have spoken of Deborah already in another work, when pointing out the Literary Attractions of the Bible, and need not introduce her here. Suffice it to say, however, in all candour, after surveying the fifteen heroes of the book of Judges, that, in all the sublime characteristics of love of country, martial enthusiasm, generous, disinterested, moral heroism, we regard Deborah as the "noblest Roman of them all."

But next to her stands Gideon. He is introduced into the sacred narrative in a way well befitting a great hero. We see him, and hear of him, for the first time, as he stands up in the threshing floor of Ophrah, face to face before an angel of the Lord, who gives him his high commission to deliver Israel from the Midianitish oppressors. The first salutation of the angel was in these pregnant words: "The Lord is with thee, thou mighty man of valour." We know not by what valiant deeds Gideon, who must have been still young, had already distinguished himself; but from that time forward his whole public career shows him to be fully entitled to this high testimonial, as both a mighty and a valiant man. We must not dwell on his heroic achievements. We can only refer to the prominent points of his history. On three different occasions he showed himself worthy of the highest honours of the patriot, and the hero. The first was when, in obedience to the command of Jehovah, and at the imminent peril of his life, he overthrew the idolatrous altar of his father, cut down the grove of Baal, and on the spot built an altar and offered sacrifice to the God of Israel. The second was when, at the head of a chosen band of three hundred, he attacked the Midianites by night, put them to flight, and followed up his advantage with such vigour, that he slew or took captive an army of 135,000 men "that drew sword." The third was when, returning from such a victory, he nobly refused to accept the honour and authority of a king over Israel. It is one of the most illustrious acts of moral heroism in history. A grateful nation was at his feet; a throne was within his grasp; a crown was ready to be placed upon his head. But he who had dethroned Baal, and crushed all the tents of Midian, was equal to this third and greater conquest—the conquest of himself. Beautifully does the sacred penman relate the heroic deed in the following brief and quiet words which follow so close upon the din of battle: "Then the men of Israel said unto Gideon, Rule thou over us, both thou and thy son, and thy son's son also; for thou hast delivered us from the hand of Midian. And Gideon said unto them, I will not rule over you, neither shall my son rule over you; the Lord shall rule over you."

No one can study these three great acts in the life of Gideon without feeling willing to accord to him the title of hero in the highest sense. His conquest over the hosts of Midian, leaving out of view all that was miraculous in his commission, would fairly entitle him to rank with the most skilful generals of ancient or modern times. And as to the success of the achievement, it has no parallel in history. The world has never grown tired of celebrating the mighty valour and "amor patriæ" of Leonidas and his heroic three hundred, who sold their lives so bravely in the pass of Thermopylæ for the salvation of Greece. But here was a leader at the head of precisely the same number of heroes, whose country, in a more desperate state than that of Greece, was already trodden by the proud invader, who did not hesitate to run the desperate, and, to all human appearance, hopeless venture of falling with such a handful upon a trained army of 135,000; and who, so far from losing a life, did not return from the pursuit till the power of Midian was more effectually crushed than was that of Xerxes at the end of the war.

"Among all the stratagems in ancient military history, which abounds in stratagems," says Dr. Kitto—"in the entire volume of instances collected by Polyænus—we find none so remarkable as that to which Gideon resorted, or having the slightest resemblance to it." "Never, surely, before or since, did a general lead three hundred men against a hundred and thirty-five thousand, with only a trumpet in one hand, and a pitcher containing a lighted torch in the other." But we must refer you to the Bible itself for further particulars in the history of this heroic man. Long must the soldiers of Israel have remembered the battle-cry of that eventful night—"The sword of the Lord and of Gideon."

IX. SAMSON THE HERO OF PHYSICAL STRENGTH.

The last, and, in some respects, the most remarkable of the fifteen judges of Israel (not counting Eli and Samuel), was a man to whom the term heroic applies in a sense altogether different from that in which it belongs to the preceding characters. Samson was the hero of physical strength. He might have been a great military leader, had he been able to conquer himself, or to inspire his countrymen with anything like confidence in his wisdom. But lacking judgment and common sense, and, although a Nazarite, greatly wanting in self-control, he was unable to control others, and accordingly frittered away his great powers on small endeavours, which resulted in little or no good to his country. Whatever, therefore, we may call him, we cannot, as in the case of Joshua or Gideon, call him either a great warrior, or a moral hero. His name is immortal as a proverb for strength, precisely as Solomon's is for wisdom or intellectual ability. It is a remarkable and instructive fact, that the strongest body and the brightest intellect which the Jewish race ever produced, should, each alike, be found in combination with so much moral weakness, as to leave the character of their possessors an enigma. Nothing could teach us more impressively, that neither intellect nor strength is the highest endowment of human nature.

Samson was the Jewish Hercules. He is evidently the original type of that class of heroes. He may have been the actual living model after which the partly real and partly fabulous hero of the Greeks was moulded. He lived, in fact, in the heroic age of the classical world—only a little preceding the celebrated Trojan war—the very age to which mythology refers the existence and wonderful exploits of the Grecian Hercules. It is worthy of remark, that almost every nation of antiquity had its heroic age—its Hercules—its giant of indomitable strength and courage, in whom the human was mingled with the supernatural and divine. Dr. Adam Clarke, quoting from a French author, tells us that Cicero enumerates six, and Varro more than forty, of these national heroes. Eminent classical scholars have maintained, that even the Grecian Hercules, the most authentic of them all, had no real existence in history, was a pure fabrication of the poets, like Jupiter or Mars, and designed to impersonate the idea of heroic strength and virtue. We do not, however, regard the Grecian Hercules as altogether a creation of the poets, though doubtless they had much to do with his manufacture. We look upon him rather as an importation from abroad, for which the Greeks were chiefly indebted to the historian and the traveller. The old Greeks, like the young Americans, were a people of great genius, great originality, and admirable inventive powers. But they never showed their original inventive genius to better purpose, than in the tact with which, in every department of science, literature, and art, they borrowed ideas from Egypt and the East; and in the facility with which they improved upon what they borrowed. It always takes original genius to do that. An uninventive race, like the Chinese, never improves, never advances, just because it has not sense enough to admit a foreign idea, or to send abroad in quest of something new. It is not the walling in of a nation, with the belief that everything it does must have an indigenous origin on the soil; but it is the free introduction of new ideas from abroad, that must stimulate the productive and inventive energies of any people. This made Greece a nation of heroes, artists, and philosophers. This made Rome the same. This is now raising our own country to the front rank of modern nations. But it so happened that ancient Israel had another, and better, mode of getting new ideas. Israel had that original stock which had come down from beyond the flood, and what was far more important, Israel was constantly receiving new ideas, not, indeed, from other nations, but directly from heaven. Hence her mission, from first to last, was not to borrow but to lend. Accordingly, true to her grand mission, she went on, ever receiving from above, and ever lending to the nations around, until her last great loan to the world was made in the form of a Divine Redeemer and a universal Christianity.

And so here, as in other things, the very ideal of a hero of indefinite physical prowess—the more than half-fabulous Hercules of the Grecian poets, may be traced up to the Jewish Samson as its great archetype, its original living embodiment. The Greeks had the idea, and they clothed it to suit their fancy.

The Jews had the incarnate reality, and they let it stand in all its native ruggedness and grandeur. To us it seems clear, from the remarkable correspondence between Samson and Hercules, that both the idea of such a personage and his wonderful feats, among the Greeks and other nations, were borrowed from the real achievements of the Jewish hero. And if any one is curious to see the proof, he may find it in the commentary of Dr. Clarke, where the parallel between the two heroes is drawn out at length. Each begins his career by slaying a lion unarmed; and each ends it by his own hand in an act of terrible vengeance on his enemies; and the resemblance descends to such minute particulars, as the fatal club of the one, and the death-dealing jaw-bone of the other. That the very heroes of classical antiquity, fabulous as well as real, should have been fashioned according to the great prototypes of character contained in the Bible, is certainly a very striking illustration of the vast extent to which the race of Abraham has influenced the characters and destinies of the nations of the earth.

The life of Samson sets before us no great military commander such as Joshua at the head of a standing army, nor moral hero such as Gideon refusing the crown of a nation just delivered by his volunteer sword; but a great champion whose name was a word of terror to the enemies of his country, and as such equal to a standing or volunteer army. He never fought a battle which he did not fight single-handed, he on one side, and the Philistines on the other. In fact, it seems, that he needed to fight only one, even of that kind. This seems to have been the purpose of Jehovah in raising him up and endowing him with supernatural strength—that he alone might defy and baffle all the powers of Philistia, and thus humble the pride of that land of idol-gods and giant men; as it was afterwards humbled in the same way, but more signally, by the stripling David. Announced beforehand by an angel, born of the tribe of Dan on the Philistine border, consecrated to Jehovah by the vow of a Nazarite, moved, at times, to deliver Israel by an irresistible spirit from the Lord, coming upon him in his early youth—with all these remarkable antecedents which promised so much, he appeared at last to have been inaugurated and acknowledged as Judge in Israel by his unexpected battle at Lehi; and from that time forward for twenty years he was equivalent to a whole standing army between Israel and her proudest foe. He stood and held all Philistia at bay, under the conviction that an army was as powerless against him, as a single man.

We need not stop to describe his varied exploits and adventures. Rending a young lion as he would a kid, slaying thirty Philistines at one time and a thousand at another, walking fearless through their capital at noon-day, and by night carrying off their city-gates with posts and bars to an adjacent hill-top, playing havoc with their ripened harvest-fields with his three hundred foxes, and finally covering himself beneath the ruins of their temple with three thousand dead bodies of the élite of all Philistia—he stands out in bold relief as one of the most extraordinary characters in the world's history, one of the enigmas of the Bible, an anomaly in human nature, and it may be a trophy and a miracle of Divine grace There is perhaps not a personage in all the Bible, whose life was in the right at all, in whose character or actions we can find so little either to love or to imitate. Yet, with all his weakness, his follies, and his crimes, by which he lost his strength, forfeited the confidence of his countrymen, and perhaps defeated the great mission on which Providence had sent him into the world, he seems at last to have become a true penitent, and to have died in the Divine favour as a victor by faith. This is evinced by the success of his last prayer, the restoration of his strength, and the honourable mention of his name in the New Testament.

But nevertheless, leaving out of view these closing scenes of his eventful and tragic career, and estimating his character solely from the actions of his whole preceding life, while we fully accord to him the daring courage of a hero, we think the judgment of Dr. Kitto not too severe, when he says: "A mere slave of the senses like him, who could repeatedly sacrifice or endanger the most important interests to a woman's sigh, was not one into whose hands the elders and warriors of Israel could entrust their lives and fortunes. Had he wrought out the possibilities of his destiny, and had his character been equal to his gifts, there is no knowing to what greatness he might not have attained; but as it is, he left a name, which is at once a miracle and a byword, a glory and a shame."

X. DAVID AND HIS MIGHTY MEN.

Passing down the current of Biblical history into the next century after Samson, we come to David, the youngest son of Jesse, and the great-grandson of Ruth the Moabitess. In him the heroic, not less than the poetic character of the Jewish race seems to reach its culminating point. It has been remarked that the age of David constitutes the great mountain ridge, the highest water-shed of Jewish national greatness and glory. This is certainly true of the joint reigns of David and Solomon. At any rate we may safely regard the life of David, as the climax of military heroism, towards which everything before him in Jewish history was constantly ascending, and from which everything after him was as constantly descending and degenerating. In him we have the rare combination of warrior and poet—the sweetest psalmist and the mightiest man of war that Israel ever produced. Nay, more: there was in him a double combination: the poet-warrior was also an inspired prophet-king; and he reached the highest distinction in all these different characters. A part of his reign was stained with a few great crimes, for which he paid the penalty in dust and ashes during an old age full of troubles. But the period of his youth and early manhood was one of unsullied honour, and of unparalleled glory both as a military and moral hero.

The career of the most celebrated generals mentioned in history—such as Alexander the Great, Hannibal, Cyrus, Cæsar, Charles XII., Frederic the Great, Marlborough, Napoleon, was each on a wider field of operation, and embraced a far more magnificent scale of war among nations of the first class, than anything to be found in the wars of David. But that being said, all is said as to their superiority. None of them was ever more successful and brilliant in the execution of his plans, or displayed more of that personal courage, bodily prowess, and intellectual tact, which must co-exist in one born to command. In the triumphs which everywhere attended his arms, in the mighty men of valour whom his genius created around him, in all the essential attributes of a great military commander, he appears equal to the foremost of them, excepting only the scale of operations; whilst neither of them can be compared to him as a moral hero, in the justice with which his wars were waged, and the magnanimity with which all his victories were crowned. There is no higher proof of the military genius of Napoleon than the wonderful manner in which he inspired all his soldiers with his own martial enthusiasm, and gathered around his person the most heroic spirits of the times, allured by the approving eye of their grand Emperor, and rewarded by the baton of "Marshal of France." The same characteristic of genius was found in David. From that bright day of his boyhood, when he triumphed over the pride of Philistia, down to the day when all the enemies of Israel were vanquished at his feet, he drew around himself, as an acknowledged chief, every man of courage and might in the nation. That personal influence, which a superior mind always exerts over kindred minds, which may be called the attraction of genius, and which is as fixed and powerful in its way as the law of gravitation itself, began with the heroic Jonathan, whose soul, we are told, from that day was knit to David like a brother. Accordingly, when, on the death of Saul, David was called to the throne, he found himself at Hebron, (as we learn from the twelfth chapter of the first book of Chronicles,) at the head of a volunteer army of more than two hundred thousand valiant, disciplined soldiers, "who kept rank." Indeed long before, whilst encamping in the wilderness, or finding quarters among the surrounding nations, to avoid a collision with Saul, he was at the head of no inconsiderable army. He eluded the grasp of the hostile and infuriated king, not because he feared him; but because he was the "Lord's anointed." Either in strategy or in open battle he would have been more than a match for him. For even then he was defended by a band of heroes, in whose presence the old imperial guard of Napoleon or the Ironsides of Cromwell, saving only their fire-arms, would have been but a company of grasshoppers.

It is curious to read the description which the sacred writer gives of that band of invincibles, in the chapter just referred to:—"And of the Gadites there separated themselves unto David, into the hold to the wilderness, men of might and men of war fit for the battle, that could handle shield and buckler, whose faces were like the faces of lions, and were as swift as the roes upon the mountains." Of those from other tribes who joined him, it is said, that they were "mighty men armed with bows, that could use both the right hand and the left, in hurling stones and shooting arrows." This was the germ of David's army. This was the nucleus around which rallied the most daring spirits of that heroic age. During the long years of his self-imposed exile, the caves and the rugged rocks of the wilderness formed the "Campus Martius" in which David trained these veterans of war. And notwithstanding his fortunes seemed to be desperate during all that period, so far from any one's deserting him, we find his cause continually gaining adherents, till he had organized an army that proved itself invincible.

We find several rolls of the names of his chief-captains, with the respective ranks of honour to which David had promoted them for their deeds of extraordinary valour. There are three great names of the first grade; then three of the second grade, who did not attain to the first; then thirty of the third rank who did not attain to the second—the whole forming a magnificent military "Order" or "Legion of Honour." And then over and above all, was the veteran and invincible Joab, David's uncle, who held the post of commander-in-chief under the king, as long as David lived. This position he won by his valour in taking Jerusalem from the Jebusites, the last stronghold of their power, which was made by David the capital of his kingdom; and this position, which he filled so well, was ever after maintained in defiance of Abner, Amasa, and all other rivals. Joab was of a fierce, rough, and unscrupulous nature; but his strong common sense and his consummate military genius always prevailed. In the course of his long eventful life, no foe, either in war or peace, ever got an advantage over him. His ends he always accomplished; by fair means if he could; but if not by fair, by such other means as he knew must insure success. That can be said of him, which cannot be said of Hannibal, or of Napoleon, or of many other great generals—he never lost a battle great or small.

But consummate as were the military abilities of Joab, heroic and invincible as were all the war-worn worthies in this ancient Legion of Honour, David himself was mightier than all. No military leader,—not Cæsar, Alexander, or Napoleon, was ever more intensely and supremely the head and front of his army. All clustered around him, and looked up to him, as to one born to command. His whole preceding history, so full of adventure, so full of wonders, was calculated to inspire his soldiers with the profoundest admiration for his heroic virtues, and the most unshaken confidence in his skill and power. First we see him as the fearless shepherd boy, feeding his flocks by day and gazing upon the stars by night—the poet of nature and the devout minstrel of the harp communing with God, utterly unconscious of the splendid destiny that awaited him, and doubtless a stranger to all political or military aspirations. A little while after we see him again, even then a stripling, as a casual messenger from his father to the camp of Israel, standing up bravely between the two contending hosts, and with his shepherd's sling and five smooth stones of the brook, attacking and triumphing over the proudest champion of Philistia that ever defied the armies of the living God. We see him next the favourite of all Israel, the anointed of the Lord, and hence the victim of Saul's anger, compelled to leave his country, and pass a series of years amidst the perils and privations of a life in the wilderness. And then we see him at the comparatively early age of thirty years called to assume the throne over the tribe of Judah; and after reigning seven years and a half over this tribe, we find him, at last, valiant in every battle, victorious over every foe, crowned king over all Israel, and commander-in-chief of two hundred thousand men; and all this before he was thirty-eight years old. Now with the antecedents of such a career fresh in the recollections of his countrymen, it is not wonderful that David should stand forth as the acknowledged soul and centre of a band of heroes, such as the world had certainly never seen before his day, and such as it has not often, if ever, seen since.

The world has had many a heroic race and nation since the son of Jesse led his invincibles to victory. The modern world has rung with a report of the brilliant achievements of Napoleon and his marshals. With thrilling interest we have all read the noble deeds of Washington and his generals in the battles of our Revolution from Bunker Hill to Yorktown. But neither on the glory-loving heroes of France, nor on the patriotic heroes of America, can we ever pronounce a higher eulogium than to say, they displayed a heroism in battle worthy of "David and his mighty men." A late writer, Gallagher, has brought out the heroic character of the times of David, in a bold and striking light, when he paraphrases the speech of Hushai the Archite before Absalom, in words like these, dissuading from a night attack:—

"And your father, says Ahithophel, if found among these veteran warriors, will be afraid! It will be the first time, aye, the first time in the history of his long eventful life. If he retreated from Saul, it was because he was conscientious about lifting his hand against the Lord's anointed. But was he ever known to tremble before an enemy of Israel? Is it forgotten that he took up the challenge of Goliath and slew him, when no other man in the twelve tribes dared attempt it? Is this the man that will be afraid? And the men that are with him will fly! Who will fly? Will Joab and Abishai fly? Will Jashobeam the Tachmonite, and Eleazar the son of Dodo fly? The Cherethites and the Pelethites, that never yet lost a battle, fly? The valiant men from Gath, that have gathered laurels on every field they have fought for twenty-five years, fly? Is this our brightest hope of success—that these men will fly? To cherish such a hope is delusion, is madness, is ruin. Has God forsaken us? Has angry heaven permitted some demon of destruction to come and mingle in our counsels and decoy us into a measure like this, with the delusive hope that these stern warriors will fly? Look for the rocks of Mount Zion to fly—look for the stream of Jordan to turn back and go foaming and thundering over the loftiest peaks of Lebanon into the sea of Tyre—look for the firm ordinances of day and night, summer and winter, to fail in their seasons—but do not look for such men as are about David, to fly when they hear the clash of arms."

Now, there are two remarks which we wish to make before leaving the character of David. The first is that David's heroism was derived from God. All his strength, his courage, his wisdom, his success, his superiority over other men, was in God. The deepest conviction of his heart, as well as the invariable confession of his lips, was that he owed all he had ever done or attained to God alone. He was distinguished from all other great warriors in many things, but most in this, that he attributed all the glory of his battles to God. He even gloried in being regarded as "vile," in the eyes of a king's daughter, that he might the more exalt the power of that God who had taken him from the sheepfold to be ruler over Israel. The Lord declared to him, "I have made thee a great name like unto the name of the great men that are in the earth;" and he seems always to have felt, that, whilst he was nothing without God, he could do all things with the help of God. Unlike the mighty conquerors of other lands, who trusted in the strength of their own swords, and in the pride of conscious genius boasted that destiny was their own, David trusted in the living God alone, and acknowledged him as "teaching his hands to war and his fingers to fight." And this strong confidence was the secret of his extraordinary courage and prowess in war.

The second remark is, that there were several brief periods in the life of David, when his faith was under a cloud, when his strong confidence in God, and with it his courage, failed him, and when he was led to exclaim, "I shall one day fall by the hand of Saul." On these occasions, when left to his fears for want of faith, he became weak like other men, resorted to human expedients for safety inconsistent with truth, and did things which were utterly unworthy of his great name as a military and moral hero. Of this character was his deception of the priests at Nob, his going to the Philistines and feigning himself mad, with other acts of deception practised on the king of Gath. But these intervals of despondency were of short duration, and when they were ended by return of his confidence in Jehovah, David was himself again.

XI. THE HEROES OF THE CAPTIVITY.

From all these warlike characters of the Old Testament history, let us now turn to look upon an example of a different kind altogether. We pass at a bound across an interval of five hundred years, from the highest pinnacle of Jewish national glory to the dark period of captivity and exile. But it was a period, of all others, best adapted to develop the moral heroism we are now to contemplate. The times no longer called for the hero of the sword, and the helmet, and battle-field, but for the hero of endurance and patient continuance in well doing—the hero of the palace and the prison, the fiery furnace and the lion's den. The providence of God seemed already to be preparing the way for the higher heroism of the New Testament, and to anticipate its sublimer teaching—"Put up thy sword, for they that take the sword shall also perish by the sword." Broad is the contrast and striking the distinction between the mighty man of war, like David, fighting his way to victory, sword in hand, and the peaceful hero of the captivity, like Daniel and his three companions, conquering only by patience, fortitude, and trust in God. These closing characters of the Old Testament form a fitting prelude and introduction to the peaceful pages of the New.

There are, indeed, many other characters of the same type, between David and Daniel. We have a noble illustration in the life of Jeremiah the prophet. In fact, this high, heroic character was exemplified in the lives of all the prophets of God from Samuel onward. Inspired of God with a clear vision of truth and duty, commissioned to bear witness for God at perilous times when all other men proved faithless, called often to stand up before wicked princes and despots, and declare the truth at the risk of their lives, they had all along, even from the days of Enoch, given the world both the conception and the impersonation of a true moral hero. They prophesied in sackcloth and ashes. In the words of the great Apostle, who himself might have sat for the picture which he draws: "They had trial of cruel mockings and scourgings; yea more, of bonds and imprisonments. They were stoned, they were sawn asunder, they were tempted, were slain with the sword; they wandered about in sheepskins and goatskins; being destitute, afflicted, tormented; of whom the world was not worthy; they wandered in deserts, and in mountains, and in dens and caves of the earth." But, as time would fail us to exhibit separately the heroic characters of this whole prophetic group, we select Daniel and his three companions in exile, as a fitting type of that heroism which, calmly planting itself on the line that duty draws, can cheerfully accept all that God appoints, and all that the rage of man can do.

In these four young men of the captivity, Daniel, Shadrach, Meshach, and Abednego, whose heroic deeds are recorded in the book of Daniel, we have a noble illustration of the two essential principles that constitute true moral heroism. The first is an unshaken faith or trust in God; the second a self-sacrificing discharge of duty. The true moral hero feels that God is his strength, that with God he is invincible, that nothing can harm him, and nothing thwart him while God is with him. "If God be for us, who can be against us?" Elisha once stood alone upon a mountain, save a single companion, while a mighty armed host of the king of Syria surrounded him with chariots and horses, cutting off all hope of escape. And yet he could say to his servant, "Fear not; for they that be with us are more than they that be with them." This is the faith, this the feeling of the true hero. At the same time he acts as if everything depended on himself. His trust in God's help does not make him fold his arms in apathy. But denying himself all forbidden indulgence, and sacrificing personal ease and enjoyment, he labours, or prays, or fights, or suffers and endures, as if the very power of God was acting in him and by him.

Thus was it with Daniel and his companions. Their first exhibition of this character was in early youth, when, being selected to receive an education suitable for the royal court in Babylon, they resolved, with patriotic piety, that they would not abandon the customs of their country, and the religion of their fathers. The account is given in the first chapter of the book of Daniel. Placed under the instruction and discipline of a skilful master, the prince of the eunuchs, furnished with supplies of the richest food by the royal order, and trained for three years in the learning and tongue of the Chaldeans, that they might excel in every bodily and mental accomplishment, they were then to stand for trial before the king—the great king Nebuchadnezzar. But, though children in years, and in a strange land, they purposed in their hearts that they would not defile themselves with the king's meat, nor the wine that he drank. And, through the kindness of Ashpenaz and Melzar, and the favouring providence of God, they were enabled to abide by this heroic determination, and at last to pass examination before the king, as more excellent than all their fellows. Thus did God put honour upon their early choice, and make them ensamples to the young of all succeeding times, of temperance, self-denial, patriotism, and piety.

But this early exhibition of manly virtue was only preparing them for those greater trials, and higher acts of heroism, to which God afterwards called them. Had they not been schooled to self-denial, courage, and trust in God, by these earlier trials, they would never have been crowned with the sublime glory of the later. God always prepares his children for what he is preparing for them. And thus Daniel was nerved for the lions' den of king Darius, and his three companions for the fiery furnace of Nebuchadnezzar. For their virtues and their rare endowments, they had been exalted to the highest stations of honour and trust in all the land of Babylon. But this exaltation exposed them to the rage of wicked men, who plotted their destruction. High as they were in office, they determined to prove faithful to their own religion. They would not worship the idols of Babylon but continued true to the God of heaven, although they knew well the penalty—for one the lions' den, for the others the sevenfold-heated furnace.

You know the story well and the result; how in spite of all the rage of their enemies, and in the very face of death in its most terrific forms, they steadfastly maintained the honour of their God; and how that God vindicated the cause of his suffering servants to the dismay and overthrow of the wicked. It was a glorious chapter in the history of the church of God. There in the lions' den, and there in the fiery furnace was the true church, and there the true succession that had come down unbroken from the Father of the faithful. And there was the great Head of the church with them—One like unto the Son of man walking in the midst of the furnace. And there is the answer to the question where is the true church to be found. She is to be found wherever her Divine Head is found. She is to be found wherever her faithful children are found—faithful even unto death for the witness of Jesus; not in Jerusalem, not in Rome, but in the dens and caves of the earth if the faithful are there.

XII. THE HEROIC CHARACTER OF PAUL.

In passing from the heroes of the Old Testament to those of the New, we shall adopt a method altogether different from that hitherto pursued. We shall select a single example, to stand as the type and exponent of the whole New Testament group. It is the highest human type. There was much of the heroic in the life and character of John the Baptist—especially in that bold and faithful preaching which led to his tragic end. We might trace the same character in the apostles of Jesus Christ, as they went forth to preach the gospel in a world of opposition, and as in defiance of prisons, privations, and countless foes, they persevered in their great work, till each had won a martyr's crown. Whatever may have been their previous character as men, it is manifest that after the day of Pentecost, as preachers and apostles, inspired of God, and armed with the whole panoply of gospel truth, they constituted a band of moral heroes, such as the world had never seen before. But instead of describing them here severally, it will suffice to exhibit one, who was worthy to be their representative. That one is Paul.

There is indeed one example far more illustrious than Paul. In the voluntary humiliation and sufferings of Him, the God-man, who died on Calvary with a martyr's zeal for truth, and with more than a martyr's agony, we behold the highest exhibition of moral courage that has ever been known amongst men. It is, however, more to our present object to select a purely human example. And such we have in the character of the great Apostle of the Gentiles. What is the hero of a hundred bloody battles, compared with this heroic man, who, with the gospel of the crucified Nazarene as his only letter of introduction to foreign nations, went forth to the work of converting the whole world to the religion of the cross! The very conception of such an enterprise, if it had not come from heaven, would have looked almost as strange and impossible to the ancients, as the proposition to create a new world in the sky. Christianity has made us familiar with the idea of one universal religion for the world. But the master minds of antiquity had never grasped it—had never heard of it—never dreamed of it, except so far as they may have caught some faint glimmerings of it in the prophecies of the Jewish Scriptures. The idea was new to the world; and to those who knew not, or believed not its Divine origin, it must have appeared bold and daring, beyond all human precedent, to think of converting all nations to one religion—and that a religion from Judea—a religion whose founder had been put to death on the cross.

Now if there has ever been such a thing as moral courage called for amongst men, it was to do such a work, preach such a religion as this. Where was the hero to be found? where the band of heroes, with moral nerve enough to encounter not only the dangers and the deaths of such an undertaking, but to endure the derision and scorn of the whole civilized world? One might venture to preach it in the synagogues of Jerusalem; but who would dare to argue the cause of the "Crucified Jew," as rightful Lord of heaven and earth, at Athens and at Rome? Paul was the man raised up and qualified for the task, not only with wisdom, but courage, from on high. The other apostles had each his share in the great work. The martyred James, and Stephen, and even John the Baptist, had a part to perform, before they passed away. But the "chosen vessel" for this great, heroic undertaking was Paul. And hence of all human lives, his is the most admirable exemplification of a sublime moral heroism.

Behold him first at Damascus, conferring not with flesh and blood, but with the zeal of a new convert, boldly preaching the religion which he had gone there to exterminate. Behold him next at Jerusalem, fearless of the attempts which had been made on his life, proclaiming the testimony of Jesus to the men who had so recently stoned Stephen. Behold him again at Antioch, reasoning mightily from the Scriptures, confounding the Jews and persuading the Gentiles, till he is compelled to shake off the dust of his feet against them, and go to other cities. Behold him then at Ephesus, anxious to adventure himself into the midst of an infuriated mob, to bear the whole blame of his doctrines; and with great difficulty dissuaded from so bold a measure. Behold him at Lystra, stoned by the Jews and left for dead; and then immediately after preaching the gospel in the adjacent cities. Behold him with Silas at Philippi, scourged, imprisoned, yet with the unconquered spirit of the hero, singing at midnight in their dungeon; strangers as they are, cut off from the sympathies of all the living world around, they hold such deep communion with things unseen and eternal, that the very earthquake lifts up its mighty voice responsive to their songs. Behold him on Mars Hill at Athens, unabashed by the brilliant wits and critics of classic Greece, preaching Jesus and the resurrection to men who were ready to laugh him to scorn at the first invasion of their received philosophy. Behold him at Cæsarea, after two years of imprisonment for conscience' sake, weary and worn out with official injustice and popular malice, taking his final appeal, in those heroic words: "If I be an offender, or have committed anything worthy of death, I refuse not to die; but if there be none of these things whereof they accuse me, no man may deliver me unto the Jews. I appeal unto Cæsar." Behold him at last, at Rome, dictating letters to all the churches, preaching the gospel alike within the prison and the palace, calmly awaiting the day of his execution, and closing his grand mission with the crown of martyrdom.

What were bonds and prisons to him, who could say on one occasion, "None of these things move me, neither count I my life dear unto myself, so that I might finish my course with joy?" What were the frowns of foes, or the cautious entreaties of friends to him who could say on another, "What mean ye to weep and break my heart; for I am ready, not only to be bound, but to die at Jerusalem for the name of the Lord Jesus?" What were dangers and deaths to him, who could say at Rome, and it may be, within hearing of the growl of Nero's wild beasts, "I am now ready to be offered, and the time of my departure is at hand. I have fought a good fight: I have finished my course: I have kept the faith: henceforth there is laid up for me a crown of righteousness which the Lord shall give me at that day?" What were the assaults of men or the gates of hell to him, who could say, "We glory in tribulations also: knowing that tribulation worketh patience, and patience experience, and experience hope, and hope maketh not ashamed?"

Take him all in all, through all his perils and privations, stripes and imprisonments, shipwrecks and stonings, labours and conflicts, and there has probably never been exhibited in human history a more eventful life, or a more heroic character, than his. Though all his battles were the bloodless battles of reason and argument, still we feel at every step of his career, that Paul was as brave a man as ever trod the earth. Of all merely human heroes, he is the most heroic, measured either by the dangers which he faced, the difficulties he surmounted, or the conquest he won. He stands, in this respect, on the culminating central point of the world's history. In him, the heroic of all antiquity, which had been steadily ascending through forty centuries, reached its zenith of glory; and to him, the heroic of all modern civilization looks back, already through eighteen centuries, as its highest noon of individual human perfection. The world has made vast progress in many things since Paul's day. Christianity has caused the race of man, as a race, to advance with giant strides, towards the goal of virtue and glory. But manifestly there has been no one man on earth since Paul, who was at all equal to Paul as a man and a hero.

XIII. CONCLUSION.

Thus have we endeavoured to point out, on a rapid survey of the vast field, some of the most striking illustrations of the heroic character, as displayed in the great men of the Bible. You are well aware, that to all readers, this is one of the most attractive elements in the history of a nation. Written history is mostly made up of the daring deeds of men, who were, or aspired to be, heroes. It is this that charms us so in the annals of Greece and Rome. It is this that gives a deathless interest to the life of Cyrus, Cæsar, Alexander, Hannibal, and Napoleon. It is this that renders immortal the names of Wallace and Bruce, Hampden and Sidney, Tell and Kosciusko. It is this that throws a halo of imperishable glory around the history of England, Scotland, and America, in the eyes of the young of every successive generation.

Now we claim for the Bible, that aside from all its other attractions, it has the charm of being the most heroic history that has ever been written. We will not stop to discuss this claim, after all that has been said; but every one can see at a glance, how the mingling of the Divine with the human in the actions of its heroes, was itself sufficient to give it this pre-eminence.

And who can estimate the influence of this most heroic history upon the formation of the individual and national character, wherever this book has been read? If modern history proves any one point beyond all controversy, it is this, that all the great heroic virtues have flourished most, among those nations where the Bible has been the book of the people. "By great and sublime virtues," says Robert Hall, "are meant those which are called into action on great and trying occasions, which demand the sacrifice of the dearest interests and prospects of human life, and sometimes of life itself; the virtues, in a word, which, by their variety and splendour, draw admiration, and have rendered illustrions the character of the patriots, martyrs, and confessors." And he argues at length, in his great sermon on "Modern Infidelity," that the world is indebted for the exhibition of these virtues, not to atheism and infidelity, nor to ancient and modern paganism, but to the religion of the Bible. We know that the sublimest exhibition of all those virtues which go to constitute moral heroism, that the world has witnessed during the last eighteen centuries, can be traced directly to the influence of the gospel. There have been three grand fields for the display of these virtues: first, that which has been occupied by the noble army of martyrs and confessors, who have sealed their testimony for Jesus with their blood: second, that which has been occupied by the missionaries of the cross, who have braved the dangers and privations of every savage land on earth, in prosecution of their arduous work: and third, that which the armed defenders of civil and religious liberty have occupied and adorned with such names as Tell, and Cromwell, and Washington. It is easy to see, how the world is indebted to the Bible for all the heroism it has to boast of in these three wide domains.

But we think it would be easy to show that all the greatest military commanders of modern Christendom, not excepting Napoleon nor the most heroic of his marshals, Macdonald, owed much of that stern grandeur which distinguished their warlike character, to their early study of the model heroes of the Bible. Take Cromwell for example, who, either as a general on the field, or a statesman in the cabinet, never failed in any thing he ever undertook, and never had, as we think, a superior in English history. In what school of heroes had Cromwell been trained? In what book of tactics, and after what fashion of a soldier, did he and his compatriots learn the art of war? The Bible and the Psalmody inspired them with courage, and furnished them with the very watchwords of battle. At the memorable battle of Dunbar, on which the fate of the Commonwealth turned as on a pivot, we are told by Carlyle, the Puritan hero led his soldiers to victory, as was his custom, by singing one of David's psalms. "The Lord General," says Hodgson, "made a halt at the foot of Doon Hill, and sang the hundred and seventeenth Psalm, till our horse could gather for the close. There we uplifted it to the tune of Bangor, or some still higher score, and rolled it great and strong against the sky." There was music, doubtless, on a lofty scale!

And there was heroism too, such as nothing but the Bible can inspire. Think of twelve thousand soldiers, such as Cromwell's Ironsides, hemmed in by the sea on a narrow peninsula, from which they knew they must cut their way, sword in hand, or perish—think of such a band of heroes under such circumstances, singing together, at the rising of the sun, this sublime psalm of God, as a preparation for the approaching battle! You know the result. They routed an army, horse, foot, and dragoons, of twenty-three thousand men, driving them from their chosen positions, and making more prisoners than their whole number. They saved the cause of liberty for England and the world.

Take another example in the celebrated Gustavus Adolphus, king of Sweden and champion of the Reformation. His military genius and his heroic character were both of the highest order. He was victorious in every battle, but the last; and in that he died like a hero, saying—"I seal with my blood the Protestant religion and the liberties of Germany." Like Cromwell, he was great as a general and great as a sovereign. Like Cromwell, he fought for civil and religious liberty. And like Cromwell, his lion-like nature had been modelled after the heroes of the Bible. The fatal battle of Lutzen, where he fell, may well remind us of the battle of Dunbar, in all save the disastrous result. In both cases, the soldiers of these great commanders were prepared for the charge by the sublime strains of sacred vocal music. The army of the Duke Wallenstein, vastly superior in numbers to that of Gustavus, quietly awaited, in their well-defended lines, the assault of the latter. "The Swedish army," says a recent, but competent authority, "then sang 'Luther's Hymn,' the king leading off in a deep, sonorous bass. The effect of forty thousand voices, thus pealing out in unison, may be easily conceived, and is described by contemporary authorities as having been awfully impressive."

But we need not multiply examples to show how much the world is indebted to the Bible, for even its greatest military characters. Infidelity itself has done homage to that influence, which the Bible has extended more or less over all men. For even the few heroic names which infidelity can boast, owe most of their greatness to those early impressions which have been unconsciously received from this book. As an illustration of this point, we may refer to an interesting incident taken from the revolutionary history of our own country, which you will find recorded in the Encyclopedia Americana, in the words following:—

"General Ethan Allen, one of the bravest of the brave, a native of Connecticut, but afterwards resident in Vermont, had, soon after the battle of Lexington, distinguished himself by the capture of two British forts, Ticonderoga and Crown Point. With eighty-three men, at the dawn of day, he made his way into fort Ticonderoga, and with uplifted sword, demanded of its as yet undressed commander, an immediate surrender. The latter asking him by whose authority: 'I demand it,' said Allen, 'in the name of the Great Jehovah and the Continental Congress.' The fort, with its stores and garrison, was at once given up; and the same day he took possession also of Crown Point. Unfortunately this heroic officer, like many others of that day, was theoretically an infidel, and published the first work that was ever published in America against Christianity, called 'Allen's Theology or the Oracles of Reason.' Long afterwards the following incident occurred, showing clearly the real conviction of the man. Whilst sitting in his library, conversing with a physician named Elliot, General Allen was informed that his daughter was dying, and desired to speak with him. He immediately repaired to her chamber followed by Dr. Elliot. His wife was distinguished for piety, and had instructed her daughter in the principles of Christianity. As soon as her father stood at her bedside, she said to him, 'I am about to die; shall I believe in the principles you have taught me, or shall I believe in what my mother has taught me?' He became greatly agitated; his chin quivered; his whole frame shook, and after waiting a few moments he replied—'Believe what your mother has taught you.'"

Suffer us, young reader, to repeat the solemn injunction to you—"Believe what your mother has taught you." If indeed you have been blest with a Christian mother who has taught you the word of God, then above all things, believe what your mother has taught you. You cannot show a nobler heroism than to live and die by what such a mother has taught you. This shield of faith is a far better equipment for life or death than that brazen shield of the Spartan mother, who arming her son for battle, said, "With this return or upon it." With this you may go forth and return a conqueror in all the battles of life. This will sustain you in the darkest hour of conflict, whether your foes be temporal or spiritual. This can never fail you, whether your heroism be tried on the red fields of war, on the arenas of political strife, in the fiery ordeals of affliction, at the distant posts of missionary duty, or in the ordinary vocations of daily life. You may be called to a career of great activity in the public affairs of life; or you may be called to endure hardness as a good soldier of Jesus Christ in the humbler walks of society; or you may be called simply to suffer and endure; for "they also serve who stand and wait." But wherever you are, and whatever you do—do it as one called and girded of God for some great thing—do it as one who feels that he has a mission to accomplish on earth—do it as feeling that it is a great thing to live and suffer and die for Christ Be a hero in the strife, and by grace a conqueror too. The greatest conquerors of earth have often been those who died in battle. The greatest of all conquerors, after Jesus Christ, is the man who wages a life-long battle against sin, and then dying wins an eternal victory over the last enemy.

With Christ strengthening me, said the heroic Paul, I can do all things. With the love of Christ constraining us, with the power of God, girding us, and the prize of eternal life inviting us, what is there we may not attempt? what is there we dare not do? Impelled by such motives, and supported by such strength from God, the very feeblest of our race, have ofttimes waxed valiant as David in the battles of the Lord, and won the conqueror's crown. How often have we seen this high and holy heroism displayed, even by naturally timid and delicate women in the annals of our modern missions! A touching but sublime instance of this character, which is all the more interesting because it is so often called for in the missionary work, is related of a wife and mother belonging to one of the Baptist stations. It became necessary, that her two little children should be separated from her and brought home, and that she should remain with her husband at the post of duty. It was a fearful struggle, but she felt that duty demanded the separation and the sacrifice. She led her little ones in each hand down to the beach, where the ship's boat waited to receive them. Taking her last loving embrace, as she gave them up, she stood, and with streaming eyes, and almost bursting heart, looked up to heaven, and said—"Lord Jesus, I can do this for thee" Ah, that is the spirit, that the motive, of all true Christian heroism. That is the noblest and the strongest principle that ever took possession of a human heart—the constraining love of Jesus. For me to live is Christ and to die is gain. Lord Jesus, I can do anything, yea all things for thee. If this love be in the heart, it matters not how, or where, or when the soldier of the cross may be called to lay down his armour. All is well. It may be like Havelock, worn out with excessive service, or Hedley Vicars in the onset of battle; it may be like Freeman in the meridian of his usefulness, or Lowrie in the bright morning of his youth, but all is well—all will be peace and joy for evermore.

"Servant of God, well done,
Rest from thy loved employ,
The battle fought, the victory won,
Enter thy Maker's joy.

At midnight came the cry,
"To meet thy God prepare!"
He woke and caught his captain's eye'
Then, strong in faith and prayer,

His spirit with a bound
Left its encumbering clay;
His tent at sunrise on the ground,
A darkened ruin lay.

The pains of death are past,
Labour and sorrow cease;
The Christian's warfare closed at last,
His soul is found in peace."

CHAPTER IV.

KINGS AND STATESMEN OF THE BIBLE.

THE kings and statesmen of the Bible, as they pass in grand and solemn procession across the broad fields of its history, may justly be regarded as constituting one of its chief attractions to the youthful mind. Though we have long since learned in America, to look upon kings and nobles, as fashioned out of no better clay than other men; still these mighty magnates of the past, so far from losing, have only gathered interest with the lapse of ages, and may furnish us with no unfruitful theme for the present occasion. Like the pyramids of Egypt to a voyager on the Nile, they stand forth as the ancient and unchangeable landmarks of human progress. They lift their unwasted peaks in stern, mysterious grandeur to the skies—the representatives of buried empires, the exponents of human folly and ambition, the monuments both of power and weakness; and the longer they stand, the more do they excite the wonder, and engage the study of mankind. It is hardly necessary to say that our present theme will confine us almost exclusively to the Old Testament. It was not the design of the New Testament history in any way to develope the genius of the statesman, or to record the deeds of the kings and nobles of the earth. It had another and a nobler King to chronicle, who was not of this world, and of whom we need not speak in this connection. But the Old Testament, which forms a sort of preparatory school to the New, is full of historical and biographical instruction, peculiarly adapted to interest the young. Amongst its most attractive characters are its kings and statesmen. We place the two together, because they are almost invariably found associated together in the Bible. It is worthy of notice, that almost every one of the mighty monarchs mentioned in the sacred history, is either connected, in some way, with a great cotemporaneous statesman, or else he supplies the place of one, like Solomon, by being a great statesman himself. From the multitude of kings, little and great, that figure on the sacred pages, let us select some of the most remarkable examples, along with their distinguished cotemporary statesmen.

I. THE PHARAOHS OF EGYPT.

At the head of the catalogue of kings stand the Pharaohs of Egypt. This was a general title given to all the Egyptian monarchs, like Cæsar to the Roman emperors. It is computed that about sixty sovereigns of that name reigned over Egypt. Of these, eleven or twelve are mentioned or referred to in different parts of the Bible. Some of them were powerful, warlike chiefs, who could lead a million of soldiers to a single campaign. They extended their conquests, at different times, from Ethiopia to the Euphrates. These are the men who, probably, built the pyramids to perpetuate their glory, and who covered Egypt with those stupendous temples and obelisks, which have stood through all time, as the most wonderful triumphs of ancient civilization. It may serve to give us some idea of the despotic power of these sons of pride, to repeat the statement of the ancient writers, that three hundred and sixty-six thousand labourers were employed twenty years in the erection of one of the pyramids. At one cent a-day for wages, allowing nothing for the cost of materials, this would make the structure cost twenty-six millions of dollars; and at our rate of fifty cents per day, thirteen hundred millions.

The Pharaohs are not the first kings mentioned in the Bible. We find other rulers before them called kings, but evidently of no great importance. And besides these petty sovereigns, we find one very remarkable character, Melchisedec, the "king of righteousness" and the "king of peace," combining both the priestly and the regal dignity, and standing forth mysteriously, in his isolation, a type of the great Messiah. But passing over all these, we may remark that the Pharaoh of Abraham's times, the first of the name in the Bible, was evidently a man of justice and integrity, one that feared God, and walked uprightly before him. The Pharaoh also, who promoted Joseph, seems to have possessed the same good qualities in a still higher degree. His deference to the will of Providence, his sagacity in recognizing superior virtue, even in a slave and a foreigner, his promptness in exalting Joseph to the office of prime minister over Egypt, his steady adherence for fourteen years to all the measures of Joseph's administration, his kind treatment of the venerable patriarch Jacob and his posterity as long as he lived, his ability to appreciate the wisdom, to follow the policy, and to reward the services of such a counsellor as Joseph—all prove Pharaoh to have been no ordinary man, whilst they illustrate both the excellence of his character and the wisdom of his reign. We scarcely know which of the two to admire most—the ability of the statesman in Joseph, or the wisdom of the monarch in Pharaoh. Such a sovereign was worthy of such a counsellor.

Two centuries later, at the birth of Moses, we find another Pharaoh on the throne, of very different character—a king that knew not Joseph, and is supposed by historians to have been of a new dynasty altogether. His policy was, by rigorous bondage and by infanticide, either to exterminate the Hebrew race from Egypt, or to reduce them to the most abject and hopeless servitude. It was his daughter who adopted Moses; and in all probability it was this same Pharaoh, who, forty years afterwards, would have killed him for slaying an Egyptian, had not Moses fled to the wilderness. His cruel overtasking of the Israelites and his inhuman destruction of their male children, have given him the unenviable distinction of being the great antitype of tyrants. He stands as the founder of the royal line of despotism. So far as history shows anything to the contrary, his successors may claim him as the head and forefather of all legitimacy, though he was probably a usurper himself. He was the first link of an iron chain, which has been extended down to our own times, and on which may be found, at irregular intervals, the Herods of Judea, the Neros and Caligulas of Rome, the Stuarts of England, and the Austrian house of Hapsburg.

But forty years later still, we find yet another Pharaoh on the throne. It is he before whom Moses stood, on his return from the wilderness, in the capacity of a messenger from Jehovah and a deliverer to Israel. This Pharaoh was as tyrannical as his predecessor; and to the tyrant he added the character of an infidel. He was a daring, defiant rebel against God. He is, perhaps, the most complete and awful impersonation of the idea of unconquerable enmity against the Almighty, which the Bible has anywhere given us, in a merely human form. His reply to Moses—"Who is the Lord, that I should obey his voice to let Israel go? I know not the Lord, neither will I let Israel go"—may well remind us of those speeches of vengeance and heaven-daring defiance which, in Paradise Lost, Milton has put into the mouths of the prince of darkness and his apostate crew. It is stated by the expositors, on the authority of Herodotus, the father of Grecian history, that Apries, one of the subsequent monarchs of Egypt, the Pharaoh Hophra, probably, of the Bible, boasted in the pride and arrogance of his heart, that there was no deity in heaven or earth strong enough to dethrone him. This seems to have been the very spirit which reigned in the Pharaoh of the ten plagues. Nothing could exhibit more strongly the proud and heaven-daring character of the man, than the fact that, after passing through all those terrific judgments which had already desolated Egypt, he should persist in marching his whole army into the channel of the sea in pursuit of Israel. Human pride, and presumption, and unbelief could go no further. Who but a madman or a fool, or a demon, after seeing what Pharaoh had seen of the power of God, would think of rushing by night upon a battle ground which had been opened for Israel on the bottom of the sea, and defended right and left by a rampart of the mighty waters?

The Scriptures every where set forth Pharaoh as an example of warning to the wicked. For this purpose he was raised up, that it might be shown to the world, how far the heart of pride would go, when left to itself, unchecked by the restraining grace of God. We cannot conceive of the amount of evil which has been prevented in this wicked world, by the exhibition of such an example of rebellion followed by its punishment, so near the fountain head of all history. The kings and despots of the earth needed just such an example to hold them in check; and if, with all the terrors of Pharaoh's doom before them, they have still been inclined to evil, who can tell what they would have done without such a warning?

Besides this important purpose of Pharaoh's standing as a warning to all transgressors, the Almighty had another great end to accomplish in raising him up, and permitting him to harden his heart in his course of rebellion. It was to show forth his own power and glory as the sovereign disposer of the nations of the earth—to vindicate his own supreme and inherent right to govern the world as he pleases. It was a right which the ancient idolaters needed much to learn. It is a right which the atheistical heart of the modern world still needs to learn. The lordly despots of the earth, from Pharaoh down to our day have ever been disposed to dispute it with the Most High. The unsanctified heart of every sinner is still ready, on every occasion, with its arm of puny pride, to join issue on the Divine sovereignty, and to quarrel and battle it out to the last, against the right of God to reign, and do what he pleases with his own. Alas for man! Alas for the sinner! If his impotence were not equal to his arrogance, and his ignorance to his presumption, he would long ago have dethroned God! Now we often fail to appreciate the dealings of Jehovah with Pharaoh, because we transfer Egypt's present insignificance, as a nation, to the ancient world. We must bear in mind that Egypt was then the leading power on earth, in arts, arms, wealth, commerce, learning, and civilization. Hence, the judgments of Jehovah in Egypt must have made a profounder impression upon the whole civilized world of that day, than they would now make, if wrought in England, France, or the United States; because no single nation of the modern world holds that place of supremacy over all others which Egypt then held. Accordingly when you read of Pharaoh and the ten plagues, you must not carry with you the associations of modern Egypt; but think of some such centre of human population, pride, and power, as London, Paris, or New York. On such a theatre of action were displayed all the dread symbols of Jehovah's power in Egypt.

II. JOSEPH AND MOSES, THE EARLIEST STATESMEN.

Contemporary with two of the Pharaohs, though separated by a long interval, we find the two earliest models of statesmanship which history affords. These are Joseph and Moses. We have already contemplated their character as young men, and need not dwell long in describing their virtues now. It is chiefly as a statesman, in his exalted seat of power, introducing and successfully carrying out a policy that saved Egypt and the surrounding nations from starvation, that the true greatness of Joseph shines forth like the sun. No premier of any civilized land from that day to this, ever wielded the helm of government with a steadier hand, and accomplished his mission with more consummate ability, than did this first of statesmen. Then, perhaps, for the first time in the history of the world was verified, in a good sense, the maxim of a "power behind the throne greater than the throne itself." Well might Pharaoh give him a name indicative of the fact that he was the "Saviour of the age." Well might he ascribe all his work to the power and wisdom of God, saying to his brethren—"God did send me before you here, to preserve life by a great deliverance." Raised up by divine providence to administer the affairs of the greatest kingdom then in the world, at the dangerous crisis of a seven years' famine, he not only carried the nation safely through the peril, but he effected a total revolution in the whole political economy of Egypt. He effected such a change as to bind every landholder in the realm, in the new relation of a tenant and supporter of the monarch's throne; so as to present the spectacle of a whole people becoming one family, and bound in gratitude to their sovereign and father for the greatest of all temporal blessings—even the preservation of life. "Joseph made it a law over the land of Egypt unto this day, that Pharaoh should have the fifth part of the produce of all the land, except the land of the priests: because he had saved the lives of all the people."

Moses must be regarded not only as the greatest of Jewish statesmen, but as the profoundest of all human lawgivers. He was under God the founder of a state, whose visible organization lived through fifteen centuries, outlasting every other state of antiquity; but more than this, he was the promulgator of laws and institutions which still survive, in all their power, in every civilized land beneath the sun. Aside from the fact that the legation of Moses was divine, who can explain for us this other fact, that from the wilderness of Mount Sinai, or if you please, from the banks of the Nile, there has gone forth a code of moral and civil law which still holds its unrelaxed supremacy over the world, and binds all nations with an authority which no law of democratic Sparta, or aristocratic Athens, or imperial Rome ever gained?

In contemplating his life and writings, his character and achievements, we feel as we always do in reference to Paul, that he has no equal out of the Bible, and but one in it. He stands at the head of all the men of the Old Testament, just as

Paul does at the head of all the mere men of the New. Both by the antiquity and the value of his writings entitled to take the honour of "Father of History" from Herodotus; by the superior wisdom and morality of his laws and institutions, entitled to take the palm of lawgiver from Solon, Lycurgus, Numa Pompilius, Justinian, and Alfred; by the extent, duration, and world-wide influence of the empire which he founded, entitled to take rank before Alexander or Romulus, Charlemagne or Cromwell, Napoleon or Washington; he stands forth confessedly as the greatest statesman, jurist, and civil ruler which the world has ever produced. And he stands thus alone in his political glory, because, in an important sense, the world did not produce either him or his institutions. He was not the natural and spontaneous product of the age in which he lived. Though he was versed in all the learning of the Egyptians, and though his laws were doubtless adjusted to suit existing customs, and habits, and even prejudices, still his political wisdom was not the legitimate and necessary off-shoot of the learning of Egypt. His wonderful civil, ecclesiastical, and moral code was no more the product of all existing and anterior learning, than was the manna which sustained the tribes in the desert, or the pillar of cloud and fire which led them through it. It was neither borrowed from Egypt, nor struck out from the deep meditations of a forty years' exile in the wilderness; and commentators only darken counsel by words without wisdom, when they try to trace it to any earthly origin. It was the product of Jehovah. It came down, like the manna, from heaven. It was graven on tables of stone with God's own finger. Its enacting clauses always ran, "Thus saith the Lord." And hence their sublime solitary grandeur.

Herder and Gilfillan have both expatiated, with beauty, upon the solitariness of Moses. "He was," says the latter, "the loneliest of men; lonely in his flight from Egypt—lonely while herding his flock in the wilderness—lonely while climbing Mount Sinai—lonely on the summit, and lonely when descending the sides of the hill—lonely in his death, and lonely in his burial. Even while mingling with the multitudes of Israel, he remained secluded and alone. As the glory which shone in his face insulated him, for a time, from men, so did all his life his majestic nature. He was among men, but not of them. Stern incarnation of the anger of omnipotence, his congenial companions were not Aaron, nor Joshua, nor Zipporah, but the rocks and caves of Horeb, the fiery pillar, the burning bush, the visible glory of the sanctuary, the lightning wreaths round Sinai's sullen brow, and all the other red symbols of Jehovah's presence."

To this remark we may add, that the loneliness of his life seems almost prophetical of that solitary and unapproachable grandeur in which, through all ages, his character has stood distinguished from all other men. It is singular, however, that one so unlike him as Napoleon Bonaparte should have been characterized by somewhat of the same loneliness both in his life and death—lonely though living in the midst of millions, and at last dying almost alone in the deepest solitudes of nature. The one was lonely and isolated from surrounding millions, because of constant communion with his God; the other was lonely because of his deep communings with his own selfish and ambitious heart; the one died mysteriously in the mountains in sight of the goal of all his hopes, and left a name of greatness for all generations to love and emulate; the other died on a rock in mid-ocean, foiled and disappointed in every object of his life, leaving a name of greatness for a terror and a warning.

The most sublime feature in the character of Moses, as a statesman, was his disinterestedness—his freedom from ambition and self-love. This was manifested in two forms during his whole life—his ardent love of God and his patriotic love of Israel—his zeal for God's glory and his devotion to Israel's welfare. These seemed to sink every selfish consideration from his view. These made him willing, like Paul, even to be "blotted from the Lord's book," for the good of his countrymen. There was never a patriotism higher than this. He flung away ambition, and gained a richer prize than ambition ever sought or found. He did what few mortals have ever done, he repeatedly refused the crown of empire. First, you remember, he refused to be called the son of Pharaoh's daughter, with all the treasures of Egypt. He might have stayed in Egypt, for aught that appears to the contrary, and become the founder of a new dynasty of kings. And when Pharaoh and all his hosts were dead in the Red Sea, what prevented Moses from returning and taking possession of Egypt? Surely the conqueror in this case had a crown within his reach; and there was nothing to prevent his grasping it, but his obedience to the will of Jehovah. Again, what prevented his assuming regal authority over Israel, a nation of three millions?

Says a learned writer in the Cyclopedia of Biblical Literature —"It is beyond a question, that the man who rescued the Jews from bondage, and conducted them to the land of Canaan, might, had he chosen, have kept the dominion in his own hands and transmitted a crown to his posterity." "If Washington," says he, "at this late period of human history, after the accumulating experience of above three thousand years has added its sanctions to the great law of disinterested benevolence, is held deserving of high honour, for having preferred to found a republic, rather than attempt to build up a throne; surely very unequal justice is done to Moses, if, as is too generally the case, we pass in neglect the extraordinary fact, that with supreme power in his hands, and to all appearance, scarcely any hindrance to the assumption of regal splendour, the great Hebrew patriot and legislator was content to die within sight of the promised land, a simple, unrewarded, unhonoured individual, content to do God's great work regardless of self."

III. SAUL, DAVID, AND SOLOMON.

Passing over all those centuries, in which the chosen people were governed by the Judges, in a pure Theocracy, with no King but Jehovah, let us pause a moment to contemplate the character of the three great kings, Saul, David, and Solomon, under whose reigns the Hebrew monarchy was founded, and raised to greatness amongst the nations of the earth. About a hundred years before the birth of Saul, there had been an abortive effort to establish a throne in Israel. Abimelech, a man of mean instincts and small abilities, and with nothing to commend him to favour but the accident of his being the son of a great father, Gideon—having ignominiously slain his seventy brethren, so as to be freed from every rival, had himself proclaimed a king on the plains of Shechem. It was on this occasion, that Jotham, the youngest and only surviving brother, who had escaped the massacre, appeared and delivered a parable, which has the double honour of being the earliest discourse of the kind on record, and at the same time, a just and merited sarcasm against all kingly government. He stood on the top of Mount Gerizim, and lifted up his voice and cried, and said unto them—"Hearken unto me, ye men of Shechem, that God may hearken unto you. The trees went forth on a time to anoint a king over them; and they said unto the olive-tree: Reign thou over us. But the olive tree said unto them: Should I leave my fatness, wherewith by me they honour God and man, and go to be promoted over the trees? And the trees said to the fig-tree: Come thou, and reign over us. But the fig-tree said unto them: Should I forsake my sweetness, and my good fruit, and go to be promoted over the trees? Then said the trees unto the vine: Come thou and reign over us. And the vine said unto them: Should I leave my wine, which cheereth God and man, and go to be promoted over the trees? Then said all the trees unto the bramble: Come thou and reign over us. And the bramble said unto the trees: If in truth ye anoint me king over you, then come and put your trust in my shadow; and if not, let fire come out from the bramble and devour the cedars of Lebanon." Three years of bitter experience were enough to satisfy the men of Shechem, that Abimelech was nothing better than a bramble. A three years' reign verified the parable and fulfilled the curse of Jotham. Alas! that three thousand years of hard bondage have not yet satisfied the world, that kings are for the most part only brambles, encumbering the ground and devouring the people!

The setting up of a throne in Israel was a virtual departure from the institutions of Moses, although it had been contemplated and provided for in the law as a contingency. The people were forewarned against the dangers of a crown; but at the same time the law of Moses prescribed the mode of choosing a king whenever the nation should determine to have one. It was however an abandonment of the great principle of the theocracy, and as such was highly displeasing to Jehovah. But the Jewish people, badly governed by their arbitrary and often incompetent judges, and ambitious of becoming like their great neighbours, the Egyptians and Assyrians, besought the Lord, through Samuel the prophet, that they might have a king for their earthly head and leader. Their request was granted, just as the desire for wealth and worldly prosperity is still often gratified in the individual, along with its accompanying influence, even "leanness in the soul."

The kingdom was set up in Saul of the tribe of Benjamin; at his death it was transferred to David of the tribe of Judah, and then transmitted to his son Solomon. Under their successive reigns, which extended through a period of one hundred and twenty years, the Hebrew monarchy trampled in the dust every enemy between Egypt and the Euphrates; and ruled without a rival over all the territory which lay between the kingdom of Tyre on the north, Assyria on the east, and Egypt on the south-west.

In Saul, David, and Solomon, we find a singular correspondence, and a still more singular diversity, both of character and fortunes. No three successive sovereigns ever sat on the Jewish throne more utterly unlike each other. And yet each of them reigned about forty years; each was called to the throne by Divine appointment without any apparent qualifications for the office; each was the "Lord's anointed," being set apart by a prophet of the Lord. Saul and David were both taken from the humblest walks of private life; David and Solomon were both alike in being younger sons.

The reign of Saul was a succession of wars and battles,

sometimes successful, sometimes doubtful, and at last unsuccessful and disastrous. The reign of David was an unbroken campaign of brilliant battles, decisive victories, and extended conquests. The reign of Solomon was a period of profound peace, illustrious for commerce, learning, art, agriculture, wealth, and luxury. It was the Augustan age of Jewish history. In reviewing the career of these three kings, we are forcibly reminded of a remark made, we believe, by Lord Bacon—"Some men are born great; some make themselves great; and some have greatness thrust upon them." Saul presents an example of greatness thrust upon a man, to which he proved himself utterly unequal. David was an instance of a man making himself great—great as a warrior, great as a sovereign, and great as a writer. Solomon was born great—great in all the endowments of that genius which makes the statesman, the philosopher, the poet, and the sovereign, besides the prestige of his father's great name.

The instances of a great father and a great son are exceedingly rare in history. We remember none so remarkable as this of David and Solomon. In ancient history we have the case of Philip of Macedon and his great son Alexander. Among modern statesmen we have the two illustrious Pitts of England, and the elder and younger Adams of our own country. In theology, we have the two Sherlocks of England, and likewise Edwards the father and son in this country, with the more recent case of the Alexanders, as, perhaps, the nearest examples. But probably ninety-nine hundreds of the great men of all ages have left no sons to perpetuate their glory. Whatever else may be inherited, it is clear that genius comes neither by blood nor entail.

In Saul we have a fearful illustration of the proverb, that "pride goeth before destruction and a haughty spirit before a fall." In the twelve tribes of Israel, there was not a young man so blest of God as Saul. He had every great and noble endowment personally that nature seemed able to bestow, to give the world assurance of a man. Being called and anointed of God to be the first king over the chosen people, he had a career of honour and glory set before him, not to say usefulness, such as had never before been offered to any descendent of Abraham. Yet in arrogant self-will he despised all his mercies, set all remonstrances at defiance, and over every opportunity of good rushed madly on to destruction. To the proud and the disobedient there is not a more fearful example in all the Bible. He is a true but sad type of the impenitent sinner in every age. He shows how near a man may come and yet miss the gate of heaven. His day of grace was gone, even before he died. "The Lord is departed from thee, and become thine enemy." It was an awful message to deliver from the Lord to a living man. And yet what impenitent sinner, long admonished, but still rejecting Christ, can say, that it is not true of him?

"There is a time, we know not when,
A point we know not where,
That marks the destiny of men
To glory or despair.

There is a line by us unseen
That crosses every path,
The hidden boundary between
God's patience and his wrath.

To pass that limit is to die—
To die as if by stealth:
It does not quench the beaming eye
Or pale the glow of health.

But on that forehead God has set
Indelibly a mark,
Unseen by man, for man as yet
Is blind and in the dark."

To David, as a sovereign, belongs the highest eulogium which is given to any man in the whole catalogue of Jewish kings. "He died in a good old age, full of days, riches, and honours. He did that which was right in the eyes of the Lord, and turned not aside from anything that he commanded him all the days of his life, save only in the matter of Uriah the Hittite." Of David, the Apostle Paul uses the following language, quoting the words of Samuel the prophet from the Old Testament—"To him God gave testimony, saying, I have found David, the son of Jesse, a man after mine own heart, who shall fulfil all my will." Now these words of high commendation touching David, were originally addressed to Saul at the time Jehovah took away the kingdom; and they were intended as a reproof to Saul for his repeated violations of the law. This fact will help us to understand their import. It was precisely in the character of sovereign, called to occupy the place which Jehovah had hitherto held as head of the nation, that Saul had proved himself a transgressor, a rebel, a traitor against God. And now he is informed, that one is called to the throne, who would do what he had always refused to do—he would obey God and conform to all the institutions of Moses. In this respect, David would be, and, in fact, proved himself to be, "a man after God's own heart." He often sinned personally—sinned grievously and repented bitterly as a man; but as the monarch of Jehovah's people he always obeyed the law to the very letter; so that he became a model, and his administration the standard, of all that succeeded him.

If, therefore, you have ever felt surprise at David's being called a man after God's own heart in the Bible, you should remember that he was so called, as an obedient king over Israel in contrast to the high-handed disobedience of Saul, and also that his conduct in the affair of Uriah is expressly mentioned as an exception to this high eulogium. With that exception he rigidly conformed to, and faithfully executed, all the laws of Jehovah, as laid down by Moses and expounded by the prophets.

Solomon's was a reign of peace and splendour—a golden age of glory coming after the iron, warlike age of his father. In him the Hebrew star of empire rose to its zenith. He was the grand monarch of his race—the Cæsar Augustus of that age—the Louis XIV. of all antiquity, saving only his wars. His authority was absolute, his wisdom unchallenged, his fame without a rival. As a sovereign he had no premier. He needed none. There was no power behind his throne greater than the throne; at least, none till he fell from his high estate and became the dupe of idolatrous women. He combined in his own person judicial, legislative, and executive power. He had early besought of God, as the supreme choice of his heart, that kind of wisdom which would enable him to govern a great nation; and the Almighty, approving his choice, accordingly bestowed on him that practical and administrative political wisdom which has made his name a proverb among all nations. His reign at the first, and for many years, was one of universal prosperity, happiness, and virtue, in Israel. In the end, it degenerated into luxury, effeminacy, sensuality, and apostasy from God. His ability as a man, and his glory as a monarch, which had gradually raised Israel to the pinnacle of national greatness, became, at last, the instruments and the measure of the awful depravity, guilt, and ruin, which his sin and folly brought upon himself, his house, his kingdom, and his people. He was great in his early rising; great in his noontide splendour; great in his lamentable fall. "Thus," to use the words of another, "he was on all sides, bright or black, equally and roundly great. Like a pyramid, the shadow he cast in one direction was as vast as the light he received on the other." He was at once a royal statesman, priest, poet, philosopher, and preacher; and so versatile were his talents, that in each department, he excelled every other man of his generation. To borrow an illustration from the eloquent Dr. Hamilton of London: Solomon may be called the century-blooming aloe of his race. Like this beautiful American plant, says he, nations sometimes require centuries to come to a head, to produce a magnificent flower, to give the world a genius of the first order. The ancient Jewish stock bore such a flower in Solomon, and then did not bloom again until He, who was greater than Solomon, appeared, whose name was "Wonderful." The French race, continues Dr. Hamilton, bloomed for the last time in Napoleon the Grand; and we may add that, having exhausted itself by that splendid product, we need not soon look for another. Whatever may be the present indications of another grand flower from the same root, it is manifestly too soon, and would be altogether out of place for the French stock to bloom again unless it be in Napoleon the Third.

But in these three great reigns of the founders of the Hebrew monarchy, we behold kingcraft at its best estate, we see it in its virgin purity, nearest the fountain head. And alas for it! What a commentary does this trio give us on the exercise of royal power! It brought the promising Saul to an untimely and unhonoured grave; it filled the old age of the heroic and devout David with unparalleled sorrows; and it led the once glorious Solomon down to the dust of humiliation, disappointment, and remorse. If these things were done in the green tree, what shall we expect in the dry?

IV. THE STATESMANSHIP OF AHITHOPHEL.

Before we leave this period of Jewish history, let us pause for a moment, to contemplate the character of a man of remarkable peculiarities, who held a high position, and acted an important part, in the kingdom of David. This is Ahithophel, the renowned counsellor, the man whose opinion in public affairs had come to be regarded, in all Israel, as an oracle of God. He is the only man mentioned in the Bible, as having attained a great reputation for political sagacity amongst the Jews. His name denotes "brother of foolishness;" and it is singular, that one so celebrated for political knowledge, should be so called. Perhaps, it was intended to stand as a sarcasm on that kind of statesmanship, for which he was so distinguished. Indeed, he comes nearer to our modern popular idea of a statesman, than any other man mentioned in the Bible, except perhaps his new master Absalom. During David's long reign, he seems to have been his familiar friend, probably the chief of his cabinet, his most tried and trusted privy-counsellor. When, however, he deserted David, and carried the whole weight of his influence over to the cause of the usurper, he sunk the character of statesman in that of the petty, time-serving politician. He evidently acted upon the principle, if principle it may be called, that discretion is the better part of valour, that expediency is the "higher law" of government, that there is a "tide in the affairs of men" which must be taken at the full. With the keen-scented discernment of one of our most thorough-going modern politicians, wide awake to all the signs of the times, and dead to every interest but the people's good, he abandons the aged king and his sinking cause—he throws himself into the arms of the popular idol—he goes with the multitude, just in time, as he thinks, to ride in upon, and direct, that current of public opinion which is bearing Absalom so smoothly on to glory. Who of all our popular statesmen, great and small, could have changed masters more opportunely, more skilfully!

When David heard of this defection of his wise counsellor, he was in dismay. He had no resource left except in the bare possibility, that, through Hushai's friendly aid, the counsel of Ahithophel might be defeated. He saw at once, that the cause which Ahithophel had adopted must indeed be strong, and would, in all human probability, succeed, unless his influence were, in some way, counteracted. And there can be no sort of doubt, that Absalom would have been entirely successful, had he followed this wily counsellor throughout, as he did at the beginning. Nothing could give us a stronger proof of the consummate sagacity of the man, than the events which followed, taken in connection with the remark of the sacred writer, that the "Lord had appointed to defeat Ahithophel's counsel." It would seem, there was no way to save David but to defeat this man; and there was none but a superhuman counsel that could defeat his. The success of his first measure with Absalom, and his conduct, when the second was set aside, demonstrate that he deserved the great reputation which he had won as a counsellor, and that he was furthermore the most unprincipled political manœuverer of his day.

When his advice was set aside, and the opposite policy adopted, he saw so clearly that all was lost to the cause of

Absalom, and that his own life must pay for his treason on the restoration of David, that he did not deem it necessary to wait for the result. Able to trace political causes to their remotest consequences, with the unerring precision of an old tactician, he anticipated the end of the first fatal step in this rebellion. He foresaw, and at once resolved to forestall his doom. Says the sacred historian, "When Ahithophel saw that his counsel was not followed, he saddled his ass, and arose and gat him home to his house, to his city, (Giloh,) and put his household in order, and hanged himself and died, and was buried in the sepulchre of his father." What an instance of a man's insight into human affairs and reliance upon his own judgment, that he should deliberately put himself to death in anticipation of an event so uncertain and contingent as the loss of a future and perhaps distant battle with the exiled king!

It is the first and only instance in the Old Testament of a purely voluntary and deliberate suicide. Saul and his armour-bearer had fallen on their swords in the battle of Gilboa, choosing self-destruction before captivity, and perhaps a lingering death. Samson had pulled down a building on his own head in order to destroy his enemies. And subsequently Zimri, one of the kings of Israel, to escape a worse fate, burnt the palace over his own head. But Ahithophel's suicide was different from all these, in being freely and deliberately chosen without constraint. Its only parallel in the Bible is the case of Judas Iscariot; with this difference, however, that Judas hung himself because his counsel had been followed. Dr. Kitto remarks that "Ahithophel is not probably the first man who hanged himself, but he bears the unenviable distinction of being the first whose hanging himself is recorded; and society would have little reason to complain, if all, who have since sentenced themselves to this doom, were as worthy of it as this father of self-suspenders."

In Ahithophel we have the Machiavelli of Jewish history. To him as the fountain-head might be traced the long and crowded succession of that well known order of politicians, whose prime principle is, that the end justifies the means, that all things are lawful which are expedient, and all expedient which promote self-interest. We take him as the great founder and exponent of that school of politics, and that stripe of theology, whose cardinal doctrine is "Vox populi vox Dei," whose chief study is to watch the winds of popularity, and box the compass of all opinions, and whose master stroke of policy, whether in church or state, is the "coup-d'état" of the usurper and the tyrant. He was to the Jewish state what the modern Jesuit has been to the Christian church—infallible in sagacity to foresee an end, because unprincipled and unscrupulous in the means of accomplishing it. Aside from his deliberate self-murder, when we weigh well the baseness of his treachery to his old friend, and his diabolical counsel to his son to kill his father after first publicly debauching his bed in the face of all Israel—we think we should do him no injustice to call him the Machiavelli, or the Benedict Arnold, or the Judas Iscariot, or the Jesuit General, of his times. Perhaps it would be no more than even justice to give him by turns the credit of all the four, along with that of our modern politician thrown into the bargain.

V. THE KINGS OF JUDAH AND ISRAEL.

Let us now descend the stream of the Hebrew royal succession. From the death of Solomon to the Babylonish captivity, a period of four centuries, the Jewish history is filled up with a long list of sovereigns, embracing almost every variety of character and fortune. As a punishment predicted by the Lord, for the great transgressions of Solomon, the kingdom, which he had brought to its highest glory, was rent asunder at his death, and became two independent and rival states. His son Rehoboam, almost as distinguished for political folly as the father had been for wisdom, succeeded to the throne of two of the tribes, constituting the kingdom of Judah, whose capital was Jerusalem; whilst Jeroboam, who had once been his servant, headed the rebellion of the ten tribes, and founded the kingdom of Israel, whose capital afterwards was Samaria. For our present purpose, we may group all these kings together. They furnish a fruitful and instructive theme, and doubtless the best commentary in the world on the whole theory and practice of monarchical government. They took an empire which had been won by the sword of David and compacted by the wisdom of Solomon, and in precisely fourteen generations, they could boast of having landed all that remained of it as an exile on the banks of the Tigris and the Euphrates. No royal succession ever had a more signal beginning or a more signal end. They began with the glory of Solomon, and they wound up with the Assyrian and Babylonish captivities. No kings ever had a fairer chance for greatness. No kings were ever more responsible for their own and their country's doom. No kings, as a body, ever made a more disastrous failure.

It is a little remarkable, that although the kingdom of Israel was destroyed by the Assyrians, more than a hundred years before Judah was destroyed by the Chaldeans, yet the number of kings in the two rival nations was exactly the same. Nineteen, all descendants of David, reigned in Jerusalem from

Rehoboam to the Chaldean captivity; and nineteen reigned over Israel, from Jeroboam to the Assyrian captivity, though of nine different dynasties. The kings of Judah, as a class, were better men than those of Israel. The descendants of David, for the most part, adhered, at least in form, to the worship of Jehovah; whilst those of Jeroboam and the constantly changing dynasties, with a few doubtful exceptions, worshipped the devil in almost every shape and form of the surrounding idolatry.

This great difference of longevity in the two successions, is a striking illustration of the proverb, that "bloody and deceitful men shall not live out half their days."

It would be tedious and perhaps tiresome to sketch the characters, or narrate even the most prominent actions, of these thirty-eight Jewish sovereigns in succession. We shall not attempt it. Let it suffice to point out some general characteristics belonging to the whole, or refer to a few prominent events recorded of the most remarkable individuals. One of the most noticeable facts connected with their history is its bloody, warlike character. Some reigns had well nigh converted into an immense standing army, a nation whose only true policy was peaceful agriculture. It is astonishing to read of the vast armies which these kings could muster for battle. In the first battle between the rival kingdoms, when the whole population of the Hebrew domains could not well have exceeded 5,000,000, Jeroboam led 800,000 soldiers against Abijah king of Judah, who was at the head of 400,000. King Asa had an army of 580,000; Uzziah, one of 307,000; and Jehoshaphat, one of 1,160,000 men that drew sword, ready for the field. What would become of us and our country, and of all the peaceful pursuits of agriculture and commerce, if, at the behest of one man, we had to muster to the field, and then maintain, such armies as these, in the United States? And yet the territory occupied by the twelve tribes of Israel, at their utmost extension, might be cut more than two hundred times out of the map of the United States!

Of the nineteen kings of Israel, not one is spoken of in the Bible as a good man, although some of them had special commissions from Jehovah, and many of them experienced signal deliverances at his hands, and saw repeated displays of his power and glory. The account of each one's reign either opens or closes with the laconic but sad memorial—"He did evil in the sight of the Lord." Not even Jehu, who had so much zeal for the Lord as to make a boast of it, can be claimed as an exception. Some of them were monsters of depravity and crime, leading their subjects into all manner of abominable idolatry. Such, for an example, was the weak and wicked Ahab, of whom it is said, that "he did evil above all that went before him." He was too weak to resist the wickedness of others; and at the same time, too prone to evil himself to shake off the besetting weakness and indolence of his nature. Although he had a friend in Elijah, he had a fiend in Jezebel. Blest with the most remarkable of all Israel's prophets, who was often at hand to hold him in check, and give him counsel, he was cursed with a presiding evil genius in his wife, who came as near being an incarnation of the spirit of evil as it is possible for woman to become. Her only compeer in the Bible is her daughter, the bloody Athaliah, queen of Judah, the only woman in fact who ever reigned alone on the throne of David. Of these two noted characters we have already spoken in a former work. In our own day, there are many who are almost turning the world upside down, in their efforts to produce strong-minded women, or to prove that all women ought to be strong-minded. Do these reformers forget, that the Bible, which gives us the earliest specimens of most things, has given us the first two strong-minded women on record? Who were ever stronger, in the sense of lording it over men, than Athaliah and Jezebel? They were as self-willed and probably as able-bodied, as they were strong-minded. They ruled all Israel with a rod of iron; and we doubt not, all Israel felt that they had enough of strong-minded women long before Jezebel and Athaliah were dead. They had no successors, at least in Israel.

The children of Israel had been forewarned by Samuel as to the evils of a kingly government; and all the successive dynasties that reigned over the northern kingdom seemed but to vie with each other in verifying the prediction. As we read the long dark catalogue of sin and folly from Jeroboam down to Hoshea, we may well remember the sarcastic voice of the faithful old prophet, saying—"This shall be the manner of your king: He will take your men servants, and your maid servants, and your goodliest young men, and your sheep, and your asses, and put them to his work. And ye shall cry out in that day, because of your king which ye have chosen; and the Lord will not hear you." The prophecy, of which this forms a part, was written by Samuel in a book, and laid up before the Lord, for the learning and admonition of all coming generations. Never did any prophecy receive a more exact fulfilment, both in the letter and the spirit. If it had been history instead of prophecy, it could not have drawn a more lifelike picture of kingcraft. It was exemplified in the lives of the nineteen kings of Israel, and, more or less, in most of the kings of Judah. With rare exceptions, it has been exemplified in every reigning dynasty on earth, from Saul down to the petty tyrants that still lord it over the Italian states, at Naples, and Rome. If there were nothing else on the subject, this fearful warning by Samuel would be enough to show, that the spirit of the Bible from the beginning has ever been opposed to monarchical, and friendly to Republican government. And if the lesson needed a living and overwhelming confirmation, we surely have it in the history of the house of Israel.

As for the house of Judah, some were good men; a few of them eminently pious men; but the great majority forsook the way in which David had walked, and "did evil in the sight of the Lord." Only eight out of the nineteen reigning descendants of David are spoken of as having "done that which was good;" namely, Asa, Jehoshaphat, Jehoash, Amaziah, Uzziah, Jotham, Hezekiah, and Josiah; and some of these fell into great errors. None of them ever attained to the integrity and excellence of their great ancestor. Jehoshaphat was distinguished as the greatest conqueror, after David, who ever sat upon the Jewish throne; Hezekiah for the remarkable prolongation of his life for fifteen years in answer to his prayer; and Josiah for his youthful piety, his great reformation, and his early, much lamented death. He ascended the throne at an earlier age than any of his race except one; and he was the only one of them all who perished in battle.

The first of the nineteen, Rehoboam, may be regarded as the earliest asserter of the doctrines of royal prerogative and the divine right of kings, to be found in history. Absolutism never had a fitter representative than this, its first propounder. He was the son, and, for aught we know to the contrary, the only son and heir of the great Solomon. 'Tis strange, indeed, that no other children should be mentioned, if others existed

The probability is, from the silence of the Bible, that none existed. Was it because heaven so frowned upon Solomon's great sin in violating the law of marriage, that at his death, the only living offspring of his thousand wives and concubines, was the feeble and foolish Rehoboam? So it would seem. This sole son of the wise man, and heir of all his glory, felt that as he was born to command, so all Israel was simply born to obey. He claimed what neither Saul, David, nor Solomon, ever dreamed of claiming—absolute power for the throne, passive obedience for the people. When he assumed the crown, and the people, petitioning for a redress of grievances, promised to serve him, if he would relax somewhat of the rigour of his father's reign, he spurned all such conditions and constitutional compacts, rejected the advice of all his father's old counsellors, and, in a tone of defiance and insult which the fabled "king of gods and men" might have envied, and which possibly the Stuarts of England may have copied, returned an answer, after three days' deliberation, in the following words—"My father made your yoke heavy, and I will add to your yoke; my father also chastised you with whips, but I will chastise you with scorpions." Alas! how soon was the prediction of good old Samuel brought to pass—that their king would come to look upon all the people as his "sheep and his asses!" Alas! poor human nature! who could have believed that a man, whose grandfather had been taken from "following the ewes great with young" on the sheep-walks of Bethlehem, could have grown to this height of imperial majesty so soon? Who could have believed that a man forty years old, unless he were a natural-born fool, could have been guilty of the amazing and stupendous arrogance, not to say infatuation, of thus addressing a great nation, whose minds were familiar with the mighty deeds of David and the political wisdom of Solomon? We need not wonder at the result. That speech cost him the sceptre of the ten tribes; and but for their loyalty to the name of David, it would have cost him the loss of the other two also. If the world needed an argument against the doctrine of polygamy, it need not go beyond Rehoboam, the feeblest of sons and the most foolish of kings. He is the legitimate product of the grandest system of polygamy the world has ever seen; and both as a man and a king he was an abortion. So was it with the children of Mohammed. So is it with the offspring of the Mormon prophets. Their harems are filled with women, the graveyards with their children—"'Tis nature's argument against polygamy."

The worst character, by far, amongst all these kings was Manasseh, whose father, Hezekiah, was one of the best. It is recorded that he filled Jerusalem with innocent blood, and caused the people of Judah and Jerusalem to do worse than the heathen, whom the Lord drove out, had ever done. He sinned with a high hand and an impious spirit. He gloried in his rebellion and iniquity. At last his pride was humbled. Being taken captive by the king of Assyria, he was carried into exile, where he repented in dust and ashes of all his past misdeeds, found favour and forgiveness in the sight of God, and was at length restored to his throne and kingdom at Jerusalem. He was a true penitent, and, like Saul of Tarsus, spent the residue of his life in the service of the Lord. He stands as one of the most signal trophies of that Divine redeeming grace, which sometimes snatches "the brand from the burning," makes the wrath of man to praise God, turns the persecutor into an apostle, and, out of publicans and sinners, chooses the vessels of mercy and the heirs of glory.

Leaving out of view Josiah, who died so young, we may regard Hezekiah as the best and most pious of all these kings of Judah. With a brief notice of a remarkable event which occurred in his reign, we must close our present sketch of them. It illustrates at once the piety of the monarch, the courage of his great prophet and minister—Isaiah, and the protecting providence of God over those that fear him.

Sennacherib, the haughty despot of Assyria and conqueror of all the surrounding nations, having overrun Israel, invades the kingdom of Judah, and, appearing before Jerusalem, threatens the destruction of the city, in the most arrogant and insulting terms. Thus far nothing has withstood his arms, and there is no fear of God or regard for man, in his heart, to restrain him. To all outward human appearance, the doom of the holy city, so long impending, seems now sealed. What earthly power can save the kingdom of Judah from the assault of a victorious army of 185,000 veteran soldiers, whose chief captain, in proud, defiant scorn, to equalize the combat, offers his feeble foe as many horses for the battle as he can set riders on? The good king Hezekiah is in dismay. He resorts himself to the prayer-hearing God; and, at the same time, sends a messenger to his faithful counsellor, Isaiah, to inform him of the peril, and lay before him all the blasphemous, reproachful words of the powerful invader. Isaiah, with a courage no doubt founded upon the message which he had received from Jehovah, and with an unshaken confidence in the word of the Lord, does not deem it necessary to go in person, but reassures the heart of the king, with a message, in these decisive words—"Thus saith the Lord concerning the king of Assyria, He shall not come into this city, nor shoot an arrow there, nor come before it with shields, nor cast a bank against it. By the way that he came, by the same shall he return, and shall not come into this city, saith the Lord. For I will defend this city to save it, for mine own sake, and for my servant David's sake."

Such was the sublime, laconic, authoritative prediction. You remember its awful, its extraordinary, its swift fulfilment. The decree was hardly announced from the eternal throne on high, ere it went forth for speedy and summary execution. The result is all told in two verses. "Then the angel of the Lord went forth, and smote in the camp of the Assyrians, an hundred, and fourscore, and five thousand: and when they arose early in the morning, behold they were all dead corpses. So Sennacherib, the king of Assyria, departed and returned to Nineveh." He returned alone, shorn of his army, bereft of his power and glory. He returned to fall by the hand of assassination. But all that vast army, whose conquering march had made the nations tremble, whose proud chieftain, Rabshakeh, had defied and blasphemed the God of Israel, was swept away in one night as with the very besom of destruction.

"Like the leaves of the forest when summer is green,
That host with their banners at sunset were seen;
Like the leaves of the forest when autumn hath blown,
That host on the morrow lay withered and strown.

For the angel of death spread his wings on the blast,
And breathed in the face of the foe as he passed;
And the eyes of the sleepers waxed deadly and chill,
And their hearts but once heaved and for ever grew still."

What a lesson to haughty ambition did that memorable morning present! what a homily for kings and conquerors was revealed in that ancient scene of death and silence! With what a voice of warning did it whisper to the hearts of all the great ones of the earth—"Thus far shalt thou go, and here shall thy proud waves be stayed!" Ah! more than once since that morning, has the same admonitory voice from God been sounded in the ears of haughty ambition. Who has not read of the mighty conqueror of modern Europe, whose young day-dream it was, to found an empire in the east, that should eclipse all the great empires of antiquity, and failing in that, next thought to make himself sole master of the nations of Europe—who, claiming to be invincible in battle, went to Russia in 1812, with the boast that destiny was his own? And who does not remember, how that grand army, whose watchword was glory, whose fiat was victory, whose idol-god was their Emperor, and whose march nothing human was able to withstand—at last perished in the snows, as silently, as hopelessly, and as fearfully, as though an angel of the Lord had smitten them in the night watches? Verily, the kings of the earth may take counsel, and the nations rage, but there is One that sitteth in the heavens, before whose throne they are all as the small dust of the balance. By the frosts of one winter, He taught the proud conqueror of destiny a lesson which man had been unable to teach him—that there was a power in the universe greater than Bonaparte. God had spoken to him, as he did to the king of Assyria. And like Sennacherib, shorn of his army, and returning to Nineveh to die, so did Napoleon to the theatre of his former glory; not indeed to die, but to outlive all his greatness; to struggle on against destiny, but no more to conquer. From that hour the sun-dial of destiny was going down against him, never more to be reversed. All his struggles—all his gigantic efforts to reverse it, were in vain. God, who had raised him up, and endowed him with such unusual powers, uttered his voice as he did of old: "Thus far shalt thou go, and here shall thy proud waves be stayed."

We know it is the fashion now in certain quarters to eulogize the character of Napoleon, to paint him in the most gorgeous colours as the very apostle and high priest of liberty, to make him out almost as much a saint as he was a hero. We admire his heroism, we accord to him the highest genius of the statesman and the military leader. But with the facts of history before us, we can go no farther. We have no sympathy with any thing belonging to the moral character of Napoleon. We believe that the key to his whole life and character is found in four words—*supreme selfishness and ambition.* The facts of history may be set in a false light; beautiful pictures of virtue may be drawn from a prolific imagination; eloquent apologists may plead the stern law of necessity for his very crimes; the tyrant's plea may be urged against the law of God and nature, to justify the worse than immolation of the best of wives—but all will not do; the judgment of mankind will still stand. The moral sense of the world and the facts of history are against Napoleon, in spite of all the eulogies. Much as the world admires his genius, it condemns the man. No fine writing can ever save such a character from that verdict of condemnation, which both history and the instinctive virtue of mankind, are compelled to pronounce against it. God forbid that it ever should! All such vindicators of fallen greatness are labouring in vain. Theirs is a hopeless and a thankless task. No bad man can be written into moral greatness, any more than a good man can be written down. It is no more possible to reverse the sentence of condemnation which has gone out through all the world against Napoleon, than it is to reverse that evil destiny which pursued him from the divorce of Josephine to the retreat from Russia, and from that to the defeat at Waterloo, and from that to his grave on St. Helena.

The history of Napoleon is a grand illustration of the doctrine of the compensatory justice of Divine Providence. The conscience of the world demands that such a career of selfish ambition should have just such a close. He reaped what he had sowed. What is called "poetic justice," but more properly the moral law of the universe, was vindicated, when the repudiator of Josephine became the exile at Helena. All history is full of such vindications, because all history is full of the justice of God. The history of the kings of Judah and Israel illustrates the same great doctrine on every page. No part of the sacred oracles, when deeply studied, is more interesting and instructive. We might have devoted a whole chapter to the illustration of these royal characters. But it is enough. No careful reader can fail to see, in this history, that eternal and immutable law of God, which connects virtue with happiness on the one hand, and sin with misery on the other. Every reign of justice, wisdom, virtue, and obedience, leads to peace, prosperity, and national greatness. Every career of sin and folly ends in degradation and woe. Through all these pages there is heard a voice, saying: "The way of the transgressor is hard"—"There is no peace to the wicked, saith my God." But here and there another voice is heard—here and there a traveller is found, crying: "Wisdom's ways are pleasantness, and all her paths are peace."

This history, also, from Jeroboam to Hoshea, and from Rehoboam to Zedekiah, strikingly displays the equity and mercy of the Divine character. We behold the condescension and forbearance of God, in waiting so long, giving so many warnings, holding out so many opportunities for repentance to his rebellious children. And then at last, when "there was no remedy"—when mercies multiplied only led to more transgressions—we behold the veracity and the justice of God for ever vindicated, in all those fearful judgments which made Jerusalem a desolation, and sent her daughters to weep in captivity under the willows of Babylon.

VI. HAMAN AND MORDECAI.

From this long and diversified panorama of Jewish sovereigns, which we have barely glanced at, let us now turn to a very different and far distant scene; to that group of characters which is revealed to us in the book of Esther. The Bible history, as it pursues its onward course, opens many a magnificent vista into the antique oriental world, now on the right hand and now on the left. Such an opening is found in the book of Esther. It introduces us to all the interior regal splendours of Shushan, the winter palace and capital of the Persian monarchs; it ushers us into the very presence of queen Esther and Ahasuerus the Great. We are permitted to look in upon the court of that luxurious and haughty despot, who, as there is good reason to believe, was none other than the celebrated Xerxes of classic story, that led his millions to the invasion of Greece. It is not our purpose however to expatiate upon the pomp and power of these oriental despots, as they are set forth in the sacred pages, in the classic historians, and in those wonderful monuments which have so recently been exhumed by Layard and others, to bear witness to the former magnificence and glory of Assyria and Persia. Recent researches have brought to light a degree of civilization and refinement in those great empires of antiquity, which, while it confirms the historical truth, both of the Bible and the Grecian writers, is marvellous in the eyes of this nineteenth century.

For the present, however, we turn to the records of the Assyrian, Chaldean, and Medo-Persian empires, not to gaze upon the regal grandeur of their monarchs, but to mark the strange vicissitudes and fortunes of some of their statesmen. Let us notice, first, that remarkable contrast, in the character and destiny of two great rival statesmen, who are brought to view in the book of Esther. These are Haman and Mordecai, who were successively the privy counsellors and prime ministers of Ahasuerus. They were both foreigners at the court of Ahasuerus, the one a Jew, the other an Amalekite. Born of rival races, inheriting all the bitter prejudices and animosities which those races entertained towards one another, and sharers in a common captivity and exile, they nevertheless had each, in turn, the good fortune to rise to the highest post of honour and responsibility in the Persian Empire. Great must have been their natural abilities, great their inborn energy, and great their skill in public affairs, thus, in despite of all the disadvantages of a foreign birth and education, to ascend to a position nearest to the throne of that great empire, of which Cyrus had been the recent founder. But so it was; and we need not detain you to repeat the familiar story of their alternate promotions and triumphs.

But let us consider, a moment, the very different orders of greatness, which characterized the career of the two rival statesmen. In Haman, we behold one of the earliest and most memorable examples of the statesman of ambition—that vaulting ambition which "o'erleaps itself and falls on th' other side." In his sudden exaltation, his accumulated honours, and his disastrous fall, we behold a vivid realization of the life and doom of many a restless, aspiring, insatiable politician. He was a man who would have all or nothing; who would gain the whole world at the risk of losing his own soul; who in grasping for more than he needed, lost all. His creed was that of the horse-leech, "Give, Give," and he was not satisfied, till he had drunk in the last drop of human applause. When he had reached what had long appeared to him the pinnacle of human glory—when he stood beside the throne of the great king, as lord of all his counsellors, and premier of one hundred and twenty-seven provinces, still he said not, "It is enough"—he was wrathful and unhappy, because there was one man, and only one, in all the kingdom, who would not bow the knee before him. He went home to his family and told his wife of all the glory of his riches, and the multitude of his children, and all the things wherein the king had promoted him above his princes and servants. "Yet," said he, "all this availeth me nothing, so long as I see Mordecai the Jew sitting at the king's gate." His soul was filled with thoughts of vengeance on the man who would not join the crowd in exalting the greatness of Haman. Too proud to wreak his vengeance on an insignificant individual, he determined to do it, by wholesale, in the extermination of the hated race of Mordecai. You remember with what success. You remember how the Providence of God, through the instrumentality of Mordecai and queen Esther, not only defeated all his plans, but reserved for him the very death which he had prepared for another, and placed his intended victim on the seat of power from which he fell.

In Mordecai, on the other hand, we behold the statesman of patriotism, consistency, and public virtue. In him we behold no mere politician and courtier who lives for himself, but a useful public servant, ready to do all, even to sacrifice all for the welfare of his people. In all the stages of his promotion, as a private citizen of Shushan, as a ruler sitting in the king's gate, and as prime minister over the empire, we see in Mordecai, a man of fearless integrity—a man of steady, consistent purpose, who, planting himself on truth and virtue, always acts from principle; who, seeing his end from the beginning, conscious of the purity of his motives, and confident of ultimate success, is willing patiently to trust in God, do the right, and abide his time. Such a statesman has ambition too; but it is ambition to excel in deeds of usefulness to his country and his fellow men. He seeks to rise; but by first deserving to rise. He seeks to rise, not by pulling others down, but by fairly climbing that ladder, on which others have ascended before him, and on which others may still ascend with him.

Haman's ruling passsion was self-love, the thirst for glory, the lust of power, the idolatry of human applause. It was that Diotrephesian spirit, which loved to have the pre-eminence, and had "rather reign in hell than serve in heaven." He exemplified the remark of one of our own great statesmen—"Possessing none of that virtue which raises mortals to the skies, he cherished only that spirit which would drag angels down." It is well for the world that the triumphing of the wicked is short. It is well for the world, that such men as Haman, being in honour, cannot abide there for ever. He fell a victim to his own envy and ambition; and his fall is a warning to the statesmen of every age and every land. In that righteous retribution of Providence which placed upon his rival's head the glory he had lost, and meted out to him the doom which he had prepared for Mordecai, we find a fitting text indeed for all those solemn admonitions, which the great poet hath put into the dying lips of Cardinal Wolsey:—

"Cromwell, I charge thee, fling away ambition,
By that sin fell the angels; how can man, then,
The image of his Maker, hope to win by it?
Love thyself last! Cherish those hearts that hate thee!
Corruption wins not more than honesty!
Still in thy right hand carry gentle peace,
To silence envious tongues! Be just and fear not!
Let all the ends thou aim'st at, be thy country's,
Thy God's, and Truth's! Then, if thou fall'st, O Cromwell!
Thou fall'st a blessed martyr."

VII. NEHEMIAH, EZRA, AND DANIEL.

But let us notice three other distinguished names in this part of Jewish history, Nehemiah, Ezra, and Daniel. In Nehemiah, "the Tirshatha," or civil governor of Judah, under King Artaxerxes, we have another example, like Mordecai, of the great and good statesman. All the ends he aimed at were his country's, his God's, and truth's. In their behalf he was not afraid to venture all; and for them he did, in fact, make large and liberal sacrifices, both in service and in money; and he did not lose his reward. Though living in perilous times, and opposed by bitter enemies, he had the glory, more than any other single man, except Ezra, of raising his fallen country and his captive race, from the dust. He had risen to high distinction at the Persian court; he stood in the most intimate relations of confidence and honour with the great king; he was blest with every thing, in the way of wealth and luxury, that heart could wish or ambition aspire to. And yet he was not happy. He had heard the sad tale of Zion's desolations.

He had continual sorrow of heart for the distant and downtrodden walls of Jerusalem. Being a faithful and devoted servant of the Most High, and impelled by an ardent and heroic patriotism to join the little band of his countrymen, who had long ago returned from the captivity, and after hard struggling had already rebuilt the temple, he besought the Persian monarch for a commission to go and rebuild the walls of Jerusalem. The request was granted; and, in a short time, he appeared at Jerusalem, attended by captains of the army and horsemen, and letters from the king, giving him full power to do all that his heart desired for the city of his fathers. Of the joyful reception which he met at the hands of his countrymen, and of the great work which he accomplished, in rebuilding the walls, in reforming abuses, in reinstating the law of Moses and the great festivals in the affections of the people, we have a full account in the book which bears his name.

Ezra may also be ranked on the list of great Jewish statesmen. Although he was professionally a priest and a scribe of the law, being a descendant of Aaron, yet he was to all intents and purposes a jurist, a legislator, and a practical civilian. He held somewhat the same relation to the Jews of the restoration, as that which Moses had held to those of the Exodus from Egypt. He was their leader, the great expounder of their laws, and the virtual restorer of all their civil and ecclesiastical institutions after the captivity. He, more than any other man, by his practical expositions of Scripture, and by his additions to its canon, impressed upon the nation that character which it bore down to the coming of the Messiah. He must have stood high in the estimation of his countrymen, both at Babylon and Jerusalem, and high in the favour and confidence of the Persian monarch, before he received his commission to visit the Holy City. We find him invested with plenary powers and laden with rich treasures, by the king, leading the second great expedition of Jews to Palestine, about seventy-five years after the first expedition had gone up under Zerubbabel, and about thirteen years before he was followed by Nehemiah. During all these latter years, until the arrival of Nehemiah, he must have been both the civil and ecclesiastical head of the nation. We have a record of a part, and probably a very small part, of the signal services which he rendered his country, in the book which bears his name, and which was, no doubt, written by him. Aided by the patriotic civil governor Nehemiah, he accomplished a great work, in rooting out the old abuses, and inaugurating the worship of Jehovah in accordance with the letter and spirit of his laws. Few names in Jewish history are held in higher honour than that of Ezra.

But the most illustrious name to be found in all these later annals of Jewish statesmanship, is confessedly that of Daniel, who flourished in Babylon during the captivity, long before Ezra and Nehemiah were born. We have referred to him once already as a model for young men, and we may have occasion to speak of him again hereafter, as a prophet of God; it is only in the character of a statesman, that we need to contemplate him now. After Moses, there is not a statesman in all the Bible, more distinguished for his virtues, his varied accomplishments, and his long life of usefulness and honour. It may be truly said of him, that "heaven gave him length of days, and he filled them up with deeds of greatness." For a man of peace, his career was remarkably diversified by great events and great trials. Descended from the royal race of his country, carried away to Babylon when but a boy, in the first year of the captivity, trained up for the service of an idolatrous court, and educated in all the learning of the Chaldees, yet from his very childhood maintaining a good conscience, and holding fast the faith of his fathers—he had the good fortune to come off conqueror in every conflict, to live through the whole seventy years of the captivity, and under two successive dynasties, to act an important part in the administration of the empire. Endowed with the wisdom of a statesman, the highest gifts of an orator, the moral courage of a hero, and the extraordinary inspiration of a prophet of God, he passed safely and triumphantly through all the seductions of a luxurious court, and all the machinations which envy and ambition had laid for his ruin; and he had the remarkable distinction—probably unparalleled in the annals of statesmanship—of keeping a clear conscience, and yet standing nearest to the throne in the reigns of Nebuchadnezzar, Belshazzar, Darius, and the great Cyrus.

By Nebuchadnezzar he was exalted, while yet a young man, to the highest post of honour in civil and ecclesiastical affairs; he became ruler of the whole province of Babylon, and chief governor of all its wise men—that is to say, premier of the state, and primate of the sacerdotal order—a position of greater responsibility than Joseph ever held in Egypt. By Belshazzar he was proclaimed third ruler of the kingdom, for services similar to those which he had before rendered to Nebuchadnezzar. By Darius he was promoted, after his deliverance from the lions' den, to be first of the three presidents of the empire. And last of all, as giving perhaps the strongest evidence of his integrity as a man and his wisdom as a statesman, we find him, at an advanced old age, high in the favour of the great Cyrus. His history, as narrated in the book which bears his name, brings his prophetic visions down to the third year of Cyrus; and it is there expressly stated, that "this Daniel prospered in the reign of Darius, and in the reign of Cyrus the Persian."

He combined in one the three styles of human greatness—he was born great, he had greatness thrust upon him, and he made himself great. Born with the highest endowments of genius, exalted to the grandeur of the Chaldean and Medo-Persian empires, he made himself great by a long life of active virtue and usefulness. He was great, because he was useful in the service both of God and man; and he was thus useful, because he was good and holy. He had, what few men have ever received—even a testimony from heaven that he was a man "greatly beloved."

There are few characters in the book of God, more perfect, and more delightful to contemplate, than Daniel's. There is no recorded flaw in his history. There is no drawback to our satisfaction, as we follow it, in the way of failure or disaster. It is a delightful picture of piety and principle winning their way to glory. All is well here, and all ends well. Vice, and pride, and power, all succumb before the sublime majesty of one humble, God-fearing man. Virtue triumphs; worldly wisdom is defeated; ambition misses its prize; malice falls into the pit which its own hands had digged; and the right always comes out right and victorious in the life of Daniel. Truth is sometimes stranger than fiction; and certainly, no novelist ever drew from the realms of imagination, any human character which so admirably vindicates the success of virtue in the world, and shows that wisdom's ways are pleasantness and peace, so fully, as is done in the career of Daniel. He stood before kings; he stood before magicians and counsellors; he stood before vindictive conspirators against his life; he stood before wild beasts; he stood for seventy years and more in the presence of dark idolaters, and despots, and blasphemers. But though he had to stand so long, and comparatively alone, he stood firm, and won the high approval of earth and heaven.

> "Servant of God, well done! well hast thou fought
> The better fight, who single hast maintained,
> Against revolted multitudes, the cause
> Of truth, in word mightier than they in arms."

VIII. CYRUS AND THE GREAT KINGS.

There are no chapters in the Bible more wonderful and attractive than those which tell the brief but graphic story of the great kings of the East. We have not space to delineate their characters now; still, a complete view of our subject requires, at least, a passing reference to the chief of them. Both the Providence and the moral government of God, over the nations, were signally illustrated in the history of these oriental rulers. It is important, that all men should observe one grand fact which is brought to light in all this history—that while Jehovah was revealing himself to Israel, and governing Israel as his chosen people, he did not leave himself without a witness to the rest of the world. He was constantly making himself known as the "God of heaven," the only "living and true God," in the great centres of human civilization; he revealed himself, by mighty signs and wonders, to the great governors of the eastern nations. As he did in Egypt, so did he in the Assyrian, Chaldean, and Medo-Persian empires, which successively ruled the ancient world. And he was then but evolving the great principles, and recording them in the Bible, by which he continues, to our day, to govern the nations of the earth. Hence, for all statesmen, and governors, and men in high authority, the history of these kings is one of the most instructive in the Bible.

We might refer to the remarkable manner in which the Almighty made himself known to the men of Nineveh, whose king and people humbled themselves, and repented, in sackcloth and ashes, at the preaching of Jonah. We have already referred to the extraordinary judgment which overwhelmed the proud host of Sennacherib, the greatest king and conqueror, that ever sat upon the Assyrian throne. We might recite the story of the mysterious "hand-writing on the wall," and the doom of the lordly and voluptuous king of Babylon. No page of Holy Writ possesses a more awful tragic interest, than the account of "Belshazzar's Feast." Poetry and painting, oratory and high art, in every age, have put forth all their powers in the effort, to depict, or re-enact the scenes of that last fearful night in Babylon. Then was it emblazoned before all the world and all the universe, that judgment follows upon the heels of transgression, that iniquity was "weighed in the balances and found wanting." We might again portray all the dramatic interest of that other eventful and memorable night in the history of Darius the Median, when no sound of music was heard in the palace, when the king fasted, and was sleepless, till the morning light, when the tabernacles of the wicked were filled with shouts of profane and premature joy, and Daniel was left to lift up his calm, confiding, courageous voice of prayer in the lions' den. Who has not waited with the sleepless king for the long dawn of such a morning? What child has not listened, with breathless interest, to the loud lamentable cry of the trembling king, as he hastens to the cave—"O Daniel, servant of the living God, is thy God, whom thou servest continually, able to deliver thee from the lions?" And who has not rejoiced with him, to catch the first sublime accents of the God-fearing prophet, bursting forth in triumphant vindication of the power of his God over all flesh—"O king, live for ever My God hath sent his angel and hath shut the lions' mouths, that they have not hurt me; forasmuch as before him innocency was found in me; and also before thee, O king, have I done no hurt." After such a night, and such a vindication, well might the king execute judgment on all the enemies of Daniel, and issue a decree, that all the nations and races of his vast empire should fear the God of Daniel. We might, in like manner, set before you the gigantic career of Nebuchadnezzar, the "Lucifer" of Isaiah's prophecy, the destroyer of nations, the despoiler of Jerusalem and the Holy Temple, by far the greatest king and conqueror of all the Chaldean monarchs—"the man that made the earth to tremble, that did shake the kingdoms; that made the world as a wilderness, and destroyed the cities thereof." "Thou hast said in thine heart, I will ascend into heaven, I will exalt my throne above the stars of God, I will ascend above the heights of the clouds, I will be like the Most High." We might tell, but it would be long to tell, all the strange fortunes and changes that passed over this mighty monarch—how he conquered the world—how he set up and put down kings—how he built and adorned "great Babylon" by the might of his power and for the honour of his majesty—how he was warned by dreams and visions and voices from heaven—how in the pride of his heart he exalted himself against Jehovah, after being the executioner of his judgments—how he was driven from the abodes of men, bereft of his reason, shorn of all his glory, his throne exchanged for the grass of the field, his proud palace for a dwelling place with the brute—how after seven years of unparalleled degradation, he lifted up his eyes to heaven in prayer, and was restored to reason, and to all his power —and how at last, an humbled and altered man, he made a public decree and proclaimed to all nations what signs and wonders the Most High had wrought, to show that "his kingdom is an everlasting kingdom, and his dominion from generation to generation." Verily, if we look for wonders, there is not a more wonderful character in history than Nebuchadnezzar; and in all the annals of human literature, saving only the story of the Cross, there is not a more wonderful chapter than the fourth of Daniel.

But of Cyrus—the great and just-minded Cyrus—the chosen instrument of Divine Providence—the restorer of Israel—the founder of the Medo-Persian empire—the subject of Isaiah's prophecies more than a hundred years before he was born, and the hero of more than one Greek historian—of Cyrus what shall we say? We did have much to say, but must forbear saying it now. What we have to say, shall be mainly from the word of God. Heathen as he was, by birth and education, he has a glory far higher than that of Socrates; he has a name, and an honourable name, recorded in the book of God. His character, his extraordinary career, and his significant name, were all set forth in the prophecy of Isaiah, not only a century before he was born, but while as yet the Persians, both as a race and nation, had not emerged from their insignificance and obscurity. He is called by name, the "servant" of the Lord; he is described as a "righteous man," raised up by the Lord for a special purpose, and he is denominated "the anointed of the Lord."

In the history of Cyrus, as revealed in the Bible, we may find, as we do in many analogous cases, a complete solution of the often disputed question, as to whether great men make great circumstances, or great circumstances create great men. It is not that great men are always the creatures on the one hand, or the creators on the other, of great events and circumstances. But the true theory is, that the Almighty shapes the two so as to meet each other; so that whenever he has a great work to be done in the world, he, at the proper time and place, raises up and qnalifies a great agent to perform it. This one truth is at least as old as the book of Daniel and the age of Cyrus—"The heavens do rule"—There is a God who governs in the affairs of men.

But let us cite two passages from the sacred oracles, and leave this remarkable man, who, for aught we know, may have been the greatest uninspired man of all antiquity—the founder, certainly, of the greatest empire that had existed in the world at his day.

The first is the proclamation for the restoration of the Jews, issued in the first year of his reign, as recorded in the first chapter of Ezra, in which he fully acknowledges himself as the agent of Jehovah—"Thus saith Cyrus, king of Persia, The Lord God of heaven hath given me all the kingdoms of the earth; and he hath charged me to build him an house at Jerusalem which is in Judah. Who is there among you of all his people? His God be with him, and let him go up to Jerusalem which is in Judah, and build the house of the Lord God of Israel (he is the God) which is in Jerusalem. And whosoever remaineth in any place where he sojourneth, let the men of his place help him with silver, and with gold, and with goods, and with beasts, besides the free-will offering for the house of God that is in Jerusalem."

The second is the beautiful and specific prophecy in the

forty-fifth chapter of Isaiah, under which Cyrus was led to make this remarkable decree, and which, no doubt, had been made known to him by Daniel, as soon as he took the kingdom. "The Lord saith of Cyrus, He is my shepherd, and shall perform all my pleasure; even saying to Jerusalem, Thou shalt be built; and to the temple: Thy foundation shall be laid. Thus saith the Lord to his anointed, to Cyrus, whose right hand I have holden, to subdue nations before him; and I will loose the loins of kings to open before him the two-leaved gates, and the gates shall not be shut. I will go before thee, and make the crooked places straight; I will break in pieces the gates of brass, and cut in sunder the bars of iron. And I will give thee the treasures of darkness, and hidden riches of secret places, that thou mayest know that I, the Lord, which call thee by thy name, am the God of Israel. For Jacob, my servant's sake, and Israel mine elect, I have even called thee by thy name. I have surnamed thee, though thou hast not known me. I am the Lord, and there is none else, there is no God besides me; I girded thee though thou hast not known me: that they may know from the rising of the sun, and from the west, that there is none besides me. I am the Lord, and there is none else. I form the light and create darkness; I make peace and create evil. I, the Lord, do all these things. I have made the earth and created man upon it: I, even my hands, have stretched out the heavens, and all their hosts have I commanded. I have raised him up in righteousness, and I will direct all his ways: he shall build my city, and he shall let go my captives, not for price nor reward, saith the Lord of hosts."

IX. KINGS AND RULERS IN THE NEW TESTAMENT.

The completeness of our survey requires that we should not wholly omit the kings and rulers that figure on the pages of the New Testament. Still we shall not find much that should detain us long. All the kings and princes, whose names are recorded in the New Testament, both Jewish and Pagan, are introduced there incidentally. They never form the main subject even of a single chapter, hardly of a verse of Scripture. Some of them had the title of Great. They were great in the world's esteem; and great in their own. It is instructive to notice, how small they appear (though there is no sort of effort made to dwarf them) when measured by the New Testament standard of character. They all sink into utter insignificance by the mere force of contact and contrast with Him, who, without any of the outward trappings of greatness, was the truly great—the King of kings and the Lord of lords.

It is remarkable that, of all the kings, princes, and civil rulers, mentioned in the New Testament (and the number is not small), not one is deserving of our commendation. If we except Festus and the two comparatively unknown Roman deputies, Gallio and Sergius Paulus, of the book of Acts, there is not one who was a good man, even on the lowest pagan or Jewish standard. Sergius Paulus is the only one that we ever read of as being converted. Felix once trembled under Paul's preaching, and Agrippa was almost persuaded. But that was all; none of them ever embraced the gospel. On the contrary, almost the whole of them were remarkable for cruelty and crime. Some of their names have become the very proverbs of infamy, as Herod and Nero. There is hardly a group of characters to be found in the records of history, who, taken altogether, are more intensely dark, and unrelieved by any trait of nobleness or virtue, than the kings and rulers of the New Testament. They are the worst of Jews and the meanest of Gentiles. They were the most depraved specimens of human nature, in an age when human nature had reached its lowest degradation. They were the efflorescence of a society which was depraved to the bottom and universally corrupt. They fulfilled, to the letter, all that Samuel had predicted of kingcraft—showed what it could do, and what it would become, when left to its legitimate and unchecked growth. And we could not ask for a keener satire on all the high pretences of monarchy and the blood royal, than that, in such a book as the New Testament, their claim should be represented by a Jewish Herod and a Roman Nero.

In the foreground of this dark picture stand the Herods. There are four of this name mentioned in the New Testament; the first Herod called the Great, the founder of the dynasty, an Idumean by birth, who, by aid of the Romans, had won his way to supreme power, and was king of Judea at the birth of our Saviour, and thought to destroy him by murdering all the young children at Bethlehem: the second, his son Herod Antipas, who was tetrarch of Galilee, and who, at the instigation of the wicked Herodias, his sister-in-law and unlawful wife, beheaded John the Baptist as a tribute of admiration for Salome's fine dancing, fit honour for such accomplishment! the third, his nephew Herod Agrippa, grandson of Herod the Great, who, as is stated in the twelfth chapter of the Acts, having slain the Apostle James, brother of John, with the sword, was about to murder Peter also, but was prevented by the hand of God, and who at last, for his great impiety, was smitten of an angel, and eaten up of worms; and the fourth, his son, king

Agrippa, before whom Paul preached with such power, that he said, "Almost thou persuadest me to be a Christian," and yet was so far from being either a Christian, a virtuous Jew, or even a decent Pagan, that he was, at the time, living in incest with his sister Bernice. It strikingly illustrates the style of Scripture history that such characters as these are set before us, only by the briefest possible statement of their deeds. Without one word of declamation or indignant denunciation, or even mention of the many other crimes and follies of these men, as related by the Jewish historians, they simply narrate facts—and only those particular facts which belonged to the matters of which they were treating. Thus we hear of the crimes of the Herods only incidentally, as they were connected with the history of Jesus, of John the Baptist, of Peter, James, and Paul. They state no other facts, they make no inferences as to character, they pass no judgments. But this is enough. With this alone, even aside from all those confirmations derived from Josephus and other writers, we are at no loss to understand the character of the Herods. The wholesale massacre at Bethlehem, the cold-blooded murder of John, the slaughter of James, and imprisonment of Peter—these were the true exponents of the heart and life of the perpetrator. So that this Herodean family may be regarded as a fair representative of their age and country—reflecting at once the highest culture of the times, conjoined with the most degraded state of moral corruption.

Next in this group of official power stand the three Roman Governors of Judea—Pontius Pilate, Portius Festus. and Felix. Festus, considering the times in which he lived, may be regarded as at least a respectable heathen, and, as a Roman governor, somewhat disposed to act the part of justice. At any rate, there is nothing impeaching his character in the sacred history. But the other two, Pilate and Felix, can stand before us in no other character, than that of the pusillanimous and cruel ruler, the unjust and mercenary judge. The cruel injustice of the one towards our Saviour is but the counterpart of the selfish cupidity and baseness of the other towards the great apostle of the Gentiles. With all the power of Rome to support his authority, Pilate, on the cowardly plea of expediency, could sacrifice an innocent man, even while pronouncing him guiltless of any crime. And for love of money in daily expectation of a bribe, Felix could hold a prisoner in chains two whole years, and then leave him bound to gratify his relentless persecutors. Roman justice was once a proverb, and to be a Roman citizen the greatest honour in the world; but Roman virtue and honour had reached a low ebb, when it appeared on the pages of the New Testament.

But in the background, behind all these royal Herods, and haughty Roman Procurators, stand the great kings, who were then masters of the world, the Roman emperors, called in the New Testament, Cæsars. Four of them are mentioned, Cæsar Augustus under whose reign Christ was born, Tiberius Cæsar under whom he was crucified, Claudius Cæsar under whom the great dearth came predicted in the Acts, and Nero to whom Paul appealed from the judgment-seat of Festus, and under whom he afterwards suffered martyrdom at Rome. The sacred writers give us no account of the characters of these great world conquerors and despots. We learn what they were from other sources. They figure in the new Testament history only as the great kings of Babylon and Egypt did in the Old. They however reached a much greater height of pride, power, and impiety. Some of them were arbitrary tyrants and monsters of depravity, who gloried in placing the iron heel of despotism upon the necks of prostrate nations. Some of them claimed and received Divine honours. They showed what human nature, left to itself and placed in power, could become, and what it could do. That which Dryden, in the song, ascribes to Alexander the Great, they thought it no blasphemy to arrogate :

> " A present deity ! they shout around ;
> A present deity ! the vaulted roofs rebound ;
> With ravished ears
> The monarch hears,
> Assumes the God,
> Affects the nod,
> And seems to shake the spheres."

X. TESTIMONY OF MODERN STATESMEN.

It is time for us to close this survey and dismiss the subject. We might have dwelt at much greater length on the diversified characters and fortunes of the kings and princes, jurists and statesmen of the Bible. It will form an appropriate close to this class of Scripture characters, to bring together here, as showing the estimate of able and impartial men, a few memorable testimonials from our modern statesmen and jurists. Rich as the Bible is, in all the great principles of human and Divine government, and diversified, as its history is, with the most striking impersonations of every style of mortal greatness, both of the evil and the good, we need not wonder, that it has always and everywhere claimed the profound study and the heartfelt admiration of the most eminent men in the world. The ablest of modern princes and civilians, the wisest of all our statesmen, the most learned of all our jurists, have been those who sat longest at the feet of the sacred writers—those who drank deepest at the fountains of Divine inspiration—those who began life with a determination to build upon the massive and eternal foundations of Bible truth

Said Mr. Webster, "I have read through the entire Bible many times. I now make a practice to go through it once a year. It is the book of all others for lawyers, as well as for divines; and I pity the man that cannot find in it a rich supply of thought, and of rules for his own conduct. It fits man for life, it prepares him for death."

Said Sir Matthew Hale, one of the greatest lights of the legal profession, "Every morning read seriously and reverently a portion of the Holy Scriptures, and acquaint yourselves with the history and doctrine thereof. It is a book full of light and wisdom, will make you wise to eternal life, and furnish you with directions and principles to guide and order your life safely and prudently. There is no book like the Bible for excellent learning, wisdom, and use."

Said that distinguished orator and statesman, Fisher Ames, "No man can be a sound lawyer, who is not well read in the laws of Moses. Marks of Divinity are stamped upon them. I will hazard the assertion, that no man ever did, or will become truly eloquent, without being a constant reader of the Bible, and an admirer of the purity, and sublimity of its language."

Said the profound jurist and master of twenty-eight languages, Sir William Jones, "I cannot refrain from adding, that the collection of tracts, which we call, from their excellence, the Scriptures, contain, independently of a Divine origin, more true sublimity, more exquisite beauty, more pure morality more important history, and finer strains both of poetry and eloquence, than could be collected within the same compass, from all other books that were ever composed in any age or in any idiom."

Said the greatest of English advocates, Lord Erskine, "I have been ever deeply devoted to the truths of Christianity; and my firm belief in the Holy Gospel is by no means owing to the prejudices of education, (though I was religiously educated by the best of parents,) but it arises from the most continued reflections of my riper years and understanding. It forms, at this moment, the great consolation of a life, which, as a shadow, must pass away; and without it, indeed, I should consider my long course of health and prosperity, perhaps too long and too uninterrupted to be good for any man, only as the dust which the wind scatters, rather as a snare than as a blessing."

"Read the Bible—read the Bible," said the dying statesman—the great and good Wilberforce, "let no religious book take its place. Through all my perplexities and distresses I never read any other book, and I never felt the want of any other. It has been my hourly study; and all my knowledge of the doctrines, and all my acquaintance with the experience and realities of religion, have been derived from the Bible only."

"The general diffusion of the Bible," says Chancellor Kent, "is the most effectual way to civilize and humanize mankind; to purify and exalt the general system of public morals; to give efficacy to the just precepts of international and municipal law; to enforce the observance of prudence, temperance, justice, and fortitude, and to improve all the relations of social and domestic life."

"I deem myself fortunate," said the venerable Ex-President of the United States, John Quincy Adams, "in having the opportunity—at a stage of a long life drawing rapidly to its close, to bear, at this place, the capital of the National Union, in the Hall of Representation of the North American people, in the chair of the presiding officer of an assembly representing the whole people, the personification of the great and mighty nation—to bear my solemn testimonial of reverence and gratitude to that Book of books, the Holy Bible. In the midst of the painful and perilous conflicts inseparable from public life, and at the eve of that moment when the grave shall close over them for ever, I may be permitted to indulge the pleasing reflection, that, having been taught in childhood the unparalleled blessings of the Christian gospel, in the maturity of manhood I associated with my brethren of that age, for spreading the light of that gospel over the face of the earth, by the simple and silent process of placing in the hands of every human being who needed, and could not otherwise procure it, the Book which contains the duties and admonitions, the promises and the rewards of the Christian gospel."

And said that eccentric, but highly gifted man, John Randolph of Roanoke, "I would not give up my slender portion of the price paid for our redemption—I would not exchange my little portion in the Son of David, for the power and glory of the Parthian or Roman empires, as described by Milton in the temptation of our Lord and Saviour—not for all with which the enemy tempted the Saviour of man." Touching Mr. Randolph's high appreciation of the word of God, we find the following interesting paragraph in Mr. Benton's recent work, the "Thirty Years' View—"The last time I saw him," says Mr. Benton, "which was in that last visit to Washington, after his return from the Russian mission, and when he was in the full view of death, I heard him read the chapter in the Revelation (of the opening of the seals), with such power and beauty of voice and delivery, and such depth of pathos, that I felt as if I had never heard the chapter read before. When he had got to the end of the opening of the sixth seal, he stopped the reading, laid the book (open at the place) on his breast, as he lay on his bed, and began a discourse upon the beauty and sublimity of the Scriptural writings, compared to which he considered all human compositions vain and empty. Going over the images presented by the opening of the seals, he averred that their divinity was in their sublimity—that no human power could take the same images, and inspire the same awe and terror, and sink ourselves into such nothingness in the presence of the 'wrath of the Lamb'—that he wanted no proof of their Divine origin but the sublime feelings they inspired."

To these we must add one more testimony. There is nothing more remarkable than the diversified tributes to the truth of Christianity, which from the beginning, have been brought by all classes of men, both friends and foes, believers and unbelievers. Witness that, for instance, of the officers of the Jewish Sanhedrim, who being sent to arrest Jesus, returned without him, bearing this report to their masters—"Never man spake like this man." Witness that of the traitor Judas, "I have sinned in that I have betrayed innocent blood." Witness that of his unjust judge, Pilate, "I find no fault in him;" and that of Pilate's wife, "Have thou nothing to do with that just man." Witness that of the Roman centurion, "Truly this man was the Son of God." Witness the celebrated confession of Rousseau, "If the life and death of Socrates were those of a sage, the life and death of Jesus are those of a God." But all things considered, perhaps, the most remarkable testimony ever borne, is that of the great Napoleon, in a conversation related by his faithful friend, the Count de Montholon.

"I know men," said Napoleon, "and I tell you, that Jesus is not a man! The religion of Christ is a mystery which subsists by its own force, and proceeds from a mind which is not a human mind. We find in it a marked individuality, which originated a train of words and maxims unknown before. Jesus borrowed nothing from our knowledge. He exhibited in himself the perfect example of his precepts. Jesus is not a philosopher; for his proofs are miracles, and from the first his disciples adored him. In fact learning and philosophy are of no use for salvation; and Jesus came into the world to reveal the mysteries of heaven and the laws of the Spirit. Alexander, Cæsar, Charlemagne, and myself founded empires; but upon what did we rest the creation of our genius? Upon *force*. Jesus Christ alone founded his empire upon *love;* and at this hour millions of men would die for him, It was not a day or a battle which achieved the triumph of the Christian religion in the world. No, it was a long war, a contest of three centuries, begun by the apostles, then continued by the flood of Christian generations. In this war all the kings and potentates of the earth were on one side; on the other I see no army, but a mysterious force: some men scattered here and there in all parts of the world, and who have no other rallying point than a common faith in the mysteries of the cross. I die before my time, and my body will be given back to the earth to become food for worms. Such is the fate which so soon awaits him who has been called the Great Napoleon. What an abyss between my deep misery, and the eternal kingdom of Christ, which is proclaimed, loved, and adored, and which is extending over the whole earth! Call you this dying? Is it not living rather? The death of Christ is the death of a God."

All these, and a great cloud of witnesses like them, from the ranks of scholars and jurists, statesmen and rulers, of past and present times, stand arrayed in the vindication of the high claims of the Bible, and of the religion it contains. In fact all the greatest names of modern civilized history, would but respond to the sentiment of Sir Isaac Newton in "accounting the Scriptures of God the most sublime philosophy," and to the memorable words of John Locke—"Therein are contained the words of eternal life. It has God for its author, salvation for its end, and truth without any mixture of error for its matter."

CHAPTER V.

THE PROPHETS AND APOSTLES OF THE BIBLE.

THE Prophets and Apostles of the Bible present us with a subject at once attractive, instructive, and important. Of whatever else we might speak, to leave these out of our survey of Scriptural characters would be to omit the most peculiar and distinguishing class of all. These may, indeed, be called the Greater Lights of Bible Character. It is only when we come to the Prophets of the Old Testament, and the Apostles of the New, that we reach the climax of Jewish history.

We have already, in our diversified illustrations of Scripture character, had occasion to portray some of these great examples, as they appeared on the stage of life and action. Some of them were poets and orators. Some were sages and statesmen. Most of them were heroes. They were endowed with many great gifts; and held many high and responsible offices amongst men. But they held a peculiar relation to God, in virtue of their own great office—a relation unshared by any other class of men. It remains now to present them in the character of Prophets and Apostles. And here we seem to breathe a higher atmosphere, to tread a holier ground. We have, indeed, ascended to the very mountain tops of Divine revelation. We do not mean to imply that there was nothing holy and Divine in all that lower ground through which we have been passing. On the contrary, we have seen marks of Divinity mingling with the human at every step. We have seen the glorious light of a Divine inspiration breaking forth everywhere in all the Scriptures, from the words and mighty deeds of heroes, sages, poets, orators, kings, statesmen, young men, and maidens. But still, it is only when we approach these holy men of old, in their prophetic and apostolic offices, that we see the light shining in its brightest splendour—shining as in its own native heaven. "For the prophecy came not in old time by the will of man; but holy men of God spake as they were moved by the Holy Ghost."

I. PROPHETICAL CHARACTERS OF THE OLD TESTAMENT.

The word Prophet is one of wide significance in the Bible. It would be tedious to mention here its many different shades of meaning. We shall point out only two—the broadest and the narrowest sense. In the widest sense, it denotes a teacher, expounder, or preacher, of the word of God, whether inspired or uninspired. In this sense Aaron was a prophet. And, in this sense, not only all the sacred writers, but all the Levites of the old dispensation, and all the preachers of the New Testament, were prophets. But in its narrower and more appropriate sense, it denotes a foreteller of the future, one inspired of God to predict coming events—a seer or foreseer of what is unknown to other men. It is only in this last restricted sense, that we shall speak of the Prophets of the Bible at present. In this sense there are about fifty true prophets of the Lord, who are either expressly mentioned by name as such, in Scripture, or are entitled to the distinction, from the fact of their foretelling things to come. Sixteen of these, from Isaiah to Malachi, hold a place in the sacred canon, being not only the speakers but the inspired writers of Divine predictions—the authors of the several books bearing their respective names, four of them called the greater and twelve the lesser prophets, according to the size of their books.

The earliest name on the roll of prophecy is that of Enoch beyond the flood. If we except Noah's prediction of the deluge, and except, also, the Divine promise of a Saviour given in the garden of Eden, Enoch's is the only prophecy which has come down to us from the antediluvian world. This we have on the authority of the Apostle Jude, in the following words—"And Enoch also, the seventh from Adam, prophesied of these also, saying, Behold, the Lord cometh with ten thousand of his saints, to execute judgment upon all, and to convince all that are ungodly among them, of all their ungodly deeds, which they have ungodly committed, and of all their hard speeches which ungodly sinners have spoken against him." There is something impressive and sublime in this ancient prophecy—a prediction of the end of time and of the last judgment, handed down, first in a voice of tradition, and then of Scripture over all the intervening ages! "It is remarkable," says an ingenious writer, "that, though the first of the prophets, he prophesied of the last event in the history of the world—the coming of the Lord—as if no event betwixt were majestic enough for him to touch, who, even on earth, was breathing the air of the upper paradise, and was, in a little while, to be caught up among the visions of God."

But to us, the most remarkable circumstance is this, that the principal prophet of each of the three great dispensations of the world's history should be translated to heaven by an ascension in the flesh. There have been three grand periods of history, as portrayed in the Bible, the Antediluvian, the Jewish, and the Christian. Each of these has had its great prophet, towering majestically above all his fellows, the three forming an ascending scale—Enoch in the first, Elijah in the second, and Jesus Christ in the third. And, as if to show how close is the connection between the seen and the unseen world—how deep an interest heaven has in earth, and earth in heaven—the great prophet of each dispensation has been taken up in a visible form, soul and body, into the heavens. If there were no other proof of the dignity of the prophetical character, this fact alone—the ascension of Enoch, Elijah, and Christ—would be enough to show to all generations what unusual honour God has conferred upon it. None but a prophet of the Lord has ever been translated from earth to heaven in the body.

II. THE PROPHECY OF JACOB.

From Enoch let us now pass to the patriarch Jacob across an interval of more than a thousand years. This long period, however, was not without its inspired prophets. We might speak of Noah preaching righteousness, and predicting the flood; and also of Abraham who foresaw the day of Christ, and is expressly called a prophet. But we pass over these, to linger for a little while near the death-bed of the venerable Jacob, as he foretells what shall befall his sons in the last days, and the coming of Shiloh, ere the sceptre should depart from Judah. This death-bed of Jacob was, perhaps, the most touching and remarkable scene of all that had occurred to him in his long and checkered life. On the approach of death, he seems to have been more signally endowed with the spirit of prophecy than his father Isaac had been on the like occasion. And he accordingly delivers a more full and beautiful prediction of the coming of the great Messiah, than had hitherto been given. It was the third stage of the Messianic prophecy. It was a great advance on the promise made to Abraham—"In thy seed shall all the families of the earth be blessed"—even as that was a great advance on the promise made to Adam—"The seed of the woman shall bruise the serpent's head."

This great forefather of the twelve tribes of Israel, whose name of honour from God gave name to the nation, was called to lead a most diversified and eventful life. In his youth the good and the evil had often struggled for the mastery; and in his old age it seemed to be an even match between adversity and prosperity, and it was long doubtful which should win the day. He was among the patriarchs what Jeremiah was among the prophets. He was the sorrowing patriarch. He had often to drink the cup of tears. And yet his life, upon the whole, and especially in its serene and peaceful issue, was a prosperous and happy one. That may be called a blessed and glorious life which ends well, notwithstanding all its dark days of trial and adversity. The sins and errors of Jacob's youth seemed but the more to display the power of that grace which at last prevailed and made him a prince with God; while the dark storms of adversity and trial that so often beat upon his head in old age, only made the sunshine of heaven's blessing appear the brighter, when once it emerged from the clouds. There is, perhaps, no one of these old Bible characters that comes nearer home to our own hearts in the experience of life, than this same tempted, erring, praying, God-fearing, hard-working, prospering, and sorrowing Jacob. He evidently lived in the same world we do: and had a nature much the same as ours. His whole career might stand as a just average of human life, at its best estate. The only difference seems to be that he had seen a little more of the world, had drunk a little longer at its mingled fountains of sorrow and joy, than we are permitted to do.

What changes of fortune and of feeling had he passed through from the time when he fled from his father's house to escape a brother's wrath, down to the day on which he stood before Pharaoh in Egypt, bowed with the weight of a hundred and thirty years, and surrounded by a posterity of three score and ten souls! An exile from home, a servant in the house of Laban for fourteen years, a pilgrim with his helpless wives and children to the land of promise; again trembling before the vengeance of Esau, and wrestling all night with the angel of the Lord, distressed in turn by the contentions in his household, and the evil report of his children—the misfortune of his only daughter, the bloody violence of Simeon and Levi, the crime of Reuben—called to lay his beloved Rachel in an early grave, to mourn for Joseph as one devoured of wild beasts; then stricken by famine, to have Benjamin torn from him and carried down into Egypt where one son is already a prisoner, and where all of them may be in danger of their lives—with all this complex scene of life in the background, Jacob is a fit subject for our tenderest sympathies, when at last brought before the king by that long-lost, but now exalted son, he responds to the question, How old art thou? with these simple and truthful words: "The days of the years of my pilgrimage are a hundred and thirty years; few and evil have the days of the years of my life been, and have not attained unto the days of the years of the life of my fathers in the days of their pilgrimage."

But through all these evil days the Lord had brought him safely. From all these troubles his ever watchful and gracious providence had delivered him. The river of his existence that had hitherto run so roughly, amid manifold obstructions, had now passed its last barrier, thenceforth to flow smoothly to the sea. His sun, which, for so much of life's day, had been hid in darkness, had at last emerged from its last cloud, so as to go down in full orbed splendour and beauty. And thus in the wonderful compensations of Divine Providence, this venerable man was permitted to linger out seventeen years in the land of Egypt, of uninterrupted peace, prosperity, and joy, blest with the companionship of all his children and grand-children, an object of interest to Pharaoh and his people, and of special love and devotion to his honoured son.

When at last his days were numbered, and the time of his departure was at hand, the sons of Israel, heads of the future tribes, were called together to see the patriarch die, and to receive his parting benedictions. It was a fitting close to such a pilgrimage. It is precisely such a winding up as all the best instincts of our nature—our sense of justice, our faith in God's providence, and our sympathy with virtue, would have demanded for the drama of such a life. Joseph was there to receive his last counsels about the burying—there to weep, to fall upon his neck and kiss him, and when all was over, to close his eyes in death. The little ones of the third generation were there to receive their share in the blessing. All were there. And when all was ready, the venerable man, endowed with that extraordinary influence which opened to his mind the far distant future, and which was the gift of the

Holy Ghost, uttered those short but graphic predictions of the career and destiny of the twelve tribes, which we have in the forty-ninth chapter of Genesis. "And Jacob called unto his sons and said, Gather yourselves together, that I may tell you that which shall befall you in the last days. Gather yourselves together, and hear, ye sons of Jacob, and hearken unto Israel your father."

But we need not repeat the predictions here. The most remarkable of them all is that in which he speaks of Judah, foretelling the power and supremacy of that tribe in Israel, and the coming of the great Deliverer, the Messiah before it shall have lost its authority. "Judah, thou art he whom thy brethren shall praise; thine hand shall be in the neck of thine enemies; thy father's children shall bow down before thee. Judah is a lion's whelp; from the prey, my son, thou art gone up; he stooped down, he couched as a lion; who shall rouse him up? The sceptre shall not depart from Judah, nor a lawgiver from between his feet, until Shiloh come, and unto him shall the gathering of the people be."

This Divine promise, which had first been as wide as the race, but was afterwards limited to the seed of Abraham, was now restricted to the posterity of Judah, and to that posterity within a given period: namely, while the sceptre of authority remained with the tribe. All this was most fully verified in Jesus Christ, who came of the royal line of Judah, and before that tribe had lost its place and power in Israel. And it is clear that unless Jesus Christ fulfilled that prophecy, by being the true Messiah, it not only never has been fulfilled, but never can. The sceptre has long ago departed from Judah, and the time foretold by the dying patriarch has gone by for ever. Nay, every other sentence of these predictions has been fulfilled long ago. And it is impossible to see, how any intelli gent Jew who receives that passage as a prediction of a Messiah at all, can resist the conviction that it has been fulfilled in Jesus Christ.

The great lesson of Jacob's life is that we should never despair of God's providence. After all, he had far more of joy than of sorrow. The darkest day he ever saw had its beams of light. The worst situation he was ever in had its mercies and its deliverances. There never was an hour of his pilgrimage when he had cause to despond or even murmur. His life brings to mind the admirable lines of Trench :

" Some murmur when their sky is clear,
And wholly bright to view,
If but one speck of dark appear
In their great heaven of blue.
And some with thankful love are filled,
If but one streak of light,
One ray of God's good mercy, gild
The darkness of their night.

In palaces are hearts that ask
In discontent and pride,
Why life is such a dreary task,
And all good things denied ;
While hearts in poorest huts admire
How love hath, in their aid,
(Love that not ever seems to tire)
Such rich provision made."

III. SAMUEL THE PROPHET.

If our object were to portray the whole course of prophetic history in the Bible, we might, in passing from Jacob, speak also of his son Joseph as a prophet of the Lord, predicting the years of plenty and famine in Egypt, and also the departure of the children of Israel to the land of promise. We might also speak of Moses, who, in addition to all his other great endowments, was a prophet of the Lord, foretelling and most graphically describing in his farewell address to Israel, the whole future history and destiny of the nation, and likewise bringing us to the fourth stage of developement in the Messianic prophecy, by those memorable words—"A prophet shall the Lord your God raise up unto you of your brethren like unto me; him shall ye hear." And we might dwell also on the strange character of Balaam, the forefather of all false prophets, reproved by the dumb beast for his error, and constrained by the Spirit of God, contrary to all his wishes, to utter a true and striking prophecy of the Messiah—"I shall see him, but not now; I shall behold him but not nigh; there shall come a star out of Jacob, and a sceptre shall rise out of Israel."

But wishing to dwell only on those who filled the true prophetic office, and whose chief distinction was the prophetic character, we pass over all these earlier prophets, and come down to the times of Samuel, from whom the whole prophetic order seems to date the beginning of a new and wider sphere of influence and endowments. As Samuel lived in that transition period when the Hebrew commonwealth passed into a regular monarchy, and had himself an important part to act in effecting the change, we find him holding several distinct offices which do not often devolve on the same man. He was a man of peace, and an inspired prophet, having from his early childhood ministered in the tabernacle of the Lord; yet we find him on one occasion acting as the military leader of the people, and for many years their virtual civil ruler. Indeed we find him alternately discharging the functions of prophet, commander, chief magistrate, minister of justice, and priest, though he did not belong to the priesthood. He was in fact the last of the Judges, a sort of irregular order of men combining both civil and military powers, who had governed Israel from the times of Joshua. He combined all these great and widely separated functions, partly because of the disorders of the times, but mainly in virtue of his prophetic office, which ever had been and continued to be the highest and holiest office in Israel. As an inspired prophet, acting by direct revelation from heaven, he had a right to do what it was treason for King Saul to do, and for the doing of which, in his arrogant self-will, he lost his kingdom. Hence we find him building an altar, and offering sacrifice, both of which were expressly forbidden by the law of God for any man to do save the priests, and even for them except at one place, where the Lord's tabernacle was. Yet Samuel did them both at Mizpeh, not only with impunity, but with heaven's blessing. We find the prophet Elijah afterwards doing the same things at Mount Carmel, and the fire of God descending at his call to consume the sacrifice. All this goes to show how sacred was the prophetic office, and how intimate was the relation between God and those who spake as they were moved by the Holy Ghost.

And so we shall find that the men who wrote the larger portions of all our Scriptures, were not priests and Scribes and kings, but in the Old Testament, the Prophets, and in the New, the Apostles who corresponded in office to them. So Moses, who wrote the first five books, was a prophet, King David was also a prophet. Samuel himself probably wrote several of the books. So the great body of Scripture was written by prophets and apostles. Now this superiority of the prophetic order over everything else in Israel, including both the priesthood and the throne, which first displayed itself so signally in the life of Samuel, and continued to do so down to the days of Malachi, was not without its great salutary purpose. The prophets were both the revealers of God's will to men, and the inspired expounders of that which was already revealed in Scripture. So their grand mission was to declare the truth, the whole counsel of God, and to call king, people, and priesthood, to a higher, holier, and more spiritual life than they had attained. The people, priests, and rulers were continually falling into a mere formal and ritual worship. The prophet's office was a standing call to repentance and faith—a testimony from God against a mere ceremonial religion, and in favour of the only saving gospel. In this spirit Samuel said to Saul, "Behold, to obey is better than sacrifice, and to hearken than the fat of rams."

IV. ELIJAH AND ELISHA.

The next great names after Samuel, on the roll of the Hebrew prophets, are those of Elijah and Elisha. These two stand intimately associated in the Bible history. They lived in perilous times. They were each in turn the head of the prophetic order. Their great mission was chiefly to the idolatrous court of Israel, when that kingdom had reached the lowest point of degeneracy. They were alike in their performance of mighty miracles. The miracles of Elijah, however, were mostly judgments of wrath against the wicked; whilst Elisha's, like those of Jesus, were nearly all miracles of mercy. The predominant characteristic of the one was a burning zeal for the Lord which seemed to raise him above the sphere of all other mortals; the distinguishing spirit of the other was his sympathizing and generous kind-heartedness.

But as our limits do not allow a full account of even all the great prophets, we select one here as the type and representative of his order. That distinction clearly belongs to Elijah. He became a sort of impersonation of the very idea of prophecy. His character was so extraordinary, his life was so full of wonders, his introduction in the history so abrupt, and his exit so sublime, that all generations looked back to him as the greatest of Israel's prophets. By Malachi, the last of the Old Testament prophets, the Lord said—"Behold I will send you Elijah the prophet, before the coming of the great and dreadful day of the Lord; and he shall turn the heart of the fathers to the children, and the heart of the children to their fathers, lest I come and smite the earth with a curse." In accordance with this promise, you remember the question of our Saviour's disciples—"How say the scribes that Elias must first come?" and his answer, that Elias had come already in the person of John the Baptist. The mysterious grandeur which enveloped his whole career on earth, was thus transmitted with his name even down to the new dispensation. His life is interwoven, like a solitary thread of light, into that thick curtain of darkness which overhung the land of Israel during the idolatrous reign of Ahab and Jezebel. His work, as indicated by his name, was to reform that wicked court; and when that had failed, to foretell and pronounce its awful doom. Suddenly he appears on the stage of Bible history, and just as suddenly disappears. "And Elijah the Tishbite, who was of the inhabitants of Gilead, said unto Ahab, As the Lord God of Israel liveth, before whom I stand, there shall not be dew nor rain these years, but according to my words." This is the first mention of his name in the Bible. Not one line does it give as to his genealogy, parentage, birth, or education. Like Melchisedec he stands on the record without beginning of days. If he had been dropped down from the skies, by that chariot of fire and cloud which ere long was to take him away, or had he been an angel incarnate, as some have absurdly conjectured, the narrative could not have been more silent as to all his human relations. Like a comet on its fiery way, so did he come into the midnight sky of Jewish history, and before the morning of a better day had dawned, he was gone—gone into the distant depths of heaven. These first recorded words of his lips, so authoritative, so laconic, so awful, evidently stand as the closing sentence of an interview which he had just held with the king. The imagination of the reader is left to supply all the rest. In the dread name of Jehovah, whose messenger he was, he proclaims a drought of indefinite duration, and disappears. How must these words have rung in the conscience of guilty Ahab during that long and terrible famine! "Elias," says the apostle James, "was a man of like passions as we are, and he prayed earnestly that it might not rain; and it rained not on the earth (the land of Israel) by the space of three years and six months." The object of this famine was to convince and reclaim Ahab and Jezebel, that they might forsake their idolatry and serve the Lord.

The scene changes from the court to the wilderness; and we next find the prophet in a solitary dell at the brook Cherith in the vale of Jordan, awaiting in retirement the great result. In this secluded spot, where he is hidden by God's command, he dwells for one year, drinking the water of the brook, receiving his morning and evening meals from the ravens of the air, and safe from the wrath of the monarch, who is searching in all the surrounding nations, for the hiding-place of this troubler of Israel.

At last the brook dries up and the scene changes again. The heavens are as brass, the earth as ashes, and the famine is sore in the land. He must find sustenance elsewhere. Though the distress has come in answer to his own prayer, and is not to be relieved, except according to his word, and though he is himself a sufferer, yet that word is not to be revoked till its purpose be accomplished. At the Lord's command, he is summoned away to the borders of Sidon, to the lowly dwelling of a poor widow of Sarepta. On her unwasting barrel of meal and unfailing cruse of oil, he is sustained all the residue of the famine; during which time he restores her son to life, the first miracle of raising the dead recorded in the Scriptures.

Again the scene changes, and we find the prophet, by the command of the Lord, in the presence of Ahab. Charged by him with being the troubler of Israel, he hurls back the charge upon the king himself, whose idolatry had caused all this distress in Israel. In virtue of his high authority as a prophet of God, he commands Ahab to call an assembly of the people. The haughty monarch, with the conscious weakness of guilt, is at once awed into acquiescence before the superior presence of the man, whom, for three years and a half, he has been hunting to destroy. Accordingly, he summons all Israel, with the prophets of Baal four hundred and fifty, and the prophets of Jezebel's table four hundred, to meet him and Elijah at Mount Carmel, for one final and decisive test of the great controversy of the day. In the presence of all Israel, king, prophets, and people, the question, Whether Baal or Jehovah be the true God, is to be publicly tried and settled by the test of fire from heaven. No test could be more appropriate, or more favourable for the Baal worshippers, who claimed that fire was the peculiar emblem of their deity—Baal being the God of the sun. The appointed day came with all its thousands and its stirring events. No battle day of Jewish history could well exceed the intense excitement and sublimity of that memorable day. You remember the wonders and the results of the whole extraordinary trial—how, when fire descended from heaven in answer to Elijah's prayer, and consumed his water drenched sacrifice, the multitudes of Israel gave forth their verdict in one unanimous shout of approval—"The Lord, he is the God; the Lord, he is the God;" how the prophets of Baal, thus publicly defeated on their own ground and in their own element, were all slain, thus meeting the fate which would have been Elijah's had they gained the day; how this solitary avenger of Israel's wrongs, having thus rid the land of its greatest abominations, then ascended to the top of the mount, and there prostrate on the ground prayed for rain, until, in the distant horizon of the great sea that rolled at the base of Carmel, a cloud at last appeared of the size of a man's hand: how it gathered in blackness over the heavens, while the royal chariot hasted away before the driving storm, and while the prophet himself, elate with the joy of a nation's deliverance, girded up his loins and ran before Ahab to the entrance of Jezreel—a harbinger of good news to the famished land, that would outstrip the very winds which had come in answer to his prayers. No statesman, king, or conqueror, however honoured by a nation's gratitude, ever had a triumphant procession like that—running himself as a footman before the sovereign, while the storm followed as a vindicator of his greatness before God!

Again the scene changes. Threatened with death by Jezebel on the next day, disappointed and indignant at the apparent failure of his mission after his signal and powerful vindication at Carmel, and despairing of doing any further good in Israel while that wicked woman held the reins of power, he flies to the wilderness of the south. Weary of his long journey, and weary of his life, murmuring and sad, being after all a man of like passions with others, he falls down exhausted under a juniper tree and craves for death. He sleeps. "Tired nature's sweet restorer." An angel awakes him. God sends a shining one to cheer the burdened spirit of his servant, and provide him food. In the strength of it he journeys forty days, and comes to Horeb the mount of God. There he dwells a solitary hermit of the cave. There amidst thunders, and lightnings, and rending rocks he is admonished and instructed by a still small voice which tells him what work there is yet for him to do in Israel, where the Lord has seven thousand true worshippers that have not bowed the knee to Baal!

But our limits would fail us to follow the wonder-working prophet through all the scenes of his eventful and mysterious life. He returned to fulfil his mission, to anoint Hazael king of Syria, Jehu king of Israel, and Elisha his successor in the prophetic office; to stand again in the presence of Ahab and of his son Ahaziah; to foretell the doom of Jezebel and all her idolatrous house; to instruct the sons of the prophets, and then, in full view of Elisha and fifty sons of the prophets, to ascend to heaven in a chariot and horses of fire.

Nothing in human history, can surpass, in sublimity, the life of Elijah. Take it in all its scenes from first to last, and there is no other life in the annals of literature that could be substituted in its place. Nothing in prose or poetry, fact or fiction, can exceed even the dramatic power with which, like an angel from the skies or a spectre from the grave, he appears before Ahab in the very scenes of his high-handed wickedness and oppression. Suddenly, unexpectedly, terribly, he stands before the haughty monarch, as one commissioned of God to expose his deepest, darkest stains of guilt. Well might he cry out, in the anguish of a guilty conscience, when after years of separation, the man of God met him again in the vineyard of murdered Naboth—"Hast thou found me, O mine enemy?" Not Banquo's ghost could inspire a greater terror in the heart of coward guilt, nor that of Hamlet's father call more fearfully for the avenging of the dead, than did this living messenger of judgment, whenever he appeared in the corrupt court of Ahab and Jezebel.

Does any one wish to see how vice meets with its just retribution; how truth, sooner or later, sweeps away all the cobwebs of hypocrisy and deception in which lordly guilt seeks to hide itself; how justice pursues its victim, and murder must come out at last; how impossible it is for crime to go unwhipt of justice while God is on the throne—he need not go for such a lesson to the Greek and Latin poets, nor to the drama ancient or modern, nor to the novels of our current literature; he will find that great truth portrayed in a far more solemn and impressive style on the sacred pages, in the fearful career and downfall of Ahab and Jezebel.

In what admirable keeping with the whole career of Elijah was its majestic close! "And it came to pass, as they still went on and talked, there appeared a chariot of fire and horses of fire, and parted them both asunder; and Elijah went up by a whirlwind into heaven. And Elisha saw it and cried, My father, my father, the chariot of Israel and the horses thereof; and he saw him no more." The scene was one of the grandest, as well as one of the most extraordinary, recorded in the Bible

Like our Saviour's ascension, it was not without spectators. It had been revealed simultaneously both to Elijah and Elisha, and the sons of the prophets at Bethel and Jericho, that Elijah should be taken away on that particular day. And with this impression Elisha would not leave him; but followed him closely from Gilgal to Bethel, thence to Jericho, and thence again to the Jordan, and even through its parted waters. "And fifty men of the sons of the prophets went, and stood to view afar off." The two friends, long bound together by many endearing ties, and feeling that the hour of separation was just at hand, paused, and stood a moment on the bank of the Jordan, probably at, or near the spot where Joshua had once led the tribes of Israel across. Endowed with miraculous powers, Elijah smote the waters with his mantle; they divided; and the two went over on dry ground. It was an hour of close and tender communion. The last petition of the disciple was now preferred; the last legacy of the master now granted, "Give me a double portion of thy spirit." It was a great gift, but it was granted, and the falling mantle with it. "And he said, Thou hast asked a hard thing; nevertheless, if thou see me when I am taken from thee, it shall be so unto thee; but, if not, it shall not be so.

> "Then forward still they went, discoursing high
> On heavenly bliss and immortality,
> When from a cloud breaks (like the purple dawn)
> By fiery steeds a fiery chariot drawn;
> A glittering convoy swift as that descends,
> And in an instant parts the embracing friends;
> To the bright car conducts the man of God,
> And mounts again the steep, ethereal road."

V. ISAIAH AND THE GREATER PROPHETICAL WRITERS.

Let us now pass to another distinct department of Scripture prophecy—from the speakers to the writers, from the prophets of deeds to the prophets of words. The prophets of whom we have thus far spoken, wrote no books of prophecy—none, at least, that have come down to us. All the prophets, from Samuel to Elisha, were actively occupied with the public affairs of the Jewish people. Their office was one peculiar to Israel, and often combined the three great elements of the Theocracy, ecclesiastical, judicial, and executive authority. They, occupied with existing home affairs, had little to do with the great contemporary nations, or the distant future. They wrought signs and wonders, proclaimed the word of the Lord to their own kings and people, and foretold events in the immediate future, which they often lived to see verified. Samuel, Elijah, and Elisha were the greatest of these prophets of the times.

But many others are mentioned, as Iddo and Gad, Nathan, Shemaiah, and Micaiah; and in the schools of the prophets we read of a hundred at a time. For you must bear in mind, that these prophets of the old dispensation had an important mission to perform to their countrymen. They were the authorized preachers of the times, standing, as a class, as much above the priesthood, as Moses stood above Aaron before the Lord. Hence we find them on certain great occasions, even performing functions which were restricted to the Aaronic priesthood, such as offering sacrifice, which they did in virtue of their higher prophetic office. They called the people, and the rulers of the people, alike, to repentance. They declared the will of the Lord without any intervention of Urim and

Thummin. They inculcated all the great spiritual and practical duties of religion, and when needful, denounced the regular sacrifices of the temple service, as vain and formal oblations—an abomination to Jehovah. "The prophetic office did for the law what preaching has done for the gospel; it supplied a living sanction, a running comment, and a quickening influence." Hence it is manifest that the apostles, preachers, and ministry in general, of the New Testament church, were designed to be the successors, and supply the place, not of the Aaronic or Levitical priesthood, but of the Old Testament prophets.

From the death of Elisha, the spirit of prophecy seemed to rise into a higher and wider sphere. While it did not let go its hold upon present and national events at home, it began, from this time, to take into its vision the horizon of the great surrounding kingdoms, and even to pierce through the gloom of a far distant future. Over the hills of coming time, it began to see the rising dawn of a brighter day—it began to exult at the prospect of Immanuel's coming, and of the latter day glory. Accordingly, as the range of prophecy was henceforth not to be confined to the prophet's own age and country, but to embrace all generations and all nations, it became necessary that it should take the form of writing—that recorded in a book it might be preserved and transmitted for the reading of after ages. Thus, from Elisha's death to Malachi, a period of some four hundred years, those sixteen greater and lesser prophets lived and wrote, whose names stand at the head of the prophetical books, and who have composed so large a part of the Old Testament Scriptures. To portray the characters, and to describe the peculiar style and excellencies of these sixteen prophetic writers, would require a volume instead of a chapter. It is not needful, however, to our present plan, which is simply to set forth, by way of illustration, a few of the most distinguished examples in each department of the Scriptures. It will be enough to do, as we have just done with the prophetical speakers—to single out the one most illustrious character, as the type and representative of his order.

At the head of this list of prophetic writers—*facile princeps*—stands Isaiah, the son of Amoz. He is the prince of all the prophetical writers, both in the beauty of his style and the sublimity of his predictions. "There are two kinds of prophets," says Dr. Kitto, "prophets of deeds and prophets of words; of the latter, the greatest is, doubtless, Isaiah; of the former, there has not been among men born of women, any greater than Elijah. Moses might be named; but he stood alone. He was mighty both in words and deeds." Isaiah has been called, by preëminence, the evangelical prophet, because of the fulness of his description of the Messiah's kingdom, and the frequency with which he has been quoted by the New Testament writers. "Of all the prophets," says Gilfillan, "who rose on aspiring pinion to meet the Sun of Righteousness, it was his—the evangelical eagle—to mount highest, and to catch on his wing the richest anticipation of his rising." He lived more than seven hundred years before Christ. He filled the prophetic office during an eventful period of fifty years under the successive reigns of four of the kings of Judah, by whom he was consulted on great and trying occasions. He was cotemporary with six of the minor prophets, Jonah, Hosea, and Amos, in the kingdom of Israel, Joel, Micah, and Obadiah, in that of Judah.

His life was closely identified with the great events of his times, and many of his earlier predictions concerning his own country he lived to see fulfilled. But his prophetic spirit, gradually rising above the current affairs of Judah and Israel, soon embraced all the great Asiatic empires in one comprehensive vision. Through all his earlier visions, he occasionally breaks away from the local and temporary, as if catching some sudden and sublime view of the Messiah and of the latter day glory; and this upward, expanding force seems to grow stronger and stronger, as he rises, till in the fortieth chapter, he reaches the summit level of the whole world of vision, where without a barrier, or a bound, or an intervening cloud, he surveys the onward course of time—beholds all nations redeemed from sin, and walking in the light of the Lord. Isaiah is characterized by great variety of style and the boldness of his imagery. His description of the fall of the king of Babylon in the fourteenth chapter, is one of the most striking examples of sublime and awful grandeur. For touching pathos and beauty we may select his minute and graphic portraiture of the suffering Messiah in his fifty-third chapter. For lofty eloquence, for glowing imagination, for broad, magnificent conceptions of Divine power and glory, nothing can exceed the fortieth chapter, or indeed the whole close of the Book. In all these last chapters, he seems to stand, like a traveller, upon the mountain's brow, where in the clear light of the setting sun, he can catch a distinct, though distant view of all that tract of country over which he expects to pass on the morrow and succeeding days. He sees the bold outline of the nearest mountain range, and whilst gazing on its beauty, a more distant range behind it rises to his view, and then a third and a fourth beyond, successively reveal their shadowy summits on the horizon, till, at last, like Bunyan's Pilgrim, he beholds the Delectable Mountains, the land of Beulah, and the very gates of the celestial city. As Moses from Pisgah's top beheld the glories of the promised land, so does Isaiah see the course of time to come, and sing the glories of Immanuel's reign.

Next to Isaiah on the roll of written prophecy stand Jeremiah and Ezekiel, though living at a later period. These, like Isaiah, are distinguished for the length of their productions, as well as the sublimity and beauty of their style. Ezekiel may be denominated the impetuous, fiery prophet. Jeremiah is ever regarded as the plaintive, weeping prophet. The one deals largely in types and symbols. The other eats the bread of afflictions, and utters a voice of lamentation. The one can look with unfaltering heart and without a tear on the valley of dry bones, or the last great battle of Gog and Magog. The other cannot survey the utter desolations of his country without the bitter cry, "Oh that my head were waters and mine eyes a fountain of tears, that I might weep day and night for the slain of the daughter of my people." They both belonged to the sacerdotal order, and were called to the prophetic office in their early youth, Ezekiel at thirty, and Jeremiah probably younger. They lived in perilous times, and were frequently exposed to extreme sufferings and danger of death by their degenerate countrymen, because of their faithful warnings. They prophesied at Jerusalem until they were carried into captivity—Jeremiah to Egypt, and Ezekiel to Babylon. Like Isaiah and Daniel, while prophets of the times, foretelling near events, they prophesied also of the great Messiah; Jeremiah speaking of him as the "righteous Branch, the Lord our Righteousness," and Ezekiel as "my servant David."

These three, Isaiah, Jeremiah, and Ezekiel, with Daniel, have been classed together and styled the Greater Prophets. This designation is given to them, not because of any superiority in official character, or style of writing, but simply as marking the greater length of their writings. Daniel indeed, though having the gift of prophecy in high perfection, and dealing largely in predictions of Messiah's coming and kingdom, is not regarded as belonging to the prophetic order in the same sense with the others. He differs from all the other prophets, as having his entire mission in the land of exile. His book is also largely historical; and partly on this account, but chiefly because of his not being called to the prophetic office in Israel, it was classed by the Jews, not with the prophets, but with that division of Scripture, called the Psalms. We however class the four together as forming the great volume of written prophecy, fulfilled and unfulfilled. For centuries they were the daily study of all those in the ancient church who looked forward to Immanuel's advent and waited for the consolation of Israel. And their unfulfilled oracles still open the broad field of meditation and of hope to all who wait for his second coming amid the scenes of the latter day glory. They have been, are, and will be, even to the end, the blessed and enrapturing theme of the church's song in the house of her pilgrimage.

"Oh, scenes surpassing fable, and yet true!
Scenes of accomplished bliss! which who can see,
Though but in distant prospect, and not feel
His soul refreshed with foretaste of the joy!
One song employs all nations; and all cry,
Worthy the Lamb, for he was slain for us;
All saints proclaim Christ King, and in their hearts
His title is engraven with a pen,
Dipped in the fountain of eternal love."

VI. JONAH AND THE MINOR PROPHETS.

Closing the volume of the Old Testament Scriptures, and occupying altogether a space less than any single one of the Greater Prophets except Daniel, stand the twelve Minor Prophets, beginning with Hosea and ending with Malachi. Jonah was however first in the order of time, going back probably to the days of Elisha. But even if he was contemporary with some of the others, these twelve prophets would still cover a period of four hundred years in the Jewish history, from the eighth to the fourth century before Christ.

Of these twelve prophetical writers, two, namely, Hosea and Amos, delivered their messages chiefly to the kingdom of Israel; three, namely, Jonah, Nahum, and Obadiah, directed their predictions against the surrounding nations, and have been called prophets of the Gentiles; whilst three others, Haggai, Zechariah, and Malachi, coming later in the history have been styled prophets of the Restoration. It is interesting to observe how all the great leading prophets of the Bible may be ranged under some appropriate and distinctive title. These have been pointed out by writers on the prophets; and it may be instructive to the young Bible reader to refer to some of them here. Thus we have Enoch, the antediluvian prophet; Jacob, the patriarchal prophet; Moses, the legislative prophet, or prophet of the law; Samuel, the prophet of the altar, or sacerdotal prophet; Elijah, the wonder-working prophet, or prophet of judgment; Elisha, the prophet of the succession, David, the royal prophet; Isaiah, the evangelical prophet; Jeremiah, the weeping prophet; Ezekiel, the prophet of the captivity; Jonah, the prophet of repentance; Daniel, the prophet of exile, or prophet of the court; Haggai, Zechariah, and Malachi, prophets of the Restoration or of the Second Temple.

One of the most ingenious and interesting views we have anywhere met with, respecting the character and office of the Old Testament prophets, has been given in a late work by Dr. T. V. Moore, on "the Prophets of the Restoration," the substance of which we will here briefly present. Answering to the three great dispensations, the Patriarchal, Mosaic, and Christian, he points out three distinct modes, which God has adopted of communicating his will to men. The first was by direct appearances or manifestations, and was the distinguishing characteristic of the Patriarchal age. As God appeared and spoke to his servants, either directly or by his angel, so the prophetic gift was seldom bestowed on men, and the prophetic office, not being needed, did not exist. And for the same reason, the miracles of this age were mostly wrought by the hand of God directly, as those of the Deluge and the destruction of Sodom. The second mode was by inspired men, who spake as they were moved by the Holy Ghost, and was the great characteristic of the Mosaic dispensation. Hence the creation of the prophetic office, as a necessary part of the Mosaic economy, and the gradual development of the prophetic character in its highest perfection, as exhibited in Samuel, Elijah, and Isaiah. The third mode was that which was to be permanent and perpetual —the written word—the "more sure word of prophecy," containing the results of all that had gone before, and inaugurated as the prophetic and apostolic office ceased, and the order of inspired men passed away. And so this written word, the result of all that God has communicated, through men who spake and wrote as they were moved by the Holy Ghost, is now the distinctive feature of the Christian dispensation. But as this scheme of revelation was gradually unfolded through so many centuries, each dispensation enjoyed some of the advantages peculiar to the others. The Patriarchal age had some inspired men as Jacob, and the Mosaic age had, from the first, portions of the written word. Even so our Christian dispensation, though unblest with any Divine appearances to men, or inspired prophets, still in the written word, enjoys the benefit of a record of all these.

The writer, just referred to, then goes on to show, how this three-fold development, which runs through all the ages, applies on a narrower scale, to what may be called distinctively the prophetic period, that is, the Mosaic dispensation; how direct manifestations of God are found in the first portion of it, from Moses to Samuel; how inspired speaking and acting prophets marked the second portion of it from Samuel to Elisha; and how the writing prophets, adding so largely to the sacred oracles, and preparing the way for the New Testament, abound in the last period from Isaiah or Jonah to Malachi. But it would be aside from our purpose to pursue the subject further.

Now, according to this classification, the twelve minor prophets belong to this closing period of the prophetic ages, in which one important function of their office was to write, and thus complete the inspired canon of the Old Testament. The longest of these is Zechariah; the shortest, Obadiah. The one whose personal history, as made known to us, is the most eventful, and whose character stands out most strikingly from his writings, is Jonah. His book, like that of Daniel, is, in large part, a history of himself, and hence we know more of his life and character, than of the others. But for prophets of the Lord, no two men could well be more unlike than Jonah and

Daniel. Jonah, in his shrinking from duty, his disobedient self-will, his anger and despondency, his want of faith in God and courage before men, as well as his unforgiving spirit at the repentance of the Ninevites, was the very opposite of Daniel. Nor is it any apology for him, to say that his appointed work was a difficult and dangerous one. His mission to Nineveh was not at all harder to perform than Daniel's in the other great idolatrous city, Babylon. The result proved that there were no dangers and hardships at Nineveh, at all to be compared with those which Daniel had to meet in Babylon. He fled from duty, deterred by the imaginary lions along the way. Daniel, in the fearless discharge of his, faced the real lions in their den, and found them harmless. The only dangers Jonah encountered were those he met in the path of disobedience. And this should teach us not to make lions of our fears. The path of duty is always the path of safety. The true way to deal with danger, even when it is real and imminent, is to look it in the face, till danger dies.

Still it cannot be questioned, that Jonah, with all his faults, was a true prophet and a real servant of the Lord. Like many since his day, he worked for the Lord, but not cheerfully, not gracefully. He was like that son in the parable, who said, I will not; but afterwards repented and went. He did his duty at last, but not until he was humbled by affliction and driven to it by severe chastisement. He records his bitter and prayerful experience, when, in the depths of the sea, and encaged within the jaws of the great fish, he cried for deliverance to that God from whose presence he had fled. It must have been a proud heart and a stubborn will that required such a correction as this; but whom the Lord loveth he chasteneth, and scourgeth every son whom he receiveth. No doubt Jonah came forth from the deep a wiser and a better man. And so we find his mission to Nineveh greatly blessed. The men of Nineveh, though dark idolaters, repented at the preaching of Jonah. But even then the blessing came in a way altogether contrary to his expectations and desires. God was still far more merciful than his servant, to whom he had lately shown such great mercy. And so he required still further lessons in the way of self-abasement, which he soon received in the symbol of the withering gourd.

Upon the whole, this story of Jonah, so full of strange adventure, of mighty judgments, of the actings of human nature, of providential corrections for his servants, and of God's good mercy to the repenting sinner, is an interesting and instructive one. In all these minor prophets, we may find much to profit us—in Hosea's earnest reproofs of sin and calls to repentance; in Joel's prediction of the outpouring of the Spirit, quoted by Peter on the day of Pentecost; in Amos the plain herdsman of Tekoa; in Obadiah's heavy burdens against Edom; in Micah's prophecy of Immanuel's birth in Bethlehem; in Nahum's description of the utter ruin of Nineveh; in Habakkuk's sublime ode; in Zephaniah's warnings to Jerusalem; in Haggai and Zechariah's exhortations for the rebuilding of the holy city and temple; and in Malachi's closing promise of the return of Elijah and coming of the Messenger of the covenant.

But time would fail us to say all that might be said on such a theme as this. We cannot linger too long on these prophets of the old dispensation. Nor can we present even an outline of the prophets of the New Testament, from that first voice of John in the wilderness, crying with the power and spirit of Elijah: "Prepare ye the way of the Lord," down to the last prediction of the Apocalypse. Men boast of successions, and long dynasties. But here in the inspired prophets of God we have the longest and grandest succession that history records. It is a line from Enoch to Samuel, from Samuel to Malachi, from Malachi to John. Suffice it to say, that the grand burden of all the Old Testament prophets was the advent of a Saviour God to die for sinners. And so the grand burden of all the New Testament prophecy is a kindred theme, the second coming of that Saviour in the clouds of heaven, to raise the dead and judge the world. The first and second advents of the Son of God are the two great facts of all prophecy. Immanuel to come was the theme of all the ancient church. And Immanuel to come is still our theme.

The several illustrations we have given are enough to show how wonderful and how exalted was the prophetic character. The spirit of prophecy was the testimony of Jesus. The prophets of the Old Testament not only pointed to Jesus by their inspired predictions, but by their lives and actions. Their office itself was typical of the Great Prophet. They were all types of Christ in that fearless fidelity with which they proclaimed the truth of God in the face of danger and death. They were often like him in their heritage of sorrow and poverty. They were like him in their patient endurance of hardship and toil. "Take the prophets," says James, "who have spoken in the name of the Lord, for an example of suffering affliction, and patience." They were sometimes like him also in their death of martyrdom for conscience' sake. Jesus himself seems to trace the resemblance, when he reminds the Jews of the blood of all the prophets, which their fathers had shed, from that of righteous Abel to that of Zacharias the son of Barachias in the temple. And it is of them particularly that the apostle Paul has given the following high and sacred memorial—"They had trial of cruel mockings and scourgings, yea, moreover, of bonds and imprisonments. They were stoned, they were sawn asunder, were tempted, were slain with the sword. They wandered about in sheepskins and goatskins; being destitute, afflicted, tormented, (of whom the world was not worthy;) they wandered in deserts, and in mountains, and in dens, and caves of the earth."

> "Their blood was shed
> In confirmation of the noblest claim
> Our claim to feed upon immortal truth,
> To walk with God, to be divinely free,
> To soar, and to anticipate the skies.
> Yet few remembered them. They lived unknown,
> Till persecution dragged them into fame,
> And chased them up to heaven. Their ashes flew—
> No marble tells us whither."

VII. THE APOSTLES OF CHRIST

From the prophets of the Old Testament, the transition is easy and natural to the apostles of the New. The apostles held the same place of supremacy in the one which the prophets held in the other. Though differing much in their official functions, and still more in the great mission to which each was called, the two orders, nevertheless, had many striking points of resemblance. The prophetic office, the highest known to the Jewish church, ceased when its great work, that of prediction, was completed. And, as it ceased, the apostolic office was instituted in its place. The one had pointed forward to Christ as an inspired oracle, the other pointed backward to Christ historically as an inspired witness. But Christ's own person was the one middle ground of meeting and union. The idea of the prophetical character reached its highest development and perfection in him, the great Prophet of Israel, and he is, at the same time, the "Apostle and High Priest of our profession," the Alpha and Omega of all apostolical authority. He accordingly stands between the prophets and the apostles of the Bible, the central object of the whole group, partaking of the peculiar character of each, and possessing all the essential glory of both. To him all the apostles bore witness. Of his salvation all the prophets spoke. "Of this salvation," says an apostle, "the prophets have inquired and searched diligently, who prophesied of the grace that should come unto you, searching what, or what manner of time the spirit of Christ which was in them did signify, when it testified beforehand the sufferings of Christ, and the glory that should follow. Unto whom it was revealed, that not unto themselves, but unto us they did minister the things which are now reported unto you, by them that have preached the gospel unto you with the Holy Ghost sent down from heaven; which things the angels desire to look into." Thus, also, the church is said to be built upon the foundation of apostles and prophets, Jesus Christ himself being the chief corner stone.

The term apostle is sometimes used in a general sense in the New Testament, to denote "one sent forth," an ambassador, messenger, or missionary. And then again it is used in a definite official sense to designate a particular class or order of men whom Jesus Christ ordained for the specific work of establishing his church on a permanent basis. It is only of the apostles in this last restricted sense that we propose now to speak; of those only who held that apostolical office, which, in point of rank and power, corresponded most nearly with the office of the ancient prophets. Of these we have fourteen names in all; these alone filled the office, and are entitled to the distinction of apostles of Jesus Christ, and of these one became an apostate. They are the twelve whom Jesus first ordained, together with Matthias chosen in the place of Judas, and Paul the apostle of the Gentiles. Besides these fourteen, there are a few others, such as Barnabas, who are occasionally called apostles in the general sense of missionary or messenger, but who did not possess the characteristic marks of an apostle.

To thirteen of this number, striking Judas from the list, was committed the great work of inaugurating the kingdom of Jesus Christ among all nations on a settled and enduring basis—preaching the gospel of the grace of God, planting and organizing the church of the new dispensation. They had a mission to perform, such as, for its difficulty and its largeness, had never before been committed to the hands of men. And, for this end, they were endowed by the Spirit of God, with those extraordinary gifts and powers which no mortals before or since could rightfully claim.

In studying the life and times of these remarkable men, you will observe three distinctly marked historical periods. The first is the period of about three years and a half, during which they were all, except Matthias and Paul, under the immediate instruction of the Master; the period of discipline and of preparation for the great work which awaited them. The second was the period of their active, energetic labours embraced in the chronology of the Acts of the Apostles; a period of about thirty years, extending from the day of Pentecost to the close of that book. Early in this period their band was reduced to eleven by the martyrdom of James, but soon restored again to its original number, twelve, by the accession of Paul. The third was the period of about thirty-five years, intervening between the close of the book of Acts, or the death of Paul, and the death of John, who was probably the last of their number, towards the close of the first century. This we may call the period of their martyrdom, but of which very little is known. It is not, however, our purpose to trace their eventful history through either of these periods; but simply to point out some of their most prominent characteristics, labours, and endowments.

It was certainly not without an object that Christ selected all his first apostles from the humble and uneducated classes. He could just as easily have called the great or the learned, as he did afterwards in the case of Saul of Tarsus. He did not, however, call illiterate men and paupers to his service. Avoiding each extreme, he chose his first disciples from what might be called the middle classes of society—still from those classes which, although respectable, have always considered themselves among the poor. Matthew, as a publican or tax-gatherer, had indeed a calling to which some degree of odium was attached among the Jews, because of the hated Roman oppression; but all the rest were either fishermen or belonged to the labouring classes, in a country where labour was held in honour to a very high degree. Paul alone belonged to the higher professional classes; so that, what was afterwards true of the church in general, was, from the start, true of its leaders—"Not many wise men after the flesh, not many mighty, not many noble are called." The reason why the apostles were chosen from the ranks of the poor, seems to have been the same that led Christ himself to assume a lowly character on coming into the world. It was that he might thereby exalt humility, and lay the axe at the root of the tree of human pride and ambition. And probably there was this further reason, that, as in all human affairs there is a law of influence by which opinion is spread and propagated naturally by working from the higher to the lower classes of society; so the Author of Christianity by reversing this order in the establishment of his religion, would render the proof of its Divine origin the more striking and complete. By beginning at the bottom and working upwards; by choosing the unlettered to confound the wise, the weak to confound the mighty, and the base the noble, he would thereby magnify the power of Divine grace, and demonstrate most triumphantly that the work was from heaven and not of men. Had it been otherwise, infidelity, through the learned and ingenious labours of her Gibbons, would have had a somewhat better success in accounting for the early spread of Christianity on merely human principles. As it is, its rapid and triumphant progress must ever stand as a demonstration of its truth. That demonstration was given as it never had been before, and as it never could have been otherwise, when twelve unlettered Galilean Jews were taken from their fishing-nets, their work-shops, and their receipts of custom, and sent forth in the name of the crucified Nazarene, to overthrow the hoary paganism of the whole classical world, and upon its ruins to inaugurate a system of religion, morality, law, and philosophy, which has lived already through eighteen centuries, and which will live to the end of time. That which was said of the Master may, with equal propriety, be applied to all his apostles except Paul—How knoweth this man letters, having never learned? The only answer which, to this day, has ever been found for the question, is the answer which was given in the rushing mighty wind, and cloven fiery tongues of the day of Pentecost. To borrow a beautiful thought from Hugh Miller, "As often as we open the New Testament and look upon this Greek of the cloven tongues—this Greek of Peter and John, James and Jude, this Greek which was never learned at school or in the nursery; it is as if we looked upon the very foot-prints of that miraculous creation of the day of Pentecost; it is as if, in this untaught Greek, we saw the proofs of a Divine agency as clear as those which the geologist finds, of animal and vegetable life, in the deep, imbedded fossils of the Old Red Sandstone."

VII. PERSONAL CHARACTERISTICS OF THE TWELVE.

Although the original twelve apostles were all chosen from the humble, uneducated walks of life, they seem nevertheless to have been chosen with a view to great diversity in their natural temper, character, and endowments. It is interesting to trace this remarkable diversity, as it was gradually developed during their three years' intercourse with our Saviour. A school is always a good place to learn character. And so the gospel history gives us a clear insight into the personal characteristics of these disciples of the great Master, while under his instruction. They were originally sent forth two by two, and they are often mentioned in pairs. Three of these couples were respectively brothers; viz., Andrew and Peter, James and John, James the less and Jude or Thaddeus, the last pair being also either brothers or cousins of the Lord Jesus. Still, after all these relationships, no twelve men could well be more unlike each other in personal peculiarities, talents, and temperament. You will observe, that they were not all, naturally, noted men, or men of mark. If they had been, they would have been very far from being true representatives of the world in general. They were all, probably, plain, common men, or, as we might say, men of mediocrity. The majority of mankind in all ages are such; and we should not suffer our admiration for genius to disparage the importance of common men. Mediocrity is even more essential to the well-going machinery of this world's business, than the highest genius; without common men to do her work, genius could make poor headway in such a world as this. God does, sometimes, but not always, employ human genius to do his greatest work. This would be a sad world indeed—much sadder than it is, if there were no others in it but your men of mark, who felt themselves born to command. Genius is a noble thing when it goes right, but it is so apt to go wrong, that we look with much more confidence upon those nine hundred and ninety-nine common men whose moderate abilities best fit them for the regular, uniform work of life, than upon your thousandth man of genius who can do nothing except in his own way and on the grandest scale. Still, we should not like to be without that thousandth man in his proper time and place. It requires hills and mountains occasionally, not less than plains and valleys, to make a world of comfort and beauty. So was it with the apostles. Paul was a man born to command anywhere—a man of consummate genius. All the others belonged by nature to a different order. Some of them, as Thaddeus and Simon Zelötes, were so little marked by strong salient points of character, that we find scarcely a word or action in the whole history by which to distinguish them from their fellow-disciples. Others, again, as Andrew and Matthew, Philip and Bartholomew, though not often prominent as speakers or actors, yet, whenever they speak or act at all, exhibit many strong, distinctive characteristics. Others still stand out on all occasions in bold relief, presenting the very extremes of human character; such as Peter, Thomas, Judas Iscariot, James, and John.

James and John, the sons of Zebedee, possessed by nature a very different spirit from that which they afterwards attained by grace. Children of an ambitious mother, they seem to have inherited her ardent, energetic character. On one occasion they wished to call down fire from heaven to consume the Samaritans; on another they ventured to forbid the casting out of devils, because it was not done in their Master's name; on another they proposed to share with him in the glory of his throne, one on the right and the other on the left. At the beginning they received from him the significant and doubtless appropriate surname of Boanerges, "Sons of thunder." But little outward indications then appeared of the loving and beloved disciple in the one, or of the first apostolic martyr in the other. How different was their destiny from that which their aspiring mother sought for them; and how different the one from the other! James the first of all the band called to verify his Master's prediction by a baptism of blood, and John tarrying to the very last!

Simon Peter, who was probably the oldest of the twelve, and withal a married man—a circumstance which seems but poorly to accord with the celibacy of his pretended successors—stands forth prominently on all occasions as the chief speaker of the band. This position he held, not by any special appointment, but simply by the force of circumstances and his own natural fitness for it. Bold, ardent, sincere, honest, generous, openhearted, zealous, energetic, impetuous, eloquent, a man of words and a man of deeds, he was eminently qualified to be a leader and a governor of his fellow men.

Some writers give a different view of his character, representing it as a strange mixture of strength and weakness, courage and cowardice, love for his master and inordinate self-love. But they certainly do him much injustice. Having nothing like concealment or hypocrisy in his character, conscious always of a sincere desire to do right, and possessing, at once, a strong mind, a warm heart, and an energetic will, he gave a full and ready expression, both by word and action, of all that was within him. And though sometimes in the wrong, he needed only to see it, in order to acknowledge and turn from the error. The promptness of his repentance was always equal to the rashness of his faults; and the decision of his actions when right far more than counterbalanced the indiscretion and self-confidence of his hasty words. The faults of Peter were mostly faults of mistaken zeal; they were such as leaned to virtue's side; we admire the character and love the man with all his faults. He is a beautiful illustration of what has been seen a thousand times in the church of God—the asperities of nature yielding to the amenities of grace—the rough disciple transformed into the loving saint—the lion mingling with the lamb. Some writer has quaintly remarked that the grace of God was as much displayed in restraining Peter from knocking his enemies down in the street, as in making John the beloved disciple.

These three the Saviour seems to have admittted to a closer intimacy with himself, than he did any of the others. They were present when he restored to life the ruler's daughter. They alone saw his glory on the mount of transfiguration. They alone witnessed his agony in the garden of Gethsemane. Of the three, John was evidently our Saviour's favourite companion and bosom friend. In all probability he was the youngest of the twelve. In him Jesus doubtless discerned, from the beginning, all those amiable and noble traits of character, which, when adorned by grace and ripened by experience, so distinguished the author of the fourth gospel history, the three epistles, and the Apocalypse. This distinction of peculiar intimacy with Jesus is manifest from his being called the disciple whom Jesus loved, from the circumstance of his cleaving to him during the night of the trial, as well as leaning on his bosom at the last supper, and from the affectionate manner in which the mother of Jesus was committed to his care amid the trying scenes of the crucifixion. There was no doubt something in the character of John, not less than in the relation of friendship between him and the Saviour, which rendered it peculiarly appropriate that he should thenceforth act the part of a son to the bereaved mother of his Lord; and the tradition of antiquity is, that he was faithful to his charge. "If we endeavour," says a biblical critic, "to picture to ourselves an image of John as drawn from his gospel and his epistles aided by a few traits of his life preserved by the fathers, he appears to have been of a wise, affectionate, and rather feminine character. It seems, that originally this softness of disposition would sometimes blaze up in wrath, as feminine characters in general feel themselves as strongly repelled as attracted. Hence it appears that love, humility, and mildness, were in John the works of transforming grace." Certainly there never was a man better fitted by nature and by grace to represent the female character and attract it to the gospel of Jesus, than the beloved disciple.

One of the most strongly marked characters in the apostolic group is that of Thomas, sometimes called the doubting disciple. It is worthy of notice that Matthew generally appears associated with him as a companion, being perhaps the nearest like him in his cast of mind. It is obvious, that these two were plain, substantial, matter-of-fact men—keen-eyed, shrewd observers, governed by the strong logic of common sense—too incredulous to be imposed upon by others, too honest to impose upon others, and too cautious and cool-tempered to be carried away by any sudden gust of fanaticism. Thomas was by nature of a sceptical, inquiring turn. Matthew must have become so by the necessities of his profession. His office, as collector of the revenues of an unpopular government, had no doubt trained him to habits of scrutiny and suspicion touching all the affairs and motives of men.

It adds greatly to our confidence in the truth of the gospel history, that Christ should have had among his apostles from the beginning, two such men as Thomas and Matthew, precisely as it does, that outside of the apostles we have an independent witness and writer like Luke, who was by birth and education, as well as by his profession as a physician, eminently qualified to give us an impartial narrative, as he has done in his Gospel and Acts of the Apostles. Our assurance of the truth is far greater when we know there were such minds as Thomas and Matthew in the college of apostles, than it would have been, had they all been like the ardent Peter and the devotional John. All the strength of their doubts now accrues to the benefit of our belief. Our conviction is all the stronger from the fact, that from the first Jesus had in his family eyewitnesses of a sceptical, inquiring turn, whose doubts were all overcome and removed by "many infallible proofs." It was important to have men like John, who was first to believe at the sepulchre, at the sea of Tiberias, and on all occasions. It was important too to have men of impulse like Peter, who was always first to act, and to reflect afterwards. It was equally important to have men like Thomas and Matthew, who would take nothing for granted, would believe nothing without evidence, and do nothing without counting the cost. Owing to their peculiar Jewish prejudices, they were all exceedingly slow of heart to believe in one fact—the resurrection of their crucified Master. But you know that, for one week after all the rest had been convinced, Thomas remained a sceptic on this point. "Except I shall see in his hands the print of the nails, and put my finger into the print of the nails, and thrust my hand into his side, I will not believe." And you remember also, with what a tone of incredulity he had said at the last supper, "Lord, we know not whither thou goest, and how can we know the way?"

He was a man who could believe, but he must have the proof for himself, and not on second hand. He was fearless and ready for action, but he must first understand the way. He would not, and could not act in the dark. You will observe that while he was slow to believe, he was prompt to act whenever his mind was once satisfied. No sooner did he see the marks on the person, and hear the voice of Jesus, saying —"Be not faithless, but believing," than he embraced the whole truth of his Divinity, and exclaimed, "My Lord and my God!" And do you not call to mind with what energetic and fearless decision, he took his stand on the report of Lazarus' sickness, when others were hesitating and dissuading Jesus from going back to Bethany, and said to his fellow disciples, "Let us also go, that we may die with him?" We see combined in Thomas the utmost caution and deliberation in making up his judgment on evidence, together with great readiness to act upon his convictions, and to be faithful even unto death. It is a noble combination of character, and, wherever it exists, constitutes a most reliable and valuable man. It has been well remarked, that "whosoever is ready to die with his Lord, will be inclined, like Thomas, to avail himself of extraordinary evidence for extraordinary facts, since nobody likes to suffer martyrdom by mistake."

Philip and Bartholomew are generally associated together, in the first three gospels, just as Philip and Nathaniel are in the last, where Bartholomew's name never occurs. From this, and other circumstances, it is evident, that Nathaniel is only another name for Bartholomew. Philip had first become a disciple; he finds his friend Nathaniel, a man of kindred spirit, who was also waiting for the consolation of Israel; he brings him to Jesus, by whose omniscience he is at once convinced that he has found the Messiah. Jesus pronounces upon him the high eulogium—"Behold an Israelite indeed in whom is no guile." The two friends follow Jesus, and are thenceforward bound together by a new tie as fellow apostles. They seem to have been of a sincere, earnest, truth-loving spirit; of a gentle and retiring, but yet firm and consistent character. Perhaps, we could not better describe their peculiar excellence, both as men and as ministers of Christ, than to call them "sons of consolation."

We must not omit to notice the character of Andrew, although he was not among the most prominent. He has received the distinction of being regarded as the first called of all the apostles. Having been a disciple of John the Baptist, he was the first to find Jesus, and to recognize in him the true Messiah of the prophets. He seems ever afterwards to have been distinguished for his active, influential zeal in leading others to Christ. With the benevolent feelings of one who wished others to share in all the good that he enjoyed, he immediately sought his brother Simon and introduced him to Jesus. He seems also to have been the chief agent in bringing his fellow-townsmen, Philip and Nathaniel, to the same happy choice. In accordance with this benevolent spirit we find him long afterwards, in connection with Philip, informing Jesus of certain Greeks at Jerusalem, who had expressed a desire to see him. Wherever Andrew is mentioned there is a beautiful consistency and verisimilitude in his character; and that character throughout is one of activity and benevolent zeal. No one better illustrated the precept of his Master, "Freely ye have received, freely give."

But the most deeply marked character in the whole group was Judas Iscariot. He was the perfect opposite of many of his fellow disciples. He was the extreme of cunning and concealment as distinguished from Peter, the embodiment of duplicity and deception as distinguished from Nathaniel, the dupe of superstition and cowardice as distinguished from Thomas, the votary and the victim of every dark malignant passion as distinguished from John—a thief, a miser, a traitor, a murderer, and a suicide as distinguished from all of them. Many ingenious theories have been advanced by learned critics, to solve the enigma of the character of Judas: such, for example, as that he was only aiming to put Jesus to the proof of his Messiahship; or again, that he had no expectation that the rulers would push matters so far as to put Jesus to death. But to us there is only one solution of his conduct: to wit, that which the Scriptures have given, that he had a devil and was mad. "Have I not chosen twelve," said the Saviour, "and one of you is a devil?" Why such a man should have been called into the family of Jesus, and made partaker of that holy apostleship, we cannot tell; unless it was, that he wished the extremes of human character there to meet, in order that thus, by the living and dying testimony of an enemy within the camp, the spotless integrity of his own life might be fully vindicated and attested to the world. Be the design what it may, such we know has been the result. It is not a little remarkable, that for the vindication of the character of Jesus, we have the testimony of the unjust judge who condemned him, of the apostate who betrayed him, and of the stern Roman soldier who commanded at his execution. Whilst the apostasy and treachery of Judas fulfilled the Scriptures, his awful death was a new and extraordinary attestation to the innocence of Jesus. His last recorded words, "I have sinned in that I have betrayed innocent blood," furnish us with precisely that argument, which infidelity would be ready enough to demand if we did not have it, even the voluntary confession of an enemy.

VIII. THE GREAT APOSTLE OF THE GENTILES.

We know far more about the personal history and character of Paul than of any other apostle of Christ: first, because we have more of his writings in the New Testament than of any other, and secondly, because the book of Acts, after the twelfth chapter, is mainly occupied with an account of his missionary labours. The probability is, that a narrative equally interesting, though on a less extended scale, might have been given of all or nearly all the rest. It seemed to be the purpose of the great Head of the Church, that the original number twelve, answering to the twelve patriarchs, and the twelve tribes of Israel, should still be kept up for a considerable time, in the apostolic band. The defection of Judas was soon supplied by the election of

Matthias; and the vacancy caused by the early martyrdom of James had already been filled by the conversion and call of Paul. It is interesting and instructive to contemplate the condition of the infant church of Jesus, at a point of time, some ten or fifteen years subsequent to the day of Pentecost. During that brief period the ranks of believers had been swelled to more than ten thousand in Jerusalem itself; the greatest cities of Palestine, Samaria and Cæsarea, had heard the word of God; the door of separation had been broken down, and the preached gospel had taken root both at Damascus and at Antioch; the church at Jerusalem had passed triumphantly through two bloody persecutions; and so far from being exterminated, even in the holy city where the persecutors had full sway, the result was, that the bloody leader of one of these persecutions, King Herod, had died a dreadful death, smitten by an angel of God; and the still fiercer leader of the other, Saul of Tarsus, arrested, converted, and transformed into an apostle, was now preaching to the Gentile world, the faith which he had so madly persecuted unto death. It would be hard to find in history a greater marvel than this. With this result before their eyes—men called "Christians" in the elegant and splendid capital of Syria, and Saul himself among the apostles—those Jewish rulers, who had set a watch over the mangled and buried body of him whom they called a "deceiver," were no doubt constrained to feel that the "last end was worse than the first." And if they had not been men who had long since taken leave of their reason, their failure, after such gigantic efforts, to keep this heresy from spreading beyond the sepulchre of Jesus, might have satisfied them, that it was from heaven and not of men.

Nothing could be more wonderful, and nothing more important, in the early history of the church, than the conversion of such a man as Paul and his commission as an apostle. A great crisis had come; a great work was to be done; the day of preparation was past; the door of the kingdom had been opened to all the nations; and there stood the vast harvest field of the ancient classical world, white and waving before the reapers. There too stood the man, called, qualified, and endowed of heaven, with his bright and polished sickle, ready and eager for the work. The head of the Jewish persecution was henceforth to be the head of Christ's ambassadors to the Gentile world.

A demonstration of what the gospel could do in the hands of unlettered men had already been made; at least, made in part. It was equally important, that the world should also have a demonstration of what this same gospel could do with a scholar, a man of genius and learning, a master in the schools of eloquence and argument. Christ needed another man, not only to take the place of the martyred James, but to do a new and peculiar work. He chose a man wholly unlike all the others—the ablest man by all odds then upon the earth. He called him in the ardour of his youthful zeal. He called him with all the resources of his learning and his commanding intellect. He took him in all the fierce and fearless energy of his lion-like nature. He took him in the very act of his daring and mad rebellion. And the conquest which the gospel made over such a man as Paul was but a prelude and a pledge of that greater conquest, which, through him, it was destined to make over the Gentile world. It has been well remarked, by Gilfillan, in reference to the conversion and apostleship of Paul, that "It was of importance to Christianity, that it should triumph over a man of culture. Simple fishermen it had in plenty; but it needed to show, how it could subdue an intellectual and educated man; how it should, in the process, reconcile the warring elements of his nature, and bring to him, what no study could ever bring, peace of conscience. In other words, the intellectual progress of the age, and the new religion must be reconciled; and they were reconciled accordingly; not merely in a compact and complete theory, but in a living man, and that man was Paul."

There can be no question, that along with his high commission from Jesus Christ, as the apostle of the Gentiles, Paul received direct and peculiar gifts from heaven, fitting him for his great work. But still it is true, that there were elements in his character, and there had been influences at work upon him from his boyhood, which did not exist in the other apostles at all, and which gave him his pre-eminent fitness and qualification for the work. His birth, education, and mode of life, were all such as to render it comparatively easy for him to become a thorough cosmopolite—"all things to all men." When he appeared upon the stage of action, the whole civilized world was pervaded and influenced by three great elements—three almost universal nationalities—the Jewish, the Grecian, and the Roman. The three races were everywhere mingled; the three civilizations were everywhere in contact; the three languages were everywhere spreading the peculiar influence of each. The Jew, the Grecian, and the Roman were confessedly the master spirits of the world; and between themselves they held the arts, the arms, the religion, the learning, the power, and destiny of the world. No man living came nearer combining all the three in one than Saul of Tarsus. A Jew, by descent, of the purest stamp, a Grecian in virtue of his nativity and early education at Tarsus, which ranked with Athens as a seat of philosophy;

he was, at the same time, by political right a "Roman citizen." He always felt and acted like a Roman; as one born for the world—born to break over the narrow conventionalities of national prejudice and prescription. All his views and feelings, as well as his early associations, partook of a world-wide character; and we are prepared, knowing his antecedents, to hear him say, even when longing with intense desire for the salvation of Israel—"I am debtor both to the Greeks and to the barbarians, both to the wise and unwise, so as much as in me is, I am ready to preach the gospel to you that are at Rome also." Yes, Rome, the proud imperial mistress of the world, was the proper field for such a man. To that grand centre we find him steadily tending from the beginning, and there at last we see his wonderful and world-wide career terminating in a death of glory.

The inspired record conducts Paul to Rome, and there leaves him. Tradition affirms, however, and there is no reason to discredit it, that, after preaching the gospel as far west as Spain, the great apostle was beheaded at Rome under Nero, about the time when Peter and Andrew were crucified at the same place. The probability is, that after the death of Paul, all the apostolic band, one after another, in their different fields of labour, suffered martyrdom in those great persecutions which wasted the church during the first century. We have no authentic history to tell us with what words of triumph, with what anticipations of celestial glory, they bore testimony with their dying breath to that gospel which it had been the labour of their lives to preach. We are, doubtless, justified in taking the last words of Paul, in view of his near departure, as a fair index of the high moral heroism, with which they all sealed their testimony with their blood. From his last letter to Timothy we know what his views and feelings were in the immediate prospect of a violent death. For thirty years and more his life had been inured to all manner of toil, he had grown familiar with suffering and privation in every possible form, he had looked death and danger in the face a thousand times. Nothing in man's experience ever transcended the moral grandeur of his life, or the sublime glory of his approach to the hour of death. Like the setting sun, his full-orbed character shone with greatest beauty, as he left the world. Like some mighty river, his life flowed with its deepest, broadest, most majestic current as he entered the ocean of eternity. Cyrus, Alexander, Hannibal, Cæsar, Charlemagne, Napoleon, were all great while living. Their grandeur ended with their lives. In death they were nothing more than common men. But here was a man whose death added infinite lustre to the greatness of his life; here was a man who could welcome death as a triumph over life itself—immortal till his work was done, and then immortal for ever. "I am now ready to be offered, and the time of my departure is at hand. I have fought a good fight, I have finished my course, I have kept the faith. Henceforth there is laid up for me a crown of righteousness, which the Lord, the righteous Judge, shall give me at that day; and not to me only, but to all them that love his appearing."

IX. THE RELATION OF THE APOSTLES TO THE CHURCH.

The apostolic office, like that of the ancient prophets, was one of special relations and extraordinary functions. Its peculiar gifts and endowments were all called for by the particular circumstances which led to the creation of the office. The

Great Head of the Church, after his ascension to heaven, needed an order of inspired and infallible men, who, as his authorized ambassadors and representatives, should complete and carry out the grand scheme of mercy whose foundation he had himself laid in the death of the cross. To do this it was necessary that the Mosaic dispensation should close, and a new order of things be introduced; that the church should be carried over from the narrow boundaries of Judaism to a gospel state as wide as the world; that it should be organized anew upon that basis which it was to occupy till the end of time, and that, by preaching, attended by mighty signs and wonders, it should be actually established among all nations. A new work was to be done, such as had never been done before. And for this end a new office was created. The men for this great work were chosen, trained, and taught by Christ himself, while he was with them in the world, and after he was gone, fully endowed and equipped for it on the day of Pentecost, by that Divine Power, which, according to his promise, should teach them all things, and bring all things to their remembrance.

The apostles, endowed with extraordinary powers, such as no man since their day has ever possessed, and commissioned to do a work such as had never been done before, filled up the measure of their high calling of God and passed away, precisely as the prophetic order had done before them. They were succeeded by the pastors, teachers, and evangelists of the ordinary Christian ministry; just as they themselves had succeeded the prophets of the Old Testament. But they continued with the church, in full possession of all their miraculous endowments as inspired teachers and infallible guides, until the church was everywhere fully indoctrinated with the knowledge of the truth as it is in Jesus, and fully organized with that uninspired and fallible, but still divinely authorized ministry, which has existed to the present hour. And, however manifold the denominations into which the church has since been divided, however diversified their modes of worship and of designating their teachers and rulers, it is safe to say, that all, everywhere, and in every age, who have held the truth as it is in Jesus, and have been called to preach it, both by the outward voice of the church and the inward voice of God, as required in the Scriptures, have been the successors of the apostles in the only sense in which they ever had any successors. And so also are they successors of the prophets, in the only sense in which any succession is possible.

While the apostles were all equal in official standing and authority, and alike responsible for the great work of preaching the gospel to all nations, still it is plain that some of them were called to act a more conspicuous and important part in the church than others. We find four of them thus distinguished: Peter the apostle of the Circumcision, Paul the apostle of the Gentiles, John the disciple whom Jesus loved, and James the brother of the Lord. The Scriptures plainly represent these four as successively taking a leading part in the church for which they were, no doubt, fitted, by superior natural endowments. We are aware that some learned men hold that James, the brother of the Lord, who is known in church history as James the Just, was a different man from James the son of Alpheus, known as James the Less, and consequently not of the number of the apostles at all. But it seems incredible to us, that one who was not an apostle at all, and not even a disciple till after the resurrection of Christ, could have held the position in the church which we find this man holding in the great synod of Jerusalem, as stated in the fifteenth chapter of the Acts.

Accordingly as he could not have been James the brother of John, whom Herod had already slain before that meeting, we can regard him only as one of the original twelve apostles, and of course identical with James the son of Alpheus. He may have been a cousin, or half-brother of our Lord; but evidently he was a pillar in the church as indicated not only by the language of Paul, but by his speech in the council and by the Epistle which bears his name.

In the first planting of the church, we find Peter acting the leading part, as he had always done during the life of Christ. He stands out prominently at the election of Matthias to fill the place of Judas; in all the scenes of the day of Pentecost; in the first miracle at the gate of the temple; in the trial before the Jewish rulers; in the judgments on Ananias and Sapphira, and on Simon Magus at Samaria; and he is the first to open the doors of the church to the Gentiles, by preaching the gospel to Cornelius. Indeed he is both the chief speaker and the chief actor in the opening chapters of the Acts of the Apostles. And it is no doubt in reference to the important part he was thus to act as a pioneer in laying the foundations of the New Testament church, both among the Jews and the Gentiles, that Christ has said, in assigning his symbolical name: "Thou art Peter, and upon this rock, I will build my church, and the gates of hell shall not prevail against it." This was precisely Peter's mission; this his great work, for which both nature and grace had so highly endowed him. He was the man to begin the work, but not the one to finish it. Accordingly, no sooner is this work of inauguration done, than others come forward and take the foremost place. Little is heard of Peter beyond the tenth chapter of the Acts, which records the opening of the kingdom to the Gentile world. In the fifteenth chapter, while the great centre of influence was still Jerusalem, we find James occupying the most prominent place. And then when the great work of the church was no longer at Jerusalem, but throughout the Gentile world, we find Paul in the foreground even to the end of the book. James yields to Paul, that pre-eminence which Peter had first yielded to him. Nor is this all. When Paul's great work was done, and sealed with martyrdom, soon after the close of the book of Acts, then we find John, the loved disciple, still tarrying, and holding the prominent position, for almost thirty years longer, even down to the close of the century. Each of the four had a great and distinctive mission to fulfil, and each of the four was in turn the prominent apostle. As to supremacy, we do not find Peter occupying any higher position, or wielding any sort of power, more than belonged in turn to the other three. On the contrary we find Paul, on one occasion, resisting and rebuking Peter, about a matter, in which, though he had once been the chief apostle, he was clearly to blame.

As it required the labours of these four great apostles, acting in turn as leaders of the church, to perfect its organization throughout the world; so also in their personal characters, and their inspired writings, taken together, we have a most symmetrical and beautiful exhibition of Christian doctrine and duty. Each apostle stands out distinctly before us, in all his writings, as presenting a noble and important illustration of Christian character, doctrine, and duty. But each apostle acts and writes as the necessary supplement of the others. Each exhibits a peculiar and essential phase of Christian character in his own person, and of gospel truth in his writings. And it is only when we put them all together, that we have that gospel in its full orbed glory, and that character in its nearest approach to the perfect virtues of the Divine Master.

For example, we have in Peter on the day of Pentecost, and thence onward, as it was needed, all the ardent, impulsive, energetic, and hopeful zeal of a pioneer and a leader, who feels that he has high responsibilities laid upon him, and a right to command the co-operation of his fellow-labourers. In James the Just, presiding with dignity over the first general council of the church, we have that calm conservative wisdom, and sterling integrity of character, which challenged the respect of Jew and Gentile, and was essential to an apostleship to be exercised at Jerusalem. In Paul again, we have all the high heroic qualities—the zeal, the energy, the courage, the faith, the love of Jesus and the love of souls—along with the highest intellectual powers and large stores of learning, which fitted him at once to plant the gospel amongst the great classical nations, and to develope and expound the whole system of revealed truth. And last of all in John, we have the deep devotion of spirit, the yearning human sympathies, the profound spiritual philosophy and intuition of Divine things, which enabled him to complete all that remained to be done, in teaching the church the supremacy of love, that God himself is love, and in adding a fourth gospel to the life of Christ, and closing the inspired canon with the Apocalypse. Nothing can be more admirable than the adaptation of these four peculiarly original and unique apostles, to each other, and to the grand end of filling up the measure of the stature of a perfect man in Christ.

Of the four, Paul and John have certainly laid us under the greatest obligations by their writings. They had occasion, more than the other two, to develope the Christian system in all its practical bearings on human life and character; and perhaps we are justified in saying, when we consider that one was caught up into paradise, and the other blessed with the sublime visions of the Apocalypse, they had a deeper insight into its mysteries. "Paul and John," says Dr. Schaff, "in their two grand systems, have laid the eternal foundations of all true theology and philosophy; and their writings, now after eighteen centuries of study, are still unfathomed. Not inaptly has Peter been styled the apostle of hope; Paul, the apostle of faith; and John, the apostle of love."

This beautiful thought, that the three cardinal graces of the gospel, faith, hope, and charity, find their fitting impersonations and exponents in the three great apostles, is only completed by adding James the Just, the author of the epistle on good works, to the list, as the apostle of evangelical obedience. For the gospel is itself a law—the law of love and perfect liberty—and obedience is essential as the test of faith, hope, and charity—the vital principle without which there can be no virtuous action and no Godlike character. And thus we trace the profound agreement of the apostles of faith, hope, love, and obedience, and find that the one grand system of doctrine and duty, revealed by them, is an unbroken circle, whose centre is the righteousness and redemption of the cross.

X. THE WORK ACCOMPLISHED BY THE APOSTLES.

We must now say a word in conclusion touching the gigantic work accomplished by the labours of these twelve men. For, after the early death of James, you will observe the number, including Matthias and Paul, was still but twelve. When did any other twelve men in the history of the world, accomplish such a work—so difficult, so vast, so important, so enduring? By the close of the first century, they had all, or nearly all, left the world. But what an influence had they left behind! what a legacy had they bequeathed to mankind! They rested from their labours; their work still went on; eighteen centuries have only spread and perpetuated their influence. Who, at that day, could have estimated the magnitude or duration of their work? Who, even now, after all these centuries of progress, can essay to calculate its value or its final result?

One great work of the apostles was to complete the canon of sacred Scripture. Six of them have written books of the New Testament: namely, Matthew and John, Paul and Peter, James and Jude. Paul is the author of fourteen separate productions, John of five, Peter of two, and the others of one each. Mark and Luke, who were not apostles, are the only two other writers in the New Testament. It is, however, the received opinion of ecclesiastical historians, that Mark wrote under the direction and approbation of Peter, whose companion he was; whilst Luke wrote under the supervision of Paul, with whom he travelled; so that, directly or indirectly, we have inspired apostolic authority for every book of the New Testament. This completion of the Divine oracles, which had been begun by Moses, and carried forward through so many centuries, was one great end of apostolic inspiration. "When he, the Spirit of truth, is come, he will teach you all things, and bring all things to your remembrance, whatsoever I have said unto you."

Great as were the active labours of the apostles, as missionaries and preachers of the cross, still greater has been their influence upon the world through their inspired writings. With their living tongues they preached Christ to the men of their own generation throughout the whole ancient world from

Arabia to Scythia, from India to the Pillars of Hercules. But by these inspired writings, they have been preaching the gospel both to the people and the preachers of all generations and of all nations and tongues. Sublime and glorious are the themes that live for ever on these sacred pages; bright and beautiful as the light; fresh and radiant as the sun of morning! Here life and immortality are brought to light, such as Grecian and Roman sages never dreamed of, such as Jewish patriarchs and prophets sought but never found! The grand inspiring theme of all the Old Testament prophecies—all its poetry, its types, its shadows, had been a Saviour to come. Even so, the one grand, soul-cheering revelation of the New, is a Saviour received—a Redeemer come from God, crucified for sin, risen again from the dead, and ascended to glory. Beginning at the point where the Old Testament ends, or where the last of the prophets laid down his burden of Messianic song, the New Testament writers take up the wondrous story, and through all their preaching, their epistles, their histories, their apocalyptic visions, their expositions of doctrine, they proclaim the glad tidings of this great salvation. Peace on earth, good will to men, redemption for Zion, glory to God, an atonement for sin, the triumph of the cross, the conversion of the world, the second coming of Christ, the resurrection of the dead, the eternal judgment, the saints' everlasting rest, the final gathering of all in one in the heavens, when God shall be all in all—these and a thousand kindred doctrines, are the themes of beauty and grandeur that glow upon the apostolic pages in all their primeval crystal purity—shining there still as bright and clear, as do the unwasting stars upon the firmament of night.

But leave out of view, if you please, that part of their work which has followed them; set aside that vast influence which has been accumulating through eighteen centuries; look now alone at the result of their labours, such as it stood at the end of a few centuries, or such as it stood before the last of them had left the world. Contrast the cause of the Nazarene, as it appeared on the night when all his followers forsook him and fled, with that same cause, as it appeared when Constantine proclaimed it as the religion of the empire; or even as John lived to see it at the close of the first century. And when did the world ever behold such a miracle of success and triumph! Measure it only by the term of a single life-time; and how wonderful the transformation! Some of the men, who, on that night of despair, forsook him and fled, indeed most of them, lived to see the gospel preached and the church planted in all the surrounding nations, that were then open to Jewish, Grecian, and Roman civilization. The man of sorrows, whom they had for three years called Master, for whom they had shed many a bitter tear as they saw him nailed to the ignominious cross, and then laid in the silent sepulchre, they now beheld, worshipped as a God, from India to Britain.

Suppose the following problem had been submitted for solution to all the wise men of the ancient world in the days of Augustus Cæsar. Given, a religion from Judæa, consisting in the worship of a crucified Jew who claimed, while living, to be an incarnation of the Deity, and for whom it was claimed after death, that he had come to life again and ascended to heaven; given also, twelve zealous, but poor and uneducated Jews from Galilee, with one of no small learning and talent from Tarsus, as the propagators of this new faith; to calculate how long it will take such a religion in such hands, to overthrow the classical mythology of the ancient Grecian literature, to supplant the venerable, established religion of the Roman empire, and to become itself the acknowledged worship of the civilized world. Mr. Gibbon, at the safe distance of a thousand years after the facts, can sit in judgment on the problem, and find nothing difficult, or wonderful, and certainly nothing Divine, in the manner in which history has solved it. We wish Mr. Gibbon and some others could have lived before the facts, and could have left on record their opinion as to the probable result of such a problem, according to the known principles of human nature. We can well imagine the cool philosophic scorn with which such a logician in the days of Augustus Cæsar, would have treated the idea, could it have been even suggested, of a religion from Jerusalem conquering the Roman world. Suppose it had been given out as a response from some old Grecian oracle, as it was by the Hebrew prophets, that a religion should go forth from the stock of Abraham and from the stem of Jesse in which all nations should be blessed—suppose some man claiming more than ordinary sagacity had asserted to Cicero or Seneca, Virgil or Horace, that a new religion from Jerusalem consisting in the apotheosis and worship of a crucified Jew should one day supplant all the gods of the Pantheon, close every splendid temple, and shiver to atoms every shrine and image of Greece and Rome—that the Sabbath worship of the Jewish synagogue, would every where on earth, in spite of all the efforts of Roman power to prevent it, take the place of that of Minerva and Diana, Jupiter and Apollo—that the simple philosophy not less than the strange religion, of the Jewish sacred books would utterly and for ever overthrow the proud philosophy of Plato, and Aristotle, and all the schools of Athens—with what lofty and contemptuous scorn, may we not suppose the old Roman to have treated such a thought!

Modern infidelity is too poor in resources, and too humble in native abilities, even to appreciate the magnificent disdain, with which the old Grecian idolater, or Roman world conqueror, would have turned up his lip at such a suggestion, and uttered the proverbial sarcasm—"Credat Judæus Apella!" And yet, if the haughty old Greek or Roman, could have come back into the world at the opening of the fourth century, or of the nineteenth, what would he have seen? He would have seen the fulfilment, and more than the fulfilment of that very prophecy which he had so despised. He would have seen what modern infidelity has so long seen with shame, and humiliation, and utter confusion of face—the defeat and extermination of all his gods both great and small, and in their place the triumph and the reign of Christianity.

The prediction of Jesus, so often reiterated, that he would rise again, is not more astounding in its fulfilment, than that other prediction which virtually runs through all the Scriptures, that his religion should rise, and spread, and increase, conquering and to conquer, until it should fill the world with its glory. The Jews thought when they had killed and buried the body of Jesus, that they had thereby killed and buried his cause with him. It seems to us that the resurrection of the religion of Jesus from such a grave, together with its whole subsequent victorious progress, is a fact about as hard to account for on infidel principles, and one which has given his modern enemies as much trouble as the resurrection of his body was difficult and troublesome to his ancient enemies. When we consider well all the circumstances of the rise and progress of this peculiar and unique religion—the vastness of the work assigned to the apostles in their great commission, the intrinsic improbability of their being able to accomplish such a work even without opposition, the accumulated obstacles in their way, the multiform dangers they had to face, the apparently feeble means and resources with which they had to work, while a world was everywhere in fierce and deadly opposition—when we consider all this in connection with the success and duration of their work, and in connection with the fact that this success was not the result of some lucky accident or after-thought, but was the one definite, avowed, proposed, and predicted object in view from the first, both of themselves and their Master—we are fully authorized in saying, that the case has no parallel in the history of man—it stands to this day the most gigantic, the most amazing, and, on rationalistic principles, the most unaccountable work that was ever undertaken and achieved among men.

There is no principle by which we can satisfactorily account for the success of Christianity in a world of sin, and against a world of sinners, at first, and often since, leagued against it, except that of its Divine truth; and of its being accompanied throughout by the mighty hand of God. For why has this religion alone of all the religious systems of Asia, and of antiquity become our religion? Why has this book alone of all the books, and creeds, and gospels, which the prolific East has produced, been incorporated as the only gospel of God into the religious belief of all Western civilized nations? Why have we this particular religion of Jerusalem, and not some other ancient religion of India, or Chaldea, or Egypt? Why this in preference to one born on European soil, ancient or modern? Why this gospel, which wages an uncompromising war against the dearest lusts and passions of man, in preference to every other more congenial system? Why this, which has come from the other side of the globe, across seas and mountains, and ten thousand national prejudices, in preference to the native religions of Woden and Thor, or to all those splendid mythologies, which had been so long enshrined in the productions of Grecian and Roman genius? Why has this oriental and Asiatic religion conquered the European and modern world, and not that of the Koran, which made the attempt to conquer and failed? Why was the false prophet unable to do with the sword what the Author of Christianity has done without any sword? Why did the Roman Empire, and with it all Europe, take a religion from Judea, and refuse one from the neighbouring nation of Arabia? Why have we here in America, a book from Jerusalem, instead of one from Mecca, to teach us all we know of God, of heaven, and of eternal life?

Manifestly but one reasonable and adequate answer can be given to these questions. The gospel is from heaven and not of men. The apostles were endued with wisdom and girded with power from on high. Christianity was founded by the hand of God; and the hand of God has sustained it against every assault of earth and hell. Its early and triumphant progress at Jerusalem, its rapid and wide-spread diffusion among the Gentiles, its onward and irresistible march in defiance of the leagued oppression of Jew and Gentile, its bold and uncompromising proclamation of its claims to all men everywhere, even to those of Cæsar's household, its passage through the fires of ten general persecutions, unscathed and victorious, its final enthronement on the very seat and citadel of the persecuting power—all this is a demonstration of its truth and Divinity, which no learning, no logic, no skill can ever invalidate. That any system of fraud, delusion, or fanaticism could have done what the gospel did in the hands of its apostles, and has since done, is utterly incredible and impossible. That any mere creed of men, or system of philosophy, could have done under the same circumstances, what this gospel did, would be to suppose an effect for which the history of the world furnishes no adequate cause. "It is an argument of great weight in favour of the gospel," says the eminent Scotch divine, Dr. Dick, "that it was published at the time when the events which it records are said to have happened; that it was submitted to the examination of those, who, had it been a human contrivance, could have easily convicted it of imposture; and that it stood this severe test, and prevailed in circumstances, which would have proved fatal to everything but truth." The success of Christianity we may certainly regard as the most remarkable phenomenon in history; and for the solution of this great historical problem, we have, as yet, but one adequate and satisfactory cause—the agency of God. *The gospel triumphed because it is of God.*

XI. CONCLUSION.

And now, as we look back over eighteen centuries of trial and of conflict during which this gospel has maintained its hold upon the world with a stronger and a stronger grasp—as from these ends of the earth and from these latter days we contemplate the great transactions recorded in the New Testament, especially the death of Christ, how wonderful, how admirable, how appropriate, does all the work of God appear! On the assumption, that the Son of God was to become incarnate, and die for man's redemption, what place on earth was so suitable for the amazing scene as Jerusalem, what time so fit, as that "fulness of time" which was chosen! Where could the Son of God make the great expiation for sin, one offering for all, so well as at the centre of all the nations and the centre of all the ages?

It has been often remarked, that the time of the Advent, was the best that could have been chosen in the annals of history. It was the very ripeness of antiquity. There was not one preparation wanting. All ancient things had come to the full, had borne their largest harvests, had culminated to their highest glory—and were ready to pass away. Philosophy had done her best. Genius had done its best. Arts, arms, and empire had done their best. The bard had sung his loftiest song. The conqueror had fought all his greatest battles and grasped his mightiest sceptre. Man had gone the whole length of his line—a line of four thousand years—and could no further go. Then it was, that God appeared. As the old world expired before him, a new stood ready to begin—and to begin at the cross. All ancient systems—the whole history of four thousand years, went down, as it were, with Jesus into the grave. With his dying breath he looked back over all the past, and cried, "It is finished." But in his resurrection a new world sprung to life, to die no more. And in the freshness of immortal youth, he looked forward over all the future and said, "Go ye into all the world and preach the gospel to every creature"—"beginning at Jerusalem." Two thousand years have not yet passed; but for aught we know there may be as many more to come. For aught we know the cross may be found at last, to have stood in the very centre of human annals, midway between man's creation and his judgment.

We have not seen it so distinctly noticed, though it is a point worthy of note, that the place for this grand event was as fittingly chosen as the time. The spot of all the earth's surface, where the Incarnate One should suffer and die for sinners, seems to have been designated of God as early as the days of Abraham. And from that time onward, for nearly two thousand years, Providence was but hallowing and preparing it, for the great immolation, prefigured by that of Isaac. There was not another spot of earth so fit, in itself and in all its associations, as Jerusalem, for such a sacrifice, and for the inauguration thereon of that kingdom of heaven which should one day fill the world with glory. Geographically and historically, socially, and politically, it stood in the very centre of the ancient world; and yet stood as a city apart, a holy, consecrated spot; in the world but not of it. It was small in itself, as compared with the great capitals and kingdoms that environed it on every side. But it was a city set on a hill that could not be hid. Its lofty seat among the mountains, twenty-five hundred feet above the Mediterranean, was but emblematic of that spiritual elevation it was destined to hold among the nations. "Beautiful for situation, the joy of the whole earth is Mount Zion, on the sides of the north, the city of the great king. God is known in her palaces for a refuge. Out of Zion the perfection of beauty God hath shined."

If you look at any map of the world as known to the ancients, you cannot fail to be struck with the central position of Jerusalem. Even now when the map of the world is so greatly changed, when the balance of power and civilization has passed away to the hands of the great Western nations, Jerusalem is still central to the earth's populations. And if Immanuel should come again, as some imagine, to establish a universal kingdom amongst men, it would be hard to find a fitter spot for such a throne than that on which he died. But in all the ancient world there was no other great city that occupied a position so central to the nations—neither Babylon, nor Alexandria, nor Athens, nor Rome, nor Constantinople in later times. Standing at the point where the three great Continents of the Eastern Hemisphere come nearest together, standing too at the head of that great middle sea which carries the world of waters into the heart of that hemisphere, giving to those continents at once intercourse with each other and outlet to all the world beyond, Jerusalem was and still is the natural centre of the Old World. All the great empires of antiquity, Egypt, Assyria, Media, Persia, Syria, Macedonia, Grecia, and Rome, rose, flourished, and, in turn, struggled for the mastery around her. Her seat was at the gate of all the nations, or where all the great highways of the world met and crossed each other. She became ere long the arena of the world's fiercest conflicts—the chosen battle ground where the nations met to wage their deadliest wars. She became the very heart of the world's population, and the life blood of nations from the circumference to the centre, could not flow at all without flowing through her.

It is all a mistake then to suppose, that, because she had lost the sceptre of political power, and was despised by her haughty Roman conqueror, Jerusalem held an insignificant place among the nations at the advent of Christ. She stood in the blazing focus of the world's light—its wealth, its learning, its commerce, its refinement. She stood like the bush which Moses saw at Horeb, ever burning and yet not consumed. She stood like the angel of the Apocalypse that St. John saw standing in the sun. She stood where the church of God, of which she was the type, and where Christianity which she gave birth to, have ever since had to stand—under the full scrutinizing gaze of the Universe. The things done in her were not done in a corner. If the Son of God had come to our world for the purpose of setting up a temporal and universal empire amongst men, no place was so fit for such a purpose as Jerusalem.

It was not less suitable for that, which he came to accomplish. He came not to reign over nations, but to die for sinners; to die in the full noonday of human history and in the public gaze of the universe; and dying to rise again and found a kingdom in the hearts of men, which should conquer all the world, and last when the world shall be no more. The result proves that the time and the place were well chosen and worthy of the grand inauguration. The result proves that no mistake was made in the history of redemption. "This is the Lord's doing; it is marvelous in our eyes." The Lord hath done all things well. The cross of the Son of God is the central object of human thought. All things rise in proof around the cross. The facts of the gospel well befit its theory; while the theory in turn explains and vindicates the facts. All things connected with it from the greatest to the most minute, are precisely what they ought to have been, and must have been, on the assumption, that it is the truth of God. Admit the facts, and we will demonstrate the truth of the theory; or admit the theory and we will demonstrate the necessity of the facts, precisely as they are alleged to have been. Admit that the Son of God lived on earth, died and rose again for the salvation of sinners, and then all other things—the most stupendous miracles, the most inscrutable doctrines, the profoundest mysteries of the Bible, become the most natural and reasonable things in the world.

CHAPTER VI.

INCIDENTAL CHARACTERS, OR THE LESSER LIGHTS OF BIBLE BIOGRAPHY.

HAVING now taken a rapid survey of what may be called the more prominent characters of the Bible or its greater lights, we pass to the contemplation of another interesting class, that seem to hold a subordinate position in the history, and may therefore be called its incidental or minor characters. They do not make up any distinct and separate group like those which we have already portrayed, but are scattered along at irregular intervals from the beginning to the end of Bible story, often forming the most beautiful episodes in the general current of the narrative. And it serves to illustrate the exceeding wealth of the Scriptures, that of all these isolated and greatly diversified characters which we are now about to introduce, not one is essential to the grand purpose for which all Scripture was written—the unfolding of the scheme of redemption. On the contrary, most of them might be left out without at all breaking the grand movement of Divine revelation, or diminishing one jot or tittle of the doctrines and duties enjoined in the Bible.

And yet we should be far from the truth, if we supposed that these minor characters were either uninteresting or useless, because they are introduced incidentally in the Bible history, and act only a subordinate part in its grand drama. The lesser lights of the firmament all add beauty and grandeur to the night, and declare both the power and wisdom of the great Architect, though many stars of the first magnitude have always been shining there. Even so these lesser lights of Bible biography, not only give all the interest and beauty of an infinite variety to its characters, but serve to illustrate in like manner with the greater, that same wisdom, power, and grace of God which are so signally displayed in the latter. One star differeth from another star in glory. But as it took the same almighty hand to make and garnish them both, so in the word of God, not less than in his works, we shall find all things beautiful and good, the least and the greatest, full of the lessons of his wisdom, power and grace.

These isolated and incidental characters, extending through the whole Bible from Genesis to Revelation, are so numerous and multiform, that we shall have to do here, as we have done in all other cases—single out a few examples to stand as types of all the rest. And in making this selection, three things shall govern our choice, namely, to present such as will be most likely to interest the young, and such as will carry our survey over the whole field of the Scriptures, and such also, whether good or bad, as promise to yield us the richest instruction.

I. LAMECH THE ANTEDILUVIAN.

We begin our sketch with a single example from beyond the flood—Lamech the seventh from Adam in the line of Cain, and probably the cotemporary of Enoch, who was translated, and was also the seventh from Adam in the line of Seth.

The chief distinction of Lamech, to which he was no doubt entitled for this mention in the sacred record, seems to have been that he was the father of a family of inventors. His moral character was evidently a very imperfect one, as we might expect in a descendant of Cain, and as we are compelled to infer, from his having two wives. For though some good men afterwards did the same thing, and an apostle of the New Testament tells us, that "the times of this ignorance God winked at," that is, overlooked and tolerated; still it was never right, it was never anything less than a flagrant violation of the original law of marriage. And from the special record which the Bible makes of the very names of Lamech's wives, Adah and Zillah, it is natural to infer, that he was the first to violate this great law. And therefore the same apology cannot be made for him, that was given for those who lived in an age when the violation had become a general custom of society.

But his children have the distinction of being the first to invent, or at least to perfect several of the most important of the fine and useful arts. He was himself probably the first writer of poetry—the first at any rate whose lines have come down to us. He recited them to his wives, and one of the sons of Adah, "the father of all such as handle the harp and organ," may have played them on his instruments. The son of Zillah, was Tubal Cain, probably the original of the Grecian god of the forge, Vulcan, and was an instructor of every artificer in copper and iron. "And the sister of Tubal Cain was Naamah." She is one of the only four women whose names are recorded before the flood. Naamah means pleasant, or beautiful; but we cannot tell whether it was descriptive of her person or character. As she belonged to a family of inventive genius, the Jewish traditions represent her as having invented the art of spinning and cloth-making. "Some," says Dr. Kitto, "ascribe to her the invention of spinning and weaving; and others, who find in her brother the Vulcan of the Greeks, recognize in her Minerva, who had among her names that of Nemanoun. But all this is bold conjecture. Her name was Naamah; her father was Lamech; her brother Tubal Cain; she lived; she died. This is all we know of her. To what she owed her fame—a fame of six thousand years—must remain inscrutable. As one finds among the ruins of time, some old gray monument, too important and distinguished to have been constructed for a person of mean note, but discovers thereon only a name which the rust of ages has left unconsumed—so it is with Lamech's illustrious daughter."

But there is not much in the life of Lamech or his family to detain us long. The record does not give us his age, nor that of any of the descendants of Cain, which forms so striking a feature in the account of the other Lamech, and all the posterity of Seth. We may infer from his song to his wives, that some at least of Cain's descendants, died by violence, even in early life. "I have slain a man to my wounding, and a young man to my hurt." The ordinary term of life in the two lines, was probably much the same, and was counted by centuries. Life has been fittingly compared to a bridge across the waters. How wonderful was life, when its bridge spanned almost a thousand years—each year forming a separate and beautiful arch! It is beautiful and glorious even now, when it reaches only three score and ten—provided only the structure be on a good foundation and of right materials. But as it is now, so was it then—there were difficulties and dangers in the crossing. One good man was taken to heaven, ere he had crossed half the bridge. Another fell as a martyr, by a brother's hand, just as he had fairly entered upon it. And no doubt the proverb was in many cases, already verified—that "bloody and deceitful men shall not live out half their days."

Nothing is more difficult than to modernize remote antiquity. The brief record of Scripture leaves us a very narrow basis on which to form a conception of this antediluvian life. It looks to us at this distance like existence in another world. It however, has one great feature in common with our own modern world—it was a world of sin and death. Human nature, with all its hopes and fears, joys and sorrows, was the same then, as now, and the end of it the same—the grave. Since sin entered into the world and death by sin, human life, even at its best estate, is but the passage of a river, the crossing of a bridge. Of human life, whether longer or shorter, modern or antediluvian, Addison has given us the true picture, in his beautiful allegory from the Vision of Mirza:

"The bridge thou seest, said he, is *Human Life;* consider it attentively. Upon a more leisurely survey of it, I found that it consisted of three-score and ten entire arches, with several broken arches, which, added to those that were entire, made up the number about a hundred. As I was counting the arches, the Genius told me, that this bridge consisted at first of a thousand arches, but that a great flood swept away the rest, and left the bridge in the ruinous condition I now beheld it. But tell me further, said he, what thou discoverest on it. I see multitudes of people passing over it, said I, and a black cloud hanging on each end of it. As I looked more attentively, I saw several of the passengers dropping through the bridge into the great tide that flowed underneath it; and upon further examination perceived, that there were innumerable trap-doors that lay concealed in the bridge, which the passengers no sooner trod upon, than they fell through into the tide, and immediately disappeared. These hidden pit-falls were set very thick at the entrance of the bridge, so that throngs of people no sooner break through the cloud than many of them fall into them. They grew thinner towards the middle, but multiplied and lay closer together towards the end of the arches that were entire. There were indeed some persons, but their number was very small, that continued a kind of hobbling march over the broken arches, but fell through, one after another, being quite tired and spent after so long a walk."

But after all, the period of our stay in this world, whether long or short, is not the great fact of our being. It is the world beyond that gives this mortal state all its import. Life is nothing, and man an empty name, apart from immortality. But with eternity in view, our allotted time of three-score years and ten, the thousand arches of the antediluvian patriarch, and the brief span of childhood's hour, are alike objects of the most solemn and impressive grandeur. The sorrow-stricken patriarch of Uz might well say, Who would live always, in view of the vanity of this life, and the glory of that which is to come? There are advantages, doubtless, in a long life. What opportunities of usefulness, what seasons for improvement, what treasured stores of wisdom, what conquests of heroic virtue would not be opened to one, even in such a world as this, by the life time of a Methuselah! And yet, how many sins, sorrows, and corroding cares to counterbalance it all! If at this distance we were called upon to select a mortal career from the lives of all the people before the flood, can we say there would be more to win us in the weary pilgrimage of Lamech or Methuselah, than in the half-finished existence of a translated Enoch, or the early doom of a martyred Abel? Why then should we think of loss and failure in the departure of our youthful or gifted dead—the young man in his noontide strength, the maiden in her womanly glory, the infant in its budding sweetness?

> "Oh hadst thou still on earth remained,
> Vision of beauty, fair as brief,
> Perhaps thy brightness had been stained
> With passion or with grief,
> Now not a sullying breath can rise,
> To dim thy glory in the skies."

II. NIMROD THE MIGHTY HUNTER.

From the flood of Noah down to the call of Abraham, a period of more than four centuries, there is but one name that figures on the sacred pages with any thing like a marked individual character. It is that of Nimrod, the great grandson of Noah through the line of Ham. Brief indeed is the notice which we have of him. But it is long enough to show, that he was the great man of his times. Though his biography in Scripture is scarcely more than an epitaph written on his tomb, yet it is the longest and fullest that remains to us of all the men who lived and died during those centuries. The venerable record is in these words—"And Cush begat Nimrod; who began to be a mighty one in the earth. He was a mighty hunter before the Lord; wherefore it is said (that is, it became a proverb to say), Even as Nimrod the mighty hunter before the Lord. And the beginning of his kingdom was Babel, and Erech, and Accad, and Calneh, in the land of Shinar."

This sets before us very vividly, both the prominence which he acquired while living, and the fame that followed him when dead. His name became a proverb for might and power. He was regarded as a sort of standard of greatness, to which his contemporaries and posterity might aspire. He was a great hunter; and doubtless excelled all others in those feats of strength and courage which such sports demand. But he was far more than a conqueror of the beasts of the field. He was the founder of a kingdom over men—evidently a man of war and a conqueror. And he has the distinction of being the first man in history, whose name was adorned with the title of Great, a title which, for the most part, has been awarded to none but those who have won it by the sword. It is a remarkable and significant fact, that along the whole line of history from Nimrod to Napoleon, the names that have borne the suffix of Great, almost without exception, have been the names of military captains and conquerors, whose garments have been rolled in the blood of their fellow-men, and whose thrones have been built upon the ruins of the fairest portions of the earth. It is a striking proof of the abnormal and apostate condition of our race, that "the Great" in man's estimation, have been those universally who proved themselves to be the greatest destroyers of their fellow-men.

Of these mighty ones—giants of ambition and despotic world conquerors—Nimrod, however excelled by his successors, was at least the pioneer. It is evident that he was the head and leader of the rebellious proceedings on the plains of Shinar—to construct a tower whose top should reach the clouds, and serve the double purpose of keeping his subjects together, and transmitting a great name to posterity. His name which means *rebellion* may have been given to him, as indicative of the spirit which prompted the undertaking, just as the tower itself was called Babel, to commemorate the judgments with which the Lord confounded the stupendous folly. The sacred writer does not, indeed, directly connect Nimrod with the building of Babel, but it is a necessary inference from the whole context, to regard him as the presiding genius of the occasion, and Babel or Babylon as the head and capital of the kingdom which he founded. Such a work could never have been attempted, or even conceived, without just such a leader; and if we take Nimrod as its prime mover, which is the natural supposition, then we see at once why he is mentioned with so much emphasis in this brief record, and understand the particular terms in which he is described. Thus he is denominated a "mighty hunter before the Lord," probably in the same sense that the men of Sodom are called "wicked and sinners before the Lord exceedingly"—that is in rebellion and in defiance of the Lord's authority. This is in accordance with the received Jewish traditions. Josephus represents Nimrod as a bold, bad man, a tyrant and a rebel against God, and does not hesitate to make him the author of all that was done at Babel.

We have a striking comment on the character of the man and his undertaking, in those boastful words which were long afterwards uttered at the same spot by one of his proud successors, Nebuchadnezzar the Great, when walking in his lordly palaces and surveying the works of his hand, he said—"Is not this great Babylon that I have built for the house of the kingdom by the might of my power, and for the honour of my majesty?" Thus Babylon, which was the centre of the first great rebellion after the flood, founded in ambition and pride, became the standing type of all those great world powers, which from Nimrod to Nebuchadnezzar, and from Nebuchadnezzar to Napoleon, have successively subjugated and desolated the earth—all for the exaltation and glory of a single individual. And so, through all the track of history, we find these world powers—Babylon, Assyria, Persia, Macedonia, Pagan and Papal Rome, with their crowned despots—ever arrayed in direct antagonism against all the rights of man, and all the interests of the church of God.

"The beginning of his kingdom was Babel, and Erech, and Accad, and Calneh, in the land of Shinar." This is the first mention of an organized kingly government in the world. Prior to that time men had probably been governed only after the patriarchal form, in their families and tribes; so that monarchy dates its origin from the time of Nimrod. It is worthy of notice, that the church of God in its outward visible organization goes back almost to the same period—being thus established first in the family of Abraham. And the two have come down through all ages, side by side, and for the most part in direct antagonism. The seat of power has often been changed, as also the form of opposition; but all the great world powers, from ancient Babylon to modern Rome, have been found in turn leagued against the true church of God. And the last form is infinitely worse than the first. It has stolen the livery of heaven to serve the devil in. It has baptized itself into the name of Christ, only the more effectually to trample upon the rights of man, and wage war against the truth of God. It is a kingdom of this world, still claiming and, to the extent of its ability, still wielding that sword of temporal power which Nimrod first unsheathed at Babel, which Nebuchadnezzar raised against the children of the captivity, and which all their successors have used in hunting and persecuting the saints of God. It is not more certain that Pagan Rome was the successor of the great oriental despotisms, both on the rolls of prophecy and of history, than that Papal Rome has succeeded to all the claims of her idolatrous namesake.

The man who sits enthroned in pride upon the seven hills, and who, if his power were but equal to his will, would crush the conscience of the world beneath his feet far more fully than Nebuchadnezzar did that of Babylon—he, we are told, is the successor of the humble fisherman of Galilee! With infinitely more propriety and probability of being legitimately in any Scriptural line at all, he might claim to be the successor of Nimrod and Nebuchadnezzar. The thing that Nimrod was aiming at so early, was conformity—implicit obedience to his own will—one great nation, one iron rule, one grand tower rising to the heavens to tell posterity of his glory. The law of his kingdom was the sword. The grand idea of Nebuchadnezzar was also conformity—absolute and unquestioning conformity in religion and politics—one wide reign of terror, and one grand idol image on the plains of Dura, to which every knee should bow on pain of death. And for this the fiery furnace was heated seven times hotter than usual, for the few saints of God that durst resist his will. And so, true to all the instincts of this ancient succession, the papal power, always and everywhere, has been a mighty hunter before the Lord; pursuing even to the dens and caves of the mountains, all who would not conform to its remorseless iron rule. It has enforced the same conformity, for the same ends, and by the same means. The parallel is complete; the chain of succession unbroken. Of the last link as truly as of the first, we have a life picture in the couplet:—

Proud Nimrod first the bloody chase began,
A mighty hunter—and his prey was man.

III. MELCHISEDEC THE KING-PRIEST.

It is only as an episode in the life of Abraham that this peculiar character is first introduced to us in the sacred history. It was when Abraham was returning victorious from the slaughter of the kings who had carried away his kinsman Lot. The incident is told in three short verses of the fourteenth chapter of Genesis: "And Melchisedec, king of Salem, brought forth bread and wine; and he was the priest of the most high God. And he blessed him and said, Blessed be Abram of the most high God, possessor of heaven and earth. And blessed be the most high God, which hath delivered thine enemies into thy hand. And he gave him tithes of all."

The next mention we find of him in the Bible, is by David in the one hundred and tenth Psalm, where he celebrates the royal dignity and kingdom of the Messiah—"The Lord hath sworn and will not repent, Thou art a priest for ever after the order of Melchisedec." These two passages of Scripture form the ground work of an argument touching the nature of the priesthood of Christ, which the Apostle Paul has presented at length in the epistle to the Hebrews. Indeed, in the course of two chapters he repeats, in one form or other, this quotation from the Psalm, some six or seven times, evidently laying much stress upon it. The argument is ingenious and striking; and the more we consider it, the more shall we see the eminent fitness of making Melchisedec the type and illustration of the priestly character of Christ.

There is first the fact, that Melchisedec is the most ancient priest mentioned in the Bible. We read of sacrifice before his time. Noah on emerging from the ark had built an altar unto the Lord, and of every clean beast and fowl, had offered burnt offerings on the altar. Abel also at the beginning had evidently offered burnt sacrifice, when he "brought of the firstlings of his flock and of the fat thereof." Still Melchisedec is the first man mentioned in history as holding the order and office of a priest. There has been much learned, but, at the same time, needless discussion on the question, who Melchisedec was. It is enough for us to let him stand for himself like other men. His typical and significant name need not destroy his individual personality, nor make it necessary to identify him with the patriarch Shem or somebody else. We take Melchisedec to be Melchisedec precisely as we take Abraham to be Abraham. We know very little about him, because it seems to have been the design of Scripture merely to give us those items of knowledge which could long afterwards be used to illustrate the priesthood of Christ.

He is accordingly not only the first priest mentioned, but a royal priest. Combining the two offices of king and priest—king of Salem and priest of the most high God—he was eminently fitted to adumbrate the royal and priestly dignity of Him, who, as Mediator between God and man, came into the world, that he might, as the great high priest of our profession, put away sins by the sacrifice of himself and obtain eternal redemption for us; while at the same time, he had power as the King of kings and Lord of lords, to conquer all his and our enemies. And thus we find David in the Psalm and Paul in the Epistle arguing from the acknowledged greatness of the royal priest Melchisedec, to the double character and still higher dignity and glory of Jesus the Son of man and the Son of God, the eternal priest and the eternal king, who by the one offering of himself hath perfected for ever them that are sanctified. To the Jewish mind there could be no higher idea of human greatness than superiority to Abraham, the friend of God and founder of the nation. But this is affirmed of Melchisedec. Abraham paid tithes to him, and received his blessing as the acknowledged superior. What a type of the Messiah then was this royal priest, who was not only greater than Aaron and the whole Levitical priesthood, but greater than the patriarch Abraham!

Again, he was a fit representative of Christ, in the nature and order of his priesthood. So far as the record shows, it was independent, unchangeable, and perpetual—that is, without predecessor or successor in office. He stands forth on the sacred record as a single, isolated priest of the most high God, having no connection with any earthly line of priesthood, and no genealogy revealed to us by which he can be linked to any one that went before or followed after. This is evidently what the apostle means, when he speaks of him as being "without father, without mother, without descent, having neither beginning of days nor end of life, but made like unto the Son of God, and abiding a priest continually." The apostle does not mean to say that he was not a mortal man, born and dying like other men; but that, as all these things are left out of his recorded history, he is as a priest, the very type of Christ's unchangeable and eternal priesthood. This indeed is the chief point in the apostle's argument. For he is seeking to show the superiority of Christ's priesthood over the whole Levitical or Aaronic priesthood, in which the Jews had so long trusted. Jesus, being made an high priest for ever after the order of Melchisedec, stands out in perfect contrast with all the priests of the Levitical order. They were many, changeable, and ever passing away by reason of death; he is one, unchangeable, having the power of an endless life, and abiding for ever, with no predecessor or successor in office. They were sinners and their offerings many; they needed daily to offer up sacrifices, first for their own sins and then for the people's; but he, by the one offering of himself in the end of the world bore the sins of many; "wherefore he is able also to save them to the uttermost that come unto God by him, seeing he ever liveth to make intercession for them. For such a high priest became us, who is holy, harmless, undefiled, separate from sinners, and made higher than the heavens."

Still further, the very names and titles of Melchisedec render him a most striking type of the priesthood of Christ. His two titles, Melchisedec and king of Salem, were both significant of the great work of the Messiah, as our Mediator; "first being by interpretation, king of righteousness, and after that also king of Salem, which is king of peace." And so righteousness and peace were wrought out for us by our great prophet, priest and king in the stupendous sacrifice of the cross. For this he took our nature, suffered and died in our stead, rose again from the dead and ascended into the heavens, even that he might bring in an everlasting righteousness for sinners, and reconcile us to God by his blood, so making peace. Thus he is called by the prophet, the "Righteous Branch, the Lord our Righteousness," and by the apostle, "the end of the law for righteousness to every one that believeth." Thus he was foretold of old, as the Prince of Peace, and heralded to the world in the songs of angels, as bringing "peace on earth and good will to men." Thus through his grand atoning work, as revealed in all the Scriptures, mercy and truth are met together, righteousness and peace have kissed each other. In the priesthood of Christ lay the problem of our eternal salvation. Without the shedding of blood there could be no remission of sin, no redemption for sinners, no righteousness that could justify, no peace with God. An adequate sacrifice must be found, and a priest adequate also to offer it. That priest was Divine, and the sacrifice being none other than himself, was of infinite worth.

> The guilt of twice ten thousand sins
> One offering takes away.

And thus we see how all the Scriptures, even in their most incidental characters, point to Christ as the Lamb of God that taketh away the sins of the world. As Melchisedec was the first priest, so Jesus is last, living and abiding for ever. Having finished his work of sacrifice on the cross, he hath ascended and entered into heaven itself, there to carry on his work of intercession to the completion of the final day.

IV. LOT, OR THE SELFISH CHOICE.

We pause to contemplate another character, incidentally brought to view in the history of Abraham. It is Lot the son of his eldest brother Haran. After the death of Haran, and that of his grandfather Terah in Mesopotamia, Lot seems to have concluded, that it was best for him to follow the fortunes of his uncle Abraham, and accordingly accompanies him to the land of promise. Whatever we may think of some of his subsequent decisions, he certainly showed good sense and wisdom in this choice. For as we learn from a passage in the book of Joshua, his ancestors even down to Terah had "served other gods;" and his choice to cleave to Abraham, and quit that land of idolatry, was virtually a choice to hold fast the only true religion.

Lot belongs to what may be called the mixed characters of the Bible, or those in which the streams of good and evil flow mingling together to such a degree that we are almost left in doubt as to the issue. His piety was of the very lowest type. He was a righteous man compared with the vile inhabitants of Sodom, but his long sojourn with them had not been without its effect on a character, not very good even at the best. "I have long regarded Lot," says Dr. Spring, "as the *worst saint* of whom we have any account in sacred history." Indeed it may be questioned whether we should have been able to look upon him as a saint at all, had it not been for the decisive testimony of one passage in the New Testament. Our Saviour, while speaking of the sinners of Sodom, and calling to remembrance the fate of Lot's wife, yet says nothing about Lot himself. Nor does Paul mention him in the list of the faithful in his Epistle to the Hebrews. Peter, however, supplies the deficiency, and speaks of him in such a way as to put it beyond question, that he was in the main a hater of iniquity and a true servant of the Lord, although his life had been so much marred by imperfection and folly. He tells us, that the Lord "delivered just Lot, vexed with the filthy conversation of the wicked. For that righteous man dwelling among them, in seeing and hearing, vexed his righteous soul from day to day with their unlawful deeds."

His whole history is full of instructive lessons both to the righteous and the wicked. It shows the folly of a selfish cupidity, the danger of mingling with the ungodly, the advantages of having even a distant connection with the faithful, the necessity of ever praying, Lead us not into temptation, the certain and fearful doom of the wicked, and the great condescension and forbearance of God towards his people however unworthy. We shall not attempt to set forth all these instructions of the succinct but pregnant narrative. There is a single point on which we would fix the reader's attention. It is one which illustrates the character of Lot most vividly, by its great contrast with the conduct of Abraham.

Lot had gone with Abraham into Egypt and returned with him. They took up their abode, together as usual, in the southern borders of the land of Canaan. But though mere pilgrims, both in Egypt and Canaan, they had been greatly blessed with an increase of wealth. Abraham, we are told, was very rich in cattle, in silver, and in gold, and Lot likewise had flocks, and herds, and tents. "The land was not able to bear them that they might dwell together; for their substance was great, so that they could not dwell together." At this juncture a strife arose between the herdmen of the two, and a separation became necessary for the sake of peace. Abraham was the first to propose it; and with that generous and noble magnanimity, which always marked his conduct—"Let there be no strife, I pray thee, between me and thee, and between my herdmen and thy herdmen: for we be brethren. Is not the whole land before thee? Separate thyself, I pray thee, from me: if thou wilt take the left hand, then I will go to the right: or if thou wilt depart to the right hand, then I will go to the left."

The experience of the world has vindicated the wisdom of this proposition. It is a good thing for brethren to dwell together in unity. But it is better to separate than to live together in strife. "Can two walk together except they be agreed?" The ancient herdman of Tekoa, Amos, thus puts the question, but the practical answer had long before been given by this more ancient herdman of Mamre. The lesson thus early illustrated in the life of the father of the faithful, is not without its value to the church in every age. The fundamental principle of all true and lasting union, is that men should be agreed and be of the same mind. No essential association is of much avail in the absence of a real heartfelt harmony and co-operation. Union is strength, if the parts be harmonious, if men be like-minded; otherwise, it is only weakness and confusion.

But we pass on to notice Lot's method of acceding to this proposition for a peaceable separation. "And Lot lifted up his eyes and beheld all the plain of Jordan, that it was well watered everywhere, before the Lord destroyed Sodom and Gomorrah, even as the garden of the Lord, like the land of Egypt as thou comest unto Zoar. Then Lot chose him all the plain of Jordan; and Lot journeyed east; and they separated themselves the one from the other. Abraham dwelt in the land of Canaan, and Lot dwelt in the cities of the plain, and pitched his tent towards Sodom. But the men of Sodom were wicked and sinners before the Lord exceedingly."

Here we have the key note to Lot's character. All the circumstances considered, this was a most ungenerous and selfish choice. Any thing like a delicate and high-toned sense of honour, not to say common justice and propriety, would have prompted him to defer to Abraham's choice. All the title that either of them had to the land, was the Divine promise, which had invariably been made to Abraham alone, and was renewed to him again most fully and emphatically after Lot's departure. It is obvious that Lot, like too many professing servants of God since his day, had too keen an eye to the good things of this world. Prompted by self-interest, he could not forego so tempting a prize as the fine pasture lands of the Jordan and the vale of Sodom. They stood upon one of those elevations, so common in the land of Palestine, from which, as modern travellers tell us, it is possible on a clear day, through its marvellously transparent atmosphere, to see distant objects with a distinctness which would be deemed incredible in other countries. "And Lot lifted up his eyes and beheld all the plain of Jordan, that it was well watered everywhere, even as the garden of the Lord." There lay the panorama of wealth and beauty, stretching away on the right, eastward to the hills of Moab, and northward to the very mountains that towered beyond the Sea of Galilee. How inviting, as contrasted with the rugged hill country on the left hand! how well watered! how admirable for pasturage! how productive of flocks and herds! how needful for one, who was now surveying it, not like Moses from Pisgah's top, with a heart just ready for that heaven of which it was the type, but with the longing eye of a cattle-grower and a grazier! What a splendid chance for a good bargain! And how eagerly did he grasp it, from the hands of that generous uncle to whom he already owed so much, and by whom he was yet more than once to be saved from utter ruin! Altogether, we think this transaction entitles Lot to the distinction of being the most ancient embodiment of the modern popular idea of a man of business—which is to get all we can, and keep all we get.

"And Lot dwelt in the cities of the plain, and pitched his tent towards Sodom." That too was the beginning of all his troubles. From the time he left the pure and simple joys of country life, his history becomes a dark and turbid stream. It was a fearful step to quit the companionship of such a man as Abraham, for the daily conversation of the inhabitants of Sodom and Gomorrah. But it was probably not taken all at once. Like all great changes in the habits of life, it was, most likely, taken very gradually. And it was all the more dangerous on that account. Temptation generally comes in that way—by small, covert, insidious approaches, like a beast of prey on its unsuspecting victim. He, no doubt, tried some of the little cities first—possibly that very Zoar, for which he afterwards pleaded, "Is it not a little one?" But like many men of our own day, when their former towns and cities become too small to hold them, he gradually worked his way into Sodom—the mighty metropolis of wealth and wickedness. It is instructive to notice that from the first, even while dwelling in the cities of the plain, "his tent was pitched toward Sodom." He was evidently smitten with a yearning after city life. While with Abraham, he had lived as a pilgrim and stranger in the land. But now we find his tent exchanged for a permanent house in Sodom, his children intermarrying with its ungodly inhabitants, and himself sitting as a judge and ruler in its gates, as occasion offered, sustaining the honour of the city in his attention to strangers. He had exactly reversed that blessedness of which the Psalmist speaks. He had first walked in the counsel of the ungodly, and then stood in the way of sinners, and at last sat down in the seat of the scornful. Nor did he come off unscathed from the association. Even then the rule stood true, that evil communications corrupt good manners. One would have thought that his captivity in the war of the kings, and deliverance by Abraham, should have cured him of this love of city life. But he had probably some real estate in Sodom, and his daughters had married there to some advantage, and he must needs return to look after these interests. Perhaps, he also reasoned as many now do, and satisfied his conscinece on the plea of being very useful in Sodom, and doing its sinners much good by mingling freely with them. We know he tried to do good; for we find him reproving them on the night before the overthrow; and the apostle tells us, that he was vexed with the filthy conversation of the wicked. "Dwelling among them, in seeing and hearing, he vexed his righteous soul from day to day with their unlawful deeds."

But it is most manifest that the Lord never blessed his labours in Sodom. He lost more than he gained. So far from converting any of its guilty inhabitants, he did not even save his own family. In answer to the earnest prayers of Abraham, he and his two daughters escaped destruction, as it were by the skin of their teeth; but he left others to perish in the doom of the city, and lost his wife on the way. And where then were all those temporal advantages—those houses and lands—those associations and alliances, and splendid luxuries of city life, on which he had so set his heart? Stripped of every thing on earth, except the merciful assurance of God's favour, and two very badly educated daughters (such was education in Sodom), he flies to the mountains, and is glad to find safety in even a more uninviting region than that which his selfish choice had long before assigned to Abraham. Truly a little with contentment is great gain. The whole story of Lot is a lesson of life to all, especially to the young. It says, "Enter not into the path of the wicked, and go not in the way of evil men. Avoid it, pass not by it, turn from it and pass away." And as it lifts this voice of warning, it points to the skies, saying, "Lay not up for yourselves treasures on earth, where moth and rust corrupt, and where thieves break through and steal, but lay up for yourselves treasures in heaven."

V. ESAU, OR THE FOOLISH CHOICE.

It is not to be denied that there were some good traits in the character of Esau, especially towards the close of his life. And on the other hand, it must be admitted that there were some things very objectionable in the conduct of Jacob. Still it is obvious that the Scriptures make a wide and radical difference between the two brothers, as they stand related to God. "Jacob have I loved, and Esau have I hated." This is the line drawn by the prophet Malachi; and the New Testament is just as explicit. In the Epistle to the Hebrews, Esau is referred to as a profane person, who, for one morsel of meat, sold his birthright. "For ye know that afterwards, when he would have inherited the blessing, he was rejected; for he found no place of repentance, though he sought it carefully with tears."

The great error of his life which indeed revealed the fatal flaw in his character, was this rejection of the birthright, and along with it, the blessing of God. As a descendant of Abraham, in whose seed all the families of the earth should be blessed, this birthright ought to have been regarded by him as an inestimable boon. Including as it did the promise of a Messiah to come, it comprehended all temporal and all spiritual blessings. His selling it therefore for one poor mess of pottage to satisfy a momentary hunger, proved him to be a man utterly indifferent to all the great things of God's salvation, and wholly under the control of present and sensual pleasures. Pinched with a little hunger at the loss of his daily venison, and too impatient to wait till food could be prepared, he thought himself ready to die, and said, What profit shall this birthright do to me? and so made the ignoble bargain, which sacrificed all the glorious and eternal future for one pitiful morsel of present indulgence. But so far from dying, he filled himself with the bread and lentiles—"did eat and drink, and rose up, and went his way; thus Esau despised his birthright." We are very far from justifying Jacob in taking advantage of his brother's extremity (supposing there was much extremity in the case). But it seems to us that the chief feature of the case was Esau's fondness for good eating, his readiness to pay any price for it, and his reckless indifference to all higher enjoyments. Jacob could no doubt have well relished this morsel himself, after taking the pains to prepare it. But perhaps reflecting, that man did not live by bread alone, and that there were some other good things in the world besides eating and drinking, he concluded to deny himself for a future and higher good, in the same spirit that afterwards prompted him to do fourteen years' hard service for his wives. The whole transaction seems a trivial one; but as it was important enough to give a new name, Edom to Esau, so it gives us a very decisive and unmistakable clue to his character.

A man of the fields, used to all the exciting pleasures of the chase, he lived solely in and for the present, with no higher aim than to gratify his appetites and passions, with whatever good each passing day might bring. Like all men of that class, he was completely under the dominion of the senses to the exclusion of all faith in things unseen and eternal. And thus we find him selling his birthright for a mess of pottage, and then weeping bitter and ineffectual tears at the loss—now moved with wrath to kill his brother, and now melted to pity on his return —alternately strong with excitement and weak with contrition. Unstable as water he could not excel. So also we find him in possession of two Hittite wives, which were a grief of mind to

Isaac and Rebekah, long before the exiled Jacob had begun to toil for Leah and Rachel in the land of Mesopotamia.

In all this want of faith and love of present enjoyment—this foolish choice of worldly good to future glory—this exaltation of the things of time and sense above the great things of God and eternity, Esau's case furnishes a vivid picture of the character of the unbelieving sinner now. Look where we will, we behold multitudes of men, who, like Esau, are completely earth-bound—intent only on the things of time and sense—living for the present as if there were no future—living for the body as if there were no soul—living for this world as if there were no God—sacrificing not only all moral character, but all hopes of immortality, for what is even more worthless and unsatisfying than one poor mess of pottage. Every man is doing this who neglects the things which are unseen and eternal, for the fleeting phantoms of sensual pleasure, or the glittering baubles of worldly treasure. The young man who, under pretence of fatiguing toil, or the cravings of nature, or any other cause, makes the wine cup or bottle his daily resort, is but another Esau, despising his birthright and selling his soul at even a harder bargain than the mess of pottage. The votary of pleasure, who says, I will eat, drink, and be merry, regardless of God's authority, who goes to the house of the strange woman and listens to her siren song of sensuality, is only another phase of this same Edomite character, which sows to the flesh and of the flesh reaps corruption. The mere man of business, whether old or young, who never lifts his eye heavenward, who thinks only of earth and earthly things, who toils for money with the eagerness of a gold-digger and worships it with the idolatry of a miser, is a genuine and worthy successor of Esau, only with the difference that the price for which he sells his soul is thirty pieces of silver instead of a mess of pottage. And so, the impenitent, unbelieving sinner, often warned and often entreated, before whom God has set the hope of immortal life and the celestial birthright of a joint heir with Christ, who still despises all God's promises, and takes the world as his portion, is only repeating the choice that Esau made, and bartering the highest boon that God can give, for that which perishes in the using.

It is to be noticed that Esau at last found out his error; but only when it was too late to profit by the discovery. As he advanced in years, and had his thoughts turned upon future and eternal things by the approaching death of his father, he came to see that the birthright, which in his impatient and unbelieving folly he had so lightly esteemed, was a great blessing. Then he sought it carefully and with tears. But it was gone never to return—lost beyond the possibility of change. What a picture of all unbelief is this! Why does the young sinner now despise his celestial birthright? Why does he scout religion, forget the wants of the soul, and ignore all the great things of God's salvation? Why does he grasp so eagerly this wretched porridge of the passing hour—this wine cup of death, this gilded morsel of sensuality, this price of iniquity? Alas! he is a sceptic—a double sceptic, both as to things which are seen, and things which are unseen. He cannot believe there is any harm in these sensual pleasures—this intoxicating bowl, this siren song, these thirty pieces of silver; and he cannot believe there is any profit, or pleasure, or truth in the great things of God's salvation. His unbelief puts him under a double delusion. But like Esau, he will not be a sceptic always. "Men may live fools, but fools they cannot die." Infidelity is always the creed of young men. It never wears the hoary crown of age. It always originates, and for the most part dies, in the foolish heart of youth. The men who die infidels always die young, with the exception of perhaps one in ten thousand, who having been a little bolder than his fellows, and aspired to be a leader, contrives to maintain a sham consistency, even as he nears the grave of fourscore years, while inward fears tell him that the creed of his youth is all a lie. As for the logic of the thing, we need not trouble ourselves to answer any man's unbelief. It will be sure to answer itself if he lives long enough. The great misfortune however is, that the answer comes too late, at least for his own good. It was so with Esau. It is so with thousands still.

VI. HOBAB, OR THE BETTER CHOICE.

The religion of God, addressed to rational beings, endowed with intellect to weigh its evidences, a heart to feel its motives, a conscience to plead for the right, and a will to choose or refuse the good, is always and everywhere, both by precept and example, appealing to us for a decision. "Choose ye this day whom ye will serve." Its voice of entreaty to all is ever that of Abraham's servant to the kinsmen of Rebekah, calling for immediate decision. "Now then, if ye will deal kindly and truly with my master tell me, and if not tell me, that I may turn to the right hand or the left." And so we have examples, throughout the Scriptures, not only of those who made a selfish choice like Lot, and a foolish choice like Esau, but of many who, like Ruth the Moabitess, or Mary at Jesus' feet, chose the good part that should never be taken from her.

One of the most striking illustrations of this better choice, is the case of Hobab, the Midianite, briefly recorded in the tenth c apter of the book of Numbers. It occurred at the time when the tribes of Israel, having been a year and a month already in the wilderness, during which time they had received God's law at Mount Sinai, were just ready to resume their journey to the promised land. The pillar of cloud by day and of fire by night, which had so long hovered over their camp—which had been with them in their passage of the Red Sea, and had guided thus far all their wanderings, was at last taken up from the tabernacle and began to move towards the wilderness of Paran, indicating at once the term and direction of their journey. Every tribe, drawn up in its appointed place, and under its appropriate standard, stood ready and waiting at the command of Moses and the sound of the silver trumpets, to take up the long line of march. After a whole year's delay, we can well imagine how eager such an army must have been to move. And we may imagine, if we can, the magnificent scene which presented itself to the eye of Moses and Hobab, as they surveyed it from one of the eminences around Mount Sinai, when six hundred thousand men, marshalled in four grand divisions, and led by the cloudy pillar, stood ready with the ark of God, to set forward with the watchword—"Rise, Lord, and let thine enemies be scattered; and let them that hate thee flee before thee."

The moment for decision had now come with Hobab, Moses' brother-in-law. Jethro or Raguel, the priest of Midian and father-in-law of Moses, who had made him a friendly visit some time before, on the first approach to Mount Sinai, bringing his wife and children to meet him, had already parted from him, after many blessings and wise counsels, and gone back to his own country. But Hobab was still there, having lingered with him through the whole year, or perhaps having come now for a last farewell. We have the interview in these words—"And

Moses said unto Hobab, We are journeying unto the place of which the Lord said, I will give it you: come thou with us, and we will do thee good; for the Lord hath spoken good concerning Israel. And he said unto him, I will not go; but I will depart to mine own land and to my kindred. And he said, Leave us not I pray thee; forasmuch as thou knowest how we are to encamp in the wilderness, and thou mayest be to us instead of eyes. And it shall be, if thou go with us, yea, it shall be that what goodness the Lord shall do unto us, the same will we do unto thee."

We are not told in this record whether he went or not. We know, however, that he did, from the mention which is made of him and his descendants in the fourth chapter of the book of Judges. Indeed, the record just quoted, seems tacitly to assume that such an invitation could not be resisted, and was accordingly accepted by Hobab. It is certainly one of the most persuasive and beautiful invitations on record, full of cordial good will, full of tender pathos, full of great promises, and breathing in every line the very spirit of the gospel of Jesus Christ in its appeal to dying men. As the whole march of Israel through the wilderness was but a type of the pilgrimage of the church in every age of the world to the heavenly Canaan; so this invitation of Moses to Hobab, to fall into the ranks of the Lord's redeemed, and go with them to the promised land, is but the ancient utterance of that beseeching voice, which is now heard in every land, as the church, through all her ministry and all her members, pleads with the dying sinner to enlist under the banners of Immanuel. Come thou and go with us. The Spirit and the bride say, Come It is the voice of God that calls: and yet it is the voice of a brother—a loving fellow-man, and a dying fellow-sinner. "Say, brother, will you meet us on Canaan's happy shore?" We are going to the place of which the Lord hath spoken. Come thou and go with us to the land where parting is no more.

Mark the motives which Moses urges upon his kinsman, and how applicable they are to us. There stood the mighty hosts of Israel, with all their waving banners and valiant men flushed with recent victory over Amalek. But he does not urge that. There too was Hobab's own native land, a sterile rock-bound desert. But he does not speak of that as a reason for going. Passing over all other considerations, he pleads with him on two grounds alone—his own good and the good of Israel—the plea of personal welfare in sharing the lot of the people of God, and the plea of duty and usefulness in aiding them on their pilgrimage. "Come thou with us and we will do thee good, for the Lord hath spoken good concerning Israel. Leave us not I pray thee, forasmuch as thou knowest how we are to encamp in the wilderness, and thou mayest be to us instead of eyes. And it shall be, if thou go with us, that what goodness the Lord shall do unto us, the same will we do unto thee." He pleads the Divine promises, We are journeying unto the place of which the Lord hath said, I will give it you: come and share in all the blessings that the Lord can give. He promises nothing in his own name, nothing in the name of Israel, but all in the name of Jehovah. And while thus sharing in all the promised blessedness of Jehovah's covenant people, Hobab at the same time shall be most useful to them as a guide through the wilderness.

And precisely so do the people of God still call upon their kinsmen according to the flesh, nay, all their fellow-men, to leave everything behind that would hinder, and go with them to the better land. We also have Divine promises to plead and a heavenly Canaan. Many things rise up to keep you back, as doubtless they did in Hobab's case. It is a long and weary way, and difficult at all times to travel. It may be attended with much toil and many dangers. But there is infinitely more to gain than to lose by this pilgrimage. There is good—infinite, eternal good at the end of it. And there is pleasure too—the pleasure of duties done and usefulness, at every step of the journey. As Moses said to Hobab, so we say to every dying sinner, "Come and go with us to this land of the blessed, in company with that innumerable host of the saints of God, who in all ages have been journeying thither. What, though earth's relationships hold you back! What, though doubts and dangers thicken on your pathway! What, though the promised inheritance lies far away beyond these deserts of life, and this Jordan of death! It is sure at last. It is God's own promise. Arise then, O doubter, and say, Hinder me not. By the grace of God I will go. If I perish I will go. I have Canaan's goodly land in view, and realms of endless day, and cannot tarry here.

"O when, thou city of my God,
Shall I thy courts ascend,
Where congregations ne'er break up,
And Sabbaths have no end?

There happier bowers than Eden's bloom,
Nor sin nor sorrow know,
Blest seats, through rude and stormy scenes,
I onward press to you."

VII. NADAB AND ABIHU, OR THE WARNING.

The tenth chapter of Leviticus contains an account of one of those awful judgments, which we find occurring in all parts of the Bible history, and which were, no doubt, needed as warnings, in order to impress the human heart with a proper reverence for Divine things. It took place while the hosts of Israel lay encamped before mount Sinai, just after Aaron and his sons had been inaugurated into their sacred office, and the whole tabernacle worship had been instituted with all its solemn and impressive ordinances. In the presence of the assembled congregation of Israel, who "drew near and stood before the Lord," Aaron had made his first offering of burnt sacrifice for himself and all the people on the great brazen altar, which stood without, before the door of the tabernacle. He lifted up his hand and blessed the people, and then, coming down from the altar, went with Moses into the tabernacle. On their coming out and again blessing the people, that remarkable manifestation, called the "glory of the Lord"—the Shekinah—the bright, visible symbol of the presence of the God of Israel, so often referred to afterwards, and even before, appeared unto all the people. "And there came a fire out from before the Lord, and consumed upon the altar the burnt-offering and the fat; which when all the people saw, they shouted and fell on their faces."

It was at this precise juncture, it would seem, when every heart was filled with profound awe at the presence of Jehovah, that Nadab and Abihu, the two eldest of Aaron's sons, committed the rash and impious act, the account of which immediately follows in these words:

"And Nadab and Abihu, the sons of Aaron, took either of them his censer, and put fire therein, and put incense thereon, and offered strange fire before the Lord which he commanded them not. And there went out fire from the Lord, and devoured them, and they died before the Lord. Then Moses said unto Aaron, This is it that the Lord spake, saying, I will be sanctified in them that come nigh me, and before all the people I will be glorified. And Aaron held his peace. And Moses called Michael and Elzaphan, the sons of Uzziel, the uncle of Aaron, and said unto them, Come near, carry your brethren from before the Sanctuary out of the camp. So they went near, and carried them in their coats out of the camp; as Moses had said. And Moses said unto Aaron, and unto Eleazar, and unto Ithamar his sons, Uncover not your heads, neither rend your clothes, lest ye die, and lest wrath come upon all the people; but let your brethren, the whole house of Israel, bewail the burning which the Lord hath kindled. And ye shall not go out from the door of the tabernacle of the congregation, lest ye die; for the anointing oil of the Lord is upon you. And they did according to the word of Moses. And the Lord spake unto Aaron, saying, Do not drink wine, nor strong drink, thou nor thy sons with thee, when ye go into the tabernacle of the congregation, lest ye die; it shall be a statute for ever throughout your generations; and that ye may put difference between holy and unholy, and betweeen clean and unclean. And that ye may teach the children of Israel all the statutes which the Lord hath spoken unto them by the hand of Moses."

From the emphatic manner in which this ordinance against wine and strong drink is here introduced, we naturally infer that these young men committed their rash act under the influence of intoxication. If so, it only aggravated their guilt. The plea of drunkenness is no mitigation of crime in the sight of God, and ought to be none at the bar of human justice. On the contrary, the man who sins because he has first reduced himself to the condition of a brute or demon, is a double sinner and will meet a double doom. But aside from this, the sin of

Nadab and Abihu was one of awful wickedness. They had just been consecrated to an office, which, above all that ever had existed, required holiness to the Lord. They had once been up with Moses, Aaron, and the seventy elders, into the holy mount, where they saw the glory of the God of Israel. If obedience to Divine authority was to be enforced at all, it is manifest that those who ministered at the altar, and stood as the representatives of God to the people, must themselves conform to the letter and spirit of the law. They rashly transgressed and died. Should any one think the judgment severe, let him remember, that to whom much is given, of him shall much be required. The greater the elevation in office, the more fearful will be the doom, if men abuse their privileges. A God of holiness must be sanctified in those who draw near to him. Even Aaron, whose heart must have been wrung with parental anguish, felt the justice of this sudden judgment, and held his peace. Such an example, moreover, of implicit conformity to God's law was essential at this opening of the ceremonial dispensation. We have a perfectly parallel case at the opening of the gospel dispensation, in the sudden and terrible execution of judgment on Ananias and Sapphira. If with these and many other fearful warnings, the church and its ministry, in both dispensations, have still been subject to the profane intrusion of worldly and wicked men, who can say what human folly and ambition would have wrought, had there been no Divine judgments to teach us that holiness becometh the house of God?

The great lesson thus early and effectually taught by the death of Aaron's first-born was that obedience was better than sacrifice—that God was, to be served in the way he had prescribed—that no rank or title or nearness of relationship to

God was to shield men from punishment who wilfully and rashly transgressed his commandments.

VIII. KORAH, DATHAN, AND ABIRAM, THE CONSPIRATORS.

In the sixteenth chapter of the book of Numbers we find a case of conspiracy and rebellion, whose tragic interest is scarcely exceeded by anything in the Scriptures. It occurred at Kadesh in the wilderness of Paran, just after the spies had brought back their report of the land of Canaan, and the people, in consequence of their long continued murmuring, had been doomed to wander forty years in the wilderness, and never to see that goodly land. There had been repeated acts of insubordination before, but on this occasion there was a deep laid plot among the chiefs of two of the leading tribes, Reuben and Levi, to renounce the authority of Moses and Aaron altogether, and place both the government and priesthood in other hands—namely, the one, probably, in the tribe of Reuben the first born of Israel, and the other, perhaps, in the family of Korah who, being a cousin of Moses and Aaron, doubtless thought himself entitled to it. Korah, as head of the Levite party, aspiring to the place of Aaron, and Dathan and Abiram, as representatives of Reuben the first born and civil head of the nation, became the leaders of this movement; and, having, after the manner of all conspirators, first contrived to hide their own ambitious ends in the guise of popular grievances, now took occasion of the general discontent at Kadesh, to carry their designs into execution. "And they rose up before Moses with certain of the children of Israel, two hundred and fifty princes of the assembly, famous in the congregation, men of renown. And they gathered themselves together against Moses and against

Aaron, and said unto them, Ye take too much upon you, seeing all the congregation are holy, every one of them, and the Lord is among them; wherefore then lift ye up yourselves above the congregation of the Lord?"

It was manifest to Moses at a glance, from the numbers and standing of the parties heading this mutiny, as well as from their determined and defiant tone, that a crisis of the utmost moment was at hand, and that the Lord himself must decide the issue. Without a moment's delay, he accordingly makes a direct appeal to the judgment of God. He prostrated himself in prayer before the Lord to ask counsel, as was his custom, and then said to Korah and his fellow conspirators—"To-morrow the Lord will show who are his, and who is holy, and will cause him to come near unto him, even him whom he hath chosen will he cause to come near unto him. This do: take you censers, Korah and all his company; and put fire therein, and put incense in them before the Lord to-morrow; and it shall be that the man whom the Lord doth choose, he shall be holy. You take too much upon you, ye sons of Levi."

With the case of Nadab and Abihu still fresh in their minds, so signally vindicating the altars of God from all unhallowed intrusion, it is not improbable that Korah and his abettors were filled with some misgivings at this proposition to decide the matter by a most solemn approach to God at the very door of the tabernacle. Still they seem to have yielded to it without objection. After some other words of severe reproof to the Levite party, charging them with rebellion not merely against Aaron, but the Lord himself, Moses sent a message to Dathan and Abiram, the Reubenites, to appear also with the others before him at the tabernacle; to which they returned the flat and decisive answer—"We will not come up," with other offensive and most reproachful terms; thus adding the sin of contumacy to that of conspiracy and rebellion.

These men, like many others in the church of God since their day, seem to have thought it was their privilege to murmur on and work in the dark, saying a thousand hard things every day, and plotting all manner of wickedness every night, against the Lord's ministers, and then the moment the iniquity was brought to light, and their own pretensions weighed in the balances of the sanctuary, that they had nothing to do but to escape all responsibility, and hide their harmless heads in their own tents. But it was a great mistake. The truth of God had to be vindicated; and whether staying away or coming they had to meet the consequences of their own evil work. Though hand join in hand the wicked shall not go unpunished. Moses, after protesting his own innocence, turns from them, and once more repeats to Korah and his company, the directions just given for their appearance with Aaron, censer in hand, before the Lord on the morrow.

The morrow came. It was a day long to be remembered in Israel. The two hundred and fifty princes of the assembly, with Korah at their head, were punctual to the appointment, and with their censers of fire all ready for the offering, stood in the door of the tabernacle side by side with Moses and Aaron. So wide spread however had been this leaven of discontent, and so confident of triumph were the conspirators, that we are told, Korah had gathered all the congregation against them unto the door of the tabernacle, no doubt thinking, by this formidable array of opposition, to outnumber, and thus carry the day against Moses and Aaron.

It must have been with dismay that they witnessed what

immediately followed. The glory of the Lord—that remarkable symbol of the Divine presence, which at times shone forth from the holy place of the tabernacle, and the cloud that hovered over it, now appeared unto all the congregation; and a voice from the Lord was heard, commanding Moses and Aaron to stand apart from the congregation, that he might consume the whole rebellious multitude in a moment.

It was an awful moment—the very turning point of destiny. It was a moment for prayer and fervent intercession of the innocent in behalf of the guilty. "And they fell upon their faces and said, O God, the God of the spirits of all flesh, shall one man sin, and wilt thou be wroth with all the congregation?" The prayer was heard, the intercession answered, and a respite given. A separation was to be made between the more and the less guilty—between a murmuring, discontented people and those artful, ambitious leaders who had sown the seeds of dissension among them. "And the Lord spake unto Moses, saying, Speak unto the congregation, saying, Get you up from about the tabernacle of Korah, Dathan, and Abiram."

As the Reubenite conspirators had refused to appear before the tabernacle with the two hundred and fifty, it became necessary for Moses, in order to execute this command, to pass over to their quarter of the encampment. It will be borne in mind, that the host of Israel, when stationary, encamped so as to form a spacious hollow square, with the tabernacle in the centre—each three of the twelve tribes constituting one of the four sides. In this arrangement, Judah as head of the first three tribes, occupied the eastern, or advanced side, and Reuben as head of the second three, lay on the south side. Moreover it so happened, that while two of the great families of Levi, bearing the tabernacle, were assigned to the eastern division with Judah, the third family, the Kohathites, to which Korah belonged, had their place on the southern side with the Reubenites. Hence we find the tents of Korah, Dathan, and Abiram, the chief instigators of this rebellion, all together in the same quarter.

Leaving the company with Korah still standing before the door of the tabernacle, Moses now, in obedience to the Divine command, advances to this south part of the encampment, followed by the seventy elders of Israel, and in a voice of solemn warning, which was instantly obeyed, cried aloud to all the congregation gathered there, "Depart, I pray you, from the tents of these wicked men, and touch nothing of theirs, lest ye be consumed in all their sins." Though in the very attitude and act of rebellion, they had too often heard the voice and felt the mighty power of their great leader, to treat his counsel with indifference now. So they fled from the tents of the rebel chiefs on every side, leaving Dathan and Abiram alone, save their families, standing in the door of their tents.

How fearful was the crisis! What a picture for the imagination—what a drama of terror was this! It must have been as if the pulse of nature stood still, while the eyes of millions were gazing on the awful scene. The chief actors of the dread drama now stood apart from the whole body of the people and from each other—Korah and his comrades before the tabernacle with Aaron—Dathan and Abiram alone, in their abandoned tents on the outer edge of the camp—and Moses with the elders, midway between the two parties. One human voice alone was now heard amid the profound and painful silence. "And Moses said, Hereby ye shall know that the Lord hath sent me to do all these works; for I have not done them of my own mind. If these men die the common death of all men, or if they be visited after the visitation of all men; then the Lord hath not sent me. But if the Lord make a new thing, and the earth open her mouth and swallow them up, with all that appertain unto them, and they go down quick into the pit; then ye shall understand that these men have provoked the Lord."

From the foundation of the world, says one, was there ever such a proposition and such a vindication as this? "Did any man ever make so bold and noble an assertion of Divine approval, or subject his claims, in the presence of a nation, to a test so immediate, so infallible?" Nor was the appeal in vain. In a moment, even "as he made an end of speaking all these words," one wild shriek of horror went up to heaven, while the earth went down with the wicked, and the whole terrified throng rushed back from the yawning chasm. For the ground that was under them cleft asunder, and "the earth opened her mouth and swallowed them up, and their houses, and all the men that appertained unto Korah, and all their goods—all went down alive into the pit, and the earth closed upon them, and they perished from the congregation. And all Israel that were round about them fled at the cry of them; for they said, Lest the earth swallow us up also."

Up to this moment, the company with Korah had remained standing at the door of the tabernacle, mute spectators of this awful scene. But they were not to escape. Like Nadab and Abihu, they perished by fire. A single verse describes their doom. "And there came out a fire from the Lord, and consumed the two hundred and fifty men that offered incense." Thus the whole band of conspirators "perished in the gainsaying of Korah." As the death of Nadab and Abihu had taught the great lesson that no unhallowed feet should intrude into the ministry of God; so this memorable example was intended as a lesson to all generations, to show that the Lord would vindicate his own true and faithful servants, and that men, however numerous or mighty, who dared to lift the tongue of slander against them, and to plot in secret for their overthrow, were themselves but as rebels against God, and worthy of a traitor's doom.

IX. BALAAM THE FALSE PROPHET.

We come now to notice one of the most singular combinations of character to be found in the Bible. There can be no doubt that Balaam was a very wicked man. The New Testament writers hold him up as a warning. They speak of him as loving the wages of unrighteousness, and running eagerly the road of transgression for reward. His great condemnation was that he knew his duty and did it not. He held the truth in unrighteousness. He saw the good clearly—approved it—admired it—commended it—and yet pursued the wrong. He attempted to do, what our Saviour has told us, no man can do—to serve God and mammon. His character, like that of King Saul in a later age, was made up of contrasts and inconsistencies.

The story of Balaam is recorded in the twenty-second and two following chapters of the book of Numbers. It is both curious and instructive. It comes in as an episode in the history of Israel, just at the point, where having reached the borders of the promised land, and conquered all who had opposed their progress, they had nothing farther to keep them from a speedy and peaceful possession, save the opposition of Moab and Midian. The rulers of these two countries seem now to have made common cause in seeking the overthrow of the invading and hitherto invincible host of the Lord. And in accordance with the prevailing superstition of those idolatrous lands, Balak, king of Moab, upon whose immediate borders Israel lay encamped, sends to the remoter land of Midian, for Balaam, a noted prophet of the times, who seems to have had some considerable knowledge of Jehovah, that he might come and utter a malediction against Israel from that very God whom Israel served. Balak had doubtless heard of all the mighty deeds which Jehovah had wrought for Israel since their departure from Egypt. Believing Balaam therefore to be a true prophet of Israel's God, he wished, at almost any expense, to secure his powerful aid in the form of a prophetic curse—saying, "I wot that he whom thou blessest is blessed, and he whom thou cursest, is cursed; come now therefore, I pray thee, curse me this people; for they are too mighty for me; peradventure I shall prevail, that we may smite them, and that I may drive them out of the land."

Balaam accordingly is waited upon by the elders of Moab and Midian, with large rewards in their hands, "the wages of divination," and with promises of honour and preferment from Balak. And when the first messenger had failed to secure him, he is importuned a second time, with still more liberal offers, and by princes more honourable than the first. At last, after many consultations with the Lord whom he professed to serve, and many noble asseverations to the messengers of Balak, that he could not, and would not go, without the Lord's bidding, he yields, and sets out on the unhallowed mission. On the way he is encountered by the angel of the Lord, who stands with drawn, but to him invisible sword, to resist his sinful progress. Thrice, as by an unseen hand, is he compelled to stop or turn from the path, and at last, when attempting to force the way, he is accosted and admonished as erring man had never been before—even the dumb beast asserting the claims of God, and with man's voice rebuking the madness of the prophet.

Still, though thus strangely arrested and convicted of his sin, he is left to follow out the strong desire of his heart, and complete the journey. From the first it had been manifest, that he loved the wages of unrighteousness, that he was bent on going if the Lord would let him; and now the final barrier is removed with one irreversible and solemn proviso—"Go with the men; but only the words that I shall speak unto thee, that shalt thou speak."

Arrived within the borders of Moab, he is received with much distinction by the king and his nobles, and conducted on the morrow to the high places of Baal, where due preparations are made for seven-fold sacrifices, and whence might be seen in the distance the mighty hosts of Israel encamped on the plains of Moab bordering the Jordan. We shall attempt no description of that ancient scene, nor of the mingled emotions of admiration, envy, and fear, with which both the king and the prophet must have surveyed it, as they stood beside their seven smoking altars on these heights of Baal. It is strange that from such a place, and on such an occasion, and even out of unhallowed lips, should issue strains of poetic beauty, of lofty sentiment, and of Divine inspired prophecy, scarcely surpassed by any in the Bible. It is more to our present design to present these inspired "parables" as they are styled—so brief, so noble, so just in feeling, so true to the whole revelation of God —which even an apostate prophet was constrained to utter. The word "parable" here, means just what it does where Job is said to "take up his parable"—not a fictitious narrative as in the New Testament, nor a dark enigmatical saying as in the Psalms, but an elevated, figurative, sententious speech, delivered in poetic numbers.

Receiving his message from the mouth of God, Balaam turned to the king, who "stood by his burnt sacrifices, he and all the princes of Moab." And he took up his parable, and said:—

"Balak, the King of Moab, hath brought me from Aram,
Out of the mountains of the East, saying,
Come, curse me, Jacob,
And come, defy Israel.
How shall I curse whom God hath not cursed?
Or how shall I defy whom the Lord hath not defied?
For from the top of the rocks I see him,
And from the hills I behold him;
Lo, the people shall dwell alone,
And shall not be reckoned among the nations.
Who can count the dust of Jacob,
And the number of the fourth part of Israel?
Let me die the death of the righteous,
And let my last end be like his."

Utterly disappointed with this first answer, and hoping to obtain one more to his mind by a change of place, the king then carried him to another position, the top of Pisgah, where he could see only a part of the camp of Israel. Seven altars being erected as before, and seven oxen and rams offered thereon, Balaam again consulted the Lord, and in terms of blessing still more emphatic, again took up his parable, saying:

"Rise up, Balak, and hear:
Hearken unto me, thou son of Zippor:
God is not a man that he should lie;
Neither the son of man that he should repent.

Hath he said, and shall he not do it?
Or hath he spoken, and shall he not make it good?
Behold, I have received commandment to bless,
And he hath blessed, and I cannot reverse it.
He hath not beheld iniquity in Jacob,
Neither hath he seen perverseness in Israel:
The Lord his God is with him,
And the shout of a king is among them.
God brought them out of Egypt,
He hath, as it were, the strength of a unicorn.
Surely there is no enchantment against Jacob,
Neither is there any divination against Israel.
According to this time it shall be said of Jacob and of Israel,
WHAT HATH GOD WROUGHT?
Behold the people shall rise up as a great lion,
And lift up himself as a young lion.
He shall not lie down until he eat of the prey,
And drink the blood of the slain."

Not satisfied yet, the king determined to make a third trial to obtain the coveted curse. Another position, the top of Peor, was chosen, and all the preparations made as before. "And when Balaam saw, that it pleased the Lord to bless Israel, he went not, as at other times, to seek for enchantments; but he set his face toward the wilderness, and lifted up his eyes, and he saw Israel abiding in their tents, according to their tribes; and the Spirit of God came upon him. And he took up his parable, and said," evidently glowing with enthusiasm under his high theme:

"Balaam the son of Beor hath said,
And the man whose eyes are open hath said:
He hath said who heard the words of God,
Which saw the vision of the Almighty,
Falling into a trance, but having his eyes open:

How goodly are thy tents, O Jacob,
And thy tabernacles, O Israel!
As the valleys are they spread forth,
As the gardens by the river side,
As the trees of lign aloes which the Lord hath planted,
And as cedar trees beside the waters.
He shall pour the waters out of his buckets,
And his seed shall be in many waters,
And his king shall be higher than Agag,
And his kingdom shall be exalted.
God brought him forth out of Egypt,
He hath, as it were, the strength of a unicorn;
He shall eat up the nations his enemies,
And shall break their bones and pierce them through with his arrows.
He couched, he lay down as a lion,
And as a great lion; who shall stir him up?
Blessed is he that blesseth thee,
And cursed is he that curseth thee."

All this was more than the king could bear, and he broke out in angry and reproachful chidings against the prophet, who had thrice blessed instead of cursing his enemies. "I thought to promote thee to great honour; but lo! the Lord hath kept thee back from honour; therefore now flee thou to thy place. And Balaam said, Spake I not to thy messengers, which thou sentest unto me, saying, If Balak would give me his house full of silver and gold, I cannot go beyond the commandment of the Lord, to do either good or bad of mine own mind; but what the Lord saith, that will I speak. And now, behold I go unto my people; come, therefore, and I will advertise thee what this people shall do to thy people in the latter days." And then, taking up his parable again, he uttered a prophecy of the coming power and glory of Israel's great Messiah, not unworthy of Isaiah's hallowed lips:

"I shall see him, but not now;
I shall behold him, but not nigh;
There shall come a Star out of Jacob,
And a Sceptre shall rise out of Israel,
And shall smite the corners of Moab,
And destroy all the children of Sheth;
And Edom shall be a possession,
Seir also shall be a possession for his enemies.
And Israel shall do valiantly.
Out of Jacob shall come He that shall have dominion,
And shall destroy him that remaineth of the city."

But having thus failed in all his attempts to turn away God's blessing from Israel; he afterwards attempted by his wicked counsel to turn away the hearts of Israel from their God. And in this, alas! he was but too successful. Through his suggestion the people were entangled in fatal alliances with the idolatrous women of Moab and strangers from God. And he whose lips had once poured forth these inspired and exalted sentiments in parables, was at last slain in battle, fighting with Midian, against the people whom he had blessed. Wretched man! the victim of conflicting passions—when blessed with the favouring breeze of a Divine inspiration, longing to die the death of the righteous; but no sooner left to his own wayward and rebellious will than found guilty of disobedience to God, covetous of worldly gain, and waging war with what he knew to be the cause of truth and righteousness. And what is he, with all his high endowments, his good resolutions, his lofty sentiments, and his malignant passions, but a picture of many a proud, impenitent sinner now, whose creed is in the right, but whose heart and life are in the wrong?

X. ELIHU, OR THE YOUNG MAN OF WISDOM.

We must here introduce a character who belongs to an earlier period than those last contemplated. The book of Job is in all probability the oldest book of all the Scriptures. There is good reason to think, from many allusions in that book, as well as from its customs and modes of thought, that Job and his three aged friends, Eliphaz, Bildad, and Zophar, along with this younger friend Elihu, lived somewhere in the period of four hundred and thirty years between Abraham and Moses; probably nearer to the former than the latter. Hence, we may regard the book and its characters as furnishing many striking illustrations of the true religion, and of the church of God as they existed in the postdiluvian and patriarchal ages. Next to the venerable, suffering patriarch who gives name to the book, and whose name has descended through all ages as a proverb for patience and steadfast trust in God, by far the most interesting and admirable character in the book, judging from his words and actions, is that of the young umpire and counsellor, Elihu the Buzite. He is a model of urbanity, courtesy, discretion, learning, piety, zeal, and eloquence. He has the logical acumen, not only to see when an argument is not good in the mouth of his compeers, but to present a better one himself. And he has the good sense, as well as the good manners, to do both without giving offence. He is evidently a believer in soft words and hard arguments—the *suaviter in modo, et fortiter in re.* For one so young, he is a remarkable example of that candour, courtesy, and skill in debate, which, if always followed, would render religious controversies as pleasant as they would be effective. Like Ephron the Hittite in his dialogue with Abraham, he stands before us, as a very ancient, but yet seasonable type of character, which all over-zealous and heated controversialists would do well to study.

Elihu seems to have been sitting by from the beginning, listening in deferential silence, and with the most fixed attention, to the great debate which Job carries on singly against his three friends, through the first thirty-one chapters of the book. There is nothing to indicate his presence, till all the others are done—vanquished and silenced by the superior earnestness and logic of the great sufferer. Never was there a more solemn or difficult theme than that which they had taken in hand to solve—to reconcile the sufferings of the righteous with the goodness of God—to tell how it could be, that Job, a professed servant of God, and hitherto unimpeached as an upright and a perfect man, should now be the greatest of sufferers under the direct judgments of the Almighty. To their minds there seemed to be no solution of the mystery, but to convict Job of great, and as yet unknown and unconfessed wickedness. This is the key note of the whole dialogue on their side—the staple of all their arguments, though brought out with different degrees of distinctness or severity. Eliphaz begins the high debate, and is followed in turn by the other two—Job, however, answering each one of the three severally as they speak. When they have all taken one round with the sufferer, without any of them being able either to prove his criminality or make him confess it, Eliphaz again opens the contest with a second speech, and is followed by the others in precisely the same order as before. Job, however, conscious of his integrity, is more than a match for them. He answers each in turn, and this second round ends with no better result than the first. Eliphaz, who through the whole discussion had been the most respectful towards Job, and the least censorious of the three, leads off now for a third round, and is answered by Job. But when now it comes to Bildad's turn, he delivers himself in five short verses of the twenty-fifth chapter, dealing in the widest and most common place generalities, evidently feeling himself in the predicament of one who could say nothing more because he had nothing to say. As for Zophar, the third speaker, he seems to have thrown up the case in despair as we hear nothing more of him. Well he might; for after Bildad's last abortive effort, Job takes up his parable through the next six chapters, in a style of impassioned eloquence, and power, and pathos that is scarcely surpassed by anything in the Bible. In glowing and unbroken numbers, as one almost, if not quite inspired, he pours forth a strain—now of sarcasm and irony—and now of devotion—now of his own heart's experiences in past times—and now of God's majesty and glory in all the works of his hands and the mysteries of his providence—that must have filled every mind with mingled admiration and awe; and did in fact silence every hearer but one.

That one was Elihu. For the first time he ventures to open his mouth. Not, however, to vindicate the three impugners of Job; for this would have been the extreme of rashness. However the case might stand with Job and his Maker, he sees clearly that they have neither answered his arguments nor made good their charges against him. His anger is kindled against the three men, because they have explained nothing, answered nothing, and yet have condemned Job, who, for aught that they can prove, is an innocent man. His anger is also excited against Job, because, in his bold and defiant vindication of himself against his unjust accusers, he seems to have justified himself rather than God. He thinks that all parties are in error; and with the zealous enthusiasm of a young man he interposes for the purpose of vindicating the truth, and setting all parties right.

His object is to show that Job may be innocent of any great iniquity, and yet God may be just and good in all these afflictions. And it is wonderful how well he succeeds, seeing that no part of our Scriptures existed at the time. His great argument is that man is weak and helpless, and must not expect to understand all the ways of God; and that these outward physical evils are intended for our spiritual good, which is the very doctrine of Paul, and all the New Testament writers. "God is greater than man. Why dost thou strive against him? for he giveth not account of any of his matters. For God speaketh once, yea twice, yet man perceiveth it not. Lo, all these things worketh God oftentimes with man, to bring back his soul from the pit, to be enlightened with the light of the living."

Nothing could be more graceful and appropriate than his introduction, "I am young, and ye are very old; wherefore I was afraid and durst not show you mine opinion. I said, Days should speak, and multitude of years should teach wisdom. But there is a spirit in man: and the inspiration of the Almighty giveth them understanding. Great men are not always wise; neither do the aged understand judgment. Therefore I said, Hearken to me: I also will show mine opinion. Behold I waited for your words, I gave ear to your reasons while ye searched out what to say. Yea, I attended unto you, and behold, there was none of you that convinced Job, or that answered his words." From this apologetic opening, he pursues his exalted discourse through the next six chapters, rising in the last of them, into the highest strain of sublimity, as with reverent awe he depicts the changes of an approaching thunderstorm, and closes his whole argument with a reiteration of its key-note—"With God is terrible majesty. Touching the Almighty, we cannot find him out; he is excellent in power and in judgment, and in plenty of justice; he will not afflict. Men do therefore fear him; he respecteth not any that are wise of heart."

At this point in the high debate, or rather in the sublime and awful drama, a new character appears. Amid the roll of the thunder and the raging of the storm, the distinct and articulate voice of the Almighty is heard, in words more majestic than mortal lips could ever essay, solving all these mighty mysteries of Providence, and deciding this great contest. And it is precisely at this point, that the book of Job rises to a degree of sublimity, which no unaided human genius has ever equalled or even approached. "Then the Lord answered Job out of the whirlwind, and said, Who is this that darkeneth counsel by words without knowledge? Gird up now thy loins like a man; for I will demand of thee, and answer thou me. Where wast thou when I laid the foundations of the earth? declare, if thou hast understanding. Who hath laid the measures thereof, if thou knowest? or who hath stretched the line upon it? Whereupon are the foundations thereof fastened? or who laid the corner stone, thereof, when the morning stars sang together, and all the sons of God shouted for joy? Or who shut up the sea with doors, when it brake forth, as if it had issued out of the womb; when I made the cloud the garment thereof, and thick darkness a swaddling band for it; and brake up for it my decreed place, and set bars and doors; and said, Hitherto shalt thou come, but no further; and here shall thy proud waves be stayed?"

But why quote we further? The next four chapters form one sublime and unbroken utterance of these mighty questionings and challenges, by their simple, naked grandeur, better befitting the majesty of God, than any thing to be found in human speech. The master poets of all ages, from Homer to Milton, have attempted these Divine impersonations; but they have always felt their pinions fail, when they have essayed to put words into the mouth of the Almighty. Here, however, in this unique, unadorned, and inimitable speech out of the whirlwind, there is not only no failure, but a revelation of the glory of the Lord, such as has inspired all generations with growing wonder, awe, and admiration.

XI. NAOMI, OR THE DESOLATE WIDOW.

The book of Ruth has always been admired, as a gem among the Scriptures, for its touching story of the young Moabitess. We must not, however, allow the superior lustre of her young and lovely life to hide from our view, the desolations and the sorrows of another character who figures there—the widowed mother-in-law, Naomi, with whose fortunes, both in grief and joy, her own were so indissolubly united. Naomi is entitled to our regards, not only on her own account and on Ruth's account, but because she stands as a type of a very large class of her sex in every age of the world. Naomi is to the bereaved and weeping wife, what Rachel is to the uncomforted, childless mother. Her sorrowing sisters are to be found in every land where death has entered the household and left the children in orphanage, the wife in desolation, and the house without a head. There is no greater woe on earth than this, and none more frequent. When the mother loses the child, there is something tender and sacred in the sorrow; for her loss is but gain to the little one, and the heart may find its consolations.

When the husband loses the wife, it is indeed a crushing blow to all the best and purest sympathies of the soul, both to the husband and the motherless children. But they may find relief in clinging the closer together; and he, in the very rush of the world's business. But when the wife loses the companion of her youth, the guide and support of her children, and finds herself, alone, or with her little ones, compelled, for the first time, to face the rude buffetings of the world, there is a vacuum in the heart and in the household, which nothing earthly can ever fill again. There is indeeed no sorrow that heaven cannot cure. But earth has no balm adequate to the healing of this wounded and widowed heart. It is a blow which breaks the charm of life, which for the most part scatters the once happy household to the four winds, leaves the future in utter darkness, and not unfrequently compels the homeless and companionless sufferer to feel that her only heritage on earth is to mourn her overwhelming and unmitigated loss. If there is any condition on earth that should touch our deepest sympathies, and elicit our utmost assistance, it is that of the desolate widow as she struggles to bear up under this great and irreparable loss. And hence God himself, when he would take one class of human affliction as a type of all the rest, and make our sympathy with it the very test and measure of our religion, has singled out this, and told us that pure religion and undefiled before God and the Father is, to visit the fatherless and widows in their affliction, and to keep ourselves unspotted from the world.

In Naomi's case, widowhood was doubly afflictive. The blow which made her a widow, was followed by another which made her childless. She was bereaved both of her husband and of her two sons; and that too in a strange land to which they had gone to escape from the famine in their own. Sad indeed was her lot, at her time of life, to bury first her husband in this land of exile, and then the two sons on whom she might have hoped to rest her declining years. All that was left to her was a companionship in widowhood—the two daughters-in-law, Orpah and Ruth, who like herself were widows. How deeply must they have mingled their tears together—three lonely women, bowed down under this three-fold grief! But even this poor consolation of companionship in widowhood, Naomi could not hope to have long. Her daughters-in-law belonged to the race of Moab, and in her own deep poverty and desolation, she felt constrained to leave them and return to her native land. All her prospects in life are blasted, all her hopes of earthly joy at an end, and with the undying instincts of a true daughter of Israel, she can think of nothing better than to go back to Bethlehem, where she may at last mingle her dust with that of her kindred. Especially was she prompted to return, when she learned that the famine was over in Israel, and her people blessed with bread.

She communicates this purpose to the two young widows. And they in turn are willing, in their desolation, to leave the graves of their husbands, and go with Naomi to a strange land. She, however, knowing from bitter experience the evils of exile, dissuades them from the choice; and with a maternal tenderness that melted them to tears, urges that they should each stay in Moab, marry again, and find rest in the house of a husband. After much weeping, and the most endearing tokens of affection on both sides, Orpah takes her advice, and bids her farewell. But Ruth is not to be dissuaded. Her heart is fixed to go and share the fortunes of Naomi. She had decided on high religious ground; and nothing but death shall ever part them. "Thy people shall be my people, and thy God my God."

Thus Ruth clave to her, and at last they found their way to Bethlehem. After so long an absence, and so great changes in her condition, Naomi was scarcely recognized, even by her old friends. On their arrival, "all the city was moved about them; and they said, Is this Naomi? But she said unto them, Call me not Naomi, call me Mara; for the Almighty hath dealt very bitterly with me. I went out full, and the Lord hath brought me home again empty. Why then call ye me Naomi, seeing the Lord hath testified against me, and the Almighty hath afflicted me?"

But we need not follow out the wonderful story. Weeping may endure for a night, but joy cometh in the morning. There is light in the clouds, or above the clouds, even the darkest day. The God of providence is ever on the throne, to watch the falling sparrow, and to take care of the desolate widow. Naomi's path through life was a thorny one; but through it all there was consolation waiting for her at the end. Her latter days were full of peace, plenty, and joy. Every Bible reader knows the sequel—how Ruth became the wife of the princely Boaz—and Boaz the father of the little Obed, and Naomi his loving nurse—and Obed the grandfather of David—and David the mighty king of Israel, the Messiah's type and progenitor.

XII. ASAPH, THE PSALMIST.

Widely different from any of the minor characters of the Bible thus far mentioned, is Asaph, the sweet singer in Israel. As we learn from the first book of Chronicles, he was one of the three chief leaders of the music, taken from the tribe of Levi, and appointed over that service by David in the regular worship of the tabernacle. There were two hundred and eighty singers and musicians in this tabernacle choir, whose business it was to "lift up their voice with joy," accompanied with psalteries, trumpets, harps, organs, and high-sounding cymbals. There was no part of the worship of Jehovah more completely organized than this. For the royal Psalmist, who was the founder of it, being himself a musician and an inspired composer, had carried into it the whole enthusiasm of his nature. The immense choir was divided into twenty equal divisions, consisting of twelve in each, and they were arranged so as at times to perform this exalted service, in responsive strains, or part answering part in recitative dialogue, as indicated by the psalms themselves. Over the whole band were Heman, Asaph, and Ethan. It may be questioned whether there ever has been any music in this world more exalted and inspiring, than when this grand choir lifted up their voices and their instruments in full chorus, to celebrate the high praises of Jehovah in his holy temple. And so great was the interest inspired by David into this whole service, that we find the same organization not only perpetuated by Solomon, but existing in all its integrity down to the days of King Hezekiah; and no doubt it continued as long as the temple stood.

Asaph was not only a musician, but an inspired composer of the songs of Zion. He is spoken of as a prophet or seer, and is doubtless to be regarded as speaking by Divine inspiration in the psalms which bear his name. Next to David, he is probably the largest writer of our present book of psalms—being the author of several of the largest and most interesting in the whole book. We cannot see that even David, though writing many more than Asaph, excels him at all in beauty of style, or justness of sentiment, or sublimity of thought, or weight of doctrine. Indeed, but for the name at the head of them, we should never have known that the Royal Psalmist did not pen them all. The name of Asaph stands at the head of the fiftieth, the seventy-third, and the ten following Psalms, making twelve in all ascribed to his hand. One of these, the seventy-eighth, is very beautiful. It consists of seventy-two verses, and is a little epic, or historical poem, recounting the wonderful dealings of Jehovah towards his chosen people. "Give ear, O my people, to my law, incline your ears to the words of my mouth. I will open my mouth in a parable, I will utter dark sayings of old; which we have heard and known, and our fathers have told us. We will not hide them from their children, showing to the generation to come the praises of the Lord, and his strength, and his wonderful works that he hath done. For he established a testimony in Jacob, and appointed a law in Israel, which he commanded our fathers, that they should make them known to their children: that the generation to come might know them, even the children which should be born; who should arise and declare them to their children: that they might set their hope in God, and not forget the works of God, but keep his commandments."

He then goes on, through the whole psalm, to tell of the mighty works of God, from the days of their deliverance in Egypt down to the establishment of David's throne. The psalms of Asaph seem to be characterized by a devout, national, and patriotic spirit, which delights to dwell on the high themes of Israel's glory. Thus he begins the eightieth psalm. "Give ear, O Shepherd of Israel, thou that leadest Joseph like a flock, thou that dwellest between the cherubim, shine forth.

Before Ephraim, and Benjamin, and Manasseh (alluding to the order of their march), stir up thy strength and come and save us." In the same spirit, he opens the eighty-first. "Sing aloud unto God our strength, make a joyful noise unto the God of Jacob. Take a psalm and bring hither the timbrel, the pleasant harp with the psaltery. Blow up the trumpet in the new moon, in the time appointed on our solemn feast-day. For this was a statute for Israel, and a law of the God of Jacob. This he ordained in Joseph for a testimony, when he went out through the land of Egypt."

But the most striking thing in the character of this sweet Psalmist is, that like David, he manifests a special care for the religious instruction and welfare of the rising generation. His most earnest desire, in writing, seems to be that the children and the children's children, through all coming ages, might learn and obey the law of the Lord. Nor was he disappointed, for how many millions upon millions, not only of Jacob's seed, but of all nations, by means of his and David's sweet songs, have been early taught to know and love these blessed commandments!

XIII. THE TWO NAMELESS PROPHETS.

The thirteenth chapter of the first book of Kings contains a record of mysterious and tragic interest. It is one which we never read without a feeling of sadness. It is one over which we would willingly drop a tear every time we read, if tears could avail to change the melancholy fate of two men, who ought to have come to a better end. And it is one which we never read without wishing it were longer and fuller. Read it to any intelligent child, however young, and he will ask you a hundred questions about it, which you would like to, but cannot answer. He will look up in your face, with the intensest curiosity, and feel that you ought to know more, and be able to tell him more, than he yet knows of this strange and curious story—something more about the prophet of Judah, something more about the old prophet, and above all something more about the lion, that would neither harm the ass, nor devour the man he had slain. And true enough, in this brief and simply told story, which rivets the attention of a child as much as if it were written only for children, there is a deep meaning which no mere child can fully fathom. It will bear the profoundest scrutiny of the learned and the wise. And like so many other things in the Bible, when the wise and learned have made it their study, they will feel that there is much yet to learn—much that they do not comprehend; still much that they do.

Whether we consider the great national event to which it relates—the setting up of idol worship at Bethel by the wicked Jeroboam, or the remarkable prediction of the man of God, or the double miracle wrought by him on the king, or the diverse and changing scenes which are made to pass before us—the public altar, the old prophet's family, the interview, the warning, the lonely journey, the sudden death, the burial, and the mourning—or all the solemn lessons taught thus as to the recompense of transgression and disobedience, or the masterly manner in which all these things are grouped together in a single chapter—we must regard the whole account as a drama of life and duty, of sin and its retribution, worthy of our profoundest study.

For aught that appears to the contrary, all the things related in the chapter took place in a single day. What a day was that at Bethel! How exciting! how eventful! how solemn in its warning to the rebel monarch! how awful in its issue to the unfaithful prophet! how sad and ominous to the old prophet who, in the garb of hospitality and with a lie in his mouth, had tempted the poor man to his undoing! Great and solemn as are the lessons of truth and duty inculcated by the chapter, we think that, even in a literary point of view, there is nothing on record which can exceed the dramatic effect with which the story is recited. The events are not so much narrated historically, as they are depicted before our eyes, in a succession of distinct and rapidly changing scenes, each of which would be an admirable subject for the artist. At the hour of morning sacrifice, we stand before the great altar which the guilty monarch had erected on one of the high places of Bethel. And there, arrayed in gorgeous robes, with a burning censer in his hand, and attended by the representatives of the ten tribes, he approaches the altar to offer incense to the golden calf, which he had substituted for Israel's God. But suddenly his hand is arrested; and every eye is riveted to the spot by an unexpected issue. An unknown stranger has made his way through the idolatrous crowd; and in notes of fearful warning from Jehovah cries against the altar—saying, "O Altar, altar! thus saith the Lord, Behold a child shall be born unto the house of David, Josiah by name; and upon thee shall he offer the priests of the high places that burn incense upon thee, and men's bones shall be burnt upon thee. And this is the sign which the Lord hath spoken, Behold the altar shall be rent, and the ashes that are upon it shall be poured out." And lo! immediately the altar was rent asunder, and the ashes of the sacrifice poured upon the ground. Nor was this all. The rebel monarch in his haughty pride had commanded his attendants to lay hold upon the stranger, who had thus intruded upon his proceedings. But in an instant, the hand of the king, stretched in anger against God's messenger, was paralyzed. Dry and rigid as a withered branch, he is unable to pull it in again; and feeling himself as powerless now, as he had just been arrogant, he humbly pleads with the man of God for its restoration. The request is granted; the prayer is offered, and the arm is restored. But the whole idolatrous worship is stopped for the day. The king, glad to be so relieved, and as if to make amends for his high handed iniquity, invites the prophet to his home, to refresh himself and take his reward. But true to Jehovah's mission, the man refuses it all; saying, "If thou wilt give me half thine house, I will not go in with thee, neither will I eat bread, nor drink water in this place. For so it was charged me by the word of the Lord, saying, Eat no bread, nor drink water, nor turn again by the same way that thou camest. So he went another way, and returned not by the way that he came to Bethel." Alas! it had been well for him had he always acted in the same spirit of uncompromising deference to Jehovah's will.

But here the scene changes. We are ushered now into a lowly dwelling on the outskirts of Bethel. It is that of an "old prophet" who lives there in seclusion, save only that his sons are with him. Who he is, what he is doing there, or how he came to be there, we are left only to conjecture. We know nothing of his former or his subsequent history. We never heard of him before and shall never hear of him again. But now he is eagerly listening to his sons, as they tell of all the strange things that had come to pass that day in Bethel, and all the words that the prophet from Judah had spoken against the king and his altar. And now, having ascertained what way the man had gone, and hastily equipped himself and his ass for the trip, he determines to pursue him and bring him back. What his motive was we cannot divine. He had evidently taken no part in the idolatrous rites of Jeroboam, that day in Bethel; and yet old as he was, he deliberately lays a plot in falsehood, for the ruin of the good man, who had so nobly fulfilled his mission to the wicked king. Like the Devil in Eden, he succeeds in his scheme. He went after the man of God, and found him sitting under an oak, perhaps for a moment resting himself from the fatigues of the way. And he said unto him, Art thou the man of God that camest from Judah? And he said, I am. Then said he, Come home with me and eat bread. But the man of God refuses the invitation, repeating to him precisely the same words, which he had spoken to the king. The old man however is not to be thwarted thus; and with that ready facility, with which temptation ever clothes itself in the form of an angel of light, and steals the livery of heaven to serve the devil in, he replies, "I am a prophet also, as thou art; and an angel spake unto me by the word of the Lord, saying, Bring him back with thee into thine house that he may eat bread and drink water." So he went back with him, and did eat bread in his house and drink water. But says the faithful record, "he lied unto him."

And now the scene changes again; from the lonely way back to the old prophet's dwelling. And now, when it is too late to retrace his steps or reverse his error—when the prophet of the Lord has disobeyed his orders, and gone in to eat bread and drink water with idolaters, there comes a revelation from the Lord himself, which exposes the tempter in all his baseness; and those old and treacherous lips, which had so lately enticed him into the sin, are opened to pronounce its imminent and terrible retribution.

But why need we multiply words, or stay to depict those other and tragic scenes that followed; as if by any description of ours, we could add ought to the matchless drama as the Bible gives it? Let every one turn for himself and read the chapter through to see what followed—how the wretched old man, as if conscious of guilt, hurries away the victim whose doom he had just predicted, as many a veteran sinner of our day is seen to do with those whom he has robbed of the last cent for the intoxicating draught—how the poor traveller, now bereft of his sense of high integrity, and an easy prey to the threatening danger, was encountered on his lonely way and slain by a lion—how, when the tidings of the calamity reached the city, the old prophet could at once explain it all, and perhaps moved with sorrow for the part he had acted, came and carried the body home to mourn for him and to bury him—how he laid him in his own sepulchre, saying, Alas! my brother, and commanded his sons when he was dead, to bury him in the same grave, and to lay his own bones beside his bones, because of his prediction against the altar, and his fidelity in rebuking Jeroboam—and how at last, in after ages, the good king Josiah fulfilled to the very letter all that he had foretold.

The moral of this story is an important one. It teaches that the way of transgressors is hard—that God will not suffer disobedience even in his own children—that sin must be punished even in the most honoured and trusted servants of the Lord. If any should think the judgment severe in this case, it is a sufficient answer to say that, in these early ages, God was teaching for all the ages to come; and mankind have always needed these signal examples, to make them feel that it is an evil and bitter thing to disobey the Lord.

XIV. THE THREE RIVAL GENERALS.

Abner, Joab, and Amasa, commanders in chief respectively under the forces of King Saul, David, and Absalom, formed a remarkable trio. We have had occasion before to refer to Joab, when speaking of David and his mighty men. The bloodiest pages to be found in all the history of David were caused by the bitter feuds and animosities of these rival chieftains. They were pre-eminently men of blood, and each of them in turn at last perished by the sword; two of them by the treacherous hand of Joab, and Joab himself by the hand of Benaiah, the chief captain of Solomon. Their fierceness and jealousy arose in a great measure out of the intimate relationship in which they stood to each other, and to their respective sovereigns. Abner was the uncle of King Saul, commanding the army during his long reign, and for seven years after his death, maintaining the cause of his son against the claims of David. Joab, and his brother warriors, Abishai and Asahel, were nephews of David, being sons of his sister Zeruiah. Amasa, who took part in Absalom's rebellion, was also a nephew of David, by his sister Abigail, and thus a cousin of Joab. How they verified the proverb, "Bloody and deceitful men shall not live out half their days!" Asahel thirsted for Abner's blood; Abner kills Asahel; Amasa and Absalom seek to kill David; Joab kills Abner, Amasa, and Absalom, and is himself killed at the very horns of the altar. So true is it, that those who take the sword shall perish by the sword.

Now it is to be observed that all this bloodshed, except in

the case of Absalom, was not the result of necessary and honourable warfare. It was the result of deep treachery and vengeance on the part of men, who thought they stood in each other's way. It began in ambition and it ended in murder. It was all utterly abhorrent to the feelings of David, except in Joab's own case, who certainly had the stain of a double murder on his soul, and deserved to die. David would have restrained the wrath of these fierce men, had he been able. But though he was king, they were too hard for him. He made a decisive effort to wrest the command of the army from Joab in Amasa's case, and was probably meditating the same thing for Abner; and it cost both men their lives. No sovereign could desire a more devoted servant, or a more prompt, energetic, and in every way competent general, than Joab through a long life proved himself to be. But if any sovereign ever had in his chieftain "a power behind the throne, greater than the throne itself," David had it in Joab. Relying upon his long and faithful services, and conscious of his own great abilities, Joab did not shrink from the responsibility of opposing the wishes of David, of reproving him sharply to his face, and, as in the death of Absalom, disobeying his express orders. Utterly unscrupulous as to the means of attaining his ends, and supported in all his plans by two brothers who were perfectly like minded, he often carried his point against the king, and was altogether more than a match for both his great rivals. On the death of Abner, to whom David seems to have been much attached, he made it a matter of public lamentation, that he was so hedged in by Joab. "Know ye not that there is a prince and a great man fallen this day in Israel! And I am this day weak, though anointed king; and these men, the sons of Zeruiah, be too hard for me."

As for moral character, it is hard to say which was the worst man of the three. In overt acts and deeds of violence Joab undoubtedly excelled his compeers. But it must not be forgotten that a man who can deliberately perpetrate one great crime is capable on occasion of many or any others. One treason was enough to blast Benedict Arnold; and we should be at no loss to estimate the moral principles of Napoleon, had we nothing to judge from but the divorce of Josephine. When Abner fell by the treacherous hand of Joab, he was himself in the act of betraying that cause for which he had been fighting forty-seven years; and that in order to avenge an insult offered to him by his former master. He was in fact the author of the barbarous and bloody duel, fought at Gibeon between his and Joab's men, as recorded in the second book of Samuel; and this desertion of Ishbosheth's cause, and betraying of the whole kingdom from Dan to Beersheba into the hands of David, simply to wipe off the stain from his own insulted dignity, which had been inflicted there by a hasty word of Ishbosheth—this very ancient example, is, we think, one of the most perfect illustrations on record, of the very spirit, and style, and temper of our most modern and approved duellist. The insulted general, conscious of innocence, would redress his sullied honour, by an act of desertion towards his sovereign, and of treason to his suffering cause. Precisely so; that is the mode; one crime shall wipe out another. And so, the modern duellist, conscious of his high claims to be a gentleman, which perhaps some trivial or ill-judged word of his best friend and companion has seemed to impugn, seeks atonement for this loss of honour, by imbruing his hands in a brother's blood, and it may be rushes into God's presence with the reduplicated guilt of a suicide and a murderer! While we abhor the crime of Joab, and commend

David for wishing to stand before the people guiltless of Abner's blood; still we think he might have spared somewhat of his grief, at the loss of such a man. He asks—"Died Abner as the fool dieth?" We should say, that so far as his death can be traced to his desertion of his old master's son for an insult, and to his own duelling spirit, he did die, precisely as a fool dieth.

And yet he was probably the best of the trio. Amasa was guilty of a worse treason, in becoming the captain of Absalom's host. In that unnatural rebellion, of the son against the father, and the nephew against the uncle, and the subject against the best of all Israel's sovereigns, he showed what a man will do, when ambition is his highest motive, and preferment in office the god of his idolatry. And as for Joab, notwithstanding all his long and faithful services for David, by entering into a plot for the crowning of Adonijah instead of Solomon, so as to thwart all the wishes of the king and the revealed purposes of God, he showed himself in heart not a whit behind the two great rival traitors whom he had slain.

XV. JEHU, OR THE REIGN OF TERROR.

Among all the kings of Israel, Ahab's was undoubtedly the most iniquitous reign; as among the kings of Judah, Manasseh's seems entitled to a similar pre-eminence. But of all the reigns in both kingdoms, that of Jehu was by far the most remarkable in the extent and severity of its judgments upon the wicked. It was emphatically a reign of terror. He was but the sword in the hand of the Lord to execute his long threatened wrath against the idolatrous house of Ahab and Jezebel, and the prophets of Baal. When the cup of their iniquity was full to the brim, and the long slumbering judgments of the Lord could sleep no longer, he raised up this son of thunder—the furious and unsparing Jehu, and had him anointed beforehand for the express purpose of inflicting those terrible curses which Elijah had been commissioned to foretell. And so far as it regards the extermination of this whole idolatrous race, never did any man fulfil his mission more rigidly to the very letter than Jehu. We shrink with horror from the scenes of cruelty and blood in which this whole royal race was utterly blotted from existence. But we must not forget the God-defying wickedness which, for generations, this accursed and incorrigible court of Israel had been perpetrating in the sight of the sun, and in defiance of all the expostulations of the greatest prophets that God ever gave to any people. In the moral government of God, great crimes demand great redress. While men continue to play the part of monsters in iniquity, we must not be surprised or shocked, if God sometimes employs other monsters as the ministers of his wrath and the executioners of his vengeance. The moral world can no more do without these sweeping and terrible outpourings of the wrath of God against iniquity, than the natural world can do without the thunder and lightning. In both, the air is purer, and men breathe freer for the storm. Hence the flood, the destruction of Sodom, the overthrow of Babylon and Jerusalem. Hence through all history God makes the wicked punish the wicked, and the wrath of man to praise him. "They are the sword, the hand is thine." Hence Cæsar had his Brutus, the Stuarts their Cromwell, the house of Judah their Nebuchadnezzar, and the court of Ahab its Jehu. "He meaneth not so, neither doth his heart think so;" but yet he executes the predictions and purposes of Jehovah.

But in Jehu's case there was no uncertainty even in his

own mind. He recognized himself as the very messenger of Jehovah's wrath. He had been called and anointed for this mission. He knew and even quoted the prophecies which demanded this strange work; and while in the midst of the carnage, he could say, "Come, see my zeal for the Lord." In his chariot of war, he drove furiously over the land from city to city, and in rapid succession, slew first the king of Israel and then his confederate the king of Judah, and then the wretched Jezebel, and seventy of Ahab's descendants, and then forty-two of the royal race of Judah, and then the whole body of the prophets of Baal, in each case exterminating the last link of life. And to crown all he broke every image and every house of Baal in the land.

And yet with all his fiery zeal, Jehu was no true servant of the Lord. We shall not stop to analyze his character, to solve its strange paradoxes, or enforce its solemn warnings. It is enough to add simply what the sacred record tells us. It is in the tenth chapter of the second book of Kings. "Howbeit, from the sins of Jeroboam, the son of Nebat, who made Israel to sin, Jehu departed not from after them, to wit, the golden calves that were in Bethel, and that were in Dan. And the Lord said unto Jehu, Because thou hast done well in executing that which is right in mine eyes, and hast done unto the house of Ahab according to all that was in mine heart, thy children of the fourth generation shall sit on the throne of Israel. But Jehu took no heed to walk in the law of the Lord God of Israel with all his heart; for he departed not from the sins of Jeroboam who made Israel to sin."

XVI. HULDAH THE PROPHETESS.

Perhaps there are some among our readers, to whom this one of the minor characters of the Bible is wholly unknown. It may be that they could not give even a good guess as to which of the books her name is to be found in. And yet two of the sacred writers have mentioned her, and both of them recorded in full a very striking prophecy of which she was the author. It is true that we know very little of her personal history and character, but her prophecy is on record, in precisely the same words, in the twenty second chapter of the second book of Kings, and the thirty-fourth chapter of the second book of Chronicles. She lived in the closing period of the kingdom of Judah, under the reign of the young and pious king Josiah, who made the last effort to reform his people and save his country from that extinction which was so near at hand in the Babylonish captivity. She is called a prophetess—one of the very few women mentioned in the Bible as exercising that high office. She was the wife of Shallum, and lived, as we are told, "in the college at Jerusalem," which probably is an expression denoting merely a particular quarter, and not an institution of the city.

At the time Huldah is introduced, the great and gifted Isaiah had already been called to his reward. The youthful Jeremiah had recently been called to the prophetical office, but was living at Anathoth. And the fact of her residence at Jerusalem is probably mentioned as the reason, why, as being just at hand, she was consulted by the great officers of state on this solemn and important occasion.

The occasion was the discovery in the temple, of the long-neglected book of the law, which Hilkiah the priest had found and given to Shaphan the Scribe; and which the latter read to the king. Nothing could give us a sadder proof of the degeneracy of Israel under the reigns of his wicked predecessors, Manasseh and Amon, covering more than half a century, than that Josiah should have been so wholly ignorant of its contents. When he heard it read, he rent his clothes in amazement and terror on account of the general violation of it, in which both he and his people had been living. He at once sent a deputation of five of his principal officers, with a solemn charge to inquire of the Lord, in behalf of himself and all other God-fearing people in Israel, concerning the words of this book.

They went directly to Huldah, the prophetess, and laid the matter before her. This is sufficient to show that she was regarded as speaking by inspiration of the Lord, and fully entitled to the prophetic office. She seems, without a moment's hesitation, to have delivered an oracle of mingled mercy and judgment, which we know from the subsequent history was exactly fulfilled. It is in these words:

"Thus saith the Lord God of Israel, Tell ye the man that sent you to me, Thus saith the Lord, Behold I will bring evil upon this place, and upon the inhabitants thereof, even all the curses that are written in the book which they have read before the king of Judah: because they have forsaken me, and have burned incense unto other gods, that they might provoke me to anger with all the works of their hands; therefore, my wrath shall be poured out upon this place, and shall not be quenched. And as for the king of Judah, who sent you to inquire of the Lord, so shall ye say unto him, Thus saith the Lord God of Israel concerning the words which thou hast heard. Because thine heart was tender, and thou didst humble thyself before God when thou heardest the words against this place, and against the inhabitants thereof, and humbledst thyself before me, and didst rend thy clothes and weep before me, I have even heard thee also, saith the Lord. Behold I will gather thee to thy fathers, and thou shalt be gathered to thy grave in peace, neither shall thine eyes see all the evil that I will bring upon this place, and upon the inhabitants of the same."

It is added, in the sequel, that Josiah immediately called together all the elders and head men of Judah and Jerusalem, and then went up to the house of the Lord, where he read from the book all the words of the Lord to priests, Levites, and people, great and small, and made a solemn covenant with the Lord which he required all the people to stand to. It was a noble effort on the part of this young sovereign, to bring up his people to the religion of their fathers. But it was too late. They were fast hastening to a final overthrow, and nothing but the bitter experience of a seventy years' exile in Babylon could ever cure them of that headstrong, and amazing tendency towards idolatry, which through all their history had been their national besetting sin.

XVII. BELSHAZZAR, OR THE HANDWRITING ON THE WALL.

Of the countless cases in the Old Testament that might swell our list of minor or incidental characters, we mention but one more. It is the impious king of Babylon, in his lordly power seeking to pour contempt upon the only living and true God. We have had occasion to trace many of the greater and the lesser lights of Bible character. Belshazzar is certainly one of its darkest shadows. The mysterious handwriting on the wall, so suddenly arresting his profane mirth and revelry, and so terribly heralding his approaching doom, has made him a proverb of warning to the wicked of all ages. Since the awful night of his judgment, many a tyrant's heart has failed him, and many a bold blasphemer's face has grown pale with fear, as conscience has called up the past and pointed him to that scroll of prophecy, overhanging all his dark future—"Thou art weighed in the balances and art found wanting."

It is, without doubt, one of the most solemn sentences in the Bible; far more so than that of Nathan the prophet to the guilty king of Israel, "Thou art the man;" because to him there was a respite given, for repentance and favour. But this is the doom of eternity. The day of life is gone; the night of death is at hand; the cup of iniquity is full. Swift, summary, and terrible was the judgment. But the impiety which called it down had been great and heaven-defying in the extreme. Belshazzar had not sinned ignorantly. He had a perfect knowledge of all the wonders God had wrought in the days of his ancestor, Nebuchadnezzar, by the hand of his servant Daniel. And yet with all these warnings before him, he deliberately, in the most public manner, undertakes to insult and defy the God of heaven.

The whole story of his high-handed sacrilege is told in a single chapter, the fifth, of the book of Daniel. It is told with wonderful simplicity, and yet with wonderful dramatic power. It comes in immediately after the account of Nebuchadnezzar's fall and restoration, whose edict closes with the following remarkable words—"Now I Nebuchadnezzar praise and extol and honour the King of heaven, all whose works are truth, and his ways judgment; and those that walk in pride he is able to abase." It was, perhaps, to illustrate this great lesson of Nebuchadnezzar that the fate of his proud and wicked grandson is so minutely recorded.

"Belshazzar the king made a great feast to a thousand of his lords and drank wine before the thousand. Belshazzar, while he tasted the wine, commanded to bring the golden and silver vessels which his father Nebuchadnezzar had taken out of the temple which was in Jerusalem, that the king and his princes, his wives and his concubines might drink therein. Then they brought the golden vessels that were taken out of the temple of the house of God which was at Jerusalem: and the king and his princes, his wives and his concubines drank in them. They drank wine, and praised the gods of gold, and of silver, of brass, of iron, of wood, and of stone. In the same hour came forth fingers of a man's hand, and wrote over against the candlestick upon the plaster of the wall of the king's palace: and the king saw the part of the hand that wrote. Then the king's countenance was changed and his thoughts troubled him, so that the joints of his loins were loosed, and his knees smote one against another."

A single unarmed hand, quietly writing on the wall! What was this, that it should have so unmanned the proudest monarch of the earth! What was this, that it should strike terror into his wine-inflamed heart, and send a thrill of amazement through all the lords and ladies of his banqueting-room! Why should the sight of fingers, tracing letters on his splendidly illuminated palace walls, make him tremble so in the presence of his mighty ones, that the sound of revelry is hushed in an instant, and the wine-cup is dropped untasted from the lips! Ah! it is coward guilt that makes him tremble. It is conscience, pointing to his own impious deeds, that now sees in the mysterious apparition, a stern reprover of his sins, and a dread messenger of the wrath to come. Conscious guilt is the father of all these sudden terrors. And he is eager to know the worst. He cries aloud for his sages and astrologers to interpret the writing; but it is beyond their skill. There is but one man in Babylon who can expound the awful secret; and he is the prophet of that God, whose worship has here been so impiously profaned. "There is a man in thy kingdom," cries the queen mother of the young monarch, "in whom is the Spirit of the holy gods; and in the days of thy father, light and understanding and wisdom like the wisdom of the gods, was found in him; whom the King Nebuchadnezzar thy father, the king, I say, thy father, made master of the magicians, astrologers, Chaldeans, and soothsayers, Daniel, whom the king named Belteshazzar. Now let Daniel be called and he will show the interpretation."

And forthwith Daniel is brought in, night though it be. Both he and his God had long been forgotten and despised by the profane revellers. But there is need for him now. Poor human nature, however arrogant and self-sufficient, is apt to call for help, even from God's despised ministers, when once it gets into trouble. And now there is trouble in the palace—trouble of a kind not to be removed by all the sages and all the gods of Chaldea. For there emblazoned on the wall is the mysterious messenger of Jehovah, and in such a presence all the instruments of music have ceased, and the throng of revellers is mute and still.

Solemn and sublime was the position of the Lord's prophet, thus summoned at midnight into the presence of the king, thus standing up to expound the decrees of heaven to that silent and awe-stricken multitude. Doubtless many an eye in that lordly throng had looked on him before. For it is that same

Daniel, who in his younger years had interpreted all the extraordinary visions of the great Nebuchadnezzar. It is that same Daniel, who had once been exalted as chief ruler over all the wise men, and governor of the Province of Babylon, and whose companions, Shadrach, Meshach, and Abednego, had passed unscathed through the fiery furnace. He it is, that now, perhaps as venerable for his years as he had ever been for his virtues, boldly reminds the young king of his transgressions, declines all his proferred honours, and foretells his imminent doom.

"Then Daniel answered and said before the king, Let thy gifts be to thyself, and give thy rewards to another; yet I will read the writing unto the king, and make known to him the interpretation. O thou king, the most high God gave Nebuchadnezzar thy father a kingdom and majesty and glory and honour. And for the majesty that he gave him, all peoples, nations, and languages, trembled and feared before him; whom he would he slew, and whom he would he kept alive, and whom he would he set up, and whom he would he put down. But when his heart was lifted up, and his mind hardened in pride, he was deposed from his kingly throne, and they took his glory from him. And he was driven from the sons of men, and his heart was made like the beasts', and his dwelling was with the wild asses; they fed him with grass like oxen, and his body was wet with the dew of heaven; till he knew that the most high God ruled in the kingdom of men, and that he appointeth over it whomsoever he will. And thou his son, O Belshazzar, hast not humbled thine heart, though thou knewest all this; but hast lifted up thyself against the Lord of heaven; and they have brought the vessels of his house before thee; and thou and thy lords, thy wives and thy concubines, have drunk wine in them; and thou hast praised the gods of silver and gold, of brass, iron, wood, and stone, which see not, nor hear, nor know; and the God in whose hand thy breath is, and whose are all thy ways, hast thou not glorified. Then was the part of the hand sent from him; and this writing was written. And this is the writing that was written, MENE, MENE, TEKEL, UPHARSIN. This is the interpretation of the thing: MENE, God hath numbered thy kingdom and finished it. TEKEL, Thou are weighed in the balances, and art found wanting. PERES, Thy kingdom is divided and given to the Medes and Persians."

Such was the solemn message! Such its faithful interpretation! Swift and terrible too was its fulfilment! For even while this strange scene is passing within the palace walls, Babylon is invaded. The victorious Cyrus, at the head of the Medo-Persian army, is already within the two-leaved gates, and the mighty city falls beneath the conqueror. "In that night," says the sacred writer, "was Belshazzar the king of the Chaldeans slain, and Darius the Median took the kingdom."

XVIII. ZACHARIAS AND ELISABETH.

In entering the New Testament Scriptures, we are compelled, for want of space, to limit our view to a comparatively small number of its many incidental or minor characters. It would be an interesting study to group and delineate them all. But we must select a few examples from the good and the bad. Prominent on the list of the former stand the venerable Zacharias and Elisabeth, honoured of God as the parents of John the Baptist, which was next to the honour of being the parents of our blessed Lord himself. It is not our purpose here to go over in detail the well known and well told story of Zacharias and Elisabeth in the first chapter of Luke. It is simply to direct attention to one or two striking points in that account. It is a remarkable testimony which the sacred writer bears to the piety and integrity of this venerable couple. "They were both righteous before God, walking in all the commandments and ordinances of the Lord blameless." Being both of the tribe of Levi and of the house of Aaron, they were devoted to the Lord's service as the great business of life, and they had already reached a goodly old age in that service, before they were selected to have a son who should be the forerunner of the Messiah. Their vocation was holy; their past lives had been eminently holy; their appointed mission as the parents of John was peculiarly holy; and in addition to this we are told that they were both filled with the Holy Ghost, and spake the inspired praises of the Lord. There is not on record, any greater and more decisive proof of the pre-eminent holiness of any two merely human beings than we have of Zacharias and Elisabeth.

And yet these two persons lived in the estate of matrimony. How does such an example rebuke the absurd and unnatural dogma, that celibacy is a higher and holier estate than marriage! And how strikingly does this case illustrate the manner in which Scripture teaches the most important doctrines by example! Here nothing is said of celibacy or marriage. But here stands before us a consecrated priest of God, ministering at his altars, and living in wedlock with one of the daughters of Aaron—and these two aged servants of Jehovah, we are told, were righteous before God, walking in all the commandments and ordinances of the Lord blameless, and afterwards filled with the Holy Ghost. And thus had it been from the beginning with all the holiest priests and ministers of God's worship. Till the apostate church of Rome, warring both against God and nature, began to forbid marriage, and extol the superior virtue of celibacy, it had never entered into the mind of man, and as certainly never into the religion of the Bible, that the ministers of God must not live in the estate of matrimony. All the ministers of religion for four thousand years had been married men. All the patriarchs and prophets who spake as they were moved by the Holy Ghost, had been married men. Nor is there a single interdict against marriage as an unholy estate in all the New Testament.

Yet the church of Rome demands celibacy as the perfection of holiness. No married man like Zacharias, or Isaiah, or David, or Samuel, or Moses, or Abraham, or Enoch, or Peter may minister at its altars. No married women, like Elisabeth, and Hannah, and Rachel, and Deborah, and the mother of our Lord, may hope to reach the highest style of piety. The church of Rome demands for saints and successors of the apostles, a class of men who have never known, from any experience of their own, the ennobling instincts of parental love, and the sweet and hallowing influences of the family. The church of Rome wages war with the first institution God ever established in the world—the family. The church of Rome wages war against the first command God ever gave to our race—that of conjugal love. The church of Rome wages war against the deepest and the most essential instinct of humanity, that on which the very existence and continuance of the race depends —the instinct of a father's and a mother's love. And if there were any danger that the church of Rome could ever succeed in such a battle against all the highest interests of God and man, it would be the duty of all men to rise up in the name of insulted and outraged human nature, and sweep such a system of tyranny and wickedness from the earth. But there is no ground to fear that doctrines so unnatural and absurd can ever overthrow the ordinance of God.

Still they exert their baneful influence on the heart and character of all who hold them. Think of a whole community of men like the Romish priesthood, cut off for ever from all the restraints and all the hopes that influence the husband and the father of a family—isolated, like icebergs in mid-ocean, from all earthly and all human ties—doomed to have but one idea, one object, and one ambition of existence, namely, church propagandism—severed utterly and for ever from the great throbbing heart of humanity, and from all the social, fraternal, patriotic instincts that spring from a country, a kindred, a posterity—uncheered by the genial presence of woman—unblest with her love—unchastened by the gentle voice of the wife whom God made as a helpmeet for man—unchecked and unmoulded by any of those tender and endearing emotions of love and sympathy that flow from the constant presence of one's children and grand-children! What would the world be! what its sympathies! what its charities! what its hopes! if all the men in it could be reduced to the condition of the Romish priesthood! Do we wonder that such a system—such a war against God and nature—should produce inquisitors and persecutors unto death! Do we wonder that every patriotic instinct, every genial sympathy, every public sentiment, every noble virtue, every impulse of a common humanity, should wither and die in hearts from which have been for ever erased all hopes of a posterity, all conjugal and all parental responsibilities, all that is tender, and blessed, and precious, in the love of wife, and mother, and child? Such a system, could it become universal, would not only ruin the world by making the present generation its last, but would blast the generation that now is by consigning it to unmitigated selfishness and cold-hearted stoicism.

If the problem were how to make man cold, selfish, tyrannical, and fiendish—to bring him by the shortest and most effective method possible into a condition, in which he should have no one feeling in common with his fellow-man, and no one tie to bind him to human society and to his country; you could not devise an expedient so likely to accomplish it as just to cut him off for ever from the companionship of woman in marriage, and from the paternal care and love of his own children in the family. Strike from his heart these two noblest instincts of his God-created nature, conjugal and paternal love; and you have divested him of the crowning glory of his manhood; you have at a blow extinguished the better half of his being; you have created in his soul a vacuum which there is nothing else on earth to fill; you have reduced him from a social to a solitary state; you have dried up in him that life-blood of existence which has been flowing from Adam; you have made him a lone and an unloved wanderer in the world, without a companion to cheer him on through life, and bless him in death. And when you have accomplished this work of annihilation on all his divinest attributes and instincts, you have prepared him to shun and abhor his fellow-men, to hate the society from which he is thus ostracised, and to look without a tear, and without an emotion, upon all the thousand scenes of human suffering and sorrow, where husbands, wives, parents, children, brothers, sisters are accustomed to weep. You have thus taken man from the sphere where God placed him, and you have made him an unfeeling stoic with a will of iron and a heart of adamant.

Who would wish to live on earth if all men were fashioned after this style? Who would be willing to trust his life or character to the tender mercies of men, whose hearts had never known, or could know the gentle influences of conjugal and parental love? Who would look for exalted patriotism, and heroic virtues, and sentiments of generosity, public spirit, and honour, in men who had thus cut themselves off from every thing that can identify man with his fellows, endear him to his country, and inspire the heart with philanthropy and enthusiasm.

Did God ever intend the ministers of religion to occupy this anomalous and unnatural position? It is a libel on the Bible to say he did. There is no such law in the Bible, and there never was in any church, until the Church of Rome forbade to marry. On the contrary, under every dispensation of his church, God intended the ministers of religion to be ensamples of the flock in all the relations of life. Aaron and the whole line of his successors in the Levitical priesthood were married men. Peter, from whom the bishops of Rome claim succession, was a married man. And even Paul, who, on account of his extraordinary vocation and the perils to which he was exposed, never married, yet asserted his right to do so, and laid down the law to Timothy in these emphatic terms—"A bishop must be blameless, the husband of one wife; one that ruleth well his own house, having his children in subjection with all gravity. For if a man know not how to rule his own house, how shall he take care of the church of God?"

Yet according to the church of Rome, celibacy is held as essential to all God's ministers, as being a higher and holier state than matrimony. There can be no question that it is precisely that estate which best answers the iron rule, and the crushing cruel despotism of the whole Romish system. For neither human nor diabolical ingenuity could well devise a more effective way to extinguish all human feeling in its ecclesiastical rulers, than thus to crush out from their hearts all conjugal and parental instincts. Such a priesthood is no doubt powerful, but it is the power of an army from whose bosoms all the best attributes of human nature have been expunged.

XIX. ANANIAS AND SAPPHIRA.

From Zacharias and Elisabeth walking in all the commandments of the Lord blameless, we turn now to a very different picture. For as the heaven-appointed relation of husband and wife may prove the greatest of all temporal blessings—the brightest picture of domestic bliss that has survived the fall—so also, where the heart is wrong, it may be abused, like all other good things, and turned into a curse. Thus was it with the unhappy Ananias and Sapphira—combining together, for selfish and covetous ends, to deceive the apostles of our Lord. This dark and fearful example of meditated wickedness was, no doubt, placed on record in the Scriptures, that it might serve as a warning to all coming generations. The shadows of Bible character are sometimes as instructive and needful as its brightest lights. They serve, by contrast, to make the pure light of heaven the more blessed and beautiful, as the dark bosom of the thunder cloud is but the better back ground to reveal the brilliance of the rainbow.

It is not often that sin meets with so sudden and terrible a rebuke, as it did in this case. But it is not often of a more daring and aggravated character. There was not only a conspiracy against the truth, but a combination of the most deliberate and inexcusable sins. These two persons had professed the religion of Christ and joined the infant church. But not content with mere membership, they were ambitious of distinction in the new fraternity on the ground of a large-hearted liberality. They aspired to be the foremost among the generous—sold their estate apparently for the good of the cause—laid a part of the proceeds at the apostles' feet as a free-will offering, and said it was the whole price.

Here then was the double sin of hypocrisy and falsehood—a deliberate bargain in iniquity, planned and executed, both in word and in deed—and that not merely to men but to God. It was direct blasphemy against the Holy Ghost—an attempt to deceive the church, and impose upon the apostles of Christ. Such an act of dissimulation and falsehood argued a total want of the faith and of the moral character which they professed as the disciples of Jesus. There is, in fact, no single element which is more essential to moral character than truth. Truth is the very basis of character. It is the life-giving aliment of all virtue. There can be no such thing as virtue or moral excellence in the absence of truth or veracity. Whatever his professions, whatever his gifts and attainments, no man can possibly be a good man who will deliberately speak or act a falsehood. All experience and observation prove, that so long as a man will stand by the truth, so long as he will neither speak nor act the lie, there is some hope of him—hope of his moral improvement, and ultimate salvation. When once that bulwark of virtue is gone, when that last link that binds him to the throne of God is sundered, there is no hope either for this world or the next. Man can be saved and improved only by means of the truth; and when he has lost all regard for the truth—when he deliberately prefers a lie to the truth, his case is hopeless, his character is wrecked, his doom is sealed beyond recall and beyond remedy. There is nothing left him but judgment and retribution. It may come speedily, or it may linger long in the distance; but soon or late it is sure to come.

In Ananias and Sapphira it was suddenly executed. The good of the infant church demanded, that those who had thus sinned, should be made an example to others. Thus they both died in one day, and by the same awful visitation of God.

XX. BARTIMEUS AND ZACCHEUS.

These two widely different characters may yet be appropriately introduced together. In one respect they had nothing in common. They stood at the extremes of mere outward condition. One was a rich man; the other was a poor blind beggar. But this very dissimilarity makes their history only the more fitting an illustration of the Saviour's grace. However unlike they had been before, both in character and worldly condition, they had much in common from the time of Christ's visit to Jericho. It is manifest that they both had a great desire to see Jesus. They had evidently heard of him before this visit; and, each in his own way, they determined not to let it pass without an effort. The one, because of his small stature preventing any chance of seeing him in the crowd, ran before, and climbed up into a sycamore tree for the purpose. The other, in his blindness, hearing the tramping of the passing crowd, cried aloud when told who it was; and though commanded to hold his peace, only cried the more vehemently, because of the opposition, "Jesus, thou Son of David, have mercy on me."

From importunity like this, so earnest and yet so humble, whether of the rich or the poor, our blessed Lord was never known to turn away. He had come into the world to seek and to save that which was lost. Here was a rich sinner who was as really lost, and as much needing his help as the poor one. He was as able and as willing to save the poor one, as the rich. He was now passing through Jericho for the last time, going up to Jerusalem to finish his great work, and make atonement for the sins of a lost world. But, though on his way to death, and bearing the great burden of such a work, he does not, he cannot, turn away from the cry of the humble, earnest suppliant for his mercy. He has time, even in a crowd, to stop for the cry of the penitent Bartimeus, and to make a visit to the house of Zaccheus, in order to carry salvation there.

How characteristic of the gospel of Christ, and how illustrative of the sovereign grace of God, that salvation should thus come on the same day to two men like these! Of the vast crowd who pressed in every direction to see Jesus, there was in all probability no one poorer and more wretched than the sightless Bartimeus. And perhaps on the other hand, there was not a richer man in Jericho than Zaccheus the publican. How little did any mortal think, when it was first announced that Jesus was on his way to Jericho, that the object, or even the result of his visit might be, to make these two unpropitious characters the very trophies of his special favour and his saving grace! But there is no case too hard for the Lord. And these extreme cases of misery and of sin, which occur so frequently in the Bible, are doubtless chosen as vessels of mercy, and their history placed on record, in order the more to magnify both God's sovereignty and his grace, by showing that he confers salvation on whom he pleases, and that the power is of God and not of man.

At the same time they illustrate, with equal clearness, the other great truth, that there is no salvation without an effort on the part of those who would be saved. The kingdom of heaven suffereth violence, and the violent take it by force. The entrance into life is through a strait gate, and they must strive who enter it. Bartimeus felt deeply his need of sight; and Zaccheus, though rich in this world's goods, no doubt, felt his need of pardon for sin. And under these felt necessities, they were ready to make exertion, when the hour of mercy was at hand—to seek the Lord when he might be found, to call upon him while he was near. Had Jesus never passed that way, or passing had he not been willing and able to save, there had been no sight for the one, and no salvation carried into the household of the other. On the other hand, however able and willing to save the chief of sinners, or to help this poor beggar, and however often he might have passed through Jericho, had Zaccheus shut himself up at home, and made no effort to see him, or had Bartimeus been deterred by those around him, and held his peace, there had been no salvation for the one or the other. God works and man works, in every work of salvation. All our Saviour's miracles of mercy, as well as his parables and his discourses, teach these two great doctrines, of man's active agency and God's sovereign power in the salvation of the soul. And we have them both strikingly displayed in these two examples at Jericho.

Just so is it now in the case of all who would be saved. There is but one power on earth that can open the eyes of the blind, or forgive sins. It is in Christ as he passes by in his mercy—as he is offered in the gospel. And he is ever passing, and ever ready to succour, where this gospel is preached, where this word of life is heard. But sinners must avail themselves of the favoured opportunity—of this day of merciful visitation. They must arise and meet him. They must break through every barrier of their own inaction, and others' opposition, and call upon him while thus he is near. If they would be healed —if they would be pardoned—if they would be made to rejoice in a good hope of salvation, they must come to Jesus as Bartimeus and Zaccheus did.

XXI. NICODEMUS AND JOSEPH OF ARIMATHEA.

John is the only one of the four Evangelists who mentions Nicodemus, but all of them speak of Joseph. They were both counsellors or rulers of the Jewish Sanhedrim. One of them is introduced near the opening, and the other near the close of the gospel history. One of them comes to Jesus by night, convinced by seeing his mighty miracles that he is a teacher come from God, and apparently inquiring for the way of life. The other comes to Pilate after the crucifixion, requesting the body of Jesus for burial, and is permitted to bury it in his own new sepulchre. Indeed John informs that Nicodemus also bore a part in this last act of kindness. He brought a hundred pounds weight of precious spices, myrrh, and aloes with which to embalm the body. And he and Joseph together wrapped it in fine linen clothes, and laid it in the tomb. There is something peculiarly striking in the fact, that these honourable counsellors, members of that very Sanhedrim which had adjudged Jesus worthy of death, should thus come to bury him.

They were in fact his disciples, though secretly for fear of the Jews. The several Evangelists speak of Joseph, as "a rich man," "an honourable counsellor," "a good man and a just," "a disciple of Jesus," as one "who waited for the kingdom of God," and "had not consented to the counsel and deed of them" that had condemned Jesus. And this last faithful and loving act shows that he deserved this tribute to his character.

Though less is said of Nicodemus, still enough is said to show that he too was a good man, a true friend and disciple of Jesus. John mentions him on three occasions: the first, when he came to Jesus by night to learn the way of life; the second, in the seventh chapter where he boldly defends the character of Jesus against the accusations of the Sanhedrim, on the ground that they had no right to assail it till they had heard him and known his works; and the third, that in which he came to take part with his fellow counsellor, in burying the body. Under such circumstances, when even our Saviour's own chosen disciples of three years' standing had forsaken him and fled, despairing of his cause, these brief notices, along with this courageous and loving act of burial, are quite sufficient to prove that Nicodemus, as well as Joseph, was a true disciple of our Lord. The probability is that after this they both ceased to attend upon the Sanhedrim, if indeed they did not lose their places by being excommunicated. On this point however the New Testament is silent.

XXII. THE TWO THIEVES IN THE CRUCIFIXION.

Here is certainly one of the most vividly drawn contrasts of character in the Bible. If there is any time when the character of a man comes out in its true colours, it is in the article of death. It is an honest hour, when, stripped of all the disguises and conventionalities of life, the lips are apt to speak out the real convictions of the heart. There is something solemn and awfully sublime, in the fact, that when the Son of God was dying for the sins of men, it should be so ordered by Providence, that two of the race should die with him; and that while one dies with the unbelieving taunt of derision on his lips, to the other he should open the gates of Paradise as an humble, believing penitent. What an illustration is it of the truth, which now, for eighteen centuries, has been verified wherever this gospel has been preached, that the point on which the destiny of men turns for eternity, is not in their external circumstances, but solely in the inward state of the heart!

To all outward appearance the condition of these two men was precisely the same—both equally guilty, equally helpless, equally wretched. It was the extreme of human guilt, impotence, and woe. They were both thieves, malefactors, and were probably selected for execution on this occasion on account of their turpitude, in order to pour the greater contempt on the Divine sufferer who hung between them. They were both alike cut off for ever from all earthly sympathy and succour, and both alike near to the only being in the Universe, who could give help or hope in death. They both died as the victims of a violated law. They both died at the cross, in sight of that blood which was flowing so freely for the guilty. That voice of sympathy and love, so near at hand, which spoke peace to the troubled heart of the one, was equally near and equally able to save the other, had he but asked it. And yet how utterly unlike, in all their feelings, in all their hopes, and in all their future destiny, were these poor dying sinners at the cross! "And one of the malefactors which were hanged, railed on him, saying, If thou be Christ, save thyself and us. But the other answering, rebuked him, saying, Dost not thou fear God, seeing thou art in the same condemnation? And we indeed justly; for we receive the due reward of our deeds; but this man hath done nothing amiss. And he said unto Jesus, Lord, remember me, when thou comest into thy kingdom. And Jesus said unto him, Verily I say unto thee, To-day shalt thou be with me in paradise."

It is sad indeed to think of any poor sinner's perishing so near the cross—perishing, without one ray of hope, in the very presence of Him who was dying for a guilty world. It is sad indeed to think that any sinner in this world should have ever perished, since the cross was first erected—that any poor, guilty soul should have clung to its unbelief and died impenitent, after even hearing of the story of the cross. But we are not to shut our eyes to the greatest facts of history, and the plainest teachings of God's word. What took place here on Calvary, in the different doom of these two dying men, has been repeated over and over again in every spot of the earth where the story of the cross has been preached. It has been a savour of life unto life to some, of death unto death to others. The same distinction, the same wide and eternal separation, which took place here, has taken place everywhere else among dying men, under the preaching of this gospel. One man hears and believes—turns his dying eyes to Calvary, and with an humble, penitent faith, cries, Lord, remember me when thou comest into thy kingdom, and is comforted with the blessed promise, This day shalt thou be with me in paradise." Another man, his nearest neighbour, his very brother, in the same condemnation, exposed to the same present and eternal woe, only rails with senseless and impotent unbelief, at the story of a Divine Saviour, and dies as he has lived in sin and despair. These two first deaths under the cross, so marked in their results and so prophetic of all subsequent history, are sufficient to show to every candid mind, the utter impossibility of accepting the modern dogma of universal salvation.

But turning from the sad picture of this malefactor, dying in impenitence and unbelief, on one side of the cross, let us ponder well the lessons of instruction and consolation, which come to us from the other. In all the affecting scenes of the crucifixion, this record of the converted thief is one of the most touching and instructive. It not only reveals the love of Jesus, and the power of his gospel; but it exhibits him as exercising the very highest powers of Godhead in the darkest hour of his humiliation as a man. Who can forgive sins but God? It is when humbling himself even unto death—it is when emptying himself of his divine glory—it is with his dying breath, when all merely human power was gone, except speech, that our Immanuel pardons sin, and opens the gates of glory to a sinner of deepest dye. What a vindication of his supreme Divinity in the very article of death—a Saviour, a Conqueror even while he dies! Nothing could better have illustrated his eternal power over sin and death, than this salvation of the dying thief. No penitent sinner need despair with such a case as this on record. And no impenitent one may presume with such an example by its side as the other.

The two most striking lessons taught by the example of the dying penitent are the efficacy of faith and the necessity of prayer. Faith alone can save—faith in Jesus—that faith which renounces all self-righteousness, all human dependence, and trusts itself confidingly into the arms of Jesus. And perhaps the Bible does not contain a more remarkable example of a true, strong, and even heroic faith, triumphing over all doubts and fears, all discouragements and drawbacks, than this faith of the dying thief. For you will observe, that it was exercised at the deepest hour of Christ's humiliation, when his cause to all human appearances was crushed for ever, and when even his long-tried disciples had all forsaken him in despair. His faith was like that of Abraham, who against hope believed in hope. It was this strong, self-renouncing, and penitent faith which led him to pray to Jesus, Lord, remember me when thou comest into thy kingdom. And thus we learn that it is prayer alone which can secure the blessing. Faith prompts the plea, and prayer offers it. In answer to the believing prayer of the humble penitent, the Son of God opens the gates of heaven. This day shalt thou be with me in paradise. How simple, how easy, how ample, how glorious is the way of salvation for the lost, thus opened by the blood of the cross, and thus secured by promise and blood to every penitent sinner who prays in faith, Lord, remember me!

"As on the cross the Saviour hung,
And wept, and bled, and died,
He poured salvation on a wretch
That languished at his side.

"His crimes with inward grief and shame,
The penitent confessed:
Then turned his dying eyes to Christ,
And thus his prayer addressed:

"'Jesus, thou Son and heir of heaven,
Thou spotless Lamb of God,
I see thee bathed in sweat and tears,
And weltering in thy blood.

"'Yet quickly from these scenes of woe
In triumph shalt thou rise,
Burst through the gloomy shades of death,
And shine above the skies.

"'Amid the glories of that world,
Dear Saviour, think on me,
And in the victories of thy death,
Let me a sharer be.'

"His prayer the dying Jesus hears,
And instantly replies,
'To-day thy parting soul shall be
With me in paradise.'"

XXIII. CORNELIUS AND AGRIPPA.

We place these two names together because of the striking contrast in character and destiny which they present. "Not many mighty, not many noble are called." Cornelius the Roman centurion, and Agrippa the Jewish king, are among the very few men of rank and power mentioned in the New Testament as being brought into immediate contact with the Gospel. Pilate the Roman governor, and Herod the Tetrarch, had, at the death of Jesus, been favoured with an occasion of salvation, which, had they embraced it, might have led them to the truth. Festus and Felix each had a similar visitation of mercy in the preaching of Paul. But none of these men of power ever profited by the blessing. In their pride and self-sufficiency they all rejected it. And so was it with King Agrippa, who was a believer in the prophets, and on his own confession to Paul, almost persuaded to be a Christian. There is not the slightest ground to hope, however, that this highly favoured and almost persuaded man ever became a real Christian. How different would have been his destiny, and how great and blessed would have been his influence on his countrymen and on the world, if he had come out boldly as a Christian, and given his life to the cause! But God had chosen humbler instruments to do his work, that the power might prove to be Divine. And it is, in this view, a significant fact, that not one of the kings and rulers mentioned in the New Testament ever embraced the gospel. The nearest approach to it was in the case of Sergius Paulus, the Roman deputy of Cyprus, under the preaching of the apostle Paul; and in the case of this good man, Cornelius the centurion, under the preaching of the apostle Peter. With these and a few other exceptions like Nicodemus and Joseph among the Jewish counsellors, all the great and the mighty men contemporary with the apostles, seem with one consent to have rejected the gospel.

Cornelius, a captain or centurion of the Italian band, and it may be, a member of the noble Cornelian family of Rome, was stationed at Cæsarea, at that time the military capital of Palestine. Prior to Peter's visit, Cornelius was a good man, worshipping Jehovah according to the knowledge which he had already gained of the Jewish religion, and through which he had probably become a proselyte of the gate. It is a high testimony which the sacred writer bears to his character—"A devout man, and one that feared God with all his house, who gave much alms to the people, and prayed to God always." This is indeed a comprehensive and beautiful description of a good man; devout in spirit, ruling his house in the fear of God, doing good to his fellow-men, and abounding in prayer. "Thy prayers, and thine alms," says the angel of the Lord, "have come up in memorial before God." And when Peter, directed by a heavenly vision, came to him from Joppa, and had heard from his own lips, the whole story of the Lord's dealings with him, he said, "Of a truth, I perceive that God is no respecter of persons, but, in every nation, he that feareth God and worketh righteousness is accepted of him."

This is the man who, though not of the seed of Abraham, had the high honour of receiving first a visit from an angel of the Lord, and then another from his apostle; of hearing the gospel preached in his own house, and of being the first Gentile admitted into the Christian church. The whole story is graphically told in the tenth chapter of the Acts. And when Peter, tracing all the steps that led to the interview, and declaring the gospel of Jesus to this good man and his assembled household, could no longer doubt that God's salvation was offered to Gentile as well as Jew, he commanded them to be baptized in the name of the Lord Jesus. For while he was preaching, the Holy Ghost came upon them with miraculous power, so that they, just as had been seen in Jerusalem on the day of Pentecost, began to speak with tongues and to magnify the Lord. Thus was the door of gospel grace opened to the Gentile world.

In striking contrast with this noble Roman and now nobler Christian, the twenty-fifth and twenty-sixth chapters of the Acts bring to our view another man of noble birth, but of widely different character. It is King Agrippa, the last one mentioned in the New Testament, of that gifted, but wicked Herodian family who played so conspicuous a part in the gospel history. Of the four whose names appear on the sacred pages: namely, Herod the Great who slew the children in Bethlehem, Herod Antipas who slew John the Baptist, Herod Agrippa who slew the Apostle James, and King Agrippa, this last of the dynasty appears to have been by far the best man. Still, he was justly chargeable with great sins, and like all his royal race, seems to have had no regard for the laws of God. When on his visit to the new Roman Governor, Festus, at Cæsarea, he was permitted to hear the gospel from the lips of the Apostle Paul. He seems to have been fascinated with the eloquence and earnestness of the prisoner, and confessed that he was almost persuaded to be a Christian. Ah! what an hour of privilege! what a golden moment of life! what an offer and opportunity of salvation was that, if he had but embraced it! It seems almost sad to think how near the gate of heaven some men come, and yet miss it; what blessings they enjoy only to despise them and turn them into curses! It had been just so with his ancestors. One of them had seen the bright star of Bethlehem; another had heard John the Baptist preach, had even heard him gladly, and had seen Jesus Christ face to face; another still might have heard it, and probably did, from the lips of James and Peter; and now this last of the royal line, is favoured with a special audience to hear of God's ancient promise fulfilled, the wondrous story of the cross, the sublime doctrines of the redemption of the soul, the resurrection of the body, and eternal life beyond the grave, as expounded by the mighty reasoning, and illustrated by the self-denying and heroic life, of the greatest preacher of that or any other age. And yet all in vain for poor Agrippa.

Cornelius, from that very city where Agrippa heard the gospel, had sent special messengers to Joppa, for Peter, that he might learn the way of life. And with his earnest, inquiring spirit, it was enough simply to hear, in order to believe and be saved with all his house. But now Agrippa has, in this same place, this same gospel expounded to him just as earnestly, as faithfully, and as eloquently as it had been to Cornelius. And yet with this rare opportunity of salvation, and with all his knowledge of the Scriptures, and with the apparent confession of their truth or power on his lips, he hears only to turn away in unbelief, and in all probability to reject the last offer of salvation that was ever made to him. Though almost persuaded, there is no evidence that he ever believed.

What a picture is this of the destiny of thousands who hear a preached gospel! Almost persuaded! Almost saved! Almost Christians! There is probably not a preacher on earth, who has been at all faithful to his Master's work, who has not had scores and hundreds of hearers, in precisely the same state of mind with Agrippa. Of all the men now living in the world, who have ever heard the gospel preached, and have not obeyed it, there is probably not one, who has not at some time felt, and even confessed, as Agrippa did—Almost thou persuadest me to be a Christian. If men are lost, it is their own fault. God hath never left himself without a witness, and a warning voice in the sinner's path. Go where he will, and do what he may, there has ever been a messenger whispering to his secret soul, urging him to leave the ways of sin, and yield his heart to God's control.

> "Something hath met thee in the path
> Of worldliness and vanity,
> And pointed to the coming wrath,
> And warned thee from that wrath to flee."

We have now completed our survey of the lesser lights of Bible character. It is of necessity a very partial one; for the field here is well nigh boundless. It would be easy to multiply examples both from the Old Testament and the New. In the latter we might speak of the virtues of the aged Simeon and

Anna, as they wait for the consolation of Israel; of the good Dorcas and Lydia, each in her sphere of life serving the cause of the Master; of Barnabas and Silas, the faithful companions of the great apostle of the Gentiles; of Philip the evangelist and the eloquent Apollos; of the zealous Aquila and Priscilla, whose house was a little sanctuary; of Lazarus of Bethany and his loving sisters; and of many others whose names are recorded in the word of God, and whose examples stand to teach us the way of life. All these—both the lights and the shadows of the picture, both the prominent and the minor characters—are given for our good, that we through them, may be able to see, and seeing to understand, and understanding to love and obey the truth of God. The least name in the kingdom of heaven is great in the sight of God; and there is no influence on earth more blessed than the memory of the good. Of these it may be said with a double emphasis—

"Lives of great men all remind us
We can make our lives sublime,
And departing leave behind us
Footsteps on the sands of time—
Footprints that perhaps another,
Sailing o'er life's solemn main,
A forlorn and shipwrecked brother,
Seeing, shall take heart again."